LIBERALISM's
LAST
HURRAH

LIBERALISM's
LAST
HURRAH

The Presidential Campaign of 1964

GARY A. DONALDSON

Skyhorse Publishing

Skyhorse Publishing books may be purchased in bulk at special discounts for sales promotion, corporate gifts, fund-raising, or educational purposes. Special editions can also be created to specifications. For details, contact the Special Sales Department, Skyhorse Publishing, 307 West 36th Street, 11th Floor, New York, NY 10018 or info@skyhorsepublishing.com.

Skyhorse® and Skyhorse Publishing® are registered trademarks of Skyhorse Publishing, Inc.®, a Delaware corporation.

Visit our website at www.skyhorsepublishing.com.

10 9 8 7 6 5 4 3 2 1

Library of Congress Cataloging-in-Publication Data is available on file.

Cover design by Rain Saukas
Cover photo credit: the Associated Press

ISBN: 978-1-5107-0236-3
Ebook ISBN: 978-1-5107-0237-0

Printed in the United States of America

Contents

Introduction

The election of 1936 was a landmark in American politics. Franklin D. Roosevelt's landslide victory over the Republican Alf Landon made it clear that the American people supported Roosevelt's New Deal programs, while at the same time they accepted the Democrats' campaign theme that the Republicans deserved the blame for the Great Depression. The 1936 election also solidified, for the first time, what is usually called the New Deal coalition, a loosely knit collection of groups that, for the most part, had little in common except that they had been the beneficiaries of New Deal programs. This coalition included such diverse groups as organized labor and farmers, urban ethnic groups and southern populists, middle-class homeowners and northeastern intellectuals. Through the remainder of Roosevelt's terms this coalition became identified as liberal, although certain groups within it, particularly farmers and southern whites, could hardly meet that classification. Nevertheless this powerful coalition held together until after the war (despite some minor defections here and there), and developed into one of the most powerful political coalitions in American history. As the 1948 election approached—the first election since Roosevelt's death and the first since the end of the war—Harry Truman tried almost desperately to keep the New Deal coalition alive. Through a series of political maneuvers, promises, statements and programs, Truman brought the often combative coalition together for what seemed to be one brief moment on November 3 and won the election.

The Republican response to five consecutive Democratic victories (including control of Congress for the twenty-year period except for two years between 1946 and 1948) was largely predictable. They turned away from their conservative leadership and nominated a series of moderate (even liberal) candidates in an attempt to follow what was apparently the national liberal trend. Led by the Northeastern Establishment, the Republicans nominated Wendell Willkie and Thomas Dewey in the three elections between 1940 and 1948—and lost. Conservative Republicans, led primarily by Ohio senator Robert Taft, complained in the wake of each defeat that the GOP had lost the election because it had lost its conservative message, that it was, in fact, offering no message beyond what they called "me-tooism," a weak argument that the Republicans, if elected, would run the New Deal programs more efficiently than the Democrats. And that, conservative Republicans insisted, was no message at all. By the late 1940s, following Dewey's second defeat, conservatives adopted a new phrase to make their point. They demanded "a choice, not an echo." They argued that the party should nominate a conservative Republican to run against the messages and programs of Democratic party liberalism. Given such a clear choice, GOP conservatives insisted, American voters would chose conservatism.

Between Dwight D. Eisenhower's election in 1952 and the 1964 campaign, the conservatives remained on the GOP sidelines while the party moderates and Northeastern Establishment ran the party and nominated the candidates. Finally, in 1964, with the rise of Barry Goldwater, the conservatives would get their chance. They would offer the nation a choice, and not an echo.

For the Democrats, major factions of the old New Deal coalition again rallied to elect John Kennedy in 1960. The 1964 campaign promised to be the first conservative–liberal political clash in over thirty years. Although it was Lyndon Johnson, and not Kennedy, who would run under the Democratic standard in 1964, Johnson accepted and fostered Kennedy's liberal base and New Deal liberalism.

While on the campaign trail in Fresno, California, in March 1964, Goldwater told a crowd that the coming election would be one of major significance in American history: "This is no stopgap election," he said. "This is not one just for the record books. This is one for the history books."[1] When the votes were counted, however, it hardly looked that way. Despite all the hoopla and promise, Goldwater pulled only a few southern states and, by only a hair's breadth, his own home state of Arizona. The rest of the nation was swept clean by the Lyndon Johnson juggernaut; even the Republican party bastion of the Midwest went for Johnson. It was a Democratic party victory that rivaled Roosevelt's trouncing of Landon in 1936—the election that confirmed the successes of the New Deal, launched an extension of New Deal political power and programs, and brought together the New Deal coalition that laid the foundations of Democratic party dominance in Washington at least until Eisenhower.

The 1964 election, however, was not as it seemed. Goldwater's campaign ended in ignominious defeat but it became the ideological basis of Ronald Reagan's 1980 victory and the foundations of Republican party ideology for much of the remaining century. Goldwater, often touted by conservatives as Reagan's John the Baptist, was the first national political figure to represent modern American conservatism. Johnson's victory, as overwhelming as it was, quickly became a mandate lost, a political tragedy of almost epic proportions. Within four years, Johnson's 1964 mandate was gone, swallowed up by the Vietnam War and the general failures of the Great Society programs. The election of 1964 was not the beginnings of some new liberal era in American history, as many pundits and observers predicted. It was instead the last hurrah of New Deal liberalism and the last great electoral success of Franklin Roosevelt's New Deal coalition—the coalition that he built in his 1936 victory over Landon. If the coalition continued in any form beyond 1964 it was considerably weakened; and never again did it wield the political power it did between 1936 and 1964.

The 1964 election also brought an end to a political process that began in 1948. In that year Truman decided that the northern urban black vote was more important than the southern white vote, that black voters in large northern cities could help deliver the big electoral vote states like Illinois, Ohio, Michigan, Pennsylvania, New York, and California. Following his aides' advice, Truman threw just enough support to the fledgling post-war civil rights movement to pull the northern black vote, and he won the election. A few Deep South states deserted the Democrats (because of their civil rights tilt) and followed Strom Thurmond and the Dixiecrats into a third party protest. This act was the beginning of the white South's slow move from the Democrats to the Republicans. By 1964, that shift was generally complete—at least in regard to national elections. In open revolt against the Democratic party's support of the Civil Rights Act of 1964, much of the white South finally abandoned the Democrats and voted Republican, now the party of Barry Goldwater and states' rights. And in the midst of that campaign, Strom Thurmond—the very symbol of southern conservatism—switched parties and became a Goldwater Republican. During most of the national elections through the remainder of the century since 1964, the South has stayed in the Republican column.

These two elections, 1948 and 1964, changed the character of both parties. The 1948 election forced the Democrats to maintain the New Deal coalition that included labor, traditional liberals, farmers, and northern African Americans—a coalition that (by 1948) excluded the needs of white southern conservatives and segregationists. It was the election of 1948 that defined the post-war Democratic party more than any other election. For the Republicans, the election of 1964 was the defining moment in their party's history. In that year they put together a geographic coalition of conservatives that included the West, the Midwest, and the South, while rejecting the old Northeast–Midwest coalition (led by northeastern moderates) that had failed the Republicans since the 1930s defeats. That Republican conservative coalition remained intact throughout the remainder of the twentieth century.

The 1964 election may not have rocked the nation at the time, but it set the foundations for American politics for the remainder of the century. It was New Deal liberalism's last hurrah and the birth of modern conservatism; the death of one and the birth of another. *Newsweek* wrote, "No one has ever seen a Presidential campaign quite like it."[2]

Liberalism's Last Hurrah

1

Conservatives in the "Modern" World of Eisenhower, and the Rise of Goldwater

The election of 1952 finally ended the Republican drought. Dwight D. Eisenhower, once he took his oath of office in January 1953, would be the first Republican in the White House since Herbert Hoover was voted out of office in 1932. For twenty long years the Democrats had controlled the presidency while the Republicans sat on the sidelines as a sort of loyal opposition to the expansion of American liberalism. "For most of a very full generation," a conservative Republican leader wrote years later, the Republican party had been "the shapeless, gutless alternative to well-formed, principled Democratic programs and candidates."[1] Another called the GOP "a satellite of the Democratic party, a political Doppelganger that moves only with the impulse of its original."[2] In an attempt to harness the American mood for themselves, Republicans had presented the nation's voters with a series of presidential candidates who promised to do the job in Washington better, more efficiently, and with a greater anti-communist commitment than the Democrats. Wendell Willkie, the 1940 Republican offering, had, in fact, voted for Roosevelt in 1936—a point that Willkie and the Republicans made often in hopes of pulling moderate votes away from Roosevelt. Tom Dewey, the Republican candidate in 1944 and again in 1948, was often referred to as a liberal, a candidate with strong ties to labor and farmers, plus a record on civil rights that was often described as progressive. By the early 1950s Dewey had become, to GOP conservatives, the symbol of Republican failure, the leader of a coalition of moderates and liberals primarily centered in the

3

Northeast who sanctioned the New Deal and touted a foreign policy of global engagement known as internationalism.

Through the twenty years of GOP drought between Hoover and Ike there had been a few bright spots for the Republicans. In the 1946 mid-term elections, the first election after the war and the first election since Roosevelt's death, the Republicans made a grand sweep of Congress. American voters seemed to be saying that the time of Democratic dominance was coming to an end, that the era of the New Deal and its federal management of the economy were over. But two years later, Harry Truman, Roosevelt's successor in the White House, rallied the Democratic forces once again and won the presidency, along with a Democratic majority in Congress. The defeat was devastating to Republicans. The voters, it seemed, had reaffirmed the New Deal and rejected the Republican alternative.

Throughout these post-war years a number of conservative Republicans led by Ohio senator Robert Taft had argued that the Republican party was constantly losing political ground to the Democrats because it offered a political philosophy that was only barely distinct from what the Democrats were offering. What voters would respond to, these conservatives argued, was a significant alternative to the liberalism of the Democratic party. That alternative was a conservative one, which was, generally, less government spending (leading to a balanced budget), less federal interference in state and local-level affairs, a staunch anti-communism, and a strong (though unilateral) national defense.

After each GOP loss through the 1940s conservatives gained control of the party apparatus and began building their strength in anticipation of running one of their own in the next election. But in each instance, as the next election neared, a liberal-moderate coalition grabbed control of the convention and won the nomination. This scenario was played out in 1940 when Willkie won the nomination, and then again in 1944 and 1948 when Dewey was nominated. After the 1948 GOP defeat, conservatives again took over the party structure and looked forward to placing Taft in nomination four years later. But as the 1952 election approached, the moderates, behind Eisenhower, steamrolled all opposition. Taft made his strongest bid yet for the nomination that year, but Ike and the moderates were simply too strong.

Electability had always been a problem for the conservatives. They had never had a charismatic, attractive figure to represent them as a presidential candidate, a character whose mere physical presence could excite the masses and send voters to the polls in swarms. Certainly, Bob Taft was not that. Taft had a distinguished career in the Senate; to be sure, he was one of the most

4

effective conservative legislators in the post-war era. But he was not an appealing figure and was never an electable presidential candidate. In 1948 Taft hired an image-maker to turn his dour personality into something that the masses would see as an appealing fatherly type. The effort was a dismal failure. It was a common refrain among Republicans in Washington in the 1940s and up until 1952 that "Taft can't win," that he simply could not match up to Eisenhower—or even Dewey, whose own personal appeal was considerably less than charismatic. As one Republican party operative noted, "Taft was . . . the first notable casualty of the age of image."[3] At the 1952 GOP convention in Chicago, Senator John Bricker of Ohio, a long-time Taft supporter, withdrew Taft's name from consideration for the third time in twelve years. And for the fifth time in as many elections, Republican conservatives were forced to compromise their principles and reluctantly get behind a moderate candidate for president. To the conservatives, the eastern-liberal-moderate wing of the party had, again, denied them a chance to run a conservative candidate.

The 1952 election was not all bad for Republican conservatives. Obviously, a Republican had won the White House for the first time since the Great Depression. In addition, Ike's coattails were enormous; he brought with him a Republican Congress, the first since the 80th Congress in 1946. But Eisenhower was a moderate on most issues (discontented conservative Republicans called him a liberal), and through the 1950s he slowly split the Republican party between the conservatives on the right and moderates on the left. Eisenhower called his political philosophy "Modern Republicanism," a plan that conservatives snubbed as little more than a validation of the New Deal plus a foreign policy of internationalism. They countered with their own policies, which they called "Real Republicanism." The distinction would not become important until after the 1956 election when Ike was a lame duck and conservatives in Congress could no longer depend on his coattails to stay in office.

Despite the Republican sweep in 1952, GOP conservatives were hurt badly in the election. Several Republican senators on the Far Right lost their seats that year, including James Kem of Missouri, Harry Cain of Washington, Zales Ecton of Wyoming, and Patrick Hurley of New Mexico. In addition, nearly all conservative senatorial candidates ran behind Eisenhower's numbers, while Republican moderates and liberals generally ran ahead of him.[4] Even Senators Joe McCarthy and William Jenner, the two most prominent figures in the Republican party's communist hunt, would probably have lost had it not been for Ike's long coattails. The political winds, it seemed, were not blowing to the right in 1952, at least within the GOP.

Among the election's bright spots for the conservatives in 1952 was Barry Goldwater's slim victory over Senate majority leader Ernest McFarland in Arizona. Goldwater was an avowed Taftite, but he was forced to attribute his November victory to Ike's popularity in Arizona. Goldwater's victory, however, was something of an affirmation of McCarthy's power. McCarthy had personally campaigned against McFarland and three other Democratic incumbents, and all four failed in their bids for reelection.

The election also showed that the South was beginning to find its way, albeit slowly, into the Republican party. The white South had made up the conservative wing of the Democratic party since the end of Reconstruction. At various times in the late 1920s and again in the late 1930s the South exhibited discontent with the Democrats, but until 1948 they stayed in the party, voting almost solidly Democratic in each presidential election. It was in 1948 that Truman pushed for the urban black vote and defeated Dewey in one of the greatest political upsets of the century. Many white southerners, however, bolted the party and joined Strom Thurmond's Dixiecrats. Thurmond took four southern states, while Truman won a large number of African-American votes in several northern urban areas. For Truman it was a good trade-off, but it meant that the Democrats had chosen northern urban black votes over southern white votes, and this left large numbers of white southerners without a political home. The result was that in 1952 Eisenhower cracked the South, and that region began its long slow journey into the Republican party. Eisenhower that year took the states that had gone for Thurmond in 1948, plus Georgia, Arkansas, North Carolina, and the border states of Kentucky and West Virginia. The Republicans would have trouble hanging on to the South in the next two elections, but it was clear as civil rights became a more volatile issue that large numbers of southern whites would vote Republican under certain circumstances.

Divisions within the Republican party also revolved around the issue of foreign and domestic communism. The Far Right was virtually engulfed in an anti-communist crusade. Led by Wisconsin senator Joseph McCarthy, they searched relentlessly for communists inside the federal government, and they considered even the slightest diplomatic concession to international communism (most specifically the Soviet Union and Communist China) to be an act of appeasement. At the 1952 GOP convention the conservatives controlled the platform committee and forced a plank into the platform that called the Democratic party's foreign policy of containment "negative, futile and immoral," because it "abandons countless human beings to a despotism and godless terrorism." Containment, they believed, was not aggressive enough. It should be replaced with a policy of liberation.[5] Although Eisenhower was nominated and then elected on this right wing–generated platform, he always steered clear of supporting such a policy, realizing that liberation of communist-held territory was much the same as invasion. The Communist Chinese intervention in Korea was, of course, the primary lesson. Many conservatives, however, saw Eisenhower's lack of aggression against international communism as weakness—appeasement of the nation's enemy.

Eisenhower rankled the right almost immediately after he came to office by nominating Charles "Chip" Bohlen to be the nation's ambassador to Moscow, obviously a sensitive post. Bohlen had been a career officer in the state department (precisely the place where Joe McCarthy was insisting there were communists giving away America's secrets), and he had been Roosevelt's translator at the Yalta Conference. Yalta had become, to the members of the Republican right, the Great Betrayal, the Democratic party's delivery of Eastern Europe into communism. To make matters worse, Bohlen testified at the Senate confirmation hearing that the problem at Yalta had not been the agreement, but that Stalin had violated the agreement—precisely the official Democratic party's stand. It looked like the issue would split the Republicans, but Taft, wanting desperately to maintain party harmony went along with the Bohlen appointment, then followed with a demand to the White House, "no more Bohlens!"[6] The incident convinced the Republicans on the right that Eisenhower would be following the Democrats on foreign policy issues, and despite Taft's surrender to harmony, the Bohlen nomination split the Republicans further. Bohlen was finally approved overwhelmingly, but in the vote on the Senate floor Jenner, Styles Bridges, Bricker, Everett Dirksen, McCarthy, and Goldwater, along with seven others on the Republican right, voted to reject Bohlen.

The situation in Korea also served to split the Republicans. As Eisenhower had promised during the campaign, he pushed quickly after his inauguration to bring an end to the war—much to the disgust of many on the GOP right. The armistice, signed in April 1953 with the North Koreans and the Chinese Communists, was perceived by conservatives as the worst kind of appeasement, an acceptance of the status quo ante, an unwillingness to confront and defeat the enemy. Republican conservatives like Jenner and George Malone of Nevada even insisted that the armistice was, in fact, a victory for international communism and a defeat for the forces of Western democracy. William Knowland, the conservative senator from California, argued that the armistice would cause the United States to "lose the balance of Asia."[7] Eisenhower's willingness to end the war in Korea was even more offensive to conservatives because two years earlier General Douglas MacArthur, the first American commander in Korea and a darling of the Republican right wing, was relieved of his command by President Truman (as many conservatives perceived it) for advocating a complete victory over communism in Asia. To those on the right, MacArthur became a martyr to the cause of anti-communism and a symbol for the conservative perception of freedom. To many right-wing Republicans, Eisenhower became an appeaser. They even went so far as to applaud South Korean president Syngman Rhee's eleventh-hour defiance of Eisenhower and the armistice.

GOP conservatives also blamed the failures in Korea on the United Nations—or more specifically, the American government's willingness to compromise its foreign policy initiatives in order to meet UN objectives. To those on the right like Taft, Jenner, House Speaker Joseph Martin, Bridges, Knowland, McCarthy, and others, America's foreign policy should always be unilateral and should never be compromised by the goals of any international organization like the UN, where the Soviet Union maintained veto power over all U.S. military action. Eisenhower's only response to such complaints from his party's right was that the United States simply could not "go it alone" in foreign affairs. The GOP right prepared to mount an attack against the president on the issue (with Taft in the lead), with the potential of causing a full breach in the party. Taft, however, fell ill with the cancer that would eventually take his life, and without his leadership the GOP conservatives pulled back from the issue. At the same time, polls showed clearly that most Americans were anxious to get out of the Korean quagmire—nearly at any cost. In fact, the armistice was a popular decision. Nevertheless, the administration's decision to end the war increased the already growing antagonisms between the GOP right and the Eisenhower moderates; and conservatives continued to oppose the nation's roll in the UN.

Anti-communism, more than any other issue, defined the Republican right in the early 1950s, and the preeminent Republican crusader against communism was Joe McCarthy, senator from Wisconsin. McCarthy had been in the public eye since 1950, holding Senate hearings and accusing any number of federal employees, mostly inside the State Department, of being communists or communist sympathizers. Eisenhower disapproved of McCarthy and his crusade, and as the Eisenhower administration matured in office, the disapproval turned to hatred. "Eisenhower came to loathe McCarthy," Stephen Ambrose has written, "almost as much as he hated Hitler."[8] McCarthy had taken a swipe at Eisenhower's friend and mentor General George Marshall following the firing of MacArthur in 1951. Marshall had supported MacArthur's dismissal, and McCarthy's response was to accuse Marshall, on the floor of the Senate, of being associated with "a conspiracy so immense and an infamy so black as to dwarf any previous such venture in the history of man."[9] It looked as though Ike and McCarthy would clash. But it was not that simple. McCarthy maintained the support of the GOP right wing while Eisenhower carried the party's moderates. Any clash over McCarthy would further divide the two wings of the party. Also, the nations' anti-communists (in and out of Congress) had come to believe that any attack on McCarthy aided the growth of communism. As late as January 1954 a full 50 percent of Americans polled by Gallup approved of what McCarthy was doing; only 29 percent disapproved.[10]

One of McCarthy's primary supporters was Arizona senator Barry Goldwater. Over the years, the two men had become good friends. They first met in the 1940s when McCarthy made occasional trips to Arizona for health reasons. A decade later in Washington, McCarthy and Goldwater became Senate colleagues and personal friends who often shared an occasional drink. As McCarthy's methods and objectives came under fire, and several even on the right abandoned him, Goldwater stood by his friend to the bitter end. Even decades later, Goldwater wrote, "I couldn't approve of some of the charges McCarthy was making, but there was a tremendous amount of evidence to support his allegations. . . . I supported McCarthy's efforts to bring this out in the open."[11] Goldwater's support of McCarthy went a long way toward straining the relationship between Eisenhower and Goldwater that was to come, and between the moderates and the right wing of the Republican party.

A clash between the conservatives led by McCarthy and the moderates led by the president seemed imminent over Eisenhower's naming of Walter Bedell Smith as Undersecretary of State. Smith, as secretary to the general staff, had been Ike's close confidant and personal friend during the war; in the Truman administration he had headed the CIA and then been appointed ambassador to the Soviet Union. But Smith had defended John Paton Davis, an advisor to Smith in Moscow and now one of McCarthy's favorite targets. Davis had been one of several "China hands" in the State Department in the late 1940s, and McCarthy and other communist hunters on the Republican right now blamed this group for the fall of China to communism in 1949. To McCarthy, Davis was a fellow traveler and Smith was his defender. Ike dealt with the problem by convincing Taft to tell McCarthy to lay off the Smith nomination.

Still, the stage seemed set for an Eisenhower–McCarthy clash, but no such clash ever really came. Ike clearly saw that any personal attack on McCarthy in the press, or through any other means, would further split the Republicans, diminish the credibility of his administration, and add fuel to McCarthy's engine. "Nothing would probably please him more," Ike wrote a friend, "than to get the publicity that would be generated by public repudiation by the President."[12] He could not, however, sit by idly and allow McCarthy to carry on as he wished. From behind the scenes (where Eisenhower often felt the most comfortable dealing with sensitive issues) the president quietly exerted executive privilege and denied to McCarthy's committee access to all aspects of the executive branch of government—including both records and people. Ike's strategy of information strangulation (along with McCarthy's own harsh image, which took a beating on national television) brought down the Wisconsin senator. In early December 1954, the Senate censured McCarthy and that era in American history came to an end.

Eisenhower's tactics in dealing with McCarthy were ultimately effective, although he is often criticized for not confronting McCarthy directly and bringing an end to the red hunts. But McCarthy's antics were generally popular, and to a growing number of conservative Americans any attack on McCarthy was tantamount to an appeasement of communism. Barry Goldwater agreed, arguing before the Senate that any assault on McCarthy or his cause by the administration "may well turn out to be a field day against America's global anti-communist policy."[13] Then, of course, there was the question of party unity. Through the entire McCarthy episode, Eisenhower maintained the appearance of staying above the fray, and that reduced the possibility of a wider split in the party. More importantly, however, McCarthy's collapse without any visible attack directly from the White House badly damaged the Republican right. Congressional conservatives were left holding the bag on the issue once McCarthy was gone and they received much of the blame for the excesses of McCarthy's actions. In 1958, and then again in 1960, the Republican right suffered badly at the polls, while Eisenhower and the moderates—generally unscathed by McCarthyism—maintained a tight grip on the party machinery.

When Eisenhower came to office in January 1953, the members of the Republican right expected their new president to lead them in a point-by-point dismantling of New Deal programs, something Taft and others on the right had promised to do at least since the war. Eisenhower, however, wanted to lead his party and the nation down the middle of the road—and not to the right. In fact, he wanted to work with the Democrats, build a bipartisan consensus, and emerge as a national president. He had no intention of going to war with the Democrats over domestic issues. This was something that the Republicans on the right simply could not abide.

There was no domestic issue more volatile among right-wing Republicans than the national budget. Democrats had shown no need to balance the budget for twenty years, a near sacrilegious travesty to those on the right who, since at least the 1890s, had come to see a balanced budget as a signal to big business that the nation's economy was sound. In the 1952 campaign the Republicans (explicitly in their party's convention platform and in several of Ike's speeches) had promised a balanced budget and with it a sound economy and economic prosperity. In April 1953 all that collapsed, however, when Eisenhower, in a briefing to Republican congressional leaders, admitted that he would be unable to balance his first budget. Taft was livid. He jumped up and pounded the table: "The one primary thing we promised the American people was reduction of expenditures! With a [budget] like this, we'll never elect a Republican Congress in 1954!" Then he added, "You're taking us down the same road Truman traveled!"[14] Both men had notorious tempers, and the fragile Republican coalition might have ended there, but Eisenhower remained calm and explained to Taft the need for certain expenditures, particularly military expenditures to maintain strength amid what was perceived as communist activity in several regions of the world. He then promised a balanced budget in 1954 and Taft calmed down. The breach was plugged.[15]

Eisenhower continued, however, to run down the middle of the road, the place he believed the American people wanted him to be, and that often meant working with the Democrats, particularly conservative Democrats. Again, the right chaffed. The president, for instance, proposed expanding Social Security, the New Deal program that many on the right considered an example of "creeping socialism" and the imminent collectivization of America. The administration's bill would have added 10 million workers to the Social Security rolls, but congressional right-wingers slapped it down in 1953. A year later, with an election looming and Democrats poised to make gains, the bill finally made its way through Congress—despite objections from the right. Eisenhower also proposed what he called "Middle Way," a plan in which the federal government would underwrite private health insurance plans, expand public housing programs, and reform the Taft–Hartley Act. These initiatives also faced strenuous opposition from the GOP right, and all were either defeated in committee or produced only innocuous legislative results.

In June 1953, the nation's conservatives were dealt a blow that damaged their cause for nearly ten years. Their leader, Robert Taft, died of cancer. Although Taft was never truly presidential material, he was the conservatives' ideological center. He was powerful enough to demand the president's ear, and it was Taft who had, over the years, maintained a close relationship with southern conservatives in the Democratic party. Without him, conservative strength diminished immediately on Capitol Hill, particularly in the face of the growing power of GOP moderates. Taft's death marked the beginning of the end of a brief moment of power for the right, and in fact the GOP right remained leaderless and weak until the rise of Barry Goldwater in the very late 1950s.

Two months after Taft's death, William Knowland, a right-winger in the Taft mold and a constant critic of the administration's foreign policy, took over Taft's place as majority leader in the Senate. Knowland was never able to fill Taft's shoes, and he was basically ineffectual in challenging the White House. Under Knowland's leadership GOP conservatives weakened. Nevertheless, as majority leader in the Senate, Knowland was possibly the second most important Republican in the nation and he immediately began to position himself as the right wing's choice for president, if not in 1956, then in 1960.

Without Taft, the right was in disarray, and within months Eisenhower began to take advantage of the opportunity to pull the party back to the middle and to purge the right. He began by making inroads in the Republican National Committee, a traditional bastion of the right. By 1956 Eisenhower loyalists controlled two-thirds of the RNC and forty-one state chairmanships. As the power of the moderates continued to grow in the late 1950s, the conservatives seemed on their way toward political extinction.

At the same time, many GOP conservatives began to see the advantages of Eisenhower's popularity. After all, they naturally reasoned, a moderate Republican in office was preferable to a Democratic president. Powerful one-time congressional leaders on the right like Dirksen, Martin, and even occasionally Knowland, all one-time Taft allies, had by 1956 begun voting the line with Eisenhower and the moderates. In the summer of that year, five months before the next election, the *National Review* (the right's primary organ by this time) complained that those still refusing to support Eisenhower were being "consigned to outer darkness. . . . With such skill have [Eisenhower] and his associates conducted the movement [and] it has become quite clear what the Republican Party is not: It is not the Party of Senator Taft."[16] Certainly, this had a great deal to do with the coming 1956 election in which Eisenhower was expected to overrun the Democrats and pull behind him some very generous coattails. By 1956, Ike's popularity and effectiveness had neutralized, quieted, or absorbed much of the Republican right wing.

Even Richard Nixon felt the shift. He had been tapped in 1952 as Eisenhower's running mate to appease the right. By 1956, however, Nixon had reinvented himself as an Eisenhower moderate. He had supported the administration on all levels through the first term, which had rattled the right-wing leadership. Nixon, however, believed he saw the future: that Eisenhower's moderation was becoming overwhelmingly popular in America, while the right wingers were on their way out the door, at least for the moment. Despite Nixon's unabashed loyalty through Ike's first term, Eisenhower felt no need to pander to the right in 1956, and he at least toyed with the idea of dumping Nixon from the ticket. Nixon, of course, remained on the ticket that year, but it was not because of any pressure put on Eisenhower from the right.

The weakness of the right in the Republican party became apparent in 1955 when Eisenhower announced he would attend the Geneva Conference for the purpose of pursuing a policy of "peaceful co-existence" with the Soviets. This to conservatives was nothing less than an accommodating relationship with the forces of international communism. Again the right chaffed. McCarthy, down but not yet out in 1955, led a right-wing fight to tie Eisenhower's hands at the Geneva Conference by passing a resolution in the Senate that would bar the president from discussing any topic with the Soviets except the liberation of Eastern Europe. The opposition to the resolution was led by Senate Democratic majority leader Lyndon Johnson. The resolution was finally forced to the floor, where the weakness of the right became all too apparent. Only three senators stood with McCarthy: Jenner from Indiana and two mavericks. Ironically, McCarthy's action united the Republicans behind Eisenhower like they had never before been united. The whole incident, however, left the GOP right gasping for air. "We have the spectacle of cannibalism holding forth," a frustrated Barry Goldwater told the Senate. "We find the Republican Party . . . busily chewing on itself."[17]

In September 1955, Eisenhower had a heart attack and the dynamic of American politics changed immediately—or at least it threatened to. One of the first rumors that began circulating on Capitol Hill and in the press was that Ike's brother Milton might be willing to step into Ike's shoes as a candidate of the moderates in 1956 if the general was not physically capable. Eisenhower himself, while he was recovering and uncertain of his own future, suggested to his press secretary, James Hagerty, that Dewey might be

13

ready. "[H]e represents my way of thinking," Eisenhower told Hagerty. After a pause, Hagerty responded that the Republican right would revolt and name their own candidate—and that the party might even split. Ike relented. "I guess you're right." The discussion then turned to Nixon. Both men agreed, however, that the vice president was not up to the job.[18]

The Republican right saw Eisenhower's heart attack as an opportunity to run one of their own if the president demurred in 1956, and they looked to Knowland, really the only leader they had. It was the editors at the *National Review*, primarily William F. Buckley, Jr., who first convinced Knowland to run in 1956. In the magazine's first issue, which came out in November 1955 (just two months after Eisenhower's heart attack), an article by Knowland assailed the president for negotiating with the Soviets and seeking peaceful coexistence at the Geneva Conference. Then on the floor of the Senate, Knowland continued to hammer at what he called the "Trojan Horse of Coexistence," and he often called for a blockade of China and an American withdrawal from the UN.[19] But all the speculation and rumors ended in February when an obviously recovered Eisenhower appeared fit on television before the nation—and then made it clear that he would run in 1956.

The GOP convention in San Francisco was a coronation for Eisenhower. It was clear that he would win the election easily, and that his coattails would be long and generous. The conservative right, of course, had nowhere to go except to jump on the winning bandwagon and support the president. At the convention, however, the right had a moment in the limelight when they conjured up, in several speeches, a tribute to "the spirit of Bob Taft." California governor Goodwin Knight announced near the end of the convention that the Republicans would leave the Cow Palace "marching arm in arm."[20] And as the campaign got under way and Republicans of all types rode the Eisenhower bandwagon to victory, the smell of unity was clearly in the air. *Life* thought it recognized a "New Republican Harmony."[21] But the party had serious problems.

Eisenhower did win big in 1956. He carried 57.3 percent of the popular vote and won forty-one states totaling 457 electoral votes to Adlai Stevenson's seven states (all in the South) and seventy-three electoral votes. It was a definite mandate for Eisenhower and his administration. Ike's coattails, however, were not quite as long as the Republicans had hoped. In a major setback, the Republicans lost control of Congress again. The message was clear. America liked Ike, but they did not necessarily like the Republicans. It was, in fact, the first time since 1848 that voters presented a newly elected president with a Congress in which his party controlled neither house. And in that election a popular general, Zachary Taylor, headed a political party, the Whigs, that was essentially in its death throes. In 1956, Congress changed little, with the Democrats picking up only one Senate seat and two House seats. In the Senate the Democratic edge was forty-nine to forty-seven; and in the House the Democratic majority remained substantial at 232 to 199. What was remarkable, of course, was that the Democrats made any gains at all, given the magnitude of Ike's victory.

On election night, Eisenhower made an appropriate acceptance speech and then headed off for a quick vacation on the Monterey Peninsula in California. But in his speech he left something for the Republican right to chew on. "America," he said, "has approved Modern Republicanism."[22] To Ike, that had been the mandate. The GOP right was now so weak, and he was so strong within the party as a result of the election mandate, that he could move forward without any concern for dissension from the right. It was truly Ike ascendant, mostly at the expense of the conservatives.

Eisenhower's concept of Modern Republicanism is difficult to define. He himself never really defined it. In 1954 he remarked to James Hagerty that he wanted to find a word "to put ahead of Republican—something like 'New' or 'Modern' or something."[23] A few liberal-minded Republicans tried to give Modern Republicanism some credence and specificity, but their ideas were never really accepted by Eisenhower or the moderate wing of the party, and some like George Aiken of Vermont insisted that the party drop the term because it was subject to any number of interpretations.[24] In fact, it is difficult to see any move by Eisenhower in his second term that was substantially new or much different from his first term. He remained generally where he had always been—in the middle of the road—and most observers simply passed off Modern Republicanism as a political catch phrase with no real definition. But the phrase stuck in the throats of the party's right wing. In fact, when Eisenhower used the phrase and then refused to follow it up with any definition or description, the right-wingers put their own definition on it. To right-wing newcomers like conservative writer William Rusher, Modern Republicanism was specific. It was not a political philosophy, but the culmination of Ike's moderation, his middle-of-the-road stance. Thus the GOP right defined Modern Republicanism by adding up the things they disliked about Eisenhower's entire administration. It was an increase in welfare spending, an expanded role of the government in the lives of individuals and institutions, reduced military spending, and a peaceful coexistence with the Soviet Union. By 1957 Modern Republicanism had a definition, but it was never Eisenhower's definition. By then Rusher and others had added to the list such things as Ike's handling of the

Suez Crisis, his failure to aid the Hungarian Revolution, and even his mishandling of *Sputnik*.[25] Modern Republicanism became all that the GOP right opposed in the party. It became the battle line for the 1960s.

William "Big Bill" Knowland was never to the conservative movement what Taft had been, but after Taft's death Knowland, from his position as Republican leader in the Senate and titular head of the Republican right, began making noises as a presidential candidate. He focused on two issues. He was a strong anti-labor conservative who lobbied hard for right-to-work laws (giving workers the right to chose if they want to join a union), and he was vehemently opposed to U.S. recognition of Communist China. Because of his passion on this issue he became known in Washington as the "Senator from Formosa." But Knowland had problems. He lacked popular appeal and, not unlike Taft, was not much of a vote-getter outside his own state. In addition, Eisenhower disliked him, a fact well known on Capitol Hill. The relationship between Ike and Taft had been one of cordial disagreement between two Republican titans. In fact, the two men got along fairly well. But Eisenhower simply refused to suffer Knowland. "[T]here seems to be no final answer to the question," Eisenhower wrote of Knowland in his diary, "How stupid can you get?"[26] Knowland had other problems. There were rumors that his wife hated Washington so much that she had threatened to move back to California and file for divorce if Big Bill insisted on running for the Senate again in 1958. To save his marriage, Knowland decided he would resign his Senate seat and jump into the California governor's race.[27] To most conservatives (not knowing Knowland's personal problems) this actually made political sense. He would run for president in 1960 from the governor's chair in California rather than as a political insider from Capitol Hill. It seemed like a perfect strategy to conservatives who intrinsically distrusted federal authority over the power of the states. Goodwin Knight, the sitting California governor, even accommodated the strategy by stepping aside and agreeing to run for Knowland's Senate seat. Both men lost.

The 1958 election was a disaster for the Republicans. It showed beyond a shadow of a doubt that the party was weak and in disarray, and that the only thing going for the GOP was Ike himself. And for conservatives the election was even more disastrous. They were even rejected by Ike. The Republicans suffered a net loss of forty-eight seats in the House and thirteen seats in the Senate—a loss far worse than the party would receive in the Democratic landslide of 1964 and the biggest Democratic party gains since 1936. They also lost thirteen of twenty-one gubernatorial contests and nearly 700 seats in state senates and lower houses.[28] Republican blood ran like it had not run

since 1948. Besides Knowland, the Republican right lost an entire generation of conservatives, men like Bricker, Jenner, Martin, McCarthy, and
Nevada's George W. "Molly" Malone. Of the Republicans who survived the
debacle, the vast majority were moderates, Eisenhower Modern Republicans. In addition, Nelson Rockefeller was elected governor of New York.
Rockefeller was a direct descendant of the Dewey–Northeastern–liberal wing
of the party and anyone following Republican party politics knew that he
would quickly become a major player in the party's immediate future. To
Brent Bozell at the *National Review*, the election was a disaster. "Let us
conservatives not look for a silver lining," he wrote. "There is none." And
Nixon responded to the events: "It was the worst defeat in history ever suffered by a party having control of the White House."[29]

With Knowland gone, the way was clear for Barry Goldwater to step into
the breach. Goldwater had supported Eisenhower against Taft at the Chicago
convention in 1952, and had ridden Ike's coattails into the Senate in that
election. Then in 1956 he had urged Eisenhower to run for a second term.
But by the spring of 1957, Goldwater was ready to break with the general,
and that break was the beginning of the modern conservative movement in
the Republican party. By 1958 the nation's conservatives believed they had
found their new leader, one who would take on the Democrats and, even
more important, one who would also attack the Modern Republicans and
take the helm of the Republican party.

The Goldwater–Eisenhower break came in April 1957, some eighteen
months before the 1958 elections. Goldwater had always been a loyal Republican, a supporter of the administration's agenda at least through 1956.[30]
That loyalty, however, did not place Goldwater in the realm of Modern
Republicanism by any means. He had always been associated with the conservative wing of the party, but at the same time was never considered way
out on the right with the likes of Jenner, McCarthy, Idaho's Herman Welker,
or even Knowland. But by April 1957 Goldwater had grown defiant. The
issue was the budget. In October 1952, candidate Eisenhower had promised to eliminate the federal deficit and lower federal expenditures to $60
billion by fiscal 1955. In 1954 and again in 1955, Ike's budgets finished in
the red with little explanation or apologies to those on the right. In 1956 he
posted a balanced budget, but conservatives like Goldwater believed he
had done so only to keep the right wing in line during an election year. In
1957 the president sent to Congress a whopping $71.8 billion budget, the
largest budget ever submitted by a president in peacetime. It included in-
creases in spending for education, public housing, foreign aid, and the

military. It was more than Goldwater could stand. Not only had Eisenhower broken his promise to the American people, as Goldwater saw it, but the president's Modern Republicanism was clearly no different than the Democratic party's philosophy of deficit spending to maintain New Deal and Fair Deal programs. The result was predictable. As Goldwater and other conservatives saw it, Modern Republicanism had taken its substantial 1952 Republican majority and turned it into a Democratic majority—in effect, handing the government over to the Democrats.

So it was, that on April 8, Barry Goldwater, standing before an almost empty Senate chamber, lashed out at the administration. He began by saying that up until then he believed that the Eisenhower administration had, in fact, "provided the responsible leadership so vital to the maintenance of a strong domestic economy which, in turn, is a vital factor in maintaining world peace." "Now," he added, "I am not so sure." Then he hit the administration hard, charging that it had been influenced by the "siren of socialism" and that it "aped New Deal antics." The 1956 budget, he said, was "a betrayal of the people's trust" and, he added, "it weakens my faith in the constant reassurances we have received from this administration that its aim was to cut spending, balance the budget, reduce the national debt, cut taxes—in short to live within our means. . . ." He went on to attack Modern Republicanism as a "splintered concept of Republican philosophy," and then promised that he would fight "against waste, extravagance, high taxes, unbalanced budgets, and deficit spending" under the Democrats, just he would battle "the same elements of fiscal responsibility in this Republican administration."[31] It was a stinging attack. A few days later, Goldwater told columnist Richard Rovere, "It was the hardest thing I ever did."[32]

In the 1958 election, as Republicans were falling left and right throughout the nation, Goldwater won an impressive victory in his reelection bid. He swamped his Democratic opponent (again Governor Ernest McFarland) by running as an anti-labor candidate who refused, as he said, to "surrender Arizona to [UAW President Walter] Reuther."[33] Goldwater's high-profile break with the Eisenhower administration in April 1957 made him a leader among conservatives in Congress, but his reelection in 1958 in a tough year for Republicans, along with Knowland's defeat that year, thrust him into the roll as the nation's leading conservative political voice.

Immediately after the election, Goldwater was approached by a group of Midwest conservatives to discuss the possibility of organizing a Goldwater-for-President committee, with an eye on the 1960 election. Goldwater undoubtedly realized that Nixon, with Eisenhower's blessing, would be unbeatable for the Republican nomination that year, and he declined the offer.[34]

It was also in this period, just after the 1958 elections, that several of Goldwater's friends encouraged him to publish a small pamphlet that would describe his conservative philosophy. The result was *The Conscience of a Conservative*, first published in 1960. It immediately became a national bestseller. *Conscience of a Conservative* was, at first, intended as a means to gain name recognition for Goldwater among potential voters and a way of raising money for a Goldwater run for the presidency—if not in 1960 then later. It was primarily Goldwater's definition of conservatism at the beginning of the 1960s and where he stood on the main issues of the time. His themes were that a limited government promotes individual freedom; that a strict construction of the Constitution is at the foundation of American freedom and individuality; and that communism is an intrinsically evil system that should be declared an outlaw, not be recognized on any level, and be "engaged" whenever and wherever possible.

It seems fairly clear that *Conscience of a Conservative* embodied Goldwater's thinking on conservatism and the issues, but he did not write the book. The author was Brent Bozell, the founder and senior editor at *National Review* and the brother-in-law of William F. Buckley, Jr. Although Bozell's name never appeared anywhere in *Conscience of a Conservative*, Goldwater always readily acknowledged Bozell's efforts, and two years later in his second book, *Why Not Victory?*, Goldwater referred to Bozell as "the guiding hand of my last book."[35]

Goldwater's primary theme in *Conscience of a Conservative* was that individuality, as fostered by limited government, is at the foundation of American freedom. The prime subverter of individuality and freedom, he argued, is the welfare state that has been under construction in the United States since the 1930s: "I do not undertake to promote welfare," he wrote as part of a type of pledge that all conservative political leaders should take, "for I propose to extend freedom."[36] At the foundation of all this was the Constitution and a national trend to misinterpret its intentions. The framers of the Constitution, Goldwater argued, wanted "effective restraints against the accumulation of power in a single authority" at the federal level. The Constitution is, in fact, he continued, "a system of restraints against the natural tendency of government to expand in the direction of absolutism."[37] The problem is that the U.S. federal government has become a "Leviathan," the very antithesis of a body promoting freedom and individuality, "a vast national authority out of touch with the people, and out of their control."[38] "I

19

am convinced," he added, "that most Americans now want to reverse the trend. I think that concern for our vanishing freedoms is genuine. I think that the people's uneasiness in the stifling omnipresence of government has turned into something approaching alarm."[39]

On the specifics of domestic affairs, Goldwater called for a "flexible and voluntary" Social Security system, the sale of the Tennessee Valley Authority (TVA) to private industry, an end to all federal farm programs, a ban on political union activities, state-level right-to-work laws, and an end to the graduated income tax that, he wrote, enforces "equality among unequal men."[40]

Possibly Goldwater's most important statement in *Conscience of a Conservative* dealt with the concept of states' rights. A proper interpretation of the Constitution, Goldwater continued, must include a return to the Jeffersonian political philosophy of states' rights. It is, he wrote, "the cornerstone of the Republic, our chief bulwark against the encroachment of individual freedom by Big Government. . . ."[41] Civil rights, he added, has become equated with opposition to the South's stand on race issues, but, he continued, states' rights is more complicated than that. "Despite the recent holding of the Supreme Court," in its *Brown v. Board of Education* decision in 1954, "I am convinced—not only that integrated schools are not required—but that the Constitution does not permit any interference whatsoever by the federal government in the field of education."[42]

In the political philosophy of Barry Goldwater, much as in the political philosophy of Jefferson and John Calhoun, there was true sincerity in the belief that the federal government did not have the constitutional authority to force a region of the nation to change its educational patterns based on race—or any other factor. The result of Goldwater's philosophy was that white southerners flocked to him. His states' rights conservatism was only a hair's breadth away from old-time southern race politics—although Goldwater never portrayed himself as a racist. As the Democrats more and more locked on to the support of northern black votes as one means of winning the electoral votes of the big northern industrial states, the South began to see a savior in Republican conservatism, a philosophy that embraced states' rights as a constitutional concept that would allow white southerners greater control over their social system. It was the beginning of the Republican party's southern strategy, which would be a part of its political philosophy well into the 1990s.

Much of this began in the 1948 campaign when Truman supported civil rights and won northern urban black votes at the expense of several Deep

South states. For Truman and the Democrats in 1948 it was a good trade, but it began the process of pushing white southerners away from the Democratic party—at least in presidential elections. Through the 1950s Eisenhower never professed a strong belief in states' rights, but nevertheless he continued to make inroads into the white southern electorate throughout his two administrations. In the 1952 elections he took Texas, Florida, Virginia, Maryland, Tennessee, and the border states of Oklahoma, Missouri, and Delaware. In 1956 he added to those states Louisiana, Kentucky, and West Virginia (although he lost Missouri). As the 1960s approached it became clear that the South, always conservative, had become fertile ground to be cultivated by the Republicans. When Barry Goldwater announced in *Conscience of a Conservative* in 1960 that states' rights was at the foundation of his political philosophy, southerners took notice. In fact, the South Carolina Republican party immediately voted unanimously to instruct their entire delegation to commit to Goldwater at the 1960 Republican National Convention. Whether or not Goldwater wanted to deal with the race issue is largely irrelevant. When he accepted states' rights as a political philosophy, he accepted the race issue.

Goldwater's primary weakness as a national political candidate in 1960 was his lack of foreign policy experience. In *Conscience of a Conservative* he intended to remedy that by explaining his view on what he called "The Soviet Menace." These expressions were the first in a series of Goldwater public statements that would allow the press to define Goldwater as a warmonger, the itchy finger on the nuclear button. No matter how hard he tried throughout the rest of his life to shake the image, he would never really succeed. Goldwater began his arguments by insisting that "overt hostilities should always be avoided," but he continued in both philosophical arguments and examples to explain that catastrophic world war must be seen as an inevitability—and that the United States should begin preparing for it. The only alternative, he continued, was to surrender to the Soviet Union. We must, he wrote, declare communism outlawed, and "withdraw diplomatic recognition from all Communist governments including the Soviet Union. . . ."[43] We should also always, he added, "engage the enemy at times and places, and with weapons, of our own choosing."[44] Singling out the 1956 Hungarian revolt, an incident that annoyed conservatives because Eisenhower refused to act on behalf of the rebels, Goldwater insisted that if the United States had threatened the use of nuclear weapons during that crisis, the Soviets would "probably" have backed down. Then he asked, in a strangely worded question, "Such a policy involves the risk of war?" and responded, "Of course."[45] The implication of Goldwater's writing was that the United States was in retreat and that something must be done immediately to prevent a complete defeat by the forces of communism. In a *New York Times Magazine* article that appeared on newsstands at nearly the same time as *Conscience of a Conservative* appeared on bookshelves, Goldwater professed to speak for America when he told a reporter "that he would rather follow the world to kingdom come than consign it to hell under Communism."[46]

Such statements were entirely too strong for the average American in the era of arms races and Soviet threats. As the 1960 election approached, and then four years later in the 1964 campaign, saber rattling of this sort seemed reckless and clearly frightened Americans. Of course, Goldwater's musings in *Conscience of a Conservative*, published in March 1960, were forever preserved on the printed page. By 1964 the nation had come close to a nuclear exchange in the Cuban Missile Crisis and both the United States and the Soviet Union were quickly approaching a mutually destructive capability that could bring an end to much of world civilization. By then, Goldwater's challenge to confront the Soviets in Hungary and other little fronts here and there represented less a showdown of wits and more a pattern for war that might easily end in the destruction of mankind. In the 1964 campaign, candidate Goldwater would have to stand by these statements, and they would be used by both political parties to destroy his credibility in dealing with foreign powers. The question was asked again and again: "Is Goldwater trigger happy?"

Barry Goldwater's *Conscience of a Conservative* still warms the hearts of America's conservatives from Newt Gingrich to William F. Buckley, Jr. It is at the foundation of modern American conservative thought. In a preface to the 1990 edition, Pat Buchanan gave some idea of the importance of *Conscience of a Conservative* to the philosophy of American conservatives. For Buchanan, and certainly for many other conservatives in America, the reaction to the book has been as much religious fervor as political philosophy. It was, he wrote, "our new testament; it contained the core beliefs of our political faith, it told us why we had failed, what we must do. We read it, memorized it, quoted it. . . . For those of us wandering in the arid desert of Eisenhower Republicanism, it hit like a rifle shot."[47] Over 3.5 million copies of *Conscience of a Conservative* have been sold since 1960, and it might well be, as conservative writer Lee Edwards has claimed, the most widely read political book of the twentieth century.[48]

The publication of *Conscience of a Conservative* made Goldwater the undisputed leader of the Republican party's right wing. Through most of the

Eisenhower 1950s, the conservatives had been generally headless under Knowland's uninspired leadership. Even after Taft's death, party conservatives still called themselves Taftites, or Taft Republicans. After 1960, however, they finally buried Taft and lined up behind Goldwater: Taft Republicans proudly became Goldwater Republicans. But how did the two men, Taft and Goldwater, compare? Was Goldwater the true descendent of Taft, or was the conservative movement under Goldwater something new and different? The answer is yes and no.

Goldwater's philosophy and policies can be measured against Taft's mostly by degree. Goldwater is usually perceived as being to the right of Taft on most issues, both foreign and domestic.[49] Taft, for instance, did not call for the elimination of New Deal programs. Goldwater did. Taft thought that the federal government had limited regulatory and fiscal obligations in social and economic matters. Generally, Goldwater did not. Taft could support federal housing legislation, as he did in 1945 when he gave his name to the Taft–Ellender–Wagner Bill that was finally killed in the House by right-wing conservatives in Taft's own party. And, after a trip to Puerto Rico forced him to see the connection between poverty and substandard education, Taft introduced a bill to authorize federal aid to education. Goldwater could never have supported either bill. As he made clear in *Conscience of a Conservative*, he believed strongly that an escalating federal bureaucracy threatened basic national freedoms.

It was on foreign affairs, however, that Taft and Goldwater disagreed most dramatically. Neither man needed to apologize to the other for their commitment to anti-communism, but Goldwater sought to confront communism abroad while Taft was more interested in fighting communism by maintaining strength (both economic and military) at home. Taft believed that the United States should limit its commitments abroad, mostly because international entanglements would overburden the national budget and ultimately damage the economy. He also argued that the United States should rid itself of the notion that it could solve the world's problems with expensive foreign aid and military might. He was not quite an isolationist, however. His policy was often called "unilateralist," a conservative post-war strategy that called for the United States to undertake its foreign policy without the assistance or burden of other nations or alliances. Most unilateralists, like Taft, had been hardcore isolationists before the war but had come to see the need for at least some degree of U.S. involvement in world affairs following Pearl Harbor. These unilateralists maintained a conservative stance in the face of Eisenhower's broad internationalism, which

23

they despised as too expensive, dangerous, and even intrusive. Goldwater, however, did not step too far from Eisenhower's internationalism, complaining mostly that the Eisenhower administration was all too willing to back away from confrontation with the Soviets. Goldwater (not unlike Eisenhower) believed strongly in an activist international foreign policy for the purpose of containing the forces of international communism—forces that Goldwater believed were inherently expansionist. To that end, he argued for a strong U.S. presence throughout the world, and that included the need for international military alliances. As the 1964 election approached, Goldwater would remind voters more and more of his support for Eisenhower's foreign policies.

Goldwater and Taft were hardly of the same mold, but Goldwater certainly built on Taft's legacy of post-war conservatism. Taft was more flexible than Goldwater on social issues, and Goldwater was more willing to involve the nation in the world's affairs. By the 1960s, however, these differences in strategy and philosophy were perceived as minor discrepancies. Goldwater, to most conservatives, became the heir apparent to Taft's conservative leadership.

Goldwater may have been steeped in the conservative political philosophy of the past, but his image was distinctly contemporary. To most conservatives, and even to most Americans, the Goldwater conservative movement was something new, even fresh. Goldwater was a dashing figure with rugged good looks, and he carried a genuine western image. He was appealing, humorous, even silly at times, often accused of "shooting from the hip," a spontaneous reaction that was often appealing to the American public. He had a fast-moving image. He flew jets and he liked sports cars. In contrast to the unelectable and dull Taft, Goldwater must have seemed like a gift from heaven to Republican conservatives. Now, for the first time in a long time, the Republican right had a likeable candidate, a vote-getter, possibly even a winner.

There was, however, a very important distinction between Taft and Goldwater, a distinction that did change the very nature of the Republican party and American conservatism itself. Taft found his voter base in the traditionally conservative Midwest and from there he tried to mollify moderate voters in the Northeast in an attempt to put together a regional coalition of those two areas. Goldwater found his base in the West, particularly in the Republican strongholds of southern California; and in the South, where his policy of states' rights meant to white southerners the retention of a segregated way of life. Most political scientists believed that if Goldwater could

24

hold the South, the West, and the Midwest, he could win in 1964, and he could win without pandering to the Dewey–Eisenhower moderate wing of the party located generally in the Northeast. Thus Goldwater appealed to a completely new and different constituency than Taft. In the final analysis, Barry Goldwater was something new, but at the same time he owed a strong legacy to Taft and the wing of the Republican party that found its antecedents in the conservatism of Hoover and Coolidge.[50]

* * *

Through most of the 1950s, American conservatives were divided. There were cultural conservatives, those traditionalists who believed that American liberalism had led to permissiveness and ultimately to the dissolution of American institutions. There were those on the right who focused on little more than the communist threat. Others were libertarians, obsessed with defending the free market, individualism, and the right of private property. If there was a commonality among them it was only that they all opposed liberalism and the New Deal that defined it in the post-war world—and subsequently opposed the acceptance of the New Deal–Fair Deal programs by the Eisenhower administrations. But there was no conservative forum, no conservative leadership to unite them, no organization to bring them together to explore whatever common ground these various philosophies and beliefs they shared. That changed in the late 1950s.

American conservatives in the post-war years often considered themselves to be misunderstood. The national press was extremely hostile, often depicting conservatives as nay-sayers, defenders of privilege, warmongers, and even racists. Taft had often complained of a need to counter what he called "New Deal bias in the press" with a conservative counterpoint. As the conservative movement grew in the mid-1950s there developed an impulse among those on the Republican right to get the word out, to explain themselves, to defend and even advertise their beliefs. Goldwater, in his *Conscience of a Conservative*, intended, at least in part, to accomplish that objective, often taking great pains to explain the validity of certain aspects of conservative philosophy as opposed to the way it was commonly perceived.

For these reasons several members of the conservative right began to see a need for a new publication that would be the mouthpiece for conservative ideas and a unifying force for a movement about to get on its feet. There had been conservative magazines. *The Freeman*, begun in 1950, showed promise, but the nation's leading conservative writers left the staff when the magazine's management chose to endorse Eisenhower in 1952 instead of Taft. By the mid-1950s *Human Events* had taken the place of *The Freeman* as the chief conservative periodical in the nation. Conservative writers such as John Chamberlain, William Henry Chamberlin, M. Stanton Evans, and James J. Kilpatrick pounded out conservative philosophy and the best of Capitol Hill politics for *Human Events*.

In 1954 a thirty-year-old William F. Buckley, Jr., decided that conservative readers needed something new, something, in fact, to challenge *The New Republic*, a slick popular weekly intellectual magazine aimed at liberals. *The New Republic* was not the only liberal magazine on newsstands in the mid-1950s. Liberals also had the *Nation*, *Commonweal*, and even a few others. Conservatives, however, had only *Human Events*. Buckley believed that a new magazine would fill a vacuum.

After a year of fund-raising among California movie types and Texas oil millionaires, Buckley's first issue of the *National Review* hit the newsstands in November 1955. For the first five years the magazine operated at a deficit of at least $100,000 per year, and was kept afloat only by infusions of cash from the Buckley family fortune. However, the *National Review* quickly became what Buckley expected it to be: the voice of American conservatism and a unifying force in the rapidly growing movement. By 1960 Buckley and the *National Review* would embrace Barry Goldwater as the leader of American conservatism, and then finally as political candidate.[51]

Buckely's wealth and New England heritage often put off conservatives from the new coalition of southerners and westerners; and, in fact, during Goldwater's 1964 run Buckley and his northeastern consorts would be unceremoniously purged from the Goldwater campaign. But Buckley (possibly more than anyone except Goldwater himself) represented the new conservative movement in America; he was a true Goldwater conservative. He shared Goldwater's conservative beliefs on everything from anti-communism to individualism. His wit and style, both on the page and off, made him a primary spokesman for conservative issues after about 1960, and thus a frequent television guest. He often appeared on evening talk shows with Johnny Carson, Dick Cavitt, and David Suskind, and Sunday morning political discussion shows like *Meet the Press* and *Issues and Answers*. During national conventions, he was often consulted and interviewed for "the conservative line" on events and issues. He was a renowned debater, and during the 1964 Republican convention was pitted against the liberal writer Gore Vidal to argue the events as they unfolded on the screen. Television impressionists even copied his distinctive mannerisms. Bill Buckley, with a pencil shoved into his chin and his eyes shot skyward, became a conservative intellectual media star.

* * *

The Republican choice for president in 1960 was pretty much a closed book. With Eisenhower behind Richard Nixon it was fairly clear that the vice president would be the party's choice in Chicago. Nixon, however, was not without his baggage and problems. Eisenhower really did not like him, and that was clear to anyone close to Republican party politics. He had been touched by a couple of scandals and was often associated with McCarthyism, discredited by 1960 in all camps except the Far Right. But nevertheless, with Eisenhower's endorsement and blessing, however reluctant and left-handed, Nixon would be the party's nominee in 1960.

The GOP right also, generally, did not like Nixon. He occasionally tilted toward conservatism, but he was never truly one of the faithful. And Nixon's attempts to appeal to conservatives, while at the same time pandering after moderate Republican votes, infuriated party conservatives. He was, however, certainly preferable to New York governor Nelson Rockefeller, who was nosing around for the nomination in the fall of 1959. Rockefeller had taken the governor's seat in the 1958 elections, defeating popular Democratic incumbent Averell Harriman. His victory in a particularly bad election year for Republicans, along with his well-recognized name, projected Rockefeller to the top of Republican party lists of future presidential timber. But to the GOP right, Rockefeller was anathema; he represented everything GOP conservatives opposed. He was a self-proclaimed Republican liberal who sat well to the left of Eisenhower on most issues. He was the darling of the northeastern moderates—the candidate of the despised New York–Dewey crowd. The right considered him the worst of the me-too Republicans and they hated his willingness to accept most New Deal–Fair Deal programs, along with the entire liberal philosophy of expanded federal programs and federal management of sectors of the economy and even society. In addition, Rockefeller supported civil rights for African Americans and he courted labor. He was, however, a talented campaigner, a genuine vote-getter with his own very deep pockets for financial support. Like Goldwater, 1960 was his first foray onto the national political scene. With Rockefeller on the left and Goldwater on the right, these two characters seemed to be preparing, in 1960, to lock horns in 1964.

Nixon wanted to bridge gaps and heal wounds between the eastern wing of the party (represented in the past by Dewey and now Rockefeller) and the newly rising conservatives now led by Goldwater. Instead, this placed Nixon in the middle—never really popular with either wing, not trusted, and generally disliked. As the 1960 convention approached, Nixon tried to mollify both sides, but in the process, when it became clear that he would have to choose one over the other, he chose to draw close to Rockefeller and the Eastern Establishment at the expense of the right. It was probably good political strategy in 1960—the conservatives had no place else to go. But in the long run it was the beginning of a break between Goldwater and Nixon that would impact the party in later years.

In December 1959 Rockefeller announced that he would not seek the Republican nomination, insisting it was "definite and final."[52] Then in May 1960 he shifted his position and announced that he would be available for a party draft at the convention, but that he would not campaign. This noncandidacy kept Rockefeller in the public eye through the summer up to the convention, and in that position he argued often for his philosophy of liberal Republicanism. It appeared he would have significant influence on the party platform. In the spring, Goldwater visited Nixon and tried to push him to support key conservative issues. "[A] number of people I've talked with," Goldwater recalled, "are disappointed with your failure to take a strong stand on some conservative issues [like] federal spending, a balanced budget, the growing bureaucracy." Nixon responded that, as a candidate, he fully intended to argue for a reduction in spending, a balanced budget, and an end to bureaucratic growth. Goldwater also asked the vice president to advocate a right-to-work plank in the Republican party platform. Nixon agreed. Then Nixon told Goldwater that he had no intention of meeting with Rockefeller until after the convention. Goldwater was satisfied. He had, he thought, won the battle for Nixon's political soul.[53]

However, Rockefeller was, at that moment, a more formidable figure in the Republican party than Goldwater. In the days just before the convention Rockefeller made it clear in press interviews that he would direct a floor fight at the convention unless Nixon came over to several of his convictions. Nixon, always the pragmatic politician, knew he needed New York to win in November, so he went for the compromise with Rockefeller in order to keep his left flank in line. On July 22, just two days before the convention opened in Chicago, Nixon traveled to Rockefeller's Manhattan apartment on Fifth Avenue, and there the two pounded out the gist of the party platform as they, together, saw it. The next morning they telephoned their decisions to the platform committee. Their plan called for federal intervention to stimulate the economy; a federally sponsored medical program for the aged; a strong civil rights plank, including specific support for the sit-in movement then sweeping across the South; and an agreement to repeal right-to-work laws under the Taft–Hartley Act. Nixon then offered to name Rockefeller as his running mate. Rockefeller declined, but he insisted that Nixon name an eastern moderate. The vice president agreed. When the specifics of the pact were announced, the language seemed to be Rockefeller's. To GOP conservatives it appeared that the New York governor had dictated the terms of the platform—and they believed they had been betrayed.[54]

Goldwater was furious. His first response was to call Nixon a "two-fisted four-square liar."[55] Years later, in reference to the same events, he called Nixon "the most dishonest individual I ever met in my life."[56] He called the Nixon–Rockefeller compact the "Munich of the Republican Party" and even "treasonous." Others on the right called it the "Surrender of Fifth Avenue." Much of the problem surrounding the Nixon–Rockefeller pact, as Goldwater and the right saw it, had to do with image. Rockefeller had summoned Nixon to his home—and Nixon (thus seemingly in a subordinate position) answered the summons and hightailed it to Rocky's lair. Then, the next morning, it was Rockefeller who announced the provisions of the agreement to the press. Nixon, it seemed, had done little more than sign on.[57]

All this changed Goldwater's mood as the opening day of the convention approached. Back in March, South Carolina Republicans had agreed to pledge their thirteen convention delegates to Goldwater, and the chairman of the South Carolina delegation convinced Goldwater that if his name were placed in nomination that, if nothing else, conservatism would be represented at the convention. Goldwater relented. "From a philosophical standpoint," he wrote later, "they were practicing what I had been practicing [so] I decided to let it stand."[58] Goldwater's home state of Arizona then followed suit. But Goldwater had no intention of upsetting the convention. In fact, he arrived in Chicago intending to withdraw his nomination and endorse Nixon. At most, he may have harbored the thought of being tapped for the second spot on the ticket.

However, following the Rockefeller–Nixon pact Goldwater decided to delay delivering his speech. The result was no conservative surge to Goldwater, but Texas released its delegates and Nixon operatives feared that Goldwater could pull as many as three hundred delegate votes in a floor count. Goldwater, however, still had no intention of taking it that far, but he would be heard. In a fiery speech (withdrawing from the nomination) Goldwater awakened the convention hall. He told his supporters on the right first to "grow up" and support Nixon's candidacy. Then he added, "If we want to take this party back, and I think we can some day, let's get to work."[59] Goldwater's statements electrified conservatives and solidified his place as the undisputed leader of American conservatism.

Nixon was nominated unanimously on the first ballot. He chose Henry Cabot Lodge, the lion of the northeastern moderates, as his running mate in what conservatives saw as a clear affront to the right, although Nixon was probably more concerned with holding the northeastern moderate wing of the party in line than jabbing at the conservatives. Thus, as the conservatives saw it, the Republican party had headed into another election with its Deweyite me-too slate and lost. Lodge's placement on the ticket had even failed to win any of the big northeastern industrial states. Conservatives complained that Nixon had tried to "out liberal Kennedy" by naming Lodge, had agreed with Kennedy on nearly every issue, and had made a deal with the devil Rockefeller—and he still made no dents in the liberal East. In addition, Nixon's pandering to the East had meant he had alienated the conservative South. For conservative analysts with an eye on 1964, the party clearly needed to abandon the northeastern liberals and develop a southern strategy.[60] Within days of the election Goldwater said, "the next election should be contested by conservatives, not by people who ape the New Deal."[61]

Nixon's 1960 defeat immediately threw the Republican party into disarray. The group most prepared to pick up the pieces was the conservatives. "All the while," *Time* noted four years later, "moderate leaders dozed complacently."[62] It also triggered a draft-Goldwater movement of almost mythical enthusiasm. The objective, of course, was 1964, an election that most expected to pit the right against the left for the first time in anyone's memory: John Kennedy and American liberalism against Barry Goldwater and the new conservatism. It would be, as Phyllis Schlafly called it, "a choice, not an echo."[63]

The 1960 Republican National Convention and following election was a turning point for the Republican right. As William Rusher has noted, the result was "a fast-growing movement with a developing set of coherent ideas, able national spokesmen, its own . . . theoretical journals, firm ties with important leaders and organizational components of the Republican party, and steadily increasing sense of unity and purpose."[64] Goldwater and the GOP right had many of the things they needed to step out into the political world. While in 1960 their ideas and dreams may have been big, their constituency was enthusiastic but small. The question for conservatives in 1960 was clear: Could they sell their convictions to the nation and turn their enthusiasm and ideas into votes in just four years?

2

The Democrats Resurgent and the Rise of the Boston–Austin Axis

The 1948 election was a monumental victory for the Democrats and their candidate Harry Truman. To anyone with the slightest eye toward politics and history, 1948 was going to be the year of the Republicans. The Democrats had had their run. America seemed to settle in for a tidal wave of Republicanism that was about to wash over Washington and the rest of the nation. Truman, however, put together a tenuous coalition of traditional liberals, organized labor, and northern urban African Americans to pull out an upset victory that seemed to surprise everyone except possibly Truman himself. And it was a solid victory. Although the popular vote was close, Truman won where it counted, in the Electoral College, with a substantial margin of 303 to 189. The Democrats routed the Republicans in Congress as well, taking back control of both houses. The Republicans were left in disarray, pointing fingers and divided again between the moderates led by the defeated presidential candidate Thomas Dewey and the conservatives led by Ohio senator Robert Taft.

Truman's win was a spectacular victory for the Democrats, but it was quickly apparent that they too were also badly divided. Truman had pulled his party together for what seemed one shining moment of unity on election day, but immediately after the election old wounds were again opened and the party found itself divided and feuding. One primary problem was civil rights, an age old issue in the party that had turned extremely volatile in the years after World War II. As the 1948 election approached, Truman (led by his advisors, particularly Clark Clifford) had concluded that black voters in northern cities were far more significant in the national electoral process than white voters in the South. Black voters in Chicago, Cleveland, and Los Angeles might deliver the electoral votes of Illinois, Ohio, and California—a total of seventy-eight electoral votes, nearly twenty votes more than the electoral votes of entire Deep South combined.[1]

The strategy may have pushed Truman over the top in 1948, but, as previously mentioned, it also divided the party by alienating the South. Truman had tried, before the election, to ride the political fence between black voters who wanted action on civil rights issues and southern whites who wanted to maintain racial segregation. By the summer of 1948, however, this strategy had succeeded in doing little more than offending both groups. African-American voters saw Truman's modest civil rights concessions as far beyond anything the Republicans were offering and gave their votes to Truman in unprecedented numbers on election day. But white southerners were not so easily bought. Most of the Alabama and Mississippi delegates bolted the Democratic National Convention when the party added a strong civil rights plank to the 1948 platform. The result was the formation of the States' Rights Democrats, or the "Dixiecrats." On August 11, they nominated South Carolina governor Strom Thurmond and Mississippi governor Fielding Wright as their candidates for president and vice president. On election day, Thurmond got a bit over 1 million popular votes and thirty-nine electoral votes in Mississippi, Louisiana, South Carolina, and Alabama.[2]

The Dixiecrat impact on the 1948 election was negligible, but after the election southern congressmen made the Democratic party pay dearly for the 1948 affront. Since the late 1930s a loose coalition had existed between conservative southern Democrats and Republicans on a few issues such as civil rights, but after 1948 that coalition turned into a southern rebellion within the Democratic party that blocked the Democrats' majorities in Congress. Southerners often voted with the Republicans against a number of Fair Deal bills, in complete disregard for the Democratic party agenda and the president's wishes. By 1952, the party was in disarray in the face of a formidable Republican party ticket of Dwight Eisenhower and Richard Nixon. The Democrats were about to take the fall that most pundits had expected them to take four years before.

The Democratic candidate-emergent in 1952 was Adlai Stevenson, the incumbent governor of Illinois. Billed as an intellectual and a liberal, he was really neither. He often called himself a moderate, and he rarely took time to read. He was an excellent speaker with an uncanny use of language and a well-developed wit. The *New York Times* described him as "slightly to the right—enough to the right to satisfy the center, but not far enough mortally to offend the left or to please the right. . . ."[3] Party liberals assumed that in office, and with the proper advice and advisors, he would prove to be liberal enough. But as a candidate, Stevenson claimed to oppose public housing, federal aid to education, federally funded medical care, and he even refused to support the repeal of Taft–Hartley, the Republican-devised law known as the "slave labor" bill to the nation's organized workers. On civil rights, Stevenson believed he would need southern votes in 1952, so he was easily persuaded at the Democratic convention to accept southern demands and concede to a moderate civil rights plank that omitted a Fair Employment Practices Commission (FEPC). The compromise alienated many blacks and liberals.[4]

Despite aggressive challenges from Tennessee senator Estes Kefauver and New York governor Averell Harriman, Stevenson was nominated on the third ballot. In an attempt to allay southern defections, he chose Alabama senator John Sparkman as his running mate. Sparkman was often described as a "southern progressive" or even a "southern liberal," but the choice of Sparkman did little to keep northern liberals from questioning Stevenson's liberalism and civil rights credentials. In the end, however, Stevenson could not overcome Eisenhower's infectious personal appeal, the nation's growing fear of domestic communism, and a nagging anxiety over the Korean War. When Eisenhower announced late in the campaign, "I will go to Korea," Stevenson was beaten. He received only eighty-nine electoral votes, all in the South.

A major chunk of the South, however, got sucked into the Eisenhower landslide. The traditional Democratic states of Texas, Tennessee, Virginia, Maryland, and Florida voted Republican. It was a slow process, but the winds in the South were changing. At least on the federal election level, southerners in ever-increasing numbers were jumping into the Republican column. In 1948 Truman had made it clear that it would be the Democrats who would carry the mantle of civil rights in the post-war era. In 1952 Stevenson essentially backed away from that pledge, but 73 percent of African Americans voted for him anyway.[5] The Democrats had become the party of civil rights. Eisenhower, however, did not ignore civil rights. He promised to end segregation in Washington, D.C., and to work for federal legislation that would put an end to lynchings and poll taxes in the South. But at the same time he also made it clear through both statements and actions that he did not believe that federal legislation could solve race problems. When the Supreme Court handed down the *Brown* decision in 1954, Eisenhower responded, "I don't believe you can change the hearts of men with laws or decisions," and "The fellow who tries to tell me that you can do these things by force is just plain nuts."[6] For those white southerners who wanted to maintain the white-dominated way of life in the South, Eisenhower was their man; and increasingly it appeared that the Republican party was (more so than the Democratic) willing to allow that way of life to exist without federal intervention.

The Democrats, however, refused to let the South leave the party without a fight. As the 1956 election approached, Democratic party leaders attempted to mend fences, to bring the white South back into the party. Again Stevenson was the party nominee. The party platform referred to civil rights only to reject "all proposals for the use of force to interfere with the orderly determination of these matters by the courts." Convinced that the civil rights issue could only damage him, and under the impression (and advice) that the election would turn on southern white votes, Stevenson steered clear of the civil rights issue; he refused to take a stand on *Brown*, even though polls showed overwhelming support among voters for the Supreme Court decision. The result was a rare moment of post-war unity between the Democratic party's northern liberal wing and southern whites. Hubert Humphrey, the Minnesota senator who rose to national prominence as a civil rights advocate, even agreed to support a civil rights plank "that is acceptable to the South."[7] And Eleanor Roosevelt, always a civil rights champion, called for reconciliation: "I think understanding and sympathy for the white people in the South," she said, "is as important as understanding and sympathy for the colored people."[8]

With Stevenson avoiding civil rights, Eisenhower had no need to engage the issue.[9] Stevenson spent most of the campaign trying to debunk the Republican party's claims of national prosperity and security. He spoke of poverty in America, a drop in farm income, deplorable schools. He called for a test ban treaty with the Soviets and an end to the draft, while at the same time accusing Eisenhower of not keeping pace with the Soviet armament buildup. The Suez Crisis, which broke out in the last days of October, and the simultaneous eruption of Soviet-dominated Eastern Europe did for Eisenhower in 1956 what the Korean War had done for him in 1952. In times of crisis, Americans wanted Eisenhower's strong hand on foreign policy in the White House. The result was a spectacular landslide. America liked Ike. He won with the largest popular vote in American history up to that time. His 57.4 percent popular vote advantage was exceeded only by Roosevelt's 1936 victory. The Republicans also won large numbers of votes from regions on the outskirts of traditionally Democratic strongholds like Chicago, Jersey City, and Milwaukee, and they attracted a large majority of the votes from Southern California. These suburban regions were growing rapidly in the 1950s, becoming increasingly affluent—and conservative. They would have a major impact on the elections in the next decade and after.

Stevenson's attempt to keep the South in line failed miserably. Although his only electoral votes came from southern states, Stevenson lost more electoral votes in the South than he won. He lost Texas, Oklahoma, Kentucky, Tennessee, Virginia, Louisiana, Florida, and Maryland. He gained Missouri, which he lost in 1952; but he lost Louisiana and Kentucky, which he had won in 1952. The Deep South remained loyal to the Democrats in 1956. By 1964, however, the civil rights issue would change the political landscape significantly in the South and finally push many of the same Deep South states into the Republican camp. The civil rights issue and southern votes (both black and white) continued to plague the Democrats into the 1960s and well beyond. In the 1930s and 1940s, Franklin Roosevelt was able to walk the fence on the civil rights issue—between southern whites who wanted to maintain a way of life built on racism and segregation, and northern liberals (together with a growing number of northern blacks). Both groups remained in the party throughout Roosevelt's tenure in office. But Harry Truman could not satisfy both sides, possibly because he was not the politician that Roosevelt was, possibly because by the late 1940s the issue was more volatile than it had been in the decades before Truman came to office. Throughout the 1950s, the Democrats tried to reconcile with the South, mostly through a weakening of party platform statements and promises of gradualism as opposed to forced desegregation. For the most part, that attempt at reconciliation failed. It would be necessary for John F. Kennedy to mend those fences in 1960.

* * *

Eisenhower's 1952 victory was sweet for Republicans. For the first time since the first two years of the Hoover administration the GOP controlled both the White House and Congress. They had been denied the White House since 1933, and they had controlled Congress for only two years between the rise of Roosevelt and the decline of Harry Truman. As is often the case with the American political pendulum, the high point of one party's successes is the exact origin of the rise of the other, and so it was in 1952. By 1954 the Democrats had won back control of Congress and their stock was on the rise as the Republicans began to divide and weaken. It was a common refrain after 1954 that Americans liked Ike, but they did not necessarily care much for the Republicans. It certainly seemed true. Even Eisenhower's huge landslide in 1956 did not bring in a Republican Congress—the first time since Zachary

Taylor that voters had elected a president whose party controlled neither house of Congress.

In 1952 black voters had gone to Stevenson in great numbers, but his efforts to appease white southerners in an attempt to keep the South in line apparently pushed large numbers of black voters back into the Republican party four years later. There may have been other reasons for the shift, however. African Americans may have seen the *Brown* decision as generated by the Eisenhower administration and delivered by a Republican chief justice who had been appointed by Eisenhower. Also, several black leaders, the most notable being New York congressman Adam Clayton Powell, came out in support of Eisenhower. This seemed to cue the pro–civil rights forces inside the Eisenhower administration to act on civil rights in hopes of building a Republican coalition for the future that might include African Americans. Fred Morrow, Eisenhower's only African-American campaign advisor, believed that a coalition of blacks, fiscal conservatives, and white suburbanites might turn the GOP into a majority party.[10] Other White House operatives and advisors, including Herbert Brownell, Maxwell Rabb, and Bryce Harlow, agreed that black votes had been part of a Republican coalition since Reconstruction and should remain so. At the same time, Democrats in Congress had come to the conclusion that Stevenson's failed policy of moderation on civil rights had caused the defection of African-American votes, clearly a primary voting bloc that the Democrats could not afford to lose to the Republicans. From these two inducements came the Civil Rights Bill of 1957, pushed by both Democratic liberals in Congress and civil rights advocates within the Eisenhower administration.

The administration had introduced a weak civil rights bill in 1956, but election year wariness stalled it in the Senate after the House approved it just before recess. The 1957 bill, as introduced by the administration, was to establish a civil rights division in the Justice Department under the leadership of a specially appointed assistant attorney general with the power to seek court injunctions against anyone obstructing the right of any citizen to vote. This portion of the bill, known as Part I, was controversial only because it gave specific powers to the federal government (as opposed to the states) to enforce voting rights. This point of contention between liberals, who supported federal intervention to regulate voting rights, and conservatives, who wanted to maintain states' rights, would be important to Goldwater supporters in 1964.

The South disliked this encroachment on their states' rights, but by the mid-1950s it was nearly impossible for moderate southerners to rationalize the old southern practice of denying African Americans the right to vote, and most southern legislators outside the Deep South states were willing to stand aside on this issue.

The bill sped through the House with few changes, passing on June 18 by vote of more than a two-to-one margin. In the Senate, majority leader Lyndon Johnson was persuaded to take leadership of the bill, despite its Republican origins. But Johnson believed the bill would pass under most any circumstances anyway, and that it was better that he control its outcome than the Republicans. Possibly more important, Johnson intended to run for his party's presidential nomination in 1960, but he was handicapped. Johnson was from Texas, and he believed that a southerner could not possibly win the Democratic nomination.[11] Consequently, he concluded that by portraying himself as more of a westerner than a southerner, and by supporting civil rights legislation, he could pull himself out from under the yoke of southern racism and possibly make himself more appealing to his party's liberals. In 1956 he was one of only three southern Senators who refused to sign what became known as the "Southern Manifesto" against the *Brown* decision, and he did not join the southern caucus in the Senate.[12] Johnson's problem with civil rights was the same problem that Democrats had grappled with since Roosevelt: he would have to perform a balancing act that would keep the always rebellious South in line without offending blacks and liberals. His plan was simple and predictable. He would lead the passage of the Civil Rights Act, but would see that it was a moderate bill, one that would not offend either side. The reward, he believed, would be a fast track to the 1960 nomination.

As Johnson had concluded, the bill would most likely pass, and that was his most persuasive argument. "[I]f you don't allow" this bill to pass, he argued to southern senators who opposed it, "you're going to lose everything . . . and your opportunity to delay or to slow down and to bring some kind of order or change will be gone."[13] Thus for southerners the objective became to influence the bill as much as possible—to weaken it. The majority of southern senators were willing to accept Part I of the bill, mostly because it was much less objectionable than the bill's other parts. It was Part III, in fact, that presented the biggest problem, the biggest threat to southern segregation. It gave broad powers to the federal government by allowing the attorney general to file a civil suit against anyone who deprived a citizen of his civil rights. Southerners saw this as nothing other than granting power to the federal government to desegregate schools in the South. Georgia's powerful senator Richard Russell led the fight against Part III, claiming that it would bring to bear "the whole might of the federal government, including the armed forces . . . to force a commingling of white and Negro children in the State supported schools of the South."[14] At the same time, Russell told Johnson privately that if Part III were not removed from the bill the South would filibuster. With that, it immediately became apparent to Johnson that southern objections to Part III would turn the bill into a political quagmire. At the same time, Eisenhower, in a press conference, announced that he had no real enthusiasm for Part III. With no support from the White House, and facing southern resistance, Johnson decided to sacrifice Part III in order to save the entire bill. An amendment orchestrated by Johnson and offered by Clinton Anderson and George Aiken removed Part III and the bill passed the Senate on August 7 by a vote of seventy-two to eighteen.

Johnson sought a second compromise on another portion of the bill, Part IV. The original bill allowed for trials by federal judges in cases involving civil rights contempt charges. Johnson became convinced (mostly by Russell) that the South would never stand for federal judges presiding over civil rights cases. The Johnson compromise that emerged was initiated in an amendment sponsored by Joe O'Mahoney of Wyoming, Estes Kefauver of Tennessee, and Frank Church of Idaho, a threesome that reflected the South–West coalition that Johnson had built to push the entire bill through the Senate. The amendment allowed for jury trials in most civil and contempt cases, which virtually emasculated the enforcement aspects of the bill because sympathetic southern juries had proven time and again that they would acquit civil rights violators. This amendment was adopted on August 2.

Naturally, liberals and civil rights advocates were infuriated by the removal of Part IV, but so was Eisenhower. He believed that Part IV would have allowed the Justice Department to obtain convictions (through decisions made by federal judges) of southern registrars who refused to allow African Americans to vote. To Eisenhower, Johnson had removed the primary voting rights aspect of the bill. On the day of the vote Eisenhower called the adoption of the amendment "one of the most serious political defeats of the past four years." The result will be, he added, that millions of "fellow Americans will continue . . . to be disenfranchised."[15] Eisenhower also criticized twelve Republicans, including Barry Goldwater, who had voted with the South on the bill.

In the final analysis, neither side particularly cared for the compromise bill, but liberals and civil rights advocates were far more disappointed than southerners. Several liberal activists and civil rights leaders like Ralph Bunche, Jackie Robinson, and A. Philip Randolph tried to convince Eisenhower that the bill was so weak it should be vetoed. Others, like the NAACP leadership and Martin Luther King, Jr., decided that a bad civil rights bill was better than none. Liberal activist Joseph Rauh said years later that the bill set back desegregation in the South seven years—because the powers of Part III were finally included in the 1964 Civil Rights Bill.[16] After the House and Senate agreed on the final bill, Eisenhower reluctantly signed it on September 2.

Instead of winning praise for his efforts, Johnson suffered a great deal within his party because of this compromise. To some liberals and civil rights leaders he had done nothing more than rallied southern power to emasculate a civil rights bill, and that cloud would hang over him until 1964 when he would push through Congress a civil rights bill that was strong enough to end legal segregation in the South. In his memoirs, Johnson wrote that he considered the Civil Rights Act of 1957 to be one of the most important accomplishments of his tenure as Senate Majority Leader. "We obtained only half a loaf in that fight," he wrote, "but it was an essential half-loaf. . . . There was no way we could have persuaded the majority of Senators to agree to [those provisions that were eventually removed]. To have pressed for the impossible would have been to destroy all hopes of the possible." As a result of the 1957 bill, he wrote, "the path was opened for later legislation extending federal protection into every area of civil rights." In an interview immediately after the bill was signed, Johnson said, "I got all I could on civil rights in 1957. Next year I'll get a little more, and the year after that I'll get a little more."[17]

There is probably no better measure of Lyndon Johnson than the Civil Rights Act of 1957. It was, in fact, probably all that was possible in 1957. And, as Johnson said, it set a precedent for the 1964 bill and the 1965 Voting Rights Act. It was also testimony to Johnson's willingness and ability to compromise on key issues. It showed his strength and agility as a legislator, possibly the greatest legislator of the twentieth century. His success on this issue showed that he, possibly better than anyone else, could be the bridge between several different political groups and sections in America. He pulled together a coalition of southerners and westerners, some Democrats and Republicans. He alienated some civil rights leaders like Roy Wilkins, but the NAACP eventually supported the bill, seeing it as a precedent for the future rather than an end. King and other civil rights moderates like Bayard Rustin saw the bill much as Johnson did: half a loaf, which was much better than none.

Johnson also kept his party together at a time when the issue of civil rights was about to tear the Democrats apart. In 1957 the Democratic party was simply no longer big enough for liberals, civil rights leaders, and white south-ern conservatives. It was fairly clear there would be an eventual realign-ment—that someone would have to go. But in the hands of Lyndon Johnson, it would not be in 1957.

The event also placed Johnson undisputedly at the head of his party—at least for a short time. By 1957 Stevenson was out of the picture as a potential candidate in 1960 and John Kennedy had not yet begun his meteoric rise. Johnson deserved the position. He had, in fact, done the seemingly impos-sible. As party leader between 1953 and 1960, Johnson had led his party through the Eisenhower years, first as minority leader and then as majority leader after the Democrats gained control of both houses of Congress in the 1954 elections. By 1960, the Democrats had regained dominance over the nation's political system. Johnson's Senate leadership, and thus party leader-ship, through this period had a great deal to do with the rise of the Democrats from division and defeat to dominance.

Johnson was not an ideologue, and an understanding of that goes a long way toward understanding his character. Hubert Humphrey called him "a rather clever, adroit, astute, pragmatist."[18] Such a characterization might have been used to describe Franklin Roosevelt, the man Johnson most admired. Johnson disliked labels and he often derided those who labeled themselves conservative or liberal, or who remained unalterably consistent in their com-mitments. To Johnson, there was no place in government for inflexibility. The American system as he saw it revolved around compromises and bar-gains. Those who insisted on fighting futile battles were impractical, unable to get things done, and were, more often than not, little more than obstruc-tionists, impediments to progress and legislative achievement. To Johnson, Barry Goldwater was the worst of this sort, uncompromising, ideological rather than pragmatic, unable or unwilling to compromise, capable of stand-ing alone in a losing fight. To Johnson this was wasted energy. Within his own party, Johnson considered Paul Douglas just as ideological on liberal legislation and, to Johnson's thinking, just as much an obstructionist as Goldwater. But Everett Dirksen, the conservative senator from Illinois, or Richard Russell, the Democrat senator from Georgia—these were men Johnson could deal with. He understood that both men had to make public stands to satisfy their constituencies (just as Johnson did), but he also knew that both men were flexible, willing to compromise, and thus helpful in mak-ing the legislative process work. Hubert Humphrey came to the Senate as something of a liberal ideologue, but under Johnson's tutelage Humphrey learned to be a player, learned to be what Johnson called a "good liberal."

Johnson, of course, would reward Humphrey for his transformation with the vice presidency in 1964.

Goldwater-the-ideologue may have annoyed Johnson-the-Majority Leader, but the feeling was not mutual. In the late 1970s, after Johnson had died, Goldwater recalled in an interview with Merle Miller that Johnson "was a very good leader. He worked the Senate. If he had a job to do, we didn't go home at five or six o'clock. We went home when we got the job done, and it might be two or three days later, having been there all night, several nights. Personally, I liked working that way. In those days at least we knew. When Lyndon Johnson said, 'this is going to be legislation,' you knew you weren't going to leave until it was legislation, until it was finished. . . . I much preferred it in every way with Lyndon Johnson."[19] Even Goldwater could not deny Johnson's effectiveness.

Johnson was also a consensus builder. His job, as he saw it, was to find areas of commonality and minimize differences, and he was famous at it. All the while, he had to hold together a political party that harbored widely divergent interests and philosophies while reaching out to moderate Republicans. During the Truman administration, a congressional coalition of Republicans and conservative Democrats (mostly from the South) laid waste to much of Truman's Fair Deal. That coalition had, in fact, emerged as early as 1936 against several New Deal programs. When Johnson took over the Senate in 1953, he began a process of turning that coalition around, building a coalition of Democrats (including the South) and moderate Republicans. That coalition, firmly in Johnson's hands, controlled the Senate through the 1950s, pushing through mounds of legislation, much of it, like the Civil Rights Act of 1957, the result of a consensus, compromised, bargained, even weakened, but passed. When Johnson left the Senate to become vice president in 1961, his tight grip on the Senate immediately loosened and the old Republican–southern conservative coalition reemerged. For three years the Kennedy administration found its hands tied, its legislation stalled, its relationship with Congress in shambles. When Johnson became president in November 1963, he immediately broke the deadlock in Congress, reestablished his old Democrat–Republican moderate consensus, and rammed through Congress some of the most important legislation of the twentieth century. To his friends he was a doer, a legislative magician. To his enemies and detractors he was an unscrupulous wheeler-dealer, an opportunist with little vision whose consensus building and compromises served to weaken, even emasculate, important legislation. Much of his Great Society legislation, for example, was passed, but Johnson was often willing to compromise on funding in order to get bills through Congress and past conservative legislators who saw the programs as too expensive. The result was that many programs failed for lack of sufficient funding.

For Johnson, the real power was at the political center, and he always considered himself a centrist while at the same time rejecting any such label. Others, however, described him as a liberal. Hubert Humphrey, seeing Johnson in something of a New Deal mold, further called him a "pragmatic liberal."[20] In Congress in the late 1930s, Johnson was associated with the New Deal and New Dealers. In the Senate in the 1950s, he continued to support relief and welfare policies, public power programs, and an interventionist foreign policy. But in the late 1940s, he deferred to his conservative Texas constituency and backed away from Truman's federal health care program and open support for organized labor. His support for Taft–Hartley nearly cost him his 1948 bid for the Senate. Before 1957, Johnson stood with the South (and again his Texas constituency) against most civil right advances, and like a number of southern Democrats through the New Deal and post–New Deal periods, he could be considered a liberal when it came to most social programs administered from Washington, but on labor and race issues he was a conservative in deference to his southern constituency.

* * *

America was surprised when John F. Kennedy chose Lyndon Johnson as his vice presidential candidate at the 1960 Democratic convention. But it should not have been a surprise. Johnson was the perfect choice. He was everything Kennedy was not—just as Kennedy was everything Johnson was not. Even the physical appearances of the two men complemented the ticket. Kennedy exuded an image of youth, intelligence, even movie-star-like glamour that appealed to a large constituency of northeastern and northern liberals and intellectuals. Johnson's image was earthy and down home—rural, even crude, often described as "corn pone." He was not that much older than Kennedy, but he appeared much older (he had already had a heart attack) and experienced, a Washington insider. Although Kennedy had been in Washington for fourteen years, he was a fresh face to the American people and easily deflected the insider image. But more important, there was no one in American politics quite like Johnson. As a legislator, he had built bridges to nearly every faction within the Democratic party. He was a southerner who had passed a civil rights bill by hammering together a coalition that included southerners, westerners, and not a few moderate Republicans. Even better, the bill was moderate and not radical, while maintaining the support of most black civil rights leaders and liberals. Kennedy needed the South to beat Nixon; Johnson could deliver the South without alienating liberals and blacks. He was the perfect running mate.

Kennedy and Johnson were, of course, not strangers in 1960. Both had served in the Senate, Johnson since 1949 and Kennedy since 1953. In the four years before Kennedy came to Washington, Johnson rose rapidly to the top of the Democratic party pecking order and was already being looked at as a presidential hopeful by party leaders. In 1952, Richard Russell encouraged Johnson to run for the presidency, and if not that, the vice presidency.[21] He was too young and not well enough known to attract much attention at the convention that year, but it was clear that Lyndon Johnson was on his way to party leadership. When Kennedy was elected to the Senate in 1952, Johnson was already an established party leader. He took on Kennedy as something of an apprentice, and soon the young senator was working easily within the various Johnson-devised coalitions, becoming, like Hubert Humphrey, a "good liberal."

In 1956 both men crossed paths as potential vice presidential candidates on what was certain to be a losing ticket with Stevenson. Kennedy tried to appeal to party leaders by arguing that Eisenhower had done extremely well with Catholics in 1952 and that a Catholic on the ticket with Stevenson would be a winner. Party delegates also found him attractive because he had just published his Pulitzer Prize–winning *Profiles in Courage*, and presented an appealing air of intellect combined with political integrity. Johnson's appeal was his southern connection. He was also distantly related to the policies of Roosevelt and the New Deal, but he was hardly considered a liberal. In fact, because of his willingness to compromise on legislation, Johnson was often bundled with the southern conservatives, an image he detested and worked through much of his life to dispel, primarily because he knew a southern conservative could never win his party's nomination for president. Rather than decide on a running mate, Stevenson decided to allow the convention delegates to make the choice, and with that all concern for voter appeal in the general election gave way to delegate counts. In the final analysis Tennessee senator Estes Kefauver was too strong for the other candidates; he had mounted a challenge to Stevenson's candidacy for the top spot and had maintained control of enough delegates from the presidential candidate nomination process to keep Johnson, Kennedy, and any other hopefuls out of serious contention. Johnson, in the final vote, threw his delegates to Kennedy. The event turned out to be good for both Kennedy and Johnson by keeping each from being identified with the losing ticket while giving both men a good shot of national exposure. Not surprisingly, they both looked immediately to 1960.

Johnson and Kennedy headed toward the 1960 election as early front-runners, but both carried the burden of a handicap that was necessary to overcome. Johnson's southern background was nearly insurmountable in the political climate of the late 1950s. The Civil Rights Act of 1957, which carried his stamp although it was an administration initiative, helped a great deal in placing him outside the realm of the southern segregationists, but southern politicians in 1960 were still considered somewhere on the fringes of American politics—good vice presidential material, but too narrow in their political and social philosophies to lead the national ticket. William Proxmier, one of only a few in the Senate who could afford Johnson as an enemy, told a group of labor leaders in Wisconsin that Johnson had "overcome his regional limitations to a remarkable degree," but he is "still a Southerner."[22] Kennedy's burden was his religion, but that was more a perceived handicap than a real one. By November 1960, Kennedy had successfully removed that factor from the campaign.

Johnson campaigned from the inside, mostly by rounding up support from the party leadership—and he did not discourage campaign activity on his behalf.[23] By early 1960, however, his support began to wane at least in part because he refused to announce his candidacy. Only on July 5, just three days before the national convention, did Johnson announce. By then, the Kennedy bandwagon had been rolling for months. Stopping it was impossible.

It is often the assumption that Johnson simply erred in 1960, that he believed he could win the nomination by carrying the support of the party leadership, that he could count on his national reputation as a legislator to win the nomination, that playing hard-to-get would be a successful strategy in a campaign where playing hard-to-get was a big mistake, that he underestimated Kennedy. It seems unlikely, however, that Johnson would make such mistakes. He was possibly the nation's most astute politician in 1960, and he certainly knew what it took to win his party's nomination. More likely, despite all Johnson's bluster and pomposity, he carried with him an incredible amount of self-doubt and insecurity. These were characteristics that would be more apparent as the 1964 election approached—an election in which Johnson was almost assured a landslide victory, but during which he managed to convince several of his advisors, and his wife, that he should drop out of the race. George Reedy, Johnson's closest advisor during his 1960 noncampaign, told an interviewer years later that Johnson really did not want to run, and Johnson's actions in 1960 seem to bear out that conclusion. "My very strong impression," Reedy said, "is that he really did not want to make the race; but that the events of all the preceding years had led him to a position where he really couldn't say no."[24] Another advisor, James Rowe, insisted that Johnson wanted the nomination "so much his tongue was hanging out," but "other parts of him said, 'This is impossible. Why get my hopes up? I'm not going to try. If I don't try I won't fail.'"[25] Bouts of self-doubt and even depression would continue to plague Johnson and color his decisions clear through 1968.

Johnson must have also realized that his southernness was nearly insurmountable in 1960. He may have concluded with good reason that the only possible hope for a southerner to become part of the national Democratic party ticket that year (and for the foreseeable future) was as vice presidential candidate. From there, possibly, a southerner like himself might ascend to the White House as heir apparent with the support of the outgoing president. It was certainly a logical conclusion. With the exception of Roosevelt's choice of Henry Wallace in 1940, the Democrats, in every election since 1928, had nominated a northerner who had, for the cause of party unity, chosen a vice presidential candidate from the South.[26] With Kennedy clearly in the driver's seat for the nomination, Johnson may have arrived at the 1960 Los Angeles convention to present himself as a strong candidate for the vice presidency.

All that seems logical—Lyndon Johnson, the southern half of a national ticket. But when Johnson arrived in Los Angeles he did not act like a candidate who was willing to settle for number two. His staff and supporters immediately began spreading several rumors about the Kennedys, one in particular that Joseph Kennedy had been an anti-Semite and a pro-Hitler isolationist before the war, an accusation that was not entirely false, but certainly exaggerated.[27] Johnson then made a number of statements before several state delegations attacking Kennedy's inexperience, his poor health, and his "soft" stance on communism. In a speech before the Washington delegation, Johnson said, "I was never any Chamberlain-umbrella-policy man," comparing himself to what many believed to be Joseph Kennedy's appeasement policies while he was ambassador to England in the years prior to World War II. "I never thought Hitler was right," he added.[28] Then, apparently to counter Kennedy's calls for youth and vigor in government, Johnson supporters John Connally and India Edwards called a press conference in Los Angeles and announced that Kennedy was not that healthy, that he, in fact, had Addison's disease. Kennedy did indeed have the disease and had tried hard to hide it, but Connally and Edwards exaggerated his condition by describing the illness as deadly.[29] The result of all this was that Kennedy's staff came to hate the Johnson people—and the feeling was clearly mutual. Quickly, it no longer seemed logical that Johnson would be considered as Kennedy's running mate.

Although Kennedy had toyed with decorating his ticket with what he called a "Midwestern liberal" (which narrowed the field for many to either Humphrey or Stuart Symington of Missouri), by as early as mid-July he seemed to have concluded that he needed Johnson in order to win in November, and that he wanted Johnson on the ticket.[30] Hubert Humphrey lobbied for a Kennedy–Johnson ticket, as did other heavyweights like *Washington Post* publisher Philip Graham and columnist Joseph Alsop.[31] And despite all the pre-convention maneuvers and rumors, Joseph Kennedy apparently saw the political advantages of a Kennedy–Johnson ticket, a fact that certainly carried a great deal of weight with the candidate. Just before the convention convened, John Kennedy made it clear that Johnson was his first choice. At a press conference he responded to a reporter's question by stating that if he could not be president he would like to see Johnson win the nomination; and he told Massachusetts congressman Tip O'Neill, "Of course I want Lyndon . . . Lyndon's the natural choice. . . ."[32] However, within the Kennedy camp there were significant dissenters. Several Kennedy family members and insiders opposed Johnson's candidacy, including political advisors Kenneth O'Donnell and Pierre Salinger, and Kennedy's brother-in-law Sargent Shriver. So did most labor leaders, particularly United Auto Workers head Walter Reuther. Most important, however, Robert Kennedy opposed Johnson and lobbied hard for his brother to take Washington senator Henry "Scoop" Jackson, who was campaigning openly for the number two position.[33] At a crucial point, Kennedy apparently wavered and allowed his brother to approach Johnson and ask him to withdraw on his own. When Johnson refused, the Kennedys decided to keep him on the ticket after all.[34] The incident, possibly one of the most notorious in the annals of post-war political history, damaged the LBJ–RFK relationship. Johnson always believed that the younger Kennedy was acting on his own; and Bobby Kennedy, who did not want Johnson on the ticket in the first place, always thought Johnson should have accepted Jack's wishes and withdrawn.[35] For the next four years, until the 1964 election, these two men would have to work closely together while truly disliking each other. Their relationship, with its beginnings in the summer of 1960, would have a major impact on the election of 1964.

Despite all the bad blood that flowed back and forth in Los Angeles in 1960, the JFK–LBJ, president–vice president relationship was one of reasonable respect. George Reedy recalled that Johnson and Jack Kennedy "always got along very well."[36] Long-time Johnson friend and advisor Abe Fortas recalled that Kennedy "was very warm toward . . . Johnson. It seemed to me there was a very good rapport between the two."[37] And Johnson did his job. In October, he toured the southern states and the ticket carried most of the region in an extremely tight race.

Johnson's job, if nothing else, was to carry Texas. As the election approached, it appeared that Texas could go either way, and the prospect of losing Texas (and then possibly the election) weighed heavily on Johnson. Texas liberals had stayed away from the campaign, and many of the state's conservative Democrats were threatening to cross over and join "Democrats for Nixon." However, on November 4, just a few days after Lady Bird's father died and just four days before the election, an event occurred in Dallas that became one of the most significant of the campaign and to many observers an election turning point in Texas. While attending a rally at the Adolphus Hotel in Dallas, Lyndon and Lady Bird were attacked by hundreds of hostile, mostly female, screaming Nixon supporters. With the entire press corps, including cameras, looking on, the vice presidential candidate and his wife were spat on, yelled at, and cursed. A hostile woman grabbed Lady Bird's gloves and threw them in a ditch. Another hit her on the head with a sign that read "Let's Ground Lady Bird," and then spit in her face. It took the Johnsons thirty minutes to move seventy-five feet through the crowd.[38]

Film of the event appeared on network news reports that evening, and on the front pages of every major newspaper in the nation the next morning. The incident worked in the favor of the Kennedy–Johnson candidacy by showing what many had come to see as growing extremism within the Republican party. It turned Johnson's image from that of a boisterous southern conservative into a sympathetic figure under attack by the far right—and, in the eyes of many, protecting his wife.[39] Immediately after the incident, and just before the election, Johnson's numbers rose rapidly in Texas and possibly pushed that state over the top for Kennedy. Johnson's stock also increased throughout the South in the last four days of the campaign. If nothing else, Georgian senator Richard Russell, reluctant to support Kennedy, came over to the campaign as a direct result of the incident and began campaigning hard for the ticket in the South.[40]

Johnson may have played a significant role in the campaign, but his role as vice president was a minor one. He was an outsider in an administration that owed little to party regulars like him. Although Johnson respected Kennedy, it is not surprising that he resented the new president's popularity, his personal wealth, even his image—all of which came to Kennedy with little effort, while Johnson had spent a lifetime trying desperately to cultivate all those things, sometimes with success and sometimes without. No two men could have been any more unalike than Kennedy and Johnson, and therein, at least on some level, was the advantage of a Kennedy–Johnson ticket. But in the context of a team in the White House, the relationship between the two men simply did not work.

Johnson's outsider status bothered him. He lacked the Harvard education, the glamorous background, the cultural appreciation. But most of that sophisticated urbanity that seemed to drape over the Kennedy crowd was at best a contrived characterization for the benefit of voters; at worst it was artificial. The Kennedys were simply not that good at Washington politics. They were not effective at building coalitions, twisting arms, and pushing legislation. By early 1963 most of the Kennedy administration's legislative agenda was moribund, dying a slow death at the hands of a conservative coalition on Capitol Hill. The press, which had accepted and agreeably disseminated the image of action, culture, and vigor in the young administration, began to reverse course and attack Kennedy for a lack of movement. By mid-summer, the administration—with justification—was being tagged a failure by the once admiring press.

As Kennedy's legislative programs foundered in Congress, Johnson came to believe, with a great deal of justification, that he had become associated with a group of rank amateurs. He was, however, never asked for advice, never a part of the Kennedy inner circle. He remained outside the administration, unfulfilled, depressed, irritable, powerless. As the press and the public fawned over the charm and culture of the Kennedys, Johnson ate too much, drank too much Cutty Sark, and courted a second heart attack. He came to believe that the Kennedys, and many of the advisors surrounding the family, had contempt for him, that they saw him as an improperly educated country hick, a Washington wheeler-dealer at best, and thus they wanted him destroyed.

Lady Bird had pushed Lyndon to accept the vice presidency. She thought the job would take some pressure off her husband, and (five years after his heart attack) that he might live longer as vice president than as the Senate Majority Leader.[41] But power was Johnson's raison d'être, and without it he simply lost his direction. He tried at least once early in the Kennedy administration to establish his own initiatives, but Kennedy ignored his plans citing confusion over authority in the White House. Johnson also tried to maintain control of the Democratic caucus in the Senate, but when questions arose over the separation of the legislative and executive branches of government, he backed away. Kennedy often brought Johnson into the administration's decision-making processes, particularly in foreign affairs. He was a member of the National Security Council, or at least attended the meetings, and was at least an observer to the primary decisions of the administration's foreign policy. As a senator, Johnson had been instrumental in establishing the National Aeronautics and Space Administration (NASA), and Kennedy gave his vice president all the power he wanted to control and direct that organization. Johnson also chaired the President's Committee on Equal Employment. But these jobs were of little significance in the greater scheme of the Kennedy administration; they failed to challenge Johnson's ego, energy, and talents.

Possibly the greatest affront to Johnson was the Kennedy administration's unwillingness to use him as a congressional liaison, to put the vice president's greatest abilities to use. Kennedy's people, in all their youth and confidence, may have concluded that they could operate in the Washington legislative arenas without Johnson, or that Johnson, the one outsider among them, had no place of any real significance in the administration's processes. While the Kennedy administration's civil rights bill limped through the summer of 1963, the vice president made an impassioned speech for civil rights in Gettysburg and then offered advice to the administration, through Kennedy advisor and speechwriter Theodore Sorensen, on how to turn the bill into a moral issue, build a coalition in Congress, and push it through.[42] Johnson's advice, however, was rejected—on this issue as well as others. He responded by doing nothing, which exasperated even Bobby Kennedy: "His ideas about how to proceed were helpful on occasion . . . but as far as making any personal effort . . . he almost invariably refused to do so."[43] By November 1963, television comics were having fun with Johnson's obscurity, asking, "Lyndon who?" and "Whatever happened to LBJ?"

A major aspect of this situation revolved around the relationship between Johnson and Robert Kennedy. The two men clearly disliked each other, but more importantly, they distrusted each other. The conflict probably originated at the 1960 convention, but it might well have been deeper than that. Johnson saw Robert Kennedy as the president's closest advisor, certainly a usurper of what might have been his own power.[44] In fact, Johnson never really understood why Bobby Kennedy disliked him, and no one else seemed to understand either. Johnson's advisor George Reedy recalled a good relationship between the president and the vice president: "Johnson and Teddy [Kennedy] got along quite well. But Johnson and Bobby . . . they were antagonists from the moment they saw each other."[45] In his own analysis,

Johnson, in his memoirs, wrote simply, "Maybe it was just a matter of chemistry."[46] For whatever reason, by 1963, Johnson had concluded that Bobby was plotting to undercut him and force him off the 1964 ticket, and that he was even conspiring to succeed his brother in 1968. The press did not help Johnson's state of mind by speculating on both possibilities.[47] In what had become a Johnson characteristic, the vice president, in his despair and depression, decided he did not want the job, that he would withdraw his name from the ticket and retire to his Texas ranch. Bobby Baker, a Johnson confidant during this period, described the vice president's obsession with the younger Kennedy as "bordered paranoia."[48]

It was, in fact, Bobby Baker who was the catalyst for much of the bad blood between Johnson and Bobby Kennedy. Baker had come to the Senate in the early 1940s as a page. By the time he was in his mid-twenties he had become secretary to the Majority Leader, a very powerful position and one extremely close to Lyndon Johnson. "I have two daughters," Johnson once said. "If I had a son, this would be the boy."[49] By 1963, however, Baker had used his powerful connections to amass a fortune of over $40 million as part owner of dozens of companies and corporations. His financial successes on a yearly salary of just $19,000 raised the curiosity of the FBI. An investigation led by Delaware senator John Williams eventually uncovered a whole series of illegal deals and sent Baker to prison on several convictions.[50] The investigators, however, wanted to cast their nets for bigger fish and tried to pull Johnson in with Baker. By October 1963 Johnson had been generally exonerated of any wrongdoing, although he and Baker had, in fact, been involved in what were clearly shady, yet minor, dealings in the 1950s.[51] The significance here is that Johnson came to the conclusion that Bobby Kennedy, the attorney general, had instigated the investigation in hopes of using its findings to destroy Johnson and remove him from the 1964 ticket.[52] There is no evidence that Bobby Kennedy instigated the investigation, and he subsequently denied several times that he wanted to use the Johnson–Baker relationship to destroy Johnson.[53] Nevertheless, if Bobby had wanted Johnson off the ticket it probably mattered little. President Kennedy needed Johnson in the approaching 1964 election for the same reason he needed him in 1960—to hold the South. In addition, Kennedy realized that to dump Johnson would be to admit that the Baker case was a serious scandal.[54] When reporter Charles Bartlett suggested to the president in 1963 that Johnson be dumped, Kennedy remarked, "Why would I do a thing like that? That would be absolutely crazy. It would . . . hurt me in Texas. That would be the most foolish thing I could do."[55] Despite the rumors, press reports, and Johnson's own misgivings,

Kennedy continued to insist during press conferences that he had no intention of removing Johnson from the 1964 ticket.

On November 12, 1963, Kennedy insiders met to chart the course for their president's 1964 reelection campaign. Those present included White House staffers Larry O'Brien, Ken O'Donnell, and Ted Sorensen. DNC members John Bailey and Richard Maguire also attended, along with Richard Scammon, a numbers-cruncher from the Census Bureau. The campaign was to be led by Stephen Smith, the president's nearly invisible brother-in-law. Smith had been quietly setting up a campaign skeleton since the spring. O'Brien was to be director of organization, doing what he did best—dealing directly with state party leaders. O'Donnell would schedule the campaign's events. Coordinators were named to deal with particularly troublesome states.[56] It was typical of the Kennedy machine: Organize early. Organize well. Besides the discussion of who would do what in the coming campaign, the group concluded from October Gallup polls that the most formidable Republican candidate would be Michigan governor George Romney. His business background, his strong civil rights record, and his moderate stance on most other issues, Kennedy believed, could make him difficult to beat. Romney's main handicap was a lack of national name recognition. The Kennedy team decided that the president should not mention Romney, thus denying him the name recognition he needed. At the other end of the political spectrum, the group decided that Goldwater would be the easiest candidate to defeat and that Kennedy would do all he could to mention Goldwater at every opportunity.[57] The only concern of the Kennedys was that Goldwater might eliminate himself. Robert Kennedy recalled later: "we knew [Goldwater] was not a very smart man" and that he might "destroy himself too early and not get the nomination."[58] If Goldwater declared his candidacy, the president was quoted in *Newsweek*, he "won't last a month." His "shoot-from-the-hip . . . or fire-at-will style," Kennedy added, would destroy him.[59]

Kennedy clearly wanted to run against Goldwater, at least because he knew he could defeat him. But Kennedy had told his friend Ben Bradlee that a run against Goldwater would give "the people a real choice."[60] And at some point, according to a Goldwater interview ten years later, the two men had met in 1963 and discussed the possibility of traveling the nation together in 1964 in a sort of national debate road show.[61] Such an event would have been a nice gesture toward informing the nation's voters, but Kennedy and his advisors certainly realized how the 1960 Nixon–Kennedy debates had raised Kennedy from the realm of being known in only a few primary states to a national political figure. It would have been unlikely that Kennedy would

51

ever have agreed to give Goldwater such equal billing for more than one or two debates—if even that. Arthur Schlesinger believed that Kennedy wanted to run against Goldwater for the expressed purpose of exposing right-wing extremism "once and for all" and in the process win an indisputable mandate for his second term.[62] Kennedy had always thought that his slim victory over Nixon in 1960 had a great deal to do with his inability to build a coalition in Congress and move legislation. A landslide, an indisputable mandate over a conservative Republican, might well grease congressional wheels.

Another topic of conversation at the November 12 meeting was a plan for the president and vice president to travel to Dallas ten days later. The events that played out there would change the nation.

3

Goldwater Ambivalence and the Decision to Run

After the 1960 defeat the Republican party was in disarray. Eisenhower could have taken the lead in reorganizing the party, but he simply refused the role, happy to occupy the background as party statesman. Nixon had been discredited a great deal by his 1960 defeat, but he had tremendous name recognition and was certainly capable of regrouping his forces and making a strong run under a united party in 1964. However, in 1962 he made an ill-advised run for the governorship of California against Democrat Pat Brown and lost. In a statement that will forever be tied to him, he told the press: "you won't have Nixon to kick around anymore," then he announced his retirement from politics and joined a prestigious Wall Street law firm. He did not, however, disappear from view. During the 1964 primary campaigns Nixon reemerged, speaking, pandering for publicity as a candidate, even occasionally running openly. He had reinvented himself as the centrist candidate in the party and, as *Newsweek* noted, the GOP might have to give Nixon the nomination in 1964 in order to "avoid a war of annihilation between the liberal wing of the party headed by Governor Nelson Rockefeller of New York, and the ultraconservatives who follow the rich, personable Senator Barry Goldwater of Arizona."

But despite a strong showing in some early polls, Nixon was never in any real position to win the 1964 GOP nomination and pull the party together.[1] It was Goldwater, of course, who would make the run under the party's banner that year, but in 1960 he seemed little more than the spokesman of a minority group within the party with a narrow philosophy that would never appeal to a majority of voters. The man to beat after 1960 was Rockefeller. Of all the Republican hopefuls, he seemed the most prepared and capable of taking over the party apparatus and getting the nomination in 1964. In addition, there were historical reasons to believe that the party would finally swing in Rockefeller's direction. After all, that had been the GOP's history: despite the consternation of the right, the Northeastern Establishment had controlled the nomination of Republican party presidential candidates at least since 1940. And the press generally agreed that Rockefeller would eventually win out.

Conservatism within the GOP was surging however, and it was Goldwater who was the catalyst in that growing phenomenon. Many of Goldwater's supporters were young, many still in or just out of college, and they provided much of the enthusiasm that surrounded their man. They were extremely persistent in advocating Goldwater's candidacy, and they brought hope and encouragement to the older members of the movement. After the 1960 election the influence of these young leaders grew, with some surprisingly talented young men pushing the movement forward. This infusion of young blood gave the conservative movement an air of freshness, eagerness, excitement. Add to that Goldwater's own youth (he was fifty-one in 1960) and his vigorous lifestyle, and the conservative movement of the 1960s left behind its stodgy image and appeared to be something new and different. These young members, however, really did not bring many new ideas to the movement. Most, in fact, believed what their parents believed, that communism was both a religious and moral offense, that the goals of the New Deal had not been achieved, and that the rapidly growing federal authority was quickly sapping the power of the states and individuality.

Just a few weeks before the 1960 election about ninety of these young Republicans met at the family estate of William F. Buckley, Jr., in Sharon, Connecticut for the purpose of forming a new organization dedicated to a conservative philosophy that they had come to associate with Goldwater and his *Conscience of a Conservative*. Many of these young conservatives had just bolted the Young Republican National Federation (often called simply the Young Republicans) because of its support of Nixon's candidacy. They saw Nixon as the purveyor of Eisenhower Modern Republicanism and, thus, much too moderate for their tastes. The result was the Young Americans for Freedom (YAF). Their manifesto, written at Sharon and known as the Sharon Statement, was influenced greatly by Goldwater's writing and thinking. The statement focused on three aspects of conservative thought. The first was states' rights: The Constitution "reserves primacy to the several states . . . in those spheres not specifically delegated to the Federal Government." The second was the free market: "[T]he market economy, allocating resources by the free play of supply and demand, is the single economic system compatible with the requirements of personal freedom and constitutional government. . . ." The third focus was communism, "the greatest single threat to [American] liberties."[2] One participant at Sharon was a young M. Stanton Evans. Writing about the movement as it took form in the months following the 1960 election, Evans clearly believed that conservatism was about to be the way of the nation's future. It was, he predicted, the beginning of something that would one day grow much larger. These young Republicans, he wrote, "will be the opinion-makers—the people who in ten, fifteen, and twenty-five years will begin to assume positions of power in America."[3]

The YAF found its greatest strength on the nation's college campuses. Within six months the organization could claim 27,000 members with chapters on at least one hundred campuses.[4] This clearly coincided with the rapid growth of conservatism in general. Subscriptions to the *National Review*, for instance, increased rapidly through the first three years of the 1960s, doubling and then tripling by 1964 to over 90,000 subscribers.[5] By then there were some 500 groups nationwide that identified themselves as conservative. On March 7, 1962, Barry Goldwater delivered the gospel of conservatism to some 18,000 supporters at a YAF rally at Madison Square Garden in New York. It was the first of a number of big rallies around the nation, mostly youth driven. It showed for the first time that conservatives might be able to produce big numbers, that they might be a force to be reckoned with in American politics.[6]

Since at least the days of Robert Taft, GOP conservatives had wanted almost desperately to offer the American people what they called a choice, not an echo, something different than the old me-tooism, something other than Republican liberalism that did little more than rephrase the liberalism of the Democratic party. Given an honest choice, conservatives believed, Americans would choose conservatism. Goldwater was to be that choice. He was, in many ways, the direct opposite of John Kennedy, the apparent Democratic candidate in 1964. Both men were young and handsome, but the similarities stopped there. Kennedy was from a well-known, well-healed northeastern Irish-American family that had been a part of the national and local political scene for at least three generations. Kennedy was Harvard educated, urbane, and a liberal whose liberalism was mostly an extension of the New Deal–Fair Deal era of two and three decades earlier. Goldwater, on the other hand, was from the West, and he carried that image of individuality at the foundations of western freedom. His character was often described as "freewheeling" in a western manner, and one of the primary criticisms as his campaign got under way was that he "shoots from the hip." Not unlike Kennedy, he was physically attractive. *Time* reported that he had "the rarest of political attributes—star quality. A tanned, trim six footer with searching blue eyes behind his dark-rimmed glasses, and a thinning shock of silver hair, Goldwater has more than his share of political sex appeal."[7] Goldwater's father was Jewish, his mother Episcopalian. He had dropped out of college. His family was well off from a successful department store business in Phoenix, but his financial status was modest compared to the Kennedy family fortune. And, of course, Goldwater was a conservative whose conservatism (despite its freshness and youthful image in 1964) found its roots in the conservative philosophy of Robert Taft and even Herbert Hoover. Goldwater and his supporters on the right were eager for a culture clash in 1964: their freewheeling conservative western businessman against the Harvard-educated northeastern blue-blood liberal. On November 3, 1964, American voters would finally have a choice and not an echo, and, conservatives believed, they would choose conservatism over liberalism, Goldwater over Kennedy.

In the months following the 1960 election several conservative grassroots political organizations formed to begin the process of grabbing the Republican nomination for Goldwater. These included Arizona's Goldwater for President Committee, Chicago's Americans for Goldwater Committee, and The Valley Forge Citizens for Goldwater. But the nucleus of what would become the most significant of the draft-Goldwater movements grew out of a meeting on October 8, 1961, at the Avenue Motel on Michigan Avenue in Chicago. This meeting of some twenty-two conservatives was called by F. Clifton White, a one-time Cornell political science instructor turned political operator who had thrown his entire soul into the Republican party and the cause of American conservatism. To White, Goldwater was the very hope for the nation's future. Working closely with White, and just as devoted to the cause, were the *National Review*'s William Rusher and Ohio congressman John Ashbrook. Other important figures included Steven Shedegg, Goldwater's campaign manager for his two Senate campaigns, and Donald Bruce, a conservative congressman from Indiana. It was White, however, who was the group's chief inspiration, and it was White who was named the committee's chairman. The group decided to conceal their purpose, deciding even not to give themselves a name for fear of immediate repudiation. And they insisted, officially, that they had no candidate. This was to become, however, the Draft-Goldwater Committee.[8]

Goldwater apparently knew nothing of these intentions. In November of 1961, White met with Goldwater and told him of the organization, insisting that its function was only to work for conservative candidates in general and to push the Republican party onto a more conservative course. Goldwater thought all this was a good idea and offered his support, but he also told White that he was fairly resigned to Rockefeller's nomination in 1964. Throughout 1962 the relationship between this group and Goldwater remained generally the same. They denied their role as a draft-Goldwater committee, and Goldwater offered his aid to the committee's stated objective of assisting in a conservative takeover of the Republican party. In the first months of 1962, White set up offices in Suite 3505 in the Chanin Building at the corner of 42nd Street and Lexington Avenue in New York. Suite 3505 would become nearly legendary among the faithful in the near-religion of right-wing conservative politics.

Meanwhile, White began building a national organization at the grassroots level to marshal conservative Republican support for Goldwater with the direct objective of building delegate strength for the 1964 convention.[9] Apparently, Goldwater knew nothing of this either. For nearly three years, up until the convention, White continued his work at the precinct, district, and state levels—at least in part because he lacked the contacts necessary to organize at the top echelons of the party. "Many of the older professionals in the GOP had lost touch completely with their grassroots," White recalled. "They were too intent on taking orders from above to notice what was happening right under their noses."[10]

* * *

The 1962 mid-term elections added up to another stunning defeat for the Republican party. The Democrats won four additional Senate seats, giving them a huge advantage of sixty-eight to the Republicans' thirty-two. They lost only two House seats, retaining their overwhelming majority of 259 to 179. For a mid-term election, when voters are almost always eager to show their disappointment with the party in the White House, it was by all accounts an impressive showing. There were, however, a few silver linings for the Republican right. The Republicans made gains in the South, where conservatives hoped to make a big impact in 1964. Five new Republican congressmen were elected from the South, and in Alabama a professed Goldwater supporter nearly upset the venerable Senate Democrat Lister Hill. There was also, in general, a sharp increase in the number of Republicans running for state and local offices throughout the South. Conservative candidates also did well in California and New York. Although Nelson Rockefeller, the nemesis of the right, won a second term as governor of New York, the newly organized New York Conservative party showed its strength by eating into his totals: he only narrowly defeated a political newcomer.[11] Nixon, never a true friend of the Republican right, lost the California gubernatorial race and insisted that he was leaving politics.

Undoubtedly, the Republicans would have done better in November 1962 had it not been for the Cuban Missile Crisis in October. President Kennedy came away from those events with what at least appeared to be a substantial victory over the Soviet Union. The result was a growing confidence in the Kennedy administration, and that produced success at the polls. Goldwater's response to the crisis was to speak boldly, even recklessly. He expressed disbelief that Kennedy had not acted with more resolve, that the president had, in fact, missed an opportunity to roll back communism. In a meeting between the president and the senator during the crisis, Goldwater counseled Kennedy to attack, "Do anything that needs to be done to get rid of that cancer. If that means war, let it mean war." Kennedy, wanting to resolve the incident without conflict, rejected the senator's advice. "I came away from the meeting," Goldwater recalled, "with the impression that no amount of Soviet provocation would ever be sufficient in Kennedy's eyes to justify any action that might lead to the use of atomic weaponry."[12] Despite Goldwater's objections, the Kennedy administration's handling of the Cuban Missile Crisis helped the Democrats at the polls.

Meanwhile, Goldwater published his second book, *Why Not Victory?*, early in 1962, in which he explained the foundations of his foreign policy convictions.[13] Like any domestic politician with presidential aspirations, Goldwater was vulnerable on foreign policy issues. At the same time, Kennedy would bring to the campaign a full term of firsthand experience in dealing with world affairs—and with the Soviets. *Why Not Victory?* was most likely designed to close that gap as much as possible and give Goldwater credibility with voters in the field of international relations. Generally, Goldwater believed (as did most conservatives) that Kennedy was too soft on the Soviets, and that the nation was losing ground against the forces of international communism.

Goldwater said little here that he had not said in the last (and longest) chapter of *Conscience of a Conservative* two years before. The Soviet Union, he wrote, was the enemy, "whose appetite is insatiable, whose creed demands slavery for everyone, Americans included. The more we give in to that enemy," he added, "the more he wants. . . ." His policies of standing up to the Soviets, Goldwater added, would not bring war, because "Every time we have stood up to the Communists they have backed down. Our trouble is we have not stood up to them enough."[14] The book was an immediate best-seller, and Goldwater's foreign policy was on record.

Throughout 1963 a series of rallies around the country advanced the conservative cause considerably. In June, right-wing leaders took back control of the Young Republicans when they elected as their president Donald "Buz" Lukens, an ardent Goldwater supporter, at their raucous San Francisco convention. Rockefeller's people were shut out. It was Goldwater himself who whipped this crowd into a near frenzy by attacking the "cynical alliance between the politicians who call themselves liberal and the corrupt big-city machines whose job it is to deliver the bloc votes of the Northern big cities."[15] A month later, on July 4, nine thousand sweaty conservatives packed the unairconditioned Washington National Guard Armory to hear conservative speakers like Texas senator John Tower, a self-described Goldwaterite. Southern partisans, complete with a band playing "Dixie" over and over, dominated the Armory rally. *Newsweek* pegged the rally as "grits and fat-back flavored," and when it was over an excited Goldwater told a UPI reporter that the event might force him to consider running for president.[16] Then in September, up to 40,000 turned out for a Goldwater rally in Los Angeles—on a night the Dodgers were fighting for the National League pennant.[17] Later that month, Steward Alsop wrote in the *Saturday Evening Post* that "Barry Goldwater is now unquestionably the man to beat for the Republican nomination. . . . [T]here is beginning to be a feeling," he added, "that Goldwater just might make it all the way to the White House. . . ."[18] William Rusher later described 1963 as "that memorable year" in the conservative movement when he realized for the first time that a conservative could beat Kennedy in 1964.[19]

Goldwater, for his part, was doing a great deal to increase his own stock. Through 1963 he was not officially a candidate, but he definitely looked and acted like one. Between 1960 and late 1963 he made nearly eight hundred speeches. He was a popular guest on college campuses and appeared on innumerable radio and television talk shows. Between 1962 and 1964 four favorable Goldwater biographies hit the newsstands along with his own *Why Not Victory?* All sold well.[20] Also, a popular syndicated column—under Barry Goldwater's byline—went out three times a week to over one hundred newspapers. Goldwater supporters actually wrote the articles, but to conservative Americans they were required reading.[21] Goldwater was moving (and to some degree being moved) toward a 1964 candidacy.

There were, however, obvious reasons not to run. Republican liberals and moderates had made impressive showings in the 1962 election, with Rockefeller winning in New York, George Romney in Michigan, and William Scranton in Pennsylvania. Goldwater also to saw Nixon's defeat in California as a bad omen. California, Goldwater believed, was necessary to the forging of a new Republican coalition of the West, the South, and parts of the Midwest, and Nixon's loss seemed to show that California would go to the Democrats in 1964. Goldwater was definitely making a splash in the party and in the press, but events and history seemed to predict that the moderates would probably push the conservatives out again and take the nomination.

* * *

In the later days of 1962, Clif White brought his unnamed, secret, draft-Goldwater group together again in Chicago. By now they numbered over fifty members. He briefed them on his organizational work under way at the state level, suggested a budget for the next year, and informed them that Goldwater was aware of their work, implying that he approved. "I was certain he would," White recalled in his memoirs, "since he had raised no objections to our activities over the past year. . . ." White's plan, then, was to go public in March.[22] But with over fifty-odd members involved, secrecy was nearly impossible, and the plan to draft Goldwater leaked to the press. On December 3, just as several newspapers were about to break the story, Walter Cronkite hit the *CBS Evening News* with his lead story of a meeting "to plot a presidential campaign for Barry Goldwater."[23] Press reports that followed branded the draft-Goldwater group as party wreckers whose main design was to stop Rockefeller. Goldwater responded immediately that he had "heard something" about the organization, but that he fully intended "to run for the Senate two years from now."[24] A month later, on January 14, 1963, White and Goldwater met again and it was clear that the leak to the press had pushed the senator away from running. "I'm not a candidate," he told White. "And I'm not going to be. I have no intention of running for the Presidency." White was crushed. He argued with Goldwater, but the senator persisted, even insisting that his wife would "leave me if I ran for this thing."[25]

Goldwater later recalled, "Few people have ever understood my fierce resistance in those days to seeking higher office. . . . [T]he whole idea was so silly . . . I had never even jokingly considered the idea."[26] Rusher recalled that White returned from the meeting "looking for a job." The senator and White met again in the first week in February; Goldwater remained adamant. He would not be pushed into running.[27]

Why? Goldwater's answer to White in February was, "You guys are just a bunch of amateurs. I haven't seen one Senator, one Congressman, or one state chairman come out for me yet and I don't see how you can expect me to take this thing seriously." That was hardly true. Considering that the organization was trying to function without a declared candidate, White had been successful in recruiting what he called "a battalion" of senators, congressmen, and state chairmen.[28] Rusher insisted the problem was that Goldwater simply did not like White, that the two had nothing in common. White was from upstate New York and had never been closely associated with Goldwater. White also had a reputation for being difficult to get along with and for not communicating with his superiors. He was reluctant to work within the Republican party structure, which was, primarily, not conservative. White and Rusher and other conservatives had concluded that it was the party establishment that had led to all the me-too candidates and to a moderation of the party ideology between 1940 and 1960, so they simply rejected the party structure as just another enemy of conservatism.[29] It also may have been that Goldwater did not like the idea of being the captive of a movement. He would undoubtedly have been more comfortable initiating and building his own campaign organization. "It [the draft-Goldwater movement] smelled like the start of something I'd not be able to control," Goldwater recalled in his memoirs.[30] Possibly for all these reasons, Goldwater had, by at least mid-December 1962, begun putting together his own group, the people who would finally run his campaign.

White and his group sulked, but they refused to die. Defiant of their man's wishes, they announced on April 8, 1963, their existence and their intent to draft Barry Goldwater. Goldwater, as adamant as ever, responded: "I'm not taking any position on this draft movement. It's their time and their money. But they're going to have to get along without any help from me." After Goldwater's "I have no intention of running" statement to White just two months earlier, this sounded pretty good to White and Rusher. Rusher pronounced it "bearable, at least bearable."[31]

Through the summer of 1963, Goldwater began quietly to put together what would become his campaign staff. To a resentful William Rusher, they were the "Arizona Mafia." Phoenix attorney Denison Kitchel arrived in Washington, billed in the press as Goldwater's campaign manager for his reelection to the Senate. *Time* called him a "wispy, introverted, hard-of-hearing mining-industry lawyer. . . ." Goldwater called him his "head honcho."[32] Kitchel, however, had no political experience at the national level. Also that same summer, Tucson attorney Dean Burch joined Goldwater's staff as administrative assistant. At age thirty-six, Burch also had little campaign experience, and like Kitchel, his chief attribute seemed to be that he was from Arizona and close to Goldwater.[33] The American Enterprise Institute's William Baroody and Washington lawyer Edward McCabe also joined. Goldwater then assigned an aide to keep an eye on White and his group.[34] This Arizona Mafia began to run Goldwater's political organization, setting the foundations for a campaign wholly in Goldwater's hands and at his direction.

While the objective seemed to be to push Goldwater into the Republican nomination, a few on the right were beginning to look at the general election. The question was, could Goldwater win? Or more specifically, could Goldwater beat Kennedy? Certainly, vast numbers of Republicans did not believe he could. In a *National Review* article in February 1963, Rusher tried to show that Goldwater was a viable candidate, in fact a winner. If Goldwater could do much of what Nixon had done in 1960, which was to carry the Midwest, upper New England, a few of the mountain states, and the Far West, he could collect about 140 electoral votes of the 270 necessary to win the election—even if he lost California. If, then, Goldwater could carry the Border States and the South, he could bring in another 165 electoral votes, well over the total needed. Rusher's philosophy was simple: Rather than try to outbid the Democrats for liberal support, give up the liberal northeastern industrial states to Kennedy. A conservative candidate like Goldwater could win the votes of conservative Americans. That would be enough, Rusher believed, for Goldwater to win the presidency in 1964.[35]

In the first week of May 1963, Republican party politics changed drastically. On May 2, Nixon announced that he was leaving politics for good. Two days later, Rockefeller telephoned Goldwater to tell him that he had just married Margaretta "Happy" Murphy. Rockefeller had divorced his first wife (of thirty years and five children) in late 1961 with no appreciable affect on the polls, but now, with his new marriage, his numbers began to fall, and Goldwater for the first time pushed past him. Many party leaders in the Midwest and West had, before now, not looked seriously at Goldwater because they believed Rockefeller was a certainty for the nomination. All that changed in the first week of May 1963. Rockefeller's remarriage did not knock him out of contention for the 1964 nomination, but it hurt him badly. Nixon also would not be out of the running in 1964, but he was clearly badly wounded and mostly out of the public eye until the primaries began.

Rockefeller continued to remain in the spotlight, but to conservatives, Rocky was anathema. His name alone conjured up in the conservative mind the personification of the Eastern Establishment, Wall Street, big money, and big government. Rockefeller courted big city voters, thus he often supported aid to education, welfare, and housing legislation at the state and federal levels. He also supported civil rights. But for many conservatives, Rockefeller was a liberal simply because he was from New York, a state perceived by conservatives as a welfare state with unnecessarily high taxes—and the home of New York City and Wall Street. As the governor of New York, Rockefeller was, by pure conservative definition, an advocate of wasteful bureaucratic spending and expanded government, the successor of Tom Dewey. And many conservatives still sneered at him for the unholy pact he made with Nixon just before the 1960 Republican convention that forced liberal planks into the Republican party platform. Rockefeller also had problems inside the party because he often played outside the Republican party structure. He had no need for party money, so he owed little to party operatives who might otherwise have been responsible for raising his campaign war chests—and thus would have demanded favors in return. Consequently, he ruffled the feathers of the party bigwigs. Eisenhower disliked him intensely, calling him "a damned egomaniac," and complained that Republicans who followed Rockefeller were "just like a herd of sheep."[36]

For about a year between 1962 and the summer of 1963, Rockefeller courted Goldwater in an obvious attempt to use Goldwater to keep a tight grip on the right. "If you can take him into [our] camp on a personal basis," Rockefeller's chief lieutenant George Hinman wrote to his boss, "it will at least do some good. When he goes around telling his people that he likes you and that there aren't great differences between you, it is much better than a fight, and it's just remotely possible," Hinman added, "that you may be able to neutralize him and his group. . . . This is a formidable man and one we need to sneak under our tent if we can."[37] Rockefeller's hand of friendship came in the form of a series of monthly breakfasts in which Rockefeller tried to convince Goldwater that he was conservative enough to work with—at least on most issues. These breakfasts, held at Rockefeller's impressive Washington residence on Foxhall Road out beyond Georgetown, seemed to have reigned Goldwater right into Rockefeller's ideological trap. "Rocky's not such a bad guy," Goldwater told his conservative friends. "He's a lot more conservative than you think." Goldwater even forgave Rockefeller for the 1960 pact with Nixon that had sold out the conservatives. Clif White and other conservative leaders chalked all this up to "Goldwater's natural gullibility."[38]

Rockefeller's remarriage to Happy in the first week of May 1963 raised eyebrows and generated a great deal of bad press. Three of Nelson's four brothers boycotted the wedding, and the groom, at fifty-four, was eighteen years older than his bride. To many observers, Rockefeller was dumping his older first wife for a newer, younger model—and the only reason he was doing it was because he could afford to. The real scandal, however, was that Happy's own divorce had been finalized only a month before the wedding and just eighteen months after Rockefeller divorced his first wife. In addition, the new Mrs. Rockefeller gave up custody of her four children from her first marriage, ages three through twelve. The quick marriage raised questions about the relationship between Rocky and Happy before their divorces, and Happy's forgoing custody of her children settled badly with many voters, who considered it morally wrong—possibly even the horrible price she had to pay for marrying Rockefeller money. It appeared that the events would damage Rockefeller's run, literally knocking him out of the campaign.

Despite the burden of his personal life, however, Rockefeller was still a formidable candidate. He had an infectious smile, deep pockets, and was a tireless and effective campaigner. His power in the Republican party came from one distinct ability: "[It] rested," wrote Theodore White, "in his sock at the polls, the fact that he could get votes."[39] He never truly challenged Goldwater for the nomination after the spring of 1964, but as the two men fought to control the political soul of the Republican party, Rockefeller damaged Goldwater badly.

The Goldwater–Rockefeller split came at least in part because of the conservative takeover of the Young Republican convention in San Francisco in June 1964 when Buz Lukens and other Goldwater supporters were unexpectedly elected to the organization's top positions and Rockefeller's people were summarily purged from office. Clif White and his people orchestrated this modest revolution with the assistance of a large number of John Birch Society members. The conservatives then pushed through a platform containing a southern strategy for the 1964 campaign that clearly rejected black votes in hopes of winning the white South. Rockefeller nearly exploded. To him this was an overt political coup designed to dominate the party infrastructure—and with it an abandonment of civil rights and an acceptance of racism. He also disliked the southern character of the Washington Armory rally on July 4. In response to both these events, as *Newsweek* reported it, Rockefeller put together a strong civil rights resolution for submission to the Governor's Conference about to meet in Miami.[40] Then, on July 14, Rockefeller lashed out at the right. The GOP, he said, was in "real danger of subversion by a radical, well-financed, and highly disciplined minority. . . . It has now become crystal clear that the vociferous and well-drilled extremist elements boring within the party utterly reject [the] fundamental principles of our heritage. . . . If Goldwater," he added, "writes off the industrial North, the big cities and the blacks," the GOP will become "a party of extremism . . . sectionalism . . . [and] racism . . . a combination that will destroy it altogether."[41] Rockefeller was clearly upset, but there was something else eating at him. His remarriage in May had turned him from a sure thing into a candidate fighting for his political life, and it had been the conservatives who had criticized him most severely for it. Now he hit back: "You can't satisfy them [the conservatives]. I've tried," he said, "and it won't work. . . . They were the first to pounce on me when the marriage was announced. They hit me when I was down." Then he added, "I'm off the unity kick."[42] *Newsweek* noted "the wraps are off." And Goldwater responded, "no more breakfasts."[43]

* * *

Who were these Goldwater Republicans? Part of the answer has to do with changing demographics, and part has to do with a rising discontent. This growing national conservative movement would not show up clearly in the election numbers until the 1968 election. That year, Nixon and George Wallace attracted an overwhelming combined vote total of 57 percent. This political shift from the Roosevelt–Truman Democratic majority to a decidedly conservative majority was a realignment in America's political history on the magnitude of the elections of 1828, 1860, 1896, and 1932. The conservative movement that became apparent in the election numbers of 1968 may have begun to emerge in some quarters immediately after World War II, appearing as early as the 1946 congressional elections. But because of a lack of organization, strategy, coherent leadership, and a general inability to fight off (or work with) Republican party liberals and moderates, the conservative movement tripped and stumbled through the 1940s and finally galvanized around McCarthy and the anti-communist movement in the 1950s while the remainder of the Republicans followed Eisenhower and Modern Republicanism. McCarthyism was generally a political dead end that alienated American moderates who might otherwise have found their way into the conservative camp for a variety of reasons. The Republican right then drifted through the late 1950s overwhelmed by Eisenhower Modern Republicanism; it was leaderless, and without much of a strategy for the future.

By 1960 the political landscape had changed. The perceived liberalism of John Kennedy's New Frontier domestic program became a rallying point for conservatives. To them, it was the New Deal reincarnated, socialism run amuck, something to be hated and fought. To conservative writers like M. Stanton Evans, the New Frontier was a "spur to conservatism. . . . With Kennedy in the White House all ideological tendencies were sharpened."[44] Under Eisenhower, conservatives in Congress often had to bite their tongues and accept initiatives from the White House that they saw as liberal. To get out of line, to take a conservative stance on any issue opposed by the White House, was to embarrass the Republican administration. Thus Kennedy's election released a pent up right-wing impulse. For the first time since Truman, the Republican right on Capitol Hill could speak its mind without running headlong into moderate opposition.

Also, by the early 1960s international communism appeared to be a palpable threat, something the Republican right had been insisting was true at least since the end of the war. The Castro revolution in Cuba brought Soviet nuclear power to America's doorstep, Southeast Asia appeared to be on the verge of being overrun by communists, and Moscow avowed that it was, in fact, expansionist. In addition, one primary issue of the 1960 presidential campaign was that the Soviets had been allowed to catch up and even surpass U.S. military might through the 1950s. This was not true, but Americans came to believe that there was, in fact, a "missile gap." Possibly most important, Americans had felt safe with Ike in control. Americans believed strongly that Eisenhower knew—undoubtedly better than anyone else—how to deal with the Russian Bear. The Democrats gave the nation no such security. For these reasons, anti-communism, one of the foundations of right-wing philosophy, was finally a viable political issue.

By the early 1960s a conservative political strategy had emerged. It revolved around a simple philosophy of pulling all conservatives into the

Republican party. GOP conservatives concluded that there were large numbers of true conservatives who voted Democratic for several reasons. Many traditional conservatives, like small farmers, blue-collar workers, and a number of urban ethnic groups had voted Democratic because they had been beneficiaries of the New Deal and other Democratic party policies. In the South, conservative white southerners voted Democratic primarily for reasons of race. Conservatives within the Republican party, then, began to put together a campaign strategy that called for winning over these various groups, particularly in the West and the South, and adding them to the already avowed conservatives in parts of the Midwest and the Great Plains. This strategy, of course, rejected the traditional Republican Establishment wing of the liberal Northeast. Kennedy's tremendous strength there in the 1960 election forced the point home that the Republican party had no real future in that region of the nation anyway. Thus Kennedy's dominance of the Northeast industrial states in 1960 weakened the northeastern liberal wing of the Republican party because they could no longer deliver that region in elections. And that, in turn, strengthened the GOP right.

The conservative movement also pulled together a variety of discontented Americans. Their numbers seemed to have grown rapidly beginning sometime in the mid-to-late 1950s and into the early 1960s. A newly affluent middle class—people with what Stewart Alsop called "new money"—was an important part of this movement. In the summer before the 1964 election, *Time* asked the question, "Who are the Goldwaterites?" and concluded that they were "troops in a middle-class revolution that borrows from Populism. . . ." Possibly their defining characteristic was that they were upwardly mobile in the post-war 1950s economic boom and that they spent much of their early lives competing for jobs and housing. Many in this group viewed the federal government as a hindrance to their personal growth, depleting their paychecks with growing taxes while spending tax money on a welfare state that they believed promoted moral decay. Small farmers and independent businessmen saw the federal government as intrusive, even a liability in their attempts to survive. They were, *Time* continued, a fed-up generation. "Fed up with economic, social and moral decay, fed up with crime-infested cities, big government, big spending, and the inability of the United States to use its power abroad." *Time* identified them as being "most obvious in the burgeoning suburbs of the South and the West that are luring the skilled technicians and the professional men, many of them from farms and from low-income families. . . ."[45]

The South was also changing. Large numbers of white voters in the

South opposed the growing strength of the civil rights movement. Their complaints had been ongoing at least since the war, but the 1954 *Brown v. Board of Education* decision turned complaints in some quarters to outright revolt. Many white Americans, particularly in the North, supported the *Brown* decision, but by the early 1960s, as the civil rights movement heated up and shifted from boycotts and protests to battles in the streets and burning cities, the call from much of white America, both in the North and in the South, was that the movement was progressing too fast. The Civil Rights Act (sent to Congress by the Kennedy administration and then passed in the summer of 1964) was widely perceived among large numbers of whites as liberal support for a movement that had gotten sorely out of hand. Goldwater constantly disavowed any tinge of racism, but his states' rights stance (which complemented his position on limited government), and his vote in the Senate against the Civil Rights Act, endeared him to conservative southern whites. He also made a number of statements that were perceived as being racist. The GOP, he told Stewart Alsop, should "stop trying to outbid the Democrats for the Negro vote [and] go hunting where the ducks are."[46] The "ducks," were widely perceived to be among the white southern segregationists. And Goldwater told *Life* magazine that "the issue is not integration. It's states' rights. I don't think it's my right to tell a southerner what to do about this thing."[47] Such statements led large numbers of white southerners to support Goldwater and the conservative movement.

This backlash against the civil rights movement was supported by a further backlash against what are often called the excesses of the 1960s. Conservatives intensely disliked the growing counterculture movement, the New Left, and the anti-war movement, all of which were beginning to emerge in the few years after 1960. These movements, conservatives believed, were directly related to the nation's moral decay. Goldwater, prior to late 1962, had focused his conservatism on anti-communism, federal economic restraint, and limited government. But by 1962 he had picked up on the moral concerns of many conservatives and began complaining of sex on television, his personal dislike of modern art, and the Supreme Court's decision to ban prayer in public schools.[48] With that, conservatism began to change. While maintaining its orthodoxy of anti-communism, economic restraint, and limited government of decades past, the Republic right took on the mantle of moral crusader, to maintain what conservative Americans believed was at the foundation of all things American and good. "The thing on which this election could turn," GOP national chairman, Dean

Burch told *Time*, "is the very broad issue of morality. We're trying to sell the idea that there's something wrong in this country. We've got riots in our cities. Our kids aren't turning out worth a darn—every other one," he added, "is a delinquent."[49] Social conservatism was beginning to develop into an issue for the GOP right.

There were other supporters of Goldwater and conservatism. First- and second-generation Eastern European immigrants in the nation's northeastern and midwestern cities liked Goldwater because he was the most anti-communist of the candidates. That group also felt threatened by the civil rights movement and the changes they believed would come from it. It was a general belief among white factory workers that civil rights advances would eventually force employers to replace white workers with black workers in order to fill racial quotas. Despite Goldwater's openly anti-union stance, he received support from steelworkers in Pittsburgh, Gary, Youngstown, and Chicago.[50] Also, anti-communist Catholics who had backed McCarthy in the 1950s supported Goldwater in the 1960s. And Goldwater appealed to the western and southwestern rugged, individualist types. It was liberal journalist I.F. Stone, however, who realized that rugged individualism had little to do with hardship in the 1960s. Their "covered wagons," he wrote, "are Cadillacs and [their] wide open spaces have been air-conditioned."[51]

There was as well in the 1960s a clear decline in confidence in the federal government, or more likely a lack of confidence in the ability of the federal government to solve problems through legislation and spending. On the left, this waning confidence manifested itself in a political youth movement, strongly critical of liberalism, known popularly as the New Left—a movement misinterpreted by the right as an extension of liberalism, a radical, left-wing (even Marxist) movement. On the right, disenchantment with federal policy translated into support for Goldwater and his philosophy of states' rights and limited federal authority. From both the left and the right the "enemy" was always the same: the Liberal Establishment. As Norman Mailer pointed out, the "basic war was between Main Street and Wall Street," a point that could have been made about aspects of both the Republican and Democratic parties in the 1960s.[52]

All of the conservative factions, groups, and philosophies coalesced around Barry Goldwater, an appealing conservative who was able to pull them together and gain control of the Republican party, if only briefly. "They don't read Robert Welch (head of the John Birch Society) or hate Negroes," *Time* wrote of the Goldwaterites. "[T]hey aren't nuclear-bomb throwers, and they don't write obscene letters to editors who disagree with them. They are, in fact, nuts about Barry Goldwater without being nutty in the process. . . . The movement injects a new thrust into U.S. politics," the article continued. "[W]in, lose or draw in November, that thrust will be felt for a long time."[53]

*   *   *

By the spring of 1963 Goldwater was on the correct path to a run for the presidency. He had yet to announce his candidacy, but he had put together a campaign staff headed by Kitchel, raised money, and built an organization. If he had ever felt doubts about running, all had passed when it became fairly clear that if he did not run the GOP would surely turn to Rockefeller. And even if Rockefeller lost in 1964, he would be in a good position to run in 1968, and that would make him a real contender against the outgoing Democrats. If Goldwater did not make a run in 1964 it was conceivable that conservatives would not have another shot at the nomination until well into the 1970s. It was an almost now-or-never situation for the GOP right. But on November 22, 1963 Kennedy was shot. Lyndon Johnson and the Democrats did all they could to keep their party and their policies on course. In the Republican party, however, the dynamics of party politics shifted dramatically on that day.

In the months before Kennedy's assassination, Rockefeller's numbers had collapsed (mostly because of his marriage to Happy) and Goldwater had pushed up hard in the polls. It looked like he could even give Kennedy a strong run in 1964. In October 1963, *Time* observed that "until recently most political observers figured that [JFK] was a sure 1964 winner . . . no matter who the GOP nominee would be. Now, many are changing their minds. . . . [A] state-by-state survey by *Time* correspondents indicates that at least Republican Barry Goldwater could give Kennedy a breathlessly close contest." *Time* gave Goldwater twenty-six states, including the entire South and the Midwest; they predicted he "could sweep the Plains easily," and take the Northwest "with small minorities." *Time* also gave Illinois to Goldwater, and declared that he was running "even" in Texas.[54]

At the same time, Goldwater was clearly looking forward to the election. He and Kennedy had always been friendly adversaries, and Goldwater was convinced that the president was just as interested as he was in offering the nation a choice between conservatism and liberalism—a choice, possibly, offered to the nation in a series of debates. "I think he kinda looked forward to it," Goldwater recalled later.[55] American voters, Goldwater thought, would see the light, see the differences between the two men, and vote Republican. By late October, the thus-far-ambivalent Goldwater had decided he would make the run.[56] But when Kennedy was assassinated everything changed. Goldwater immediately ordered all campaign work on his behalf to stop, and he confided to his wife that under the circumstances he did not believe he could beat Johnson. "To heck with the presidential thing," he recalled a year later. "[A]ll the desire left me because I couldn't see Johnson able to draw the fine line" between liberalism and conservatism.[57] So in late November, just days after Dallas and a year before the election, he decided he would not make the run, and on December 8 he announced that decision to his supporters.[58]

The problem for Goldwater was that Johnson appealed to many of the groups he expected to pull into his own coalition of conservatives. History has tagged Lyndon Johnson a liberal, but up until the first years of the 1960s he was considered a southern conservative, or at least a moderate—on the 1960 ticket to balance the perceived Kennedy liberalism. William Rusher later wrote that Johnson was "identified with the relatively conservative Southern wing of the Democratic Party," and he was "pronouncedly more conservative" than Goldwater. Johnson was also perceived as a southwesterner, "and one bigger in almost every dimension at that," Rusher added. He could not, in any way, be linked to the nation's youth culture, or (at that time) to the civil rights movement. Rusher wrote: "Goldwater . . . would never be able to persuade most American voters that Lyndon Johnson represented any of the new tendencies in the country which so many of them feared and opposed."[59] Most of the factors that had made Kennedy a target of the right were rubbed out by Johnson's politics, character, background, and the region of the nation he represented. The "choice" that Goldwater and the conservatives had hoped to offer the nation was now just a big blur.

To make matters worse, Johnson quickly took the mantle of continuing Kennedy's policies. And although Kennedy was dead, his image lived on—not necessarily in the un-Kennedy-like Johnson, but in the administration that most of America saw as Kennedy's men and ideas headed up by Johnson. "Let us continue," marked the beginning of Johnson's first message to the nation as president, a nation that would never accept three presidents in just fourteen months. As a candidate, Goldwater would be in the horrible situation of having to fight against the electrifying character of the Kennedy image, headed now by a moderate leadership with western and southern influences. Also, Johnson had immediately placed himself in the position of chief griever at the head of a nation of grievers. It was a tremendously popular position. Then, on top of everything else, the murder in Dallas was widely perceived as the work of extremists—and most likely, right-wing extremists—and the press constantly referred to Dallas as a center for right-wing extremism. Goldwater was already being marked as an extremist—mostly by the Rockefeller camp. All this fell on Goldwater's shoulders at once. He would not run.

But it was, in several ways, too late not to run. The organization was there, the movement was rolling, and Goldwater had committed. As he began to step away from the campaign, his friends appealed to his sense of duty to the movement and the nation. They argued that if he did not run in 1964 he might never again have the opportunity and the movement would die. Besides, with Goldwater out of the campaign the nomination would surely go to Rockefeller by default. With a final nod from his wife, who told him "I don't particularly want you to run, but I'm not going to stand in your way," Goldwater decided, reluctantly, to take the plunge. "I just finally said to myself, you've got to do it. I realized that I had a responsibility to conservatism and to the young people who had become interested in it and I felt too that if I didn't do it that these people who were voting, many of them for the first time, might drift away. . . . I felt if [I did not run] that would be the end of conservatism in the party."[60] On January 3, just two days after his fifty-fifth birthday, Goldwater announced that he would run. In his announcement speech from his home outside Phoenix, he said he was not a "me-too Republican," and that he would "offer a choice, not an echo."[61]

Goldwater named Kitchel as his campaign manager and Richard Kleindienst, another old friend, as his advisor in charge of field operations. Clif White, despite three years of devotion and work, was cut out, demoted to Kleindienst's aide. White had orchestrated a successful grassroots Goldwater-for-president movement, but he had ultimately failed to win over his candidate. To Goldwater, White was a political technician, a northeastern intellectual surrounded by the haughty and the Harvard-degreed. Not surprisingly, Goldwater wanted to be advised by what he considered his own people—western businessmen types who saw the world as he did.

At the same time, White had from the beginning worked outside Goldwater's plans and intentions, establishing an organization and moving to draft Goldwater into it. Goldwater's critics, especially Rockefeller, had accused Goldwater of being the dupe of the far right, of being a product of the movement rather than its initiator—and White's committee was, in many ways, a right-wing movement looking to draft a leader. It might not be surprising that Goldwater was uncomfortable in that position. He wanted the campaign to be his own, run by people he knew and trusted. White was thus relegated to "the far sidelines," as Rusher called it.[62] White's three-year-old staff was also out. A few were given jobs inside Kitchel's hierarchy, but most were not. The message to White and his group was crystal clear.

This may have been an understandable decision, but it was also a bad one. Kitchel had no experience running a national campaign; he had no contacts of any significance outside of Arizona; and he was unwilling to learn (possibly at Goldwater's insistence) from White's experience and organization. Kleindienst had had some experience at the national level inside Nixon's 1960 campaign organization as a delegate hunter, but Nixon's nomination that year was never in question and Kleindienst's job was hardly crucial to Nixon's nomination.[63] So it was that three years of growth and organization under White's direction that were cut off; Kitchel and Kleindienst set out to reinvent the wheel.

A somewhat bitter William Rusher recalled: "We all realized by now . . . that he would lose."[64] That realization was probably clear to most Goldwater insiders very early; defeating Johnson under the post-assassination circumstances would be insurmountable. Thus, the objective shifted almost immediately from a campaign to elect a president to an ideological campaign to gain control of the Republican party and, in the fall campaign, spread the gospel to the nation. Goldwater would be a sacrificial lamb to the cause of conservatism. As he later recalled, "I knew, and said privately from the start, that I would lose to President Johnson. . . . From my perspective, the race itself—explaining the conservative viewpoint—had greater historical value and meaning than winning."[65]

* * *

Goldwater's most powerful challenger was, of course, Nelson Rockefeller. He had announced his candidacy on November 6, 1963, to very little fanfare. He represented the wing of the Republican party that had achieved the most success in nominating candidates in the past, but, as Goldwater and the right continually pointed out, they were generally losers. Immediately after his marriage to Happy, Rockefeller's approval ratings began slipping badly. He had tried something of a comeback by attacking Goldwater and the Young

Republicans, and then he had gone abroad in September 1963 in an attempt to display himself as an international statesman. Neither attempt really attracted much press attention or brought his numbers up. His only recourse seemed to be to mount an attack on Goldwater in the primaries, and possibly go to the convention as the chief party vote-getter, the candidate who could show the most muscle at the polls. He planned to enter the nation's first primary in New Hampshire on March 10, then in Oregon on May 15, and on to the big stakes in California on June 2. When he announced his candidacy in November, he was no longer the sure thing he had been six months earlier, but he was still a formidable candidate. He also remained the Republican candidate favored in the press—particularly the eastern press, and that was a powerful ally.

When Rockefeller announced his marriage, and saw his numbers slip in the polls as a result, he was perceived as vulnerable and several other Republicans pandered about, letting anyone know who was listening that if the right support came forward they would make a run. One of those was Richard Nixon. After eight years at the feet of Ike and then as the party's 1960 standard-bearer, he obviously had national name recognition and had shown that Republicans would vote for him. All that placed him at the very top of the party hierarchy and in a good position to win the 1964 nomination. But much of that changed in 1962 when his defeat in the California gubernatorial race added to his reputation as a loser. His response was to blame the press and announce his resignation from politics. But as the 1964 election approached, Nixon emerged as something of a noncandidate, ready to step off the sidelines if given the opportunity. He did not make a concerted effort to pick up delegates, but he made it clear that he would accept the nomination if the convention became deadlocked between the two undesirables on the left and the right, Rockefeller and Goldwater. He would then emerge as the moderate, the party healer. His strategy was clear: "When I say that I don't want to be a candidate," Nixon told the press, "I mean [it, but] if the opportunity should come again, I would accept it."[66]

The real prize for any Republican candidate was an Eisenhower endorsement. It was, in fact, perceived as the only true route to the nomination. Running without it, when another candidate had it, was a sure loser. But Ike decided to remain aloof, wanting apparently to stay above the politics with no great desire to become a kingmaker. He did, however, encourage at least two candidates to run. But it became clear throughout 1964 that Ike's encouragement was not necessarily an endorsement. He had originally hoped that the party would turn to his brother, Milton, but in December 1963, when party leaders proved disinterested in a second Eisenhower, the general approached Henry Cabot Lodge, then serving the Kennedy administration as ambassador to South Vietnam. It seemed to bother Eisenhower that Lodge (along with another of his presidential appointees, Douglas Dillon) had accepted such a high position in the Democratic administration, and he tried to persuade Lodge to give up the post and come home and campaign. But Lodge, citing the volatile political situation in Saigon, refused.[67]

Lodge, like Rockefeller, simply reeked Eastern Establishment. He carried significant national name recognition, but as a party liberal with an aloof demeanor he almost always offended party conservatives from the South, the West, and the Far West. He was also a notoriously poor campaigner, whose vice presidential bid on the ticket with Nixon in 1960 was perceived by party regulars as weak, even damaging to the ticket. In January 1964, just a month after Ike approached Lodge to run, several prominent New Englanders began organizing a Lodge-for-president write-in campaign in anticipation of the New Hampshire primary in March. Lodge, however, again refused to return from Saigon to campaign, but he also did not object. The press then called him a candidate. Lodge responded from Saigon: "Naturally, I would consider it my duty to run for the presidency if nominated."[68] At least in New Hampshire, Lodge, in absentia, would be a serious contender.

Just a week after Eisenhower approached Lodge, he apparently asked William Scranton, governor of Pennsylvania, to run. Scranton was definitely on a fast track through the ranks of the Republican party, but Ike's insistence that he run in 1964 quickly pushed him to the top. He had served only one term in Congress before running for and winning the Pennsylvania governor's seat in 1962—at Eisenhower's suggestion.[69] With only a year's experience there, he was already being viewed as a presidential contender. Scranton had one of the most desirable of political characteristics: a fresh face. He was also young and handsome, with an attractive wife, good-looking kids, and an Ivy League degree—all qualities usually attributed to the Kennedys. In fact, as the election year began, *Newsweek* placed Scranton's picture on its cover with the tag line "coming up fast," and in its feature story referred to Scranton as a "GOP Kennedy" who has "vigor," a word used relentlessly in the press to describe Kennedy and his administration. Scranton had, in fact, even dated the president's sister, Kathleen, a point that the press repeated over and over.[70] He had a good war record, and he had experience in the State Department under John Foster Dulles's tutelage. But Scranton was faced with the same dilemma as Lodge. Did Eisenhower's encouragement add up to an endorsement? Without an answer (and he never got one), Scranton understandably waffled. Just before the New Hampshire primary he tried to answer the question "Will you run?": "I am not now and do not intend to become a candidate," he said. "It would, however, be less than honest for me . . . to say that under no circumstance would I accept the nomination."[71] When he finally did throw his hat into the ring, it was too late to stop the Goldwater express.

Eisenhower claimed several times that both Lodge and Scranton had "common sense," a term he had begun to use instead of the now much-maligned descriptive words such as "modern," "moderate," "progressive," or "middle of the road." But the encouraging words never amounted to an endorsement. Eisenhower, however, had no encouraging words for Goldwater who, *Newsweek* reported, "had barely snagged an uncomfortable berth on Ike's bulging carriage of 'modern Republican' candidates."[72]

There were still other interested parties. George Romney, the newly elected governor of Michigan, also made it clear that he would consider a run under the right conditions. Romney had jumped into politics from his position as president of American Motors. Not unlike Scranton, Romney seemed on a fast track to the top of the Republican party candidate list, and when Kennedy's advisors first began looking at the 1964 election they saw Romney as a real threat.[73] Several of Nixon's 1960 campaign people had tried to launch Romney as a national political figure in early 1963, but the effort never got off the ground. In early January 1964, *Newsweek* described Romney as "near-forgotten." However, he was always there, clearly ready to run for the nomination if given the support and the opportunity.[74]

The only other Republican candidate of consequence was Margaret Chase Smith from Maine. She would make a reasonable run in the New Hampshire primary. Her most significant campaign statement was that she had more government experience than any of the other candidates. She came to the House following her husband's death in 1940 and then won a seat in the Senate in 1948. She described herself as a moderate: "I'm to the left of Goldwater and to the right of Rockefeller," she told the press.[75] More than anything else, her significance is that she was the first woman in the nation's history to actively campaign for the nomination of a major party, and the first woman to be nominated at a major party convention. At age sixty-six she was capable and experienced. The press and the Republican party, however, treated her as little more than a campaign novelty.

As the Republicans began to roll, it was Goldwater who was clearly the front-runner from the beginning of 1964. Rockefeller had been the choice through much of 1963. His nomination, at least as the press saw it that year, was a foregone conclusion. But the outcry over his marriage (along with his insistence on continually antagonizing his party's right wing) pushed him nearly out of the running. Nixon refused to commit and run while Lodge, Scranton, and Romney waited in vain for an endorsement from Eisenhower. Goldwater was there, at the head of a growing conservative movement, prepared to step into the breach and take control of the party. His opponents (both Democrat and Republican) would destroy him. But by the beginning of 1964 Goldwater had placed himself at the head of a new and growing movement that was just finding itself and its leadership.

4

Early Republican
Battlegrounds and the Rise of
George Wallace

For the Republicans, the approaching 1964 primary season meant the exposure of a party in disarray, while Johnson and the Democrats, it seemed, would be unbeatable in November. Polls showed that the president was running so far ahead of all the GOP comers that some Republicans began to speculate that only the possibility of Johnson's failing health could bring a Republican victory in November. As early as January, the president was a runaway with a 75 to 20 percent margin ahead of Goldwater and a 74 to 17 percent lead on Rockefeller.[1] Emmet John Hughes, writing in *Newsweek*, observed that "the 1964 Republican Presidential nomination looks to most observers like the least enviable political prize since Alf Landon won his chance to be humiliated by FDR in 1936."[2] Consequently, several potential candidates considered making the run, but finally demurred. Most of these were moderates holding out in vain for an Eisenhower endorsement: Nixon, Lodge, Scranton, and even Romney all seemed to be waiting for Ike to weigh in. When he refused, they were left dangling, not powerful enough to win the party nomination without his blessing, nor terribly interested in running against Johnson in November without the general on board. What remained was Rockefeller on the left and Goldwater on the right. The Republicans ended their primary season and headed toward their convention divided and angry.

On January 8, the party regulars held their breath. Eisenhower was due to release a statement in the press that most thought would end the deadlock and name a successor, a moderate, who would then take over the Republican party and move to the top of the polls. Would it be Lodge? Scranton? Instead, Ike called for an unnamed candidate who stood for what he called "the responsible, forward-looking Republicanism I tried to espouse as President. . . ." This candidate, he added, should support the civil rights movement, reject what Eisenhower called a simple foreign policy, support the United Nations, and accept Ike's basic premise that there was no "room for impulsiveness" in dealing with international affairs. The press immediately concluded that the general's comments were intended as a direct attack on Goldwater rather than an endorsement of any particular candidate. Goldwater, of course, was an outspoken critic of the Civil Rights Act. He had also said, on *Meet the Press*, that America's Cold War objective should "be simple . . . the only alternative to victory is defeat."[3] And he had argued against U.S. involvement in world affairs through the UN. Whatever Eisenhower's intentions had been, he did not do what moderate Republicans had hoped: give his blessing to a candidate who would derail Goldwater.

Goldwater began his primary campaign at the first of the year in New Hampshire, and with a comfortable lead over Rockefeller, who was still reeling from the affects of his marriage to Happy.[4] But as the New Hampshire campaign progressed, it became clear that Goldwater had problems. His campaign stalled almost immediately, and he began a rapid decline in the polls. It was finally determined that the campaign was, from the very beginning, poorly conceived, and that Goldwater's campaign style was not winning over voters. Much of the blame can be directed at Kitchel and Kleindienst, Goldwater's inexperienced campaign managers, who seemed to stumble even on the basics. They neglected to distribute enough campaign literature in New Hampshire and they failed to schedule enough television or radio time to put their candidate's face (and voice) in front of the people of the state. At the same time, they overbooked Goldwater at public appearances, even to the point of wearing him out. "For more than three weeks, from dawn to dusk," Goldwater recalled years later, "I sloshed through the snow for as long as eighteen hours a day. We flew up and down the state in random leaps that made no sense, sometimes spending more time in planes and cars than campaigning. I often spoke to as few as a dozen people. I fell into bed most nights completely exhausted. . . . Just about everything we did was extemporaneous."[5]

Possibly more importantly, Goldwater's handlers allowed him to speak to the press at any time and any place along the campaign trail without any preparation or briefing. The result was a whole series of gaffes that hit the national press, one after another, over a series of weeks. By the end of the New Hampshire campaign, Goldwater was way down in the polls, and most of America believed, as William Rusher put it, that he "was a fire-breathing monster who would repeal Social Security and plunge the world into nuclear war."[6] Goldwater understood the organizational and planning problems in New Hampshire, but he never quite seemed to realize the political repercussions of his remarks. "I goofed up somewhere," he told the press.[7]

The problem was that as long as Goldwater spoke in general terms about the abuses of federal authority, the inefficiency of a bloated bureaucracy, and individualism and self-reliance, he appealed to the conservative mind. But when he spoke in specifics, he raised eyebrows and disturbed voters. He said that the United States should attack Cuba, that U.S. missiles were "undependable," and that he approved of an escalation of the situation in Vietnam. He also said that the progressive income tax should be repealed in favor of a flat tax and that the Social Security system should be made voluntary.[8] No matter what the circumstances were when Goldwater made these statements, they all left him open to charges of extremism—and Rockefeller began using them against him. In response to Goldwater's statement that he would make Social Security a voluntary program, Rockefeller said that it would "bankrupt the Social Security system and be a personal disaster to millions of senior citizens and their families."[9] Earlier in the year, the Cubans had turned off the water supply to the U.S. base at Guantanamo. Goldwater had said that he would use force to get the water turned back on. He also suggested that NATO commanders in Europe be given the authority to use nuclear weapons.[10] Rockefeller hit back hard, calling these statements irresponsible, responses that could lead to war with the Soviets.[11] Such "Goldwaterisms," as they were being called in the press, made it easy for Rockefeller to move to the center and label Goldwater an extremist. "I want to build a Republican Party that rejects the extremism of both the left and the right," Rockefeller said.[12] By February, Goldwater had fallen in the polls from a 53 percent approval rating to 46 percent, while Rockefeller had jumped six points from 33 to 39 percent.[13]

On top of all this, Goldwater was sick. Just before New Hampshire he had had a painful heel spur removed and had headed into the campaign with his leg in a heavy plaster cast. As he hobbled around on crutches in the wet New Hampshire snow, facing a press corps that had turned against him, he became surly and angry. "He was irritable [and] withdrawn," *Time* wrote, "generally reluctant to fare forth to meet we-the-people." When asked about his less-than-cordial style, Goldwater growled, "I'm no baby-kissing, handshaking, blintz-eating candidate."[14] By contrast, Rockefeller was all that; he was truly in his element. He was an effective, tireless campaigner, and that made him a formidable one. Rockefeller, *Newsweek* reported, is "tirelessly jouncing, winking, clasping, bounding, clutching, and grinning."[15] Rockefeller had little chance for a big victory in New Hampshire (a full 38 percent of New Hampshire Republicans in a pre-election poll said they disapproved of his personal life), but as the campaign progressed beyond straight-laced New Hampshire, campaign style could easily make a difference; the grumpy Goldwater might be overtaken by the enthusiastic Rockefeller.[16]

Goldwater had problems with the press throughout the 1964 campaign. But in most cases, there was no one to blame but himself. He simply said things he should not have said, and before he realized how his words would be treated in the press. For instance, along with his musing on the Social Security system and Castro, Goldwater often said that he welcomed the support of the John Birch Society, that he believed NATO commanders should have the authority to launch nuclear weapons (without an order from the president), and that low-yield nuclear weapons should be dropped on supply lines inside southern China. To many Americans such statements were frightening. On January 7, following one of these off-the-cuff, impromptu press conferences, the headline in the *Concord Daily Monitor* read, GOLDWATER SETS GOALS: END SOCIAL SECURITY; HIT CASTRO.[17] He never seemed to understand how his statements would be used in the press, or how his opponents (Rockefeller in the primaries and later Johnson in the general election) would be able to convince voters that he wanted to destroy Social Security, become an ally of the radical right, and start a world war.

"For all his charm," *Newsweek* noted, "Goldwater [is] still the fastest gun in the West—too fast even for some of his friends." In the same article a "GOP committeeman" was quoted as saying, "I'm glad he has one foot in a cast or he'd have that one in his mouth too."[18] The members of the press corps saw this flaw in Goldwater-the-candidate, apparently, long before Goldwater. Theodore White observed: "How could one be fair to Goldwater—by quoting what he said or by explaining what he thought? To quote him directly was manifestly unfair, but if he insisted on speaking thus in public, how could one resist quoting him?" In New Hampshire, White added "it was difficult for anyone to believe that any Presidential candidate could be so innocent of the importance and attention of the national press in a major campaign. Goldwater's irresistible candor, translated by the reporters into print and then fed back out to the electorate by Rockefeller's research staff, was, ultimately, the work of his destruction."[19]

Goldwater on the campaign trail. His rugged good looks, energetic style, and forthright personality appealed to many voters. *(Arizona Historical Foundation)*

Edwin Canham of the *Christian Science Monitor* wrote after the election that "I have never met a public figure who is more difficult to cover fairly. You have to work very hard to protect the man against his own indiscretions."[20] And, of course, it was the unfriendly reporters who were willing to give Goldwater the least room for error. As one such reporter told Karl Hess, a Goldwater speechwriter, it "was great. All we had to do was keep hitting him with questions and then wait until he slipped and we had our headline." After New Hampshire, Goldwater finally learned to speak less and watch what he said more.[21] He would also make better use of prepared television and radio speeches and announcements.

Years later, Goldwater tried to defend himself, but even then he was still clearly naive about the relationship between a political candidate and the press. "I sometimes said things for immediate effect, to get people on my side by making them listen or laugh. And I made too many joking references. . . . [S]ome of my off-the-cuff quips hit the evening television news or national headlines the following morning. I had to be more careful. . . . It wasn't like back home in Arizona. A lot of these reporters had no sense of humor. And many didn't like conservative Republicans."[22] Goldwater learned from events in New Hampshire, and throughout the rest of the campaign he avoided casual conversations with the press. But the damage had already been done and, as Goldwater would find, no amount of retraction or denial could kill the image that came from the old statements and stories. Rockefeller used many of the New Hampshire statements and misstatements to label Goldwater a right-wing extremist. That strategy was picked up by the Johnson campaign staff in the general election and used to browbeat Goldwater right up until November. It was Rockefeller more than anyone else who destroyed Goldwater and the conservative movement in 1964, but it was Goldwater who gave Rockefeller the ammunition to do it. And it all began in New Hampshire.

Where were the other candidates? Lodge was in Saigon, refusing to return to run, despite Eisenhower's suggestion that he do so. At least three times Rockefeller made calls to Lodge in Saigon insisting that he withdraw, arguing that his candidacy would split the moderate vote and throw the election to Goldwater. But Lodge refused to take his name out of the running.[23] Lodge had tremendous appeal in New Hampshire, mainly because of his nearby Massachusetts address and his association with the moderation of the Eisenhower administration—although he still fell short of an Eisenhower endorsement.

Lodge's real strength came from the enthusiasm of four extremely resourceful amateurs who had set out in late 1963 to push him into the Republican primaries—completely without their candidate's knowledge or approval. Paul Grindle, David Goldberg, Sally Saltstall, and Caroline Williams had almost no prior political experience. Grindle was forty-three; the women were both in their early twenties. Theodore White described them as "simple and childlike." He characterized the women as "fresh with first bloom," and at one point he referred to the group as "the four pranksters." Nevertheless, they were all public relations people who did have significant experience with direct mail. During the first month of 1964, from a storefront in Concord, they initiated a saturation mail campaign on Lodge's behalf and, with only about 100,000 potential voters in the state, produced some surprising results. With some 9,000 respondents to their mail campaign they built several statewide organizations and volunteer groups that spearheaded an amazingly successful Lodge-for-President write-in campaign.[24]

When the New Hampshire snow settled on March 10, Lodge had won the big prize. Considering that he had refused to leave Saigon for the effort, this was a major victory. New Hampshire was a big defeat for both Rockefeller and Goldwater, and it threatened to derail their campaigns. They had, it seemed, canceled each other out. Rockefeller had succeeded in destroying Goldwater by labeling him an extremist, a strategy he would continue using throughout the remainder of the primary season. At the same time, New Hampshire voters were unwilling to accept Rockefeller, most likely because of his personal life, and decided to look elsewhere. Apparently, they found Lodge somewhere in the middle.

The press saw little in the outcome of the New Hampshire primary. It was, wrote *Newsweek*, "an expensive, inconclusive exercise in the politics of frustration."[25] Another observer, quoted by Theodore White, called it a "kickoff in a driving rain on a muddy field of no decision."[26] But some things had been sorted out—although it was only a temporary sorting. Lodge had won but his victory was expected, and an expected victory in a primary is usually no real victory. He was the New England candidate, and New Hampshire voters have traditionally thrown their support to a New Englander if the option is available. Despite *Newsweek*'s gushing pronouncement that Lodge had a "dramatic, possibly decisive lead," and that he was "within striking distance" of Johnson, Lodge realized the fleeting character of his New Hampshire victory and continued to refuse to return from Saigon to take control of his campaign. He had received 35.7 percent of the vote.[27]

Rockefeller was probably hurt the worst in New Hampshire. He received a paltry 21.1 percent of the vote, which severely diminished his chances of

Nelson Rockefeller was an exciting campaigner. While Goldwater complained about the weather and the rigors of campaigning in New Hampshire, Rockefeller relished it. Here he slogs through a snowy New Hampshire town pulling along supporters, the press, and a three-piece marching band. *(Rockefeller Archive Center)*

becoming the Republican party nominee. Even the New York delegation threatened to desert him.[28] But Rockefeller continued on, believing with good reason that he would eventually rally the majority of the GOP against Goldwater's right-wing candidacy. He hoped that with a win in California he could go to the convention and lead the party moderates in a partywide stop-Goldwater movement.

It was, of course, Eisenhower who still held the key to any such movement. Had he stepped forward and endorsed a successor to Modern Republicanism, the moderates would have rallied, but the general continued to sit on the sidelines, content to maintain a place above the fray and stay out of the mud hole of politics. In mid-February, Eisenhower was scheduled to speak at a nationwide fundraiser for Republicans. Again, the party seemed poised for the general to anoint a successor, an heir apparent, but, as *Newsweek* reported, "he did little to speed the selection of a candidate."[29]

Goldwater was hurt in New Hampshire as well. He received only 22.4 percent of the vote, just a short bump ahead of Rockefeller. Probably Goldwater's biggest problem with the New Hampshire outcome was that he made the mistake of predicting a 40 percent victory over all the candidates, an act that can only be chalked up to his (and his advisors') inexperience. For several reasons, however, Goldwater's defeat in New Hampshire was not nearly as bad as it appeared. He had no real chance of winning there. As a westerner, he had little local appeal. He lacked the name recognition that Nixon, Rockefeller, and Lodge carried. He had also campaigned badly. But Goldwater's strategy in 1964 had little to do with winning primaries. There were only nine Republican primaries in the nation that year, and although primary wins are important in building momentum and establishing name recognition, most of the GOP convention delegates were quietly chosen in state party caucuses. While the nation was transfixed on the outcomes of a few raucous primaries, Goldwater's people were slowly wracking up delegates in the states without primaries. By the time the California primary rolled around in the first week of June, Clif White and his grassroots organizers could claim some 550 delegates committed to Goldwater through state convention votes and state caucuses around the country.[30] They had completed this feat largely on their own, nearly clandestinely, with very little assistance or encouragement from Goldwater, Kleindienst, Kitchel, or any of the other members of the "Arizona Mafia." Conceivably, had Goldwater lost in California or had a moderate candidate emerged with Eisenhower's blessing, many of these delegates might have deserted Goldwater before or at the convention. But that did not happen.

Long before the convention, even long before California, Goldwater had the nomination largely wrapped up.

Nixon was the clearest casualty of New Hampshire. His write-in campaign, led by former New Hampshire governor Wesley Powell, was a failure. He pulled just under 17 percent of the vote, and although he often looked good in the polls and continued to sniff around for the nomination in the case of a convention deadlock, he was effectively out of the running. Nixon's main problem, as *Newsweek* pointed out the week before the New Hampshire vote, was "his own lack of enthusiasm for his candidacy."[31] The only other serious candidate was Margaret Chase Smith, who was running what *Newsweek* called a "shoestring Presidential drive," pointing out that she was touring New Hampshire with her two aides in a 1961 sedan.[32] The press continued to treat her run as little more than a curiosity.

Just after the New Hampshire primary a Louis Harris poll showed that the nation's voters had a long way to go before they settled on a Republican candidate. It also showed that Johnson was still nearly unbeatable. Lodge held an impressive lead with a 41 percent approval rating—up from 14 percent in February. Nixon followed with 28 percent, down from 44 percent in February. Goldwater tallied a weak 10 percent and Rockefeller was at rock bottom with 6 percent. Lodge, according to the poll, would do the best against Johnson, losing with an embarrassing 33 percent of the vote to the president's 52 percent. Rockefeller would do the worst, with 23 percent to Johnson's 69 percent.[33] It looked as though it was going to be a bad year for Republicans no matter whom they chose in San Francisco.

Just a few days before the New Hampshire vote, at a rally in Manchester, Goldwater supporters ran a film of actor Ronald Reagan speaking on Goldwater's behalf. He was introduced as "the Gipper." Reagan had not yet decided on politics as a second career, but in 1964 he was working to repeal California's Rumford Fair Housing Act, passed the year before, and his political leaning had brought him to Goldwater's side. The event was hardly noticed in the press, but it was a portent for the future of American conservatism.[34]

* * *

It was in the middle of the New Hampshire primary that the bill that would become the Civil Rights Act of 1964 passed the House of Representatives. Goldwater had begun speaking out against the bill, citing mostly the constitutional issue of federal infringement of state and local authority. His stand

Maine senator Margaret Chase Smith was the first woman to run for president as a candidate for either of the major parties. However, she had very little money, and she was not taken seriously by her party or by the press. Here she waves to supporters outside the 1964 Republican National Convention in San Francisco. (*Margaret Chase Smith Library, Skowhegan, Maine*)

on the Civil Rights Act would give him southern support along with charges of racism from Democrats and moderate Republicans. It was a charge that was difficult to shake, and it would impact the campaign.

The charge of racism was misguided. Goldwater had, in fact, voted for the civil rights bills of 1957 and 1960, both with few trepidations or concerns, and in 1961 he insisted that the federal government "should act even if it means with troops" to ensure voting rights.[35] In fact, Goldwater made his local political reputation as a member of the Phoenix city council who fought to desegregate Phoenix public schools and lunch counters; and he was instrumental in establishing an integrated Arizona Air National Guard in 1946, two years before Truman desegregated the U.S. armed forces. He was at that time a member of the NAACP, and contributed generously to that organization. In addition, his first legislative assistant on his Senate staff was an African-American woman. For Goldwater, race was never the issue; he opposed what would become the Civil Rights Act of 1964 primarily on constitutional grounds.

However, the question of civil rights in the 1964 election had little to do with convictions or the backgrounds of the politicians. It was a political issue. One party would receive the votes of a large majority of the white South; the other party would receive the votes from African Americans in the northern urban centers. Clearly, neither party was broad-based enough to capture both groups, a fact that had been apparent since the 1948 election. In that election year, Truman and the Democrats pushed civil rights issues and abandoned the white South in hopes of bringing in black voters in the northern cities. That strategy probably gave Truman the big electoral states of Illinois, Ohio, and California; he nearly won New York. At the same time, most of the South remained in the Democratic column. Truman's surprising victory that year seemed to have taught the Democrats the lesson that the South would generally stay put while the party courted northern black votes with civil rights initiatives. But as civil rights became a hot issue in the 1950s it was soon clear that the Democratic party could not control both groups; one or the other would have to conform or find a new home. The 1952 national election returns showed that white southerners were making a slow but steady move from the Democrats to the Republicans. That year Eisenhower picked up Oklahoma, Texas, Florida, Missouri, Tennessee, Virginia, Maryland, and Delaware. Four years later, the trend continued. Eisenhower added Louisiana, Kentucky, and West Virginia (although he lost Missouri). In both elections, Ike controlled the rest of the nation. The Deep South (the Carolinas, Georgia, Alabama, Mississippi, and Arkansas) was the only region he could not control during his eight years in office. His response was to salve southern needs with at least some hope that the South would ultimately join a powerful Republican coalition. At the same time, Eisenhower's personal convictions swung in that direction anyway. Throughout his eight years in office, he often repeated his personal conviction that he supported improved race relations, but that he believed racial harmony would never come as a result of federal legislation. In the same vein, he continually reassured southern governors that his administration would not interfere in southern social attitudes toward race. Even following the incident at Little Rock in 1957, when he sent in federal troops to stop riots and ultimately integrate the city's high school, he reassured southern governors that he acted as a president protecting the lives of citizens and not as a federal authority forcing a social agenda on the South. Consequently, when Eisenhower left office he believed he had done a great deal to bring the white South into the Republican camp—either through his own convictions or through political maneuvering.

In 1960, Nixon continued Ike's southern strategy. By then, however, large numbers of African Americans in the South were defying southern mores and making their way to the polls; the South was no longer simply the white South. Nixon retained control of Florida, Virginia, Kentucky, Oklahoma, and Tennessee, but he lost Texas, Louisiana, Missouri, West Virginia, Maryland, and Delaware (states that Eisenhower had won), along with the other states of the Deep South that Eisenhower never did control. As racial tensions increased in the early 1960s, the Kennedy administration found itself time and again allied with the civil rights movement. Finally, following several violent incidents in the South, the Kennedy administration sent to Congress the Civil Rights Bill that would become the Civil Rights Act of 1964.

The administration's first recommendation, sent to Congress in February 1963, asked for strong legislation on voting rights, financial assistance to schools that were then in the process of desegregating, and a strengthened civil rights commission. On top of these requests, Kennedy, following the riots in Birmingham in the spring, asked Congress to pass a stronger bill that would include a ban on discrimination in all public accommodations, such as hotels, restaurants, theaters, sports arenas, retail stores, gas stations, and lunch counters. The stronger bill would also give the attorney general the authority to initiate proceedings against segregated schools, and give the president the power to cut funds to government-supported projects that refused to desegregate.[36] Vice President Johnson pushed Kennedy to introduce an even stronger bill, one that would, he told the president, make "a bigot out of nearly anybody that's against it."[37] Throughout the spring and summer of 1963 the bill hit a series of roadblocks and finally became bottled up in the House Judiciary Committee.

During the summer months, Kennedy had tried desperately to move the bill through Congress. The administration's objective was to obtain the vote of two-thirds of the Senate, sixty-seven votes, enough to evoke cloture and bring an end to an impending southern filibuster. There were, in fact, exactly sixty-seven Democrats in the Senate, but southern Democrats, of course, led the fight against the bill. Kennedy, then, was forced to turn to moderate Republicans. In June, the president met with Eisenhower in hopes of enlisting him in the civil rights cause—which would, of course, greatly influence Republican moderates. But the general continued to argue his long-time position that race relations could not be legislated, and he refused to help the administration. At the end of June, the president could count only forty-seven sure votes.[38]

Another part of the Kennedy strategy on the Civil Rights Bill was to soften several moderate southern senators, men like Lister Hill of Alabama and J. William Fulbright of Arkansas. To accomplish that, Kennedy believed he would have to quiet the civil rights movement. The president's advisors argued that civil rights direct action, particularly the type used by King in Birmingham, provoked a backlash in the South that put pressure on southern legislators in Washington to vote against the bill. Kennedy hoped that a less aggressive movement would take that pressure off southern moderates in the Senate and allow them to support the bill. In a June 19 message to Congress, Kennedy said that "Unruly tactics or pressures will not help and may hinder the effective consideration of" the civil rights bill. "I urge all community leaders, Negro and white, to do their utmost to lessen tensions and to exercise self-restraint. The Congress should have an opportunity to freely work its will."[39] Kennedy had reason to suspect an escalation of violence. In the ten-week period since he announced his plan to send a civil rights bill to Congress, there had been some 20,000 arrests and ten deaths in demonstrations across the South.

The response from civil rights leaders was the opposite of the administration's request for restraint. They planned a march on Washington for August 28, an event that was expected to be at least confrontational, possibly even violent. At a White House meeting in late June, Kennedy tried desperately to persuade the nation's leading civil rights leaders to call off the march. "We want success in Congress," Kennedy told King, Whitney Young,

A. Philip Randolph, and others present, "not just a big show at the Capitol. Some [congressmen] are looking for an excuse to be against us. I don't want to give any of them a chance to say, 'Yes, I'm for the bill, but I'm dammed if I'll vote for it at the point of a gun!'"[40] Kennedy lost the argument and 250,000 African Americans and their white supporters converged on the Mall and at the foot of the Lincoln Memorial on August 28 to hear speeches by civil rights leaders, including King's memorable "I Have A Dream" speech. The march was the crowning glory of the civil rights movement, a call for a final victory over de jure segregation in the South. But Kennedy was right—at least from a political standpoint: it probably did little to aid in the passage of the Civil Rights Bill.

Kennedy continued to lobby for the bill during the summer and fall of 1963. By the fall, his support of civil rights and the Civil Rights Bill had made him a hero among liberals and won him tremendous respect from all but the most militant members of the civil rights movement. However, in late October, when it appeared the bill could not muster the required vote to end cloture, the president surrendered to the power of the coalition of conservative Republicans and southerners and a new, more moderate version of the bill was sent to the House Judiciary Committee and adopted. A month later, the compromise bill was reported out of Judiciary and sent to the House Rules Committee. Then on November 22, Kennedy was assassinated, and the situation changed.

Civil rights leaders feared that Lyndon Johnson would destroy the bill altogether, but in the days and weeks following Kennedy's death, Johnson met privately with civil rights leaders and assured each that he would carry on Kennedy's commitment to civil rights and to the passage of the Civil Rights Bill. Then, in his first address to Congress, Johnson told a grieving nation: "No memorial oration or eulogy could more eloquently honor President Kennedy's memory than the earliest possible passage of the civil rights bill for which he fought so long."[41] In his first State of the Union message Johnson followed up on his commitment: "It is a moral issue," he told the nation. "Today, Americans of all races stand side by side in Berlin and Vietnam. They died side by side in Korea. Surely they can work and eat and travel side by side in their own country."[42]

As a result of Johnson's appeal for public support and a great deal of Johnson-style arm twisting, the bill passed the House and headed to the Senate in February 1964, smack in the middle of the New Hampshire primary. There seemed to be a sense of urgency in the air. "There can be no question," wrote Kenneth Crawford for *Newsweek*, "that the racial outrages of the last year have convinced Congress . . . that something must be done about the just grievances of the Negroes and about violence in the streets."[43] Goldwater most likely would have agreed, but his stand on the issue of civil rights was constitutional, which translated into a strong states' rights stance— a stance that appealed to the South. Not many in New Hampshire shared the southern attitude toward states' rights in 1964 (that federal authority should not abridge a state's right to maintain a racially segregated system), but the idea that the federal government should not interfere in the private affairs of individuals did appeal to New Hampshire conservatives. Throughout the New Hampshire primary Goldwater complained about the bill, primarily Title VII, which dealt with discrimination in housing. "Simply put," Goldwater argued, the act "said you couldn't refuse to rent your house to anybody. . . . That aspect of the bill was unconstitutional. . . ."[44] He also opposed the public accommodations provision because it would, he said, "force you to admit drunks, a known murderer or an insane person into your place of business." The fair employment provision similarly would, he believed, force employers to hire "incompetent" employees whether they wanted to or not.[45] Although Goldwater believed that job discrimination was morally wrong, he did not believe that it was the proper role of the federal government to attempt to eliminate it. He said that if the government "can forbid such discrimination, it is a real possibility that sometime in the future the same government can require people to discriminate in hiring on the basis of color or race or religion."[46]

It was, however, George Wallace who, in 1964, got the most political mileage from the Civil Rights Bill (and the fears that whites had developed) as a result of the national debate over the issue. Wallace, the newly elected governor of Alabama, had attracted a smattering of national attention by trying to stop the desegregation of the University of Alabama. But in the Civil Rights Bill, and in the civil rights movement itself, Wallace saw a growing backlash. He identified it, exploited it, and then turned it over to Barry Goldwater and the Republican right.

* * *

On January 14, 1963, George Corley Wallace jumped onto the American political scene, and for most of the rest of the twentieth century national politics would not be quite the same. On that day, Wallace was inaugurated governor of Alabama in Montgomery, and in his inaugural address he made it clear that he had bigger plans than to be simply the governor of a southern

94

state. In his most famous statement from that address, Wallace said, "I draw the line in the dust and toss the gauntlet before the feet of tyranny, and I say, Segregation now! Segregation tomorrow! Segregation forever!" They were strong words, but he also said, "[L]et us send this message back to Washington by our representatives who are with us today that from this day we are standing up, and the heel of tyranny does not fit the neck of an upright man, that we intend to take the offensive and carry our fight for freedom across the nation, wielding the balance of power we know we possess in the Southland that we, not the insipid bloc votes of some section, will determine in the next elections who shall sit in the White House of these United States." Then he concluded: "[F]rom this day, from this hour, from this minute, we give the word of a race of honor that we will tolerate their boot in our face no longer, and let those certain judges put that in their opium pipes and smoke it."[47] It was an amazing speech, a call to southern arms. It was also defiance shouted directly at the hated Kennedys in Washington.

It was clear from the start that George Wallace would not, as a reporter at the *Nation* wrote, be "placed beside that old broken musketeer, Ross Barnett, in Dixie's wax museum."[48] His message was for the nation. In his youth, he had gone from bantamweight boxer into the army to fly B-24s over the Pacific, and then afterward into Alabama state politics. His boxing career has become both metaphor and myth. He was to his supporters the scrappy fighter, unvanquished, like the South, always ready to rise and fight again. He was a small, feisty man, who in 1964 was described by Theodore White as a "narrow-minded grotesquely provincial man," with hair "in a ducktail slicked back with brilliantine, like the cartoons of Senator Claghorn," dressed in the "undertaker's uniform—dark suit, narrow black necktie—of Southern courthouse politicians. . . ."[49] Wallace brought out extreme emotions in people: he was either loved or hated. Whites in Alabama and the rest of the white South loved him. He would find in 1964 that many in the North loved him too. He would be the first politician to sense the existence of a large group of voters who came to be known by many names: the white backlash, the silent majority, the alienated voters.

Throughout the 1962 campaign for Alabama governor, and before that in his 1958 loss, Wallace had learned the new lessons of race in the post-*Brown* South. In 1958, Wallace ran as a relative moderate on the race issue—and was soundly beaten. He had spoken out against the 1957 Civil Rights Act and accused his opponent John Patterson of not doing enough to keep Alabama's busses segregated, but standing against an overt racism expounded by Patterson that transcended code and innuendo, Wallace had come across to Alabama

95

voters as maintaining an insufficient devotion to the cause of white supremacy in the state. He had, in fact, denounced the Klan. After the election, surrounded by close friends while waiting to give his concession speech, Wallace seemed to reach an epiphany, one of several in his political life. "John Patterson," he said, "out-nigguhed me. And boys, I'm not goin' to be out nigguhed again."[50] Wallace always denied using those words, but a few days later James "Big Jim" Folsom, Alabama's governor for two terms in the late 1940s and 1950s, made the point that it was less important what words Wallace used than what he had learned from the campaign, a lesson that would impact his political career for decades to come. "Patterson out-niggered George in that race," Folsom told a newsman in 1964. "And old George resolved he wouldn't let that happen again. That's when he got to be so monomaniacal on the race thing. [He] felt like he had to hang six Negroes from every stump every time he made a speech."[51]

By the 1962 campaign for governor the competition was less than steep. Wallace's primary contender was Folsom, who was plying the waters for a third term. But corruption, liquor, and an erratic message on the race issue nullified Folsom and allowed Wallace to be a moderate on the race issue again—if he had wished. But as the campaign continued, Wallace came to realize that it was race that awoke his crowds, that when he spoke about race issues he made the jump from just a political candidate with a message to southern messiah. This time around, Wallace refused to denounce the Klan, and by all accounts welcomed Klan support. Folsom managed to get drunk and self-destruct before an Alabama television audience the night before the Democratic primary, and the next day voters denied him a place in the runoff. In November, Wallace won in a landslide against an ineffectual candidate, with 56 percent of the popular vote while carrying 56 of the state's 67 counties.

Wallace came to office at the very height of the nation's post-war racial problems—directly in the throes of Birmingham. In April 1963, Martin Luther King, Jr., at the head of the Southern Christian Leadership Conference (SCLC), began orchestrating sit-in demonstrations to desegregate downtown Birmingham's restaurants. King deliberately chose Birmingham because of the potential for the city's police department to respond brutally to the protests. And, not surprisingly, the protests drew the desired violence. In full view of the nation's television cameras, high-pressure water hoses and attack dogs were turned on peaceful demonstrators, many of whom were children. Bombs exploded throughout the city, including at the Gaston Hotel, where King's operation was centered, and at the home of King's brother. In the final analysis it was a tremendous victory for King and the civil rights movement because it made apparent for the first time to many northern whites (particularly northern white liberals and moderates) that blacks in the South were oppressed by whites, and that the situation needed rectification—no matter what the cost. Wallace emerged as the southern challenger to this new national attitude toward race.

Much of Wallace's success had to do with his speaking ability. He could work a crowd into a fervor, particularly when he thumped the issue of race and denounced northern liberals. It was Asa Carter who wrote many of Wallace's fire-eating speeches through the early 1960s. Carter had spent most of his life at the well of southern white supremacy; he was an avowed anti-Semite and even made an occasional tip to Hitler's "final solution." He was a White Citizens Council leader and the organizer of a paramilitary force that he called the Original Ku Klux Klan of the Confederacy. Carter edited the *Southerner* magazine, possibly the most racist organ of the 1950s, and occasionally showed up on radio programs to denounce "mongrelism" as a threat to white supremacy. Carter, however, often crossed the line from big words and threats and turned to action. He was connected to several acts of terror throughout Alabama in the 1950s and early 1960s, including an assault on Nat "King" Cole as he sang to an all-white audience in Birmingham, and the beating of Birmingham civil rights leader Fred Shuttlesworth and his wife.[52] Wallace wisely kept Carter in the background during his campaign for governor in 1962, but it was Carter's hard-hitting speeches (including Wallace's denunciatory inaugural address) that brought Alabama audiences to their feet during the campaign.

Throughout the 1962 campaign, Wallace had said several times that he would "stand in the schoolhouse door" if necessary to stop the segregation of Alabama's schools. It became one of his best applause lines, and as the campaign progressed he used it more and more to rally the faithful. In early June 1963, less than five months after Wallace's inauguration as governor, two black students, Vivian Malone and Jimmy Hood, were scheduled to register at the University of Alabama under the protection of a federal court order. On *Meet the Press* on June 2, 1963, Wallace threatened to bar the students from registering.[53] And from that, a confrontation grew that would pit (if only for a brief moment and for the benefit of television cameras) the forces of the federal government against the forces of the State of Alabama.

The incidents themselves that were finally played out at the University of Alabama on June 11, 1963, are hardly worth recounting—except that they had an important political impact. What appeared to the nation as little more than another racist southern governor trying to hold onto a bygone era was, in fact, the emergence of a formidable national political force that would threaten to siphon conservative votes from the candidates of the two major parties for the next three presidential campaigns.

Wallace had made it clear that he would confront the federal government on the issue, and the press, expecting (or possibly hoping for) the worst, congregated as dupes of the Alabama governor. Just two months before, the Kennedy administration had come away bloodied in its handling of the desegregation of the University of Mississippi. That incident deteriorated into what became known as the "Battle of Oxford," resulting in two deaths and over three hundred injuries. The press, and possibly the nation, expected no less from the University of Alabama.

Some four hundred reporters and television crews showed up at Tuscaloosa on June 11 expecting to witness another "battle" over the question of desegregation. But Wallace had other plans. He had no intention of being counted among the other southern governors who had stood for segregation and against federal authority and then lost.

On the evening news, 68 million Americans watched as Assistant Attorney General Nicholas Katzenbach strode up the steps of Foster Auditorium to where Wallace stood, literally, in the schoolhouse door. In dramatic fashion, Wallace stuck his hand out in a "stop" gesture. Katzenbach stopped, and Wallace made his speech before the cameras. In a thousand words read in fifteen minutes in the sweltering June heat, he spoke of the "unwelcome, unwanted, unwarranted, and force-induced intrusion upon the campus of the University of Alabama" by "the central government." The event, he added, "offers a frightful example of oppression of the rights, privileges, and sovereignty of this state by the officers of the federal government." It is an "intrusion," he concluded, that "results solely from force, undignified by any reasonable application of the principle of law, reason, and justice."[54]

It was dramatic enough, staged for the nation like a theatrical publicity stunt. Wallace had chosen the constitutional question over the racial issue. And that is where he would stand over the next months in his campaign for the presidency, a campaign he never intended to win but that would make a statement of conservatism and awaken—or draw out—a conservative spirit that was becoming more and more pervasive in the nation.

The incident at Tuscaloosa ended quickly following Wallace's statement. The White House had nationalized the Alabama National Guard in anticipation of violence. Malone and Hood were registered without incident, and Wallace returned to the Governor's Mansion in Montgomery. At the time, few looked deeply into the event. But it had given Wallace a national forum and thus national stature. In the weeks that followed, Wallace received over 100,000 congratulatory telegrams and letters.[55] Almost all supported his stand, and well over half were from outside the South. Again, Wallace experienced an epiphany. There were, he realized, Americans with southern values and beliefs outside the South.

Wallace clearly had tapped into something significant, and just as clearly he knew it. And the race issue was only part of it. All the change that was engulfing the 1960s, Wallace realized, was more than many Americans could absorb. He saw that large numbers of white Americans were alienated by the new liberalism. If nothing else, many Americans believed that civil rights was moving much too fast. The events at Tuscaloosa convinced Wallace that there was a large constituency awaiting a champion, and he began to plan for a national campaign to tap into that constituency. On the very day Wallace made his stand in the schoolhouse door, the Kennedy administration delivered its Civil Rights Bill to Congress.

For Wallace and his supporters, however, the Civil Rights Act was a call to arms, evidence that the federal government had gone too far in dealing with state issues. At this point, and over this issue, the ideas of George Wallace and Barry Goldwater converged. Both men delivered much the same message, often even using the same words: the federal government must not usurp the authority of the states. Goldwater voted against the bill in the Senate, claiming that it was not a matter of race or racism, but a matter of state sovereignty over federal authority. Wallace, as he traveled around the nation on various speaking engagements, made the same point, arguing that the states have the right to maintain their own internal affairs without fear of federal interference. The philosophies of the two men had different origins, and certainly different objectives in the sense of what the outcomes should be. Goldwater founded his statements in the philosophy of Thomas Jefferson. He could be called a classical eighteenth-century liberal in the Jeffersonian-Madisonian mold, believing that any attempt by the federal authority to regulate private enterprise, as the Civil Rights Act threatened to do, was not only unconstitutional but a giant step toward the abolition of private property. Although Wallace would have been more likely to cite Calhoun than Jefferson, he made many of the same points. The Civil Rights Act, he said, "is an assassin's knife stuck in the back of liberty."[56] The differences, however indiscernible through the words the two men used, should have been clear to anyone capable of distinguishing Wallace's southern accent. States' rights to Wallace, of course, meant the right of the states over the right of the federal government to segregate the races as the nation's state governments wished—or did not wish, as Wallace would often argue in the North. "I will campaign for the defeat of the so-called Civil Rights bill," Wallace told a Wisconsin audience, "which will destroy Wisconsin's right to control [their] schools, private enterprise and private property."[57]

But Wallace's real message was always segregation and ultimately race. His need to get that message across to his audiences (while using the inoffensive constitutional language of states' rights) led to the use of code words and phrases in American politics. Wallace was the first of any national candidate to refer to law and order as a code for cracking down on black-on-white street crime. In March 1964, for instance, he complained in Wisconsin about the situations in large sections of the nation's northern cities "where grown men are afraid to walk, and taxi drivers refuse to ply their trade." In many cities, he added, "We are subjected to roving bands of irresponsible street rioters. . . . Wallace often used Washington, D.C., as the nation's worst example of a crime-ridden city, a "jungle," he often called it, "where citizens fear to walk the streets at night."[57]

This is considerably different from Strom Thurmond's message in his run for the presidency on the States' Rights ticket in 1948. Thurmond made many of the same states' rights arguments in that election as Wallace did in 1964, but Thurmond realized in 1948 that a political party that clung only to issues of race would have no future in American politics. Thus he spoke on states' rights—not as a way to mask the race issue, but to avoid it. He hoped that by avoiding race he would broaden his party's electoral base by drawing in a growing group of southern urban middle- and upper-income types who had come to define the New South in the immediate post-war years. If nothing else, this was where the money was in the South in 1948, and these new leaders could furnish the funds Thurmond needed to carry on his campaign. This group had also come to dislike the South's image as an economic, political, social, and cultural backwater. Race issues (as sociologists, historians, and others were beginning to say at that time) were at the foundation of all those problems in the South, and these new leaders were beginning to shy away from the Old South's racial hard line founded in the age-old issues that had emerged from Reconstruction.[58]

Wallace never actually spoke about the Civil Rights Act in terms of race. Instead, he almost always referred to the public accommodation section of the act. You will not be able, he said, "to refuse to serve anyone without fear of violating this act." "[F]ederal agencies," he added, will be able to "destroy the homogeneous neighborhood and dictate who you shall sell your real estate to, who you shall rent a room to, who will be your lease tenant." And he often promised that the act would establish quota systems for hiring. Then, when confronted with the issue of race, he would reply. "In all my speeches I have never spoken one word of evil or demagoguery against any race. . . ."[59] Just as Wallace hoped, the coded message of race was always clear to anyone who wanted to hear it. At the same time, there was another message for anyone who was offended by the race issue but who sympathized with the constitutional question.

At least on one level this defines Wallace's support in the 1964 primaries: racists who read the code as racism, and conservatives who were drawn by the constitutional question. Wallace was instrumental in flushing out the first group, not only in the several primary states he entered, but nationwide through national media coverage of his primary campaigns. When Wallace left the campaign and it became apparent that the constitutional question espoused by Goldwater also encompassed the racial concerns of this group, they cast their lot with Goldwater. Wallace knew what he had done. He had identified the backlash and handed it to the Republicans for the remainder of the century. In what can be considered another use of the race code, Wallace, in the days just before the November election, made a simple statement with a monumental meaning: I "brought out the conservative vote within the Democratic Party."[60]

* * *

Before finally entering the 1964 primaries, Wallace tested the national waters with a series of speaking engagements. In September 1963 Wallace announced that he had been invited to speak at Harvard. He would take the southern cause directly to the house of the hated Kennedys. He had nothing to lose. If the crowds were discourteous or disrespectful, he would receive sympathy at home as a lamb torn by wolves. If he were received well, his stature would be enhanced significantly outside the South. Wallace succeeded at Harvard. There were the signs, boos, and hecklers, and the tires on his limousine were slit, but for the most part Wallace was treated with respect. During a question-and-answer period a black man stood up and announced that he would be running for president in 1964. Wallace brought the house down when he responded, "Between you and me, we might get rid of that crowd in Washington. We might even run on the same ticket." From Harvard he went on to speak at Dartmouth, Smith, and Brown. And just as at Harvard, the crowds were surprisingly cordial, even entertained by Wallace. The crowds

101

erupted into boos and catcalls only when questions from the floor forced Wallace into defending southern racial customs. Throughout his week inside the bowels of northeastern liberalism Wallace also spoke to the people of New England through a series of television and radio statements and interviews. He returned home something of a conquering hero, while the student bodies of the northeastern schools patted themselves on the backs for their broadmindedness. It was all a good lesson for the governor; he could be effective outside the South.[61]

Following Kennedy's assassination in November 1963, Wallace went on a swing of five Western states at the beginning of the new year. He spoke in Colorado, Washington, Oregon, Arizona, and California. As in the Northeast, he took time to speak at the major universities in the region, where he was generally received well. Ostensibly, the trip was to find new industry for Alabama, but clearly, Wallace was still testing the waters for a national campaign. Finally, in Phoenix, the home of Barry Goldwater, Wallace announced that he was considering a run in the New Hampshire, Indiana, Ohio, and Maryland primaries.[62]

Through the spring months of 1964, Lyndon Johnson refused to declare that he would be a candidate in November and thus he refused to enter any Democratic primaries. At the same time, he carried forward the Kennedy administration's policies, including the commitment to the Civil Rights Bill introduced in 1963. The new president threw his total support behind the bill, and together with a coalition of liberal lawmakers, labor leaders, and civil rights and religious groups, he was able to strengthen the bill considerably. To Wallace, the Civil Rights Act opened doors. A campaign needs an opponent. The Civil Rights Act would be George Wallace's opponent.

5

Lyndon Johnson and
the Reins of Power

In 1963 the Democratic party in Texas was, as usual, in turmoil. The all-powerful Democrats had split between the oil-money conservatives, led by Lyndon Johnson's close friend Governor John Connally, and the labor-liberal coalition that Connally hated led by Texas senator Ralph Yarborough. Despite Johnson's place on the Kennedy ticket, Texas was by no means a sure thing in the 1964 election. *Time* reported, in fact, that Kennedy's chances in Texas "can only be rated even."[1] In addition, conservative forces in Texas were growing rapidly. Senator John Tower was leading a strong Goldwater drive in the state, and there was speculation in the Kennedy camp that if conservative Democrats followed Tower and voted for Goldwater that Kennedy could lose the state. To shore up his base in Texas, Kennedy decided to visit the state in November and show his support for Connally and the Texas conservatives. That, he hoped, would weaken Yarborough's support enough to unite the party behind Connally and allow Kennedy to carry the state in the national election. All this planning was done, however, without consulting either Johnson or Connally, and neither man believed that Kennedy's appeal was strong enough in late 1963 to pull the state's Democrats together by simply making an appearance. In fact, Kennedy's appeal in November 1963 was on the wane in Texas—a state where the president's organization had few strong connections beyond Lyndon Johnson. Several Kennedy advisors suggested that Kennedy might be a more powerful party leader in the coming spring or summer as the convention approached. But brother Bobby insisted on the Texas trip and the need to pull that state into line before the campaigning moved into higher gear after the New Year. It was a decision that most likely haunted Robert Kennedy for the rest of his life.[2]

The tragedy of the assassination, recounted many times, stunned the nation. It also changed the face of the coming election. For the Republicans, the death of Kennedy and the ascension of Lyndon Johnson altered the political dynamic completely. Goldwater had expected to take on Kennedy, the eastern liberal, but now he was pitted against a southerner who had strong support in the West and, because of his ties to the Kennedy administration, would probably be strong in the Northeast as well. If Johnson could maintain that coalition, he would be unbeatable in 1964. Added to that, Johnson would surely build political capital out of the national tragedy by trying to absorb some of the Kennedy mystique, by becoming the new carrier of the torch. The drastic turn of events soured Goldwater on the campaign to the point that he considered dropping out of the race. For the Democrats, however, Kennedy's assassination, despite the obvious horror of it, was little more than a bump in the political road. Johnson lacked all the charisma, the style, the apparent vigor of the Kennedys, but the new president saw his role in history clearly. He would have to restore the nation's confidence in its government, and he would have to do it as quickly as possible. The theme that he picked up and conveyed immediately was continuity—at every level. He would carry on the policies of his predecessor, for, not unlike Harry Truman who came to office under much the same circumstances, Johnson had not been elected president of the United States, and he believed he had a moral obligation to carry on the policies of the man who had been elected to the office. It was a natural response and it resulted in a fairly smooth transition. Within eight months, he had taken control of the Democratic party apparatus, pushed through Congress much of the Kennedy domestic agenda, and placed himself out in front of a grieving nation. By August 1964 he went into the Democratic convention unchallenged and on his way to one of the biggest political landslides in American history. It was a brilliant display of political skill and national leadership.

For most of America the defining moment for the nation's future came on November 27, less than a week following the assassination, when Lyndon Johnson spoke for the first time to Congress and the nation as president of the United States.[3] What America saw over its millions of television sets was something of a shock. There before them, in the place of the jaunty good looks of John Kennedy, was the saggy-faced Lyndon Johnson. And instead of the crisp accent of New England wealth they heard Johnson's drawn out Texas drawl. Few Americans knew much about their new president. Those who did most likely harbored the wheeler-dealer southern pol image that he carried his entire life. His reputation as a giant among senators and a master legislator was largely unknown outside of Washington, and even those who may have followed his career, or some aspect of it, probably had little regard for him. Americans on November 27 may well have wondered whether their new president was capable of leading the nation through the immediate crisis—and through the national crises that most believed were sure to come.

Johnson's speech that evening, written by Kennedy's speechwriter Ted Sorensen, could not, however, have been more reassuring, more certain. "All I have," he began so softly that few in the great hall could hear him, "I would have given gladly not be standing here today." Then, calling on one of many memorable moments from Kennedy's 1961 inaugural speech in which Kennedy said, "Let us begin anew," Johnson said with great emotion, "Let us continue." For Americans who approved of the way the nation was progressing under John Kennedy, Johnson's words were soothing. The new president also had comforting words for liberals, those in his party most disturbed by the ascension of Lyndon Johnson. He would, he said, in the name of the dead president, call for a continuation of the administration's agenda, including Medicare for the elderly, federal aid to education, aid to the nation's mentally ill, the continued quest to conquer outer space, and "above all," he added, the dream of equal rights for all Americans whatever their race or color. Most southerners and Republicans that evening in the Senate Chamber sat on their hands, but for liberals the speech was a relief. Kennedy had had the vision but not the skill. Here, clearly, was a man, now president, who had inherited the vision and had proven his skill in the legislative arena. He ended his speech with the last four lines from "America the Beautiful."[4] He received a thunderous standing ovation. Lyndon Johnson was no John Kennedy, and for many Americans he never would be. But here, on Thanksgiving eve 1963, he calmed the nerves of a jittery nation during a time of monumental crisis.

To Robert Kennedy, and to several members of the Kennedy family and a few of John Kennedy's aides, all this was simply too much too soon. Immediately, Kennedy White House aide Arthur Schlesinger had taken the lead in discontinuity. Within twenty-four hours of the assassination, Schlesinger had called a gathering of Kennedy aides at a restaurant near the White House. John Kenneth Galbraith, renowned liberal economist and John Kennedy's ambassador to India, attended the meeting and kept notes. Schlesinger, he wrote, "was reacting far too quickly to the chemistry of the moment and was dwelling on the possibility of a ticket in 1964 headed by Bob Kennedy and Hubert Humphrey. This of course is fantasy, unless of course Johnson stumbles unbelievably."[5] Some of John Kennedy's people were willing to work inside what was now the new administration; others, like Schlesinger, were not.

Johnson realized, as had Truman, that one way to maintain continuity, or at least the appearance of continuity, was to keep on his predecessors' aides, advisors, and cabinet members. Clark Clifford advised Johnson to proceed slowly, allowing the Kennedy people to leave their office spaces at their own pace, and to retain as many Kennedy people as possible.[6] Clifford was an influential Washington lawyer who had advised Truman during his first term and helped orchestrate Truman's 1948 upset victory. He had seen Truman sit in Johnson's place, and his advice to the new president was invaluable. Clifford had also seen how most of the New Dealers had abandoned Truman, and how as the 1948 election approached they had flirted with forming a government-in-exile behind Henry Wallace. In 1948 that plan collapsed for a variety of reasons. In 1963, Clifford warned Johnson that if the political situation was not handled properly that a disgruntled Kennedy government-in-exile might emerge with Robert Kennedy at its head and gain enough power to challenge Johnson for the party's nomination later the next summer.[7]

Under Clifford's advisement, Johnson postponed his move into the White House until December 7, a date that was still much too soon for Robert Kennedy, who simply could not accept Johnson's presence in the Oval Office. Among the Kennedy administration's key people, Ken O'Donnell, Sorensen, and Schlesinger could not bring themselves to work for Johnson. Larry O'Brien, however, stayed on as White House congressional liaison, and Kennedy's main foreign policy people continued to occupy their seats in the cabinet. Dean Rusk stayed on at State, Robert McNamara continued at Defense, and McGeorge Bundy remained on as National Security Advisor. Johnson, not particularly astute at foreign policy, was duly impressed with all three men.[8] Robert Kennedy stayed on as attorney general, but as the year passed it became clear that he could not remain in that position for long. Nevertheless, the lack of an overhaul of personnel in Washington reassured the public that Johnson would keep the Kennedy balls rolling in the same direction. Johnson, of course, brought in his own people, most notably Jack Valenti, George Reedy, Walter Jenkins, and Bill Moyers. According to Kenneth O'Donnell, the two staffs (Kennedy's people and Johnson's people) got along well.[9]

But Lyndon and Bobby did not. The feud between these two men went back to at least the 1960 presidential nomination, and most likely well before that. They simply clashed. Throughout the Kennedy administration, they seldom crossed paths. Bobby saw Johnson as an interloper, an outsider, an old-time pol in the new dynamic administration of young doers. At the same time, Johnson clearly resented Bobby's access to the president just as he resented being relegated to a position outside the immediate decision-making processes. But when John Kennedy was killed, the two men could no longer ignore each other. They either had to work together or work against each other. Eventually, they would do both. "There is only one undisputable fact about their relationship," wrote one of Robert Kennedy's advisors; "they mistrusted each other almost from the beginning, and their mistrust turned to bitter enmity at the end."[10]

Exacerbating all this was Johnson's own lack of self-confidence and an accompanying fear that Bobby at the head of a Kennedy family political juggernaut was conspiring to damage him and ultimately to take the presidency (and his potential legacy as president of the United States) away from him. Bobby, on the other side of the equation, foundered badly in the months after Dallas. He seemed unable to decide what to do with himself, as if his brother had been his compass. He had a great deal of difficulty dealing with his brother's death and he seemed to believe that the torch had been passed to him—and that somehow he needed to carry on the Kennedy legacy. He also, apparently, saw Johnson as somehow blocking the way of all the intended Kennedy achievements. The conflict between the two men grew to enormous proportions and had major ramifications for the political events coming in the summer of 1964. For Johnson, the "Bobby problem," as he called it, had to be solved before the convention. For his part Bobby simply needed to find his way, to serve the nation in some capacity, to carry on his brother's work in some form. From the moment of John Kennedy's death through the summer of 1964 the relationship between the president and the younger Kennedy would be extremely difficult, and it would impact the election.

Lyndon Johnson harbored an amazing lack of confidence in himself, particularly so for a man who had achieved so much success in the political arena. It was this lack of confidence that made him constantly look over his shoulder, expecting somehow to see Robert Kennedy undermining his presidency and conspiring against him. "I was . . . illegitimate," Johnson told historian Doris Kearns of how he believed the Kennedys and the nation's liberals saw him, "a naked man with no Presidential covering, a pretender to the throne, an illegal usurper."[11] The groups he worried about most, the ones he believed were strong enough to take his presidency away from him, were what he often called the "Kennedy crowd," the Eastern Estab-

107

lishment, the "eastern intellectuals."[12] "[T]o them my name is shit and always has been and always will be. . . ."[13] His insecurities fed his jealousies, and all that was made worse by the nation's adulation for the Kennedy family, an adulation that he always felt was undeserved. Even after the "Bobby problem" was solved, he still carried the weight of self-doubt. He told George Reedy and Zephyr Wright that he would not run in 1964, and both men were convinced at times that Johnson meant what he said.[14] His lack of confidence would continue to weigh heavily through the spring and summer of 1964.

Robert Kennedy's dislike for Johnson apparently pre-dated the 1960 election, although the two men had had no significant dealings with each other before the 1960 Democratic Convention. The incidents that occurred there simply punctuated Bobby's dislike for the majority leader. Following John Kennedy's assassination in November 1963, the relationship deteriorated almost immediately. Clark Clifford recalled that "Bobby Kennedy seemed at the beginning very much to resent President Johnson. It was a curious attitude, completely illogical, wholly emotional. It seemed to irritate Bobby Kennedy when he saw President Johnson as President."[15] One immediate problem was that Bobby expected Johnson to be conservative, to come into the office and shut down the Kennedy initiatives. "People just don't realize how conservative Lyndon is," Kennedy told his own advisor Edwin Guthman. "There are," he added, "going to be a lot of changes."[16] In a remarkably candid interview with Bartow Martin in the spring of 1964, Bobby held nothing back in expressing his feelings for Johnson. John Kennedy, he told Martin, "was a gentleman and a human being." Johnson, in contrast, is "mean, bitter, vicious—an animal in many ways." He's "got this other side of him in his relationship with human beings which makes it very difficult, unless you want to kiss his behind all the time. . . . The fact is," he continued, "he's able to eat people up, even people who are considered rather strong figures."[17]

To the Kennedys, and many of their supporters in Washington, Johnson was crude and uncultured. He was certainly recognized as a heavyweight in the legislative arena, but in polite society he was someone to be avoided—and their opinions were not much of a secret. A combination of rumors and jokes spread from coast to coast almost immediately after Johnson took office. Did he really have a telephone installed in the Oval Office bathroom so that he could talk while sitting on the toilet? In his first month in office he startled newsmen by graphically describing the sex lives of his prize bulls—and then comparing it to his own sexual prowess. He urinated on his own grave site, belched aloud, told dirty jokes and racist jokes.[18] When these incidents turned up in the press, he seemed amazed. "Inappropriate presidential behavior," was the description most often used. Perhaps none of this would have mattered much had it not been not for the sharp contrast between the new president and the image of the urbane, cultured Kennedys. Also, the press seemed to attack Johnson even more harshly because his actions were at such a wide variance from the stable, solid public image he was trying to portray before the nation. Almost desperately, Johnson responded by trying to soften his image. He placed himself at the appropriate cultural events, named his friend Abe Fortas as director for the arts, and tried to shed some of his Texas corn pone. Nothing worked. He was accused of trying to be a Kennedy, of trying to woo intellectuals—intellectuals who would not be wooed. He had never had image problems before, and it was something that he dealt with badly. All of this tore at Johnson's thin skin and increased his insecurity and self-doubt.

* * *

Robert Kennedy in 1964 was not yet forty years old. He had experienced extreme power at a very young age, and now, because of his brother's death, he was outside the power structure, outside of the political loop. He was, in fact, in almost the same place Johnson had found himself in Kennedy's administration. It was clearly a frustrating position for the young Kennedy. What may have been even more frustrating was that, in the minds of many Americans who had become infatuated with the Kennedys, he became a sort of surrogate Jack, the man who was expected to carry on the family name, the legislative agenda, the image, and the high hopes his followers had pinned on John. In addition, many Americans certainly wanted him to succeed his brother and become president. Almost immediately after Dallas there was talk of a Johnson–Kennedy ticket in 1964. It seemed a logical progression. A Kennedy–Johnson ticket had worked in 1960. For many of the same reasons, a Johnson–Kennedy ticket should succeed in 1964. In January, *Newsweek* speculated on the 1964 Democratic match-up, referring to the appeal of the "Boston–Austin Axis," and how the "cool intellectualism" of Robert Kennedy would be offset nicely by the "warm folksiness" of Lyndon Johnson. The tone was clear—and probably pervasive among Democrats. If it could not be John Kennedy and Lyndon Johnson, then the next best thing was Lyndon Johnson and Robert Kennedy.

Throughout much of the summer of 1964, and despite the growing conflict with the president, Bobby considered accepting the second spot on the Democratic ticket. In that position, he surely thought, he could carry on the Kennedy legacy in the White House while maintaining control of what was being called the "Kennedy wing" of the Democratic party and fostering its growth for the future. Then, in 1968, older and better prepared, he could succeed Johnson. If all went well, it would be a sixteen-year Kennedy–Johnson–Kennedy run by the Democrats.

Bobby was also willing to be Johnson's vice president because he felt an obligation to his brother's men. Bobby saw himself now as their leader, the one whose job it was to fulfill the expectations that his brother had brought to Washington in 1961. At the same time, many of these Kennedy men wanted Bobby to stay on and influence Johnson's programs, and possibly push the new president to the left. Bobby as vice president and as leader of the Kennedy people might keep the administration focused on John Kennedy's agenda—an agenda that many saw as a national vision. Ken O'Donnell, an important operative on John Kennedy's staff and a Kennedy family insider, wanted Bobby to accept the vice presidency. So did UAW chief Walter Reuther, Chicago mayor Richard Daly, and John Kenneth Galbraith.[19] Bobby's wife Ethel was also of this mind, and Jacqueline Kennedy approved.[20]

Certainly the American people liked the idea as well. In an April 1964 Gallup poll 47 percent of Democrats polled said they wanted Robert Kennedy as their next vice president. Coming in a distant second and third were Adlai Stevenson with 18 percent and Hubert Humphrey with a paltry 10 percent.[21]

Bobby may also have harbored thoughts that Lyndon Johnson would not live through the next term. "To put it coldly and bluntly," Clark Clifford recalled later, "it was well known that President Johnson had had a serious coronary attack years before, so I think the job [of vice president] was eagerly sought."[22] In late February, Bobby met with Douglas MacArthur, whose advice was definitely blunt: "Take it," he told Bobby. "He won't live. He gambled on your brother and won. You gamble on him and you'll win."[23] Bobby, of course, would never have expressed any such thoughts publicly, but it was common knowledge that Johnson was not healthy, and even Lady Bird feared that he might not live out the term.

Lyndon Johnson's "Bobby problem" crystallized in the issue of the 1964 Democratic ticket. Just three weeks after Dallas, and with the upcoming election and his own legacy as president of the United States in mind, Johnson told Ken O'Donnell of his dilemma: "I don't want history to say I was elected to this office because I had Bobby on the ticket with me. . . .

110

I don't want to go down in history as the guy to have the dog wagged by the tail and have the Vice President elect me, because that's what they're going to write. Bobby and I don't get along, and that's neither one of our faults. . . ."[24] Johnson later told Doris Kearns, "With Bobby on the ticket, I'd never know if I could be elected on my own."[25] As the problem began to burden Johnson, he again sought the advice of Clark Clifford. In his memoirs, Clifford recalled a discussion with the president: "If Bobby became Vice President, the President told me, he would be forever sandwiched between the two Kennedy brothers, unable to command public support for his programs."[26]

At the same time, Johnson accepted the realization that he may need Bobby on the ticket to win in 1964, particularly if it was necessary to control the Northeast industrial states, or win the votes of organized labor, African Americans, or possibly even eastern intellectuals, young voters, or Catholics. Whom the Republicans nominate would decide all of this. For instance, Nelson Rockefeller, a northeastern liberal with strong connections to labor and black voters, might offer a real challenge to Johnson, who was generally perceived as a conservative southerner with few ties to black issues, industry, or labor, and who was certainly weak in the northeastern industrial corridor. Along with Rockefeller, the Republican field was littered with strong liberal-to-moderate candidates. George Romney had a respectable civil rights record, was popular in the Midwest and among the nation's industry leaders. Henry Cabot Lodge and William Scranton were both northeastern moderates who appealed to industry leaders, black voters, and to some extent, organized labor. Scranton, who was a young wealthy northeasterner, was often touted in the press as the Republican Kennedy. A Scranton candidacy might pull away the young voters who had flooded into the Kennedy camp in 1960. Any of these men at the head of a Republican ticket might do a great deal of damage to the Democratic appeal among a number of important national groups. Robert Kennedy might, for Johnson, be a necessary evil. "Look," Johnson told O'Donnell, "if I need Robert Kennedy, I'll take him."[27] Kennedy, however, remained unsure of what to do. Family members, including his wife, wanted him to push for the vice presidency to remain close to the center of power, while he felt a deep obligation to those who had helped elect his brother and who served in the Kennedy administration for three years. According to Edwin Guthman, possibly the aide closest to him during those months, Kennedy decided not to decide. He would keep his options open, wait and see.[28]

The relationship between Johnson and Kennedy had been bad, but it seemed to get worse after the beginning of 1964 when Bobby began to act like a candidate by touring the nation. Most likely, Bobby hoped to show Johnson that he could campaign, that (although he had never run for any elected office) he was a vote-getter, that he had inherited the Kennedy mystique, the national and international appeal. Kennedy focused his tours on the North and West, regions where he could most easily exhibit his popularity and his vote-pulling power, where he could, Guthman has argued, show that his appeal in those areas "would more than offset the liability he would be in the South."[29] He began in Charleston, West Virginia, where his brother's candidacy had taken off in 1960, and traveled from there throughout much of the country. He spoke at urban housing projects, old folks' homes, before the American Jewish Committee, the American Bar Association, the Business Council, the U.S. Conference of Mayors, the United Auto Workers' national convention, and the American Society of Newspaper Editors.[30] By early summer, Kennedy had convinced himself that, despite all the problems and consequences, Johnson needed him on the ticket and that he would accept the vice presidency. But because both Kennedy and Johnson avoided each other and communicated little during this period, the insecure Johnson, not surprisingly, saw this "campaigning" as a threat to his own candidacy. Guthman, who traveled with Bobby at the time, wrote later, "the rising tide of political activity, with its . . . pervasive memories of President Kennedy, began to sweep him into an unannounced, unrestrained campaign for the Vice Presidential nomination. He allowed himself to drift into it even though he felt instinctively—and correctly—that Lyndon Johnson didn't want any part of him. . . ."[31]

Kennedy continued to vacillate through the spring and early summer of 1964. At times he seemed to want the spot on the ticket; at other times he did not. One sticking point was that the position itself was historically weak, even a political dead end. As Kennedy told an interviewer in May, "I don't think [the vice president] can have any influence. Lyndon Johnson didn't have any influence. . . . And as Vice President, I'm not going to have any influence. He's not going to have to pay any attention to me whatsoever. . . . I would lose all ability to ever take any independent positions on matters."[32] Kennedy also told a friend, "I'd be climbing the walls in three months."[33] And then there was the concern that seemed apparent to just about everyone in Washington: Lyndon Johnson's vice president would have to be more than just a loyal lieutenant. According to Arthur Schlesinger, Johnson often remarked of his vice president, "whoever he is, I want his pecker in my pocket."[34] Kennedy himself realized just how subordinate Johnson's vice president would be, and this notion must certainly have pushed Kennedy away from accepting the position.

Somewhere in the confusion of this decision-making process, Kennedy began looking at still other options. In April he considered running for governor of Massachusetts, a job that would get him away from the Washington microscope and Lyndon Johnson. It would also give him experience and keep him in the national spotlight. But the governor of Massachusetts is one of the weakest in the nation, the state was deeply in debt, and the Massachusetts legislature was embroiled in political turmoil. He rejected that option quickly. Younger brother Ted (who was now a senator from Massachusetts) suggested that Bobby run for a New York Senate seat. Steve Smith, their brother-in-law and Kennedy family political advisor, agreed. But here again there were problems. The New York state Democratic party was badly divided, and although Bobby had lived most of his life in New York, he knew he would be accused of being a carpetbagger, a political interloper.[35] But the idea definitely intrigued him. In mid-June, Kennedy headed off in a completely different direction when he asked Johnson to make him Ambassador to Vietnam, replacing the retiring Henry Cabot Lodge. Clark Clifford, who discussed the matter with Kennedy, called this "an utterly sincere act," but he added that it was "from a man still deeply depressed over his brother's death," apparently implying that Kennedy, in these few months after Dallas, was not quite thinking clearly. Clifford, Rusk, McNamara, and Johnson discussed the possibility of a Kennedy ambassadorship but rejected it outright, primarily for reasons of Kennedy's personal security.[36]

There may have been options, but Kennedy seemed directionless, unable to find his way. In an interview with *Newsweek* editor and Kennedy family friend Bill Bradlee that appeared in early July, Kennedy was even willing to tell the nation of his own dilemmas and the weight he was carrying as the younger brother of a martyr. "It's important," he said, "that the striving for excellence continue, that there be an end to mediocrity. The torch really has been passed to a new generation. People are still looking for all that idealism. It permeated young people all over the globe. And I became sort of a symbol, not just as an individual." Then he added, "If I could figure out some course for me that would keep all that alive and utilize it for the country, that's what I'd do."[37] While Kennedy looked for his place in history, Johnson knew exactly where he stood. He had two problems: One was to remove Robert Kennedy from contention for the vice presidency. The other was to choose a vice presidential candidate. He could move forward on neither point, however, until the Republicans chose their candidate.

* * *

Not unlike Truman, or any other president who succeeded to the presidency as a result of his predecessor's death, Lyndon Johnson felt a need to complete the agenda of the man elected by the American people. At the same time, that agenda, primarily liberal in nature, fit Johnson's needs well. Perceived mostly as a conservative southerner with a narrow outlook on national politics, Johnson relished the thought of pushing through Kennedy-initiated liberal legislation. The feat would both transform him into a national-level politician outside his narrow southern image, and, he hoped, allow him to capture some of that almost mystical Kennedy aura—a commodity that he respected but did not understand. The objective, however, was always clear: to capture the biggest victory possible in the 1964 election.

John Kennedy had initiated four pieces of legislation that together had come to define his domestic agenda. By the time of Kennedy's death, however, all four bills had become bogged down in Congress and, it appeared, would finally fail to pass. The press had even begun muttering quietly that the Kennedy administration, with all its promise and hope, might actually come up a failure. Among these bills, civil rights legislation was possibly the most important, for reasons that ranged from political to moral. The other three included a tax cut, federal aid to education, and Medicare. Lyndon Johnson set his sights on all four. He would carry on the Kennedy legacy (and thus, he hoped, make it his own), enhance his place among liberals in the Democratic party, shed his own southern conservative image, and then cut down the Republican opposition in November.

Just four days after Dallas, and before Johnson jumped headlong into these four pieces of legislation, the new president placed Congress on notice that the three-year-old logjam was about to be cut loose. While the government planned Kennedy's funeral and the nation mourned, Johnson shoved through the Senate a controversial foreign aid bill that included the sale of surplus wheat to the Soviet Union. Conservatives, led by Republican senator Karl Mundt of South Dakota, had been fighting to kill the bill by adding amendments that would disallow any such trade with all communist countries. After two days of hard work, the bill passed the Senate on November 26, the day after Kennedy's funeral. The events put a great deal of strain on White House personnel as they shuttled between funeral events and legislative activity. But to Johnson, the vote was imperative and it even took a back seat to Kennedy's funeral. "We could not afford to lose a vote like that," he recalled in his memoirs. "If those legislators had tasted blood then, they would have run over us like a steamroller when they returned in January, when much more than foreign aid would depend on their actions."[38] In the House–Senate conference committee, however, the bill stalled again when House Republicans tried one more time to attach anti-communist restrictions to the bill. With no decision, Congress headed home for Christmas. Johnson, however, was not about to let that stand. On December 21, he called the legislators back to an arm-twisting Christmas party at the White House. Finally, on Christmas Eve at 7:00 A.M., the conference report was accepted without the anti-communist restrictions, the bill passed, and the president got what he wanted. "At that moment," Johnson recalled, "the power of the federal government began flowing back to the White House."[39]

The Kennedy $11 billion tax cut bill had already cleared the House when Johnson took office in late November 1963.[40] But the bill had become bottled up in the Senate for some ten months at the hands of conservatives who believed it would increase the federal deficit and drag down the economy. Liberals countered in classical Keynesian language that a tax cut would fuel the economy; the resulting economic growth would create more tax revenue, thus reducing the deficit. As vice president, Johnson had opposed the bill, clinging to his conservative belief that a balanced budget increased business confidence. But Kennedy's economic advisors promised that the cut would produce a $30 billion expansion in the gross national product in 1964 and head off a recession. They added possibly the most compelling argument: restrictive monetary policies in the late Eisenhower administration had brought on a recession in late 1959 and 1960, a recession that may well have cost Nixon the election. Johnson was won over. He could not head into an election year with a weak economy and high unemployment. He may also have thought that a major tax cut would damage Republican arguments that the Democrats were eager to tax and spend to fund social programs. A tax cut in an election year would be good for the health of the nation, the Democratic party, and for the legacy of Lyndon Johnson.

The problem with cutting taxes in 1964 was the budget. Kennedy's budget for that year (which included the tax cut) was at just above $102 billion with revenue estimates at only $93 billion. The Senate Finance Committee, chaired by Virginia senator and Democrat Harry Byrd, simply would not accept a $9 billion budget deficit. The key, of course, was Byrd. During an Oval Office lunch in late December, Johnson and Byrd sat face-to-face and hammered out a compromise. The wheeling and dealing produced a Johnson promise to reduce the budget to below $100 billion. In exchange, Byrd would get the bill to the floor for a vote—but he refused to support it or vote for it himself. Johnson agreed, but his Keynesian economic advisors led by Walter Heller and Douglas Dillon argued that cuts in the budget would simply offset the tax cut, decrease the deficit, and slow the economy. Johnson's response was to take it or leave it. He told them "they could have their budget intact or they could have their tax cut, but that Congress would not give them both." You "might be able to sell me on the New Economics," he added, "but not Harry Byrd."[41] Following a great deal of cutting, slashing, and teeth gnashing among Johnson's economic advisors, the administration produced a budget at just under $98 billion. Byrd kept his promise and released the bill to the Senate floor where every manner of special interest threatened to reduce the bill to senatorial pork. Senator Bourke Hickenlooper of Iowa wanted to remove the tax on ballpoint pens produced in his state. John Pastore wanted to reduce the excise tax to aid the production of jewelry in his state of Rhode Island. Senator Russell Long from oil-producing Louisiana wanted to cut taxes on oil. But Byrd, while making it clear that he opposed the measure, saw to it that the bill was not significantly changed. Finally, on February 26 the bill passed. It had languished in Congress for thirteen months; Johnson had untied the knots and pushed the bill through in only ninety days. He signed it that evening.[42] Just a few days later, the president, speaking at a fund raiser at the Fountainbleau Hotel in Miami, bathed in his victory: "I intend," he said, to prove "that Government can be progressive without being radical, prudent without being reactionary."[43]

* * *

There were two groups of voters that were extremely important to a Johnson victory in November 1964: the traditional liberals and the African Americans, particularly those African-American voters living in northern cities. Johnson would win the enthusiastic support of both groups by passing a far-reaching civil rights bill (which had been initiated in the Kennedy administration), and the Economic Opportunity Act, better known as the War on Poverty Bill. Together, these two bills would solidify Johnson's reputation as a liberal and an advocate of minority rights.

In the few months before Dallas, Kennedy had convinced House leaders to compromise on a civil rights bill that would outlaw segregation in public accommodations and public schools. The bill also included a Fair Employment Practices Commission and a provision that permitted the Department of Justice to intervene in civil rights cases. This Civil Rights Bill received approval from the House Judiciary Committee in October 1963 and was before the House Rules Committee when Kennedy was assassinated. In mid-February 1964, just days before President Johnson signed the tax bill, the Civil Rights Bill was approved by the House and sent to the Senate—where a filibuster led by southern senators would, as most observers predicted, either kill the bill outright or force a series of amendments that would gut it.

Civil rights was an extremely volatile issue in 1963 and 1964. The events of those two years had brought the movement to a dramatic crescendo. At Birmingham, in the spring of 1963, Martin Luther King had pushed the movement out of the South and into the nation's living rooms, and for many Americans it was an introduction to the brutality of southern racism. In late August 1963, the March on Washington (MOW) was something of a crowning glory to the entire movement, a celebration of success, a consolidation of victories. The MOW was also intended to bring to bear the power and numbers of the African-American community, to pressure Congress into passing the Civil Rights Bill, at that time stuck in the House. The MOW was a spectacular event. It received extensive national media coverage and it gave King a national audience for one of the greatest speeches made by an American in the twentieth century. But despite the 200,000 participants before the Lincoln Memorial, the event failed to shake the bill loose.

Part of the problem was that the Kennedy administration had not pushed the bill hard enough. Both Kennedy brothers believed the bill would never clear a Senate filibuster and that there was little use in spending presidential currency to support a bill that would either die or be severely weakened at the hands of powerful southern leaders (in coalition with conservative Republicans) in the Senate. In addition, John Kennedy had not run on a civil rights platform in 1960, and he had made no real promises to civil rights leaders—mostly hoping to keep southern members of Congress from emasculating his legislative agenda. As the major events of the modern civil rights movement unfolded between January 1961 and November 1963, the Kennedy administration generally reacted to these events rather than leading them. For the most part, however, they sided with the movement while trying to calm the confrontational aspects of it.

The next summer, the summer of 1964, erupted into street violence. It began in Jacksonville, Florida. On the last day of March 1964, Mayor Hayden Burns ordered African Americans to stop picketing and demonstrating against segregation and discrimination in the city's hotels and restaurants. The result was a race riot, the first of a series that continued through several summers over the next five years. The press barely noticed the events in Jacksonville.[44] In July, however, a New York City policeman shot and killed a young black man, James Powell, during an altercation in Harlem. For five nights parts of New York raged. "Harlem rattled to gunfire," Theodore White recalled, "and Negroes by the thousands were in the streets, smashing, looting, burning in a series of riots. . . ."[45] The riot spread quickly to Brooklyn's Bedford-Stuyvesant district and then upstate to Rochester. Later that summer, riots broke out in three New Jersey cities.[46] These events were on the cusp of change in America, marking the beginnings of a shift in the civil rights movement away from the church-based nonviolent strategy led by King and other activists in the South, and toward a mostly leaderless movement that was centered in northern cities and marked by violence, frustration, and confrontation. And it identified a change in the nature of the political backlash. The term *backlash* had been used first in 1963 to mean racial competition for diminishing blue-collar jobs. But by the summer of 1964 the definition of the backlash had changed in the white mind. The riots, the Civil Rights Bill (and often, a misunderstanding of it), and George Wallace's run in the three Democratic primaries in the spring transformed the idea of the backlash into a broader one encompassing white fear of urban blacks, a group that many whites were beginning to associate directly with crime, looting, burning, and destruction. This fear was not only played out in the work place, but also in neighborhoods where the white inhabitants feared black encroachment—encroachment that would bring, as many saw it, crime and blight. Theodore White observed the change in 1964 as he wrote about the coming election and the impact this new backlash was beginning to have on white America. The nation, White wrote, is "witnessing in the black ghettos . . . one of the great population explosions of all time. Something has to give," he added. "In Chicago white people had hoped to hold [blacks] to a few small beachheads north of the Chicago River, [dividing] the city into a white north and black south. By 1964 the beachheads had enlarged into total breakthrough. . . . In New York, 96th Street was to be the line protecting the East Side of Manhattan. But Negroes are now crossing the line into the Eighties. In Boston 'they' were supposed to stop at Franklin Park; 'they' have by now completely outflanked the park in Dorchester and have closed in on Blue Hill Avenue. In Los Angeles, in Philadelphia, in Cleveland" he added, "—everywhere the FOR RENT and FOR SALE signs on lawns and apartment houses mark the moving edge of a Negro frontier." As whites fled to the suburbs, White continued, the "'white noose' tightens about an inner city becoming more and more rapidly Negro, while within the strangulating city a turmoil begins that feeds on fear and hate."[47] Theodore White's analysis reflected the fears and anxieties of white America in the mid-1960s, fear of a black tide on the rise, pushing at both physical and social boundaries, demanding equality when a large portion of white America was not yet quite willing to give it.

On November 27, in his address to the Joint Session of Congress, his first address to the nation as president, Lyndon Johnson expressed his intentions on the question of civil rights: "We have talked long enough in this country about equal rights. . . . It is time now to write the next chapter—to write it in the books of laws."[48] The Civil Rights Bill was passed by the House on February 10, after little debate and some strengthening in the area of the attorney general's role in initiating suits. A week later the Senate received the House-approved Civil Rights Bill.

It was Georgia's Richard Russell who headed the opposition in the Senate. Russell thought he could destroy the bill because he believed Johnson would not let the Democratic party go into the election in November split over an issue as volatile and divisive as civil rights. The president, however, saw the situation differently. "I knew," he told Doris Kearns, "that if I didn't get out in front of this issue, [the liberals] would get me. They'd turn my background against me, they'd use it to prove that I was incapable of bringing unity to the land. . . . I couldn't let that happen. I had to produce a civil rights bill that was even stronger than the one they'd have gotten if Kennedy had lived. Without this, I'd be dead before I could even begin."[49] As a southerner, and lacking Kennedy's credibility as a civil rights president, Johnson knew he had to push the bill through. A new climate of opinion permitted it. Kennedy's assassination, together with the actions of racists in the South against the rights movement and the roll of the press in showing the nation the horrors of racism, all generated a wave of sympathy for the movement itself and for civil rights legislation that would, much of America believed, right the wrongs of de jure segregation and bring an end to race discrimination.

A parliamentary maneuver by Democratic majority leader Mike Mansfield pushed the bill past the Senate Judiciary Committee, chaired by Mississippi senator James Eastland. Eastland's committee had become the designated graveyard for civil rights legislation, and many observers thought the bill would die an untimely death there. Mansfield's maneuver, however, placed the bill directly on the Senate calendar. By March, all the preliminary maneuvering in the Senate had run out, and the bill headed for a southern filibuster at Russell's direction. The Russell-run filibuster was a well-orchestrated event staffed by eighteen soldier-senators in Russell's anti–civil rights army. He rotated six senators in and out each day for fifty-seven days, a Senate record.

While Russell and his cohorts chatted away on the floor of the Senate, Lyndon Johnson and Everett Dirksen were quietly coming to terms—and in many ways pounding out the future of American race relations. Dirksen was the Republican leader in the Senate, a craggy, disheveled man with wild white hair, a mellow baritone voice, and a sharp intellect. One colleague described him as "the most accomplished thespian who ever trod."[50] He was a conservative, a long-time Taft supporter, a defender of Joseph McCarthy a decade before, and an early supporter of Goldwater for president. But Dirksen and Johnson were cut from much the same cloth. Both men, through years of experience on Capitol Hill, had come to realize the significance of moderation, compromise, and the benefits of acquiring half a loaf. They could work together. It would be their relationship that would finally bring about the passage of the 1964 Civil Rights Act.

The Democrats had enough votes in the Senate for a simple majority, enough to pass the bill, but it took a two-thirds vote of the body to force cloture of the filibuster and send the bill to the floor for a vote. For that, Johnson and the Democrats would need the aid of Senate Republicans. It was Dirksen who held the key to those votes.

The Johnson–Dirksen relationship was one of legend. As Eric Goldman recalled, "the men were like two veterans of the ring . . . showing thorough respect for a fellow pro, recognizing that the other man was doing his job even if it included bloodying your face. . . ."[51] "It was a unique arrangement," Jack Valenti observed, "because they could negotiate. . . . A lot of good things happened in this country . . . because these two men were able to negotiate out their differences." Lady Bird later recalled that "[T]here was something terrifically right about watching them talk to each other."[52]

As events surrounding the Civil Rights Bill unfolded, Dirksen began to see that it would be the Republicans, now enjoined in filibuster with southern Democrats, who would be blamed for trying to kill the Civil Rights Bill, a bill that would probably pass—at least in some form. The result might be that the Republicans could be tagged in the coming election as the party of racism. Dirksen clearly felt the heat. In his personal writings he complained bitterly of editorials and political cartoons that predicted, as he saw it, an "odious demise" of the Republican party if it did not provide the votes necessary for cloture.[53] It was also clear to Dirksen that if the Republicans joined the South in opposing civil rights, the GOP might easily lose its moderate base. The Republicans and southern Democrats had joined in the past on a number of issues, but here in 1964 the Civil Rights Bill was generally a popular piece of legislation. If the Republicans allowed the administration to pin the badge of racism on them because of their association with southern Democrats here (and with George Wallace's candidacy and opposition to the bill) the results could be devastating in future elections. The Republicans might, in fact, become the party of the South, and that would be an extremely weak political base. Dirksen saw the future. The Republicans could not afford to stand with the racist South in opposition to the Civil Rights Bill, even if some Republicans (like Goldwater) opposed the bill for reasons of states' rights. As Dirksen knew, states' rights had long been a thinly veiled code for racism in the South, and of course Wallace had used just that argument against the bill in his primary runs earlier in the year. Dirksen came to believe that he simply could not allow his party to take responsibility for the defeat of the Civil Rights Bill. In a number of position papers, he tried to remind the nation that the Civil Rights Bill was Democratic legislation and that the Democrats had a solid majority in Congress. It would not, he argued, be the fault of the Republicans if the bill failed to pass.[54]

Johnson needed Republican votes to invoke cloture and then finally to pass the bill, but he also knew he needed Republicans for other reasons. A bipartisan bill would, of course, carry more weight with the public than a bill pushed through by a Democratic majority. It would also make it easier to enforce the bill, and that issue concerned Johnson. In May, he told Humphrey that simply passing the law might not be enough. "The thing we are more afraid of than anything else is that we will have real revolution in this country when this bill goes into effect. . . . Unless we have the Republicans joinin' us . . . we'll have mutiny in this goddamn country. So we've got to make this an American bill and not just a Democratic bill. . . . It doesn't do any good to have a law like the Volstead Act if you can't enforce it."[55] So, Johnson believed, it would take Dirksen and the Republicans to make this controversial piece of legislation both palatable and enforceable.

Johnson, of course, pushed Dirksen hard on the issue, but Dirksen probably needed little persuasion. According to Valenti, Johnson believed he had convinced Dirksen that the winds of time were changing, "that it was in Dirksen's long-range best interest to go along with this. . . . I think he really convinced Dirksen that this would be sort of like a Vandenburg changing on foreign relations; that this would be a great thing for Dirksen, a statesman-like attitude."[56] Arthur Vandenburg, a Republican senator from Michigan in the 1930s and 1940s, was a staunch isolationist until the Japanese attack on Pearl Harbor convinced him to support a foreign policy of internationalism in the post-war years. His willingness to make such an about-face change in his opinion placed him in the category of a great statesman—at least to the internationalists in both parties.

Generally, the Senate Republicans were divided three ways on the Civil Rights Bill. The conservatives, led by Goldwater and followed by John Tower of Texas, Ed Mecham of New Mexico, Milward Simpson of Wyoming, Wallace Bennett of Utah, and Milton Young of North Dakota, would give their support to the South and not vote to end debate. Northeastern liberals in the party like Jacob Javits of New York and Clifford Case of New Jersey had large black urban constituencies and would vote for cloture. In between was a group of midwestern senators with very few African-American constituents who generally saw the Civil Rights Bill as little more than massive government encroachment. Names here included Bourke Hickenlooper of Iowa, Len B. Jordan of Idaho, Karl Mundt of South Dakota, and Carl Curtis and Roman L. Hruska, both of Nebraska. This group generally voted with the conservatives on most issues, but Dirksen believed that they had no great desire to be associated with the preservation of racism and segregation in the South. It became Dirksen's objective to add amendments to the Civil Rights Bill that would make it acceptable to this group.

In May, Humphrey and Dirksen entered into negotiations. In an effort to satisfy the limited-government Republicans, Dirksen proposed an amendment that would eliminate the attorney general's power to initiate court actions in individual cases of discrimination. A second amendment would defer complaints about public accommodation and fair employment to state agencies before they became a Justice Department concern. These amendments removed some of the federal authority from the bill, making it easier for the limited-government Republicans to vote for cloture. Humphrey agreed to all terms.[57] According to Joseph Rauh, who attended the Dirksen–Humphrey sessions, "concessions had been made to Senator Dirksen in language, and on occasion in substance, but the basic structure of the House-passed bill remained intact."[58]

After two months of the southern filibuster, the craggy senator from Illinois (knowing that he had the votes he needed for cloture) spoke to his fellow senators just before he filed the cloture petition. "There are many reasons," he said, "why cloture should be invoked and a good civil rights measure enacted. First," he continued, "it is said that on the night he died, Victor Hugo wrote in his diary, substantially this sentiment: 'Stronger than all the armies is an idea whose time has come.'" Then Dirksen added what seemed to be a truth to everyone except the most stalwart and the most racist:

"The time has come for equality of opportunity in sharing in government, in education, and in employment. It will not be stayed or denied. It is here."[59] The vote came on June 12. The final tally was 71 to 29, 4 votes more than the 67 needed to invoke cloture. Dirksen delivered 27 of the 33 Republican votes, and thereby avoided—in an election year—having the Republicans saddled with standing in opposition to civil rights.[60]

Goldwater, however, saw it all differently. Referring often to a critique of the bill written by Yale law professor Robert Bork, Goldwater railed on the Senate floor against the proposed legislation, and then voted with five other Senate Republicans and the southerners against cloture. He followed up by offering amendments that would remove from the bill those sections that prohibited discrimination in public accommodations and mandated fair employment practices. In an argument he had made over and over, Goldwater claimed in a press interview that the bill "would force you to admit drunks, a known murderer or an insane person into your place of business," and would require the hiring of "incompetent" employees.[61] He also stated his belief that legislation could not change social mores. "You cannot pass a law that will make me like you—or you like me. This is something that can only happen in our hearts."[62] One week later, the Senate adopted the bill, and again Goldwater voted against it, claiming, "If my vote is misconstrued," I will "suffer its consequences. . . ."[63]

Goldwater was no segregationist. He opposed the Civil Rights Bill because he believed strongly in the need to limit federal authority and he saw the bill as trouncing on the powers of state and local governments. However, by this time, Goldwater's campaign strategy had begun to change. He had seen the backlash. He had come to realize the votes it could garner in the South, but more importantly he realized that there were votes to be won among whites in the northern cities. Polls had begun to show that many whites, as a direct result of the civil rights movement, had come to fear blacks and their encroachments into neighborhoods, schools, and the job market.[64] By the summer of 1964, Goldwater had even learned the code of race, words he no doubt picked up from Wallace. At a rally in Springfield, Illinois, he made a Wallace-like coded statement that was clearly intended to strike a nerve in those whites who saw predatory street crime and urban riots as reasons to fear racial violence against white women. "Every wife and mother, yes every woman and girl," he said, "knows what I mean, knows what I'm talking about." The *New York Times* noted that these statements "seemed to be well understood by the audience." [65] In a speech later in his campaign, he added: "Choose the way of the present administration and you have the way of the mobs in the streets, restrained only by the plea that they wait until election time to ignite violence again."[66]

When it came to the philosophy of the race issue, Goldwater and the white South did not exactly see eye to eye. But Goldwater's states' rights stance was good enough for white southerners; they cared little about the reasoning. Goldwater had made it clear that he would allow the states, and not the federal government, to deal with race issues. As the election approached, Goldwater and the white South believed they needed each other to survive.

On the evening of July 2, President Johnson signed the Civil Rights Bill before a national television audience in the East Room of the White House. It was 223 days after Dallas. Looking on were senators from both parties and the nation's most prominent civil rights leaders. It was the most far-reaching piece of civil rights legislation in the nation's history, and certainly one of the most significant bills to pass Congress in the twentieth century. It would, in fact, change the social structure of the South, and would do so through the authority of the federal government. "Let us close the springs of racial poison," the president said in one of his most flowery speeches.[67] Just two weeks after the signing ceremony, Goldwater accepted his party's nomination for the presidency.

The signing ceremony was itself a political event, indicative of the wounds that were festering below the surface between the president and Bobby Kennedy. On national television, Johnson intentionally treated Bobby Kennedy badly by giving him a handful of signing pens to be distributed among Justice Department officials. To many observers, the president seemed to be sending Bobby on an errand; and Bobby, sort of sheepishly, with pens in hand, faded into the crowd surrounding the president. The incident was telling. The bill may have originated as a Kennedy bill, and Johnson may have used the Kennedy legacy to push it through Congress, but to Lyndon Johnson the Civil Rights Act of 1964 was his bill and he was not about to share the glory. In what may have been something of a personal act of defiance, Bobby Kennedy finally had one of the pens framed. Under it was carved the inscription, "Pen used to sign President Kennedy's civil rights bill."[68]

Moments later, just after the bill was signed and the crowds left, Johnson turned to one of his aides, Bill Moyers, and delivered an aphorism. "I think we just delivered the South to the Republican party for a long time to come."[69] With only a couple of exceptions, he was correct for the remainder of the twentieth century.

* * *

Johnson's key social program was the War on Poverty, a $3.6 billion increase in health, education, and poverty programs. The Kennedy administration had begun work on a similar program, but it had never really advanced beyond the planning stages. This gave Johnson the chance to seize the initiative and make the program his own. With no credit to Kennedy, Johnson, in his State of the Union address on January 8, 1964, spoke promisingly of an anti-poverty program calling for an "unconditional war on poverty in America." At other times he spoke of a "sound investment" for the nation, and argued that "$1,000 invested in salvaging an unemployable youth today can return $40,000 or more in his lifetime."[70] The point was clear: the successes that Johnson would draw from these anti-poverty programs would be his own.

The key, Johnson believed, in passing such sweeping social legislation, was to sell Congress and the nation on a program (or a series of programs) that would ultimately benefit all Americans and not just the few who needed the assistance—specifically the inner-city African-American population who made up a significant part of the nation's poor. Johnson believed that the American people would not accept a program that simply taxed the rich to benefit the poor, or any program that might be described as make-work. Several of the president's economic advisors had convinced him that an expanding economy would provide the necessary revenue to pay for such an expensive program.[71] Columnist Walter Lippmann made the argument in favor of the president's plan: "[I]n this generation a revolutionary idea has taken hold. The size of the pie can be increased by . . . organized fiscal policy and the whole society, not just one part of it, will grow richer."[72]

Bobby Kennedy, who was still looking for his place in the new administration in the early months of 1964, made it clear that he wanted to head the anti-poverty program. He apparently saw it as one way to carry on his brother's legacy. Johnson, however, saw the position as a possible stepping-stone to a Kennedy vice presidential candidacy that he could not control, and rejected the idea. At the same time, the president saw a need to keep the Kennedy name attached to the anti-poverty initiative, so he chose Sargent Shriver to head the program. Shriver had directed the Peace Corps, possibly the most successful and visible of all the Kennedy administration programs. He was also a Kennedy family member—the husband of the Kennedy brothers' sister, Eunice.

The bill went to Congress in March as the Economic Opportunity Act.[73] It proposed the creation of a Job Corps, a jobs training program; VISTA, Volunteers in Service to America, a sort of domestic Peace Corps; and the Community Action Program, designed to give individual communities the resources to deal with their own poverty. The bill also proposed college work-study programs, grants for low-income college students, and loans to businesses that would agree to hire the unemployed. These were all designed as self-help programs that provided training, but stopped short of providing jobs. The entire plan was to be administered from the Office of Economic Opportunity.[74]

On May 22, before a mammoth crowd of 90,000 at the University of Michigan football stadium, Johnson first used the phrase "Great Society" to identify his program. "[W]ill you," Johnson asked in Kennedyesque fashion, "join the battle to give every citizen the full equality which God enjoins and the law requires, whatever his belief, or race, or the color of his skin? Will you join in the battle to give every citizen an escape from the crushing weight of poverty? Will you join in the battle to make it possible for all nations to live in enduring peace—as neighbors and not as mortal enemies? Will you join in the battle to build a Great Society?"[75]

For Richard Goodwin, a Johnson aide and speechwriter, the University of Michigan speech was a defining moment in the Johnson administration. "[S]tanding before the graduating class at the peaceful Ann Arbor campus, speaking for thirty minutes, interrupted constantly by applause, the president left the almost completed Kennedy legacy behind and struck out on his own."[76]

The bill, with an appropriation at just under $1 billion, passed the Senate in an almost two-to-one vote. In the House the margin was 226 to 184.[77] On August 20, the president signed the bill into law at a Rose Garden ceremony. It will provide, he said, an "opportunity and not an opiate."[78] Goldwater, who had voted against the bill as a member of the Senate Labor and Public Welfare Committee, called the bill Johnson's "Wizard of Oz philosophy," and a "Madison Avenue trick to win the election."[79]

It was hardly a trick, but it was definitely designed to beat Goldwater in November. The Economic Opportunity Act was, not unlike the Civil Rights Act being debated in Congress at the same time, an attempt by Johnson to pull himself away from the stereotype of a southern conservative. As the election approached, he knew he would need the support of the northeastern liberals—the Kennedy wing of the party. And he hoped that by selling the program as good for the country as a whole he could play on the nation's good graces while maintaining control of the political center. All of this worked. By November Johnson was his own man with his own agenda who had succeeded at convincing the electorate that he wanted badly to be president of all the people.

Between the tragedy of November 1963 and the summer of 1964 Lyndon Johnson had transformed himself. For his means of transformation, he looked to his strengths. Through legislation and his ability to manipulate, compromise, and massage literally every aspect of the legislative process, Johnson had proved himself a giant. About the only thing that stood in his path to a November victory was his own self-doubt.

6

Conservatism Triumphant: Wallace and Goldwater in the Primary Season

George Wallace was looking and acting like a candidate as early as the fall of 1963. But in February 1964 he again experienced something of an epiphany. While at the University of Wisconsin in Madison during a speaking tour, he received a telephone call from a Wisconsin right-wing politico from Oshkosh named Lloyd Herbstreith who insisted that if Wallace ran in the Wisconsin primary the next month that he would pull up to one-third of the Republican vote in the state. "George didn't say nothing," Wallace aide Oscar Harper recalled. "Sometimes you couldn't tell if he was interested or if he was ignoring you."[1]

It became immediately apparent that the governor was, in fact, interested. But just as apparent was the obvious problem that Wallace knew nothing of Wisconsin politics. One editor later commented that the governor might not even be able to locate Wisconsin on a map.[2] Herbstreith, however, convinced Wallace that a successful run in Wisconsin was entirely possible. The primary was open, so voters could cross over party lines allowing Wallace to pull votes from conservatives in both parties. Herbstreith, a long-time supporter of Wisconsin senator Joseph McCarthy, insisted that Wallace would make a strong showing against the state's Democratic governor, John Reynolds, who would be running as a favorite son stand-in for President Johnson. Reynolds had become increasingly unpopular, Herbstreith argued, with large numbers of white upper-middle income suburbanites around Milwaukee and with white ethnic-working-class groups in the inner city because of his strong support for a statewide open housing law. At the same time, Reynolds represented the Johnson administration's support for the Civil Rights Act, then being debated in Congress. For Herbstreith, Wallace was the perfect candidate to oppose the state's Democratic liberalism, plus he carried the race card, which Herbstreith certainly realized was at the heart of all the discontent in and around Milwaukee. In addition, Herbstreith promised that all the old McCarthyite Republicans in the state would rally to Wallace's message of anti-communism and limited central government. Wallace agreed. As absurd as it must have seemed at the time, George Wallace, the figure that the press had typecast as a race-baiting Dixie demagogue, would run for president of the United States in the Wisconsin primary.[3]

Wallace flew into Madison on filing day, March 6. His old state-owned Lockheed Lodestar twin-engine prop plane had been refashioned to reflect the candidate's new national focus. The Confederate battle flag and the words "Stand up for Alabama" that had once decorated the plane's fuselage now sported an American flag and new words, "Stand up for America."[4] The governor opened his campaign, at Herbstreith's suggestion, in McCarthy's hometown of Appleton, where (again at Herbstreith's suggestion) Wallace spoke on such topics as communists in the state department and the Yalta betrayal—topics no doubt as foreign to Wallace as the sub-zero weather on the afternoon he spoke.[5] But it was not the fear of communism or even Wallace's well-known racism that would fuel the Alabama governor's success in Wisconsin. Wallace would find for himself in various pockets of disenchantment in Wisconsin the seeds of a new conservatism. In other parts of the country that same movement was coalescing around Barry Goldwater; in Wisconsin it was coalescing around George Wallace.

It was the wide-open nature of the Wisconsin primary that makes Wallace's appeal definable in the 1964 election. He appealed to conservatives. And Wallace (and clearly Herbstreith as well) had reached the conclusion that there were conservatives in both parties, that in fact larger numbers of Americans (or at least in this case Wisconsin voters) were more conservative than anyone believed in this era of supposed growing American liberalism. Wallace uncovered large groups of conservatives. There were some who believed in limited federal authority, some who feared for the racial contamination of their neighborhoods, others who feared the expansion of communism at home and abroad, and still other conservatives who worried that the Civil Rights Act would take away their jobs and their right to live as they wished. Another group of Wallace conservatives may well have bemoaned what was perceived widely as the moral decay of a newly permissive society. Many were Republicans; clearly, others were Democrats. The discontent of the backlash was rising in early 1964, and Wallace laid his hands on it in—of all places—Wisconsin, the dairy state.

Wallace's entrance into the Wisconsin primary immediately drove the state's politics wild, with the predictable result that Wallace was attacked from nearly every angle. All the major state organizations condemned him, including the Catholic hierarchy, the Protestant establishment, organized labor, and finally the Wisconsin Democratic party leadership. Even the Republican party, fearing a loss of support as their conservative members crossed over to vote for Wallace, felt a need to attack the Alabama governor.[6] The strategy for all these groups was to expose Wallace as an interloper, someone who clearly had no business trying to capture any Wisconsin votes for any reason. On the day after Wallace qualified to run in the primary, Louis Hanson, the state Democratic party chairman said, "This man [Wallace] is being supported by extreme right-wing elements who are even kookier than he is."[7] The next day, Governor Reynolds said, "Next to South Africa, Alabama has the worst civil rights record in the world."[8] Later in the campaign, the state's heavy hitters weighed in from Washington. Wisconsin senator Gaylord Nelson said, "we must repudiate the record of racist violence [and] suppression of personal liberty . . . which Wallace brings with him from Alabama." Wisconsin's other senator, William Proxmier, added that Wallace represents a state that is "the shame of the nation."[9] After the election Wallace recalled that his enemies in Wisconsin "made me out a fiend with horns and a tail, a hatemonger, a bigot and a racist. . . . [T]hey made [me] out to be some sort of ogre."[10] Wallace's response to these attacks was to blame a liberal conspiracy against his candidacy, a conspiracy of federal authority against his message of states' rights for Wisconsin. "I am no racist," he often claimed. "But I am a segregationist. . . . If Wisconsin believes in integration, that is Wisconsin's business, not mine. . . . And the Central Government in Washington has no right to tell either Alabama or Wisconsin what to do."[11]

Wallace immediately left behind the McCarthyite rhetoric of rural Wisconsin for the urban politics of Milwaukee. There he hoped to find disenchantment among homeowners who feared for their property values, and various white working-class groups who feared for their jobs. The issue, of course, was the Civil Rights Act, then being debated in Congress—and in the media before the nation.

In the nearly twenty years since the end of World War II the black neighborhoods throughout Milwaukee had expanded rapidly, bumping up against lower- and middle-income white neighborhoods, most of which comprised first- and second-generation ethnic Eastern Europeans. Governor Reynolds was pushing hard for a tough new statewide open housing law; the Civil Rights Act would give federal support to Reynolds's state law. By the time Wallace marched into the Wisconsin primary, this large Milwaukee Eastern European working-class community was nearly up in arms. But America was not paying much attention to the political events in Wisconsin. In fact, Wallace was getting very little news coverage outside of Wisconsin and Alabama, but something became very clear very quickly. This was Wallace country.

Much of this became apparent on April 1 when Wallace spoke at the Milwaukee Southside Serbian Memorial Hall. This little community center was jammed well beyond capacity to hear Wallace speak, and several hundred more Wallace supporters congregated outside the building to listen to Wallace's message over loudspeakers. Before the governor got to the podium a verbal brawl broke out between two black protesters in the audience and the majority crowd of whites. When the two protesters began heckling Wallace, a Wallace supporter grabbed the microphone and began to rave against what he perceived as a growing crime problem related directly to blacks moving into white neighborhoods. "Three weeks ago tonight a friend of mine was assaulted by three [blacks]," he screamed. "They beat up old ladies . . . rape our womenfolk. They mug people. They won't work. They are on relief. How long can we tolerate this? Did I go to Guadalcanal and come back to something like this?" The statement was followed by thunderous applause and the two black protesters slowly made their way out of the auditorium amid jeers, taunts, and even physical abuse. Then Wallace spoke. The crowd was charged, and Wallace's style whipped them up even further. They interrupted him with applause and standing ovations thirty-four times in forty minutes.[12] At least for that moment and that place, Wallace had found a constituency.

When Wallace entered the campaign the Wisconsin press predicted that he would pull possibly 5 percent of the vote. Three weeks before the election, Governor Reynolds predicted that Wallace might pick up something closer to 10 percent. Herbstreith, in trying to convince Wallace to run, promised the governor as much as a third of the popular vote. As election day got closer, Governor Reynolds finally realized that Wallace's support was growing rapidly. He gritted his teeth and admitted to the press that Wallace might pull as many as 100,000 votes, considerably more than anyone expected, and a number that Reynolds called "dangerously high" because it might "give heart to hate-mongers from coast to coast." In response to Reynolds's prediction, Wallace said that if he pulled that many votes it would "shake the eyeteeth of leaders in both national parties."[13] On election day, Wallace reeled in a whopping 264,000 votes—over a third of the ballots cast in the Democratic primary and 25 percent of the total vote. It was a far greater blow than anyone anticipated. Expectations are often the gauge of victory or defeat in primary campaigns. In the 1964 Wisconsin primary, George Wallace had far exceeded anyone's expectations. It was a tremendous victory.[14]

The fallout of the Wisconsin primary ultimately brought down Reynolds. Following the election he offered his analysis that all George Wallace had demonstrated in Wisconsin was "what we've known all along," that there are "a lot of people who are prejudiced." The statement came back to haunt him in his campaign for reelection that fall. Despite President Johnson's generous coattails, Reynolds was defeated. After the election he told Johnson that he believed he had lost because he had been irreparably damaged in his March run against Wallace. As apparent compensation, Johnson awarded Reynolds with a circuit judgeship.[15]

Wallace's biggest victories came in and around Milwaukee. In the city's working class suburbs on the Southside he received close to 42 percent of the vote. But it was in the middle-income suburbs, areas that had gone heavily Republican in the past, where his popularity was the most surprising. There his numbers reached even higher at 44 percent. In River Hills, one of Milwaukee's wealthiest suburbs, he took 66 percent of the vote. There was a backlash that was apparent in the Wisconsin primary. It was among white working-class ethnic minorities who, *Newsweek* explained, had developed an "edginess about the specter of Negroes moving in next door."[16] But it was also strong among upper middle-income whites, a group that was at the very foundations of the national Republican party. In fact, the Wallace numbers in Wisconsin closely resembled the normal Republican voting patterns in the state.[17] His own analysis of the election was far simpler, but probably not far from being correct: "It was a vote against those wild-eyed, far-out pinko liberals who, under the false guise of civil rights, are trying to control all your property and dictate every detail of your lives." "We have," he told a crowd back in Montgomery following the Wisconsin primary, "shaken the eyeteeth of every liberal in the country."[18]

* * *

Following the New Hampshire primary, the several Republican candidates set their sites on the big prize, the June 3 California primary. But before California there was Oregon. A win in Oregon would not make much difference in the overall delegate count, but the Oregon primary was seen as the gateway to California, and it was believed that a win in Oregon meant that a California victory was not far behind. Success in Oregon also meant a strong foothold in the West. Most likely it was just as important that it was possible for candidates to campaign in California while also campaigning nearby in Oregon.

In April, *Newsweek* reported a surge in the polls for Lodge, still ensconced at the American Embassy in Saigon and unwilling to return to take charge of his campaign. Pre-Oregon predictions gave Lodge a substantial lead of 46 percent over the rest of the Republican field. The other Republican candidates each polled less than 20 percent of the vote.[19]

Lodge's popularity was growing rapidly with voters because he was perceived as a moderate who fell somewhere between the conservative Goldwater and the liberal Rockefeller. He was also a fresh face. Although he had been dragged down to defeat in 1960 as Nixon's running mate, most voters recognized him as Eisenhower's ambassador to the United Nations. Now, in 1964, he was a major player in the Democratic administration, thus obviously a moderate and appealing to centrists in the Republican party who were by now sick of the haggling between the party's right and left wings.

Lodge, however, was facing several major problems. First of all, he was still in Saigon and not visible on the campaign trail, a noncandidate whose absence would eventually eliminate him if he continued to stay away. He was also disliked by Republican party leaders, who saw him as aloof and affected, and perhaps most importantly believed he was much too independent and unwilling to work within the party structure. The party leadership also marked him as a notoriously poor campaigner. In 1960 he had done little to aid the Nixon–Lodge ticket, and party bigwigs had little interest in backing someone who had not shown any ability or willingness to go toe-to-toe with Johnson in that election. Also, Lodge had made a couple of costly blunders in the 1960 campaign. In a speech in Harlem he had promised that a Nixon administration would name a black cabinet member, end segregation in the public schools and public facilities, and enact new legislation that would guarantee blacks voting rights. "[I]t is part of our program and it is offered as a pledge," he promised.[20] Such statements, made without Nixon's approval, threatened to upset the Republican party's newly developing southern strategy, and Nixon, in order to shore up his southern defenses, had to publicly refute the statement. Polls showed that the incident hurt Nixon's standing among both white southerners and northern blacks. As the 1964 primary season moved on to Oregon, Lodge was still pulling some impressive numbers in the polls, but his absentee campaign with almost no party support and no party money was headed for a predictable collapse. In Oregon, it was apparent that Lodge's time was up.

Oregon was a must-win for Rockefeller. Following his embarrassing defeat in New Hampshire he had to show he could win votes by running ahead of predictions in Oregon or his campaign in California would be damaged— possibly beyond repair. Rockefeller's strategy was to target Lodge by accusing him of orchestrating the administration's failures in Vietnam.[21] He also set out to buy the election. By some accounts, he paid as much as three dollars per vote in Oregon, an enormous sum.

The real wildcard in Oregon was Nixon. Nixon's write-in campaign in New Hampshire had kept him in the running with a respectable 17 percent of the total, about half of what Lodge, the front-runner, received and just a few percentage points behind Goldwater. This outcome encouraged Nixon enough to enlarge his campaign staff, while still insisting that he was not a serious candidate. In May, he entered the Nebraska primary as a write-in candidate and did well against Goldwater, the only candidate on the ballot. From there he hoped to carry some significant momentum into the Oregon campaign. A good showing there would place him in good stead for California, his home state. Although he had lost the 1962 gubernatorial election in California, Nixon felt confident that he could beat either Rockefeller or Goldwater on his home turf, and then head toward the convention as the choice among party moderates. Just days before the Oregon primary, Rockefeller strategists still believed that Nixon would be the man to beat at the convention, expecting him to step forward as, what they called, a "toned down Goldwater." And a *Newsweek* poll targeting so-called "party regulars" showed growing support for Goldwater, but the majority polled said they still expected Nixon finally to pull ahead and win the nomination.[22]

Goldwater decided to stay away from Oregon.[23] The best he could hope for there was that Lodge would beat Rockefeller and knock him out of the running before California. Instead of stumping Oregon, Goldwater entered the Illinois primary—"Goldwater country," as the press called it. He was expected to win there by 80 percent of the vote and show himself to be a vote-getter among the all-important midwestern conservatives. But Margaret Chase Smith raised eyebrows and embarrassed Goldwater with 25 percent of the vote after only two appearances in the state and spending less than $1,000. Goldwater "can't stand many more victories like this," a GOP leader told *Newsweek*.[24] Goldwater also won the Indiana and Texas primaries, again with only token opposition. The press claimed that these victories were un-

The Rockefeller campaign style. (*Rockefeller Archive Center*)

important in showing Goldwater's strength because his opposition was insignificant, but clearly the other candidates stayed away from these minor contests to avoid being crushed by Goldwater in these conservative states. They were also important because Goldwater collected the delegates while Rockefeller and the other candidates focused on a few highly visible primary states like New Hampshire and California.

With the other candidates on the periphery of the Oregon campaign, Rockefeller hit the state hard. With deep pockets and an effective campaign slogan, "He cared enough to come," Rockefeller won in Oregon and kept his campaign alive long enough to enter the California primary with some momentum to challenge Goldwater. Rockefeller received 33 percent of the vote to Lodge's 27 percent. Goldwater as a no-show pulled a respectable 18 percent. Nixon came in fourth, one point behind Goldwater. Nixon's poor showing following a significant effort effectively removed him from the running, although he continued to harbor thoughts of a deadlocked convention coming to him as the moderate unifier of the party, standing between Rockefeller and Goldwater. Lodge, despite the numbers, was still a noncandidate, and as long as he remained in Saigon and made no effort to organize a major campaign, raise money, or work with GOP pols he would remain a noncandidate with no chance of winning the nomination. That left Goldwater and Rockefeller in the ring, and in the post-Oregon polls neither man appeared strong. Despite Rockefeller's flash-in-the-pan Oregon victory it was clear that it had taken a great deal of money to achieve it. In addition, Rockefeller had accumulated only about one hundred delegates nationwide. He would need over five times that many to win the GOP nomination.[25] Goldwater had lost in New Hampshire and Oregon, and he had been embarrassed by Smith in Illinois. His poll numbers were down after Rockefeller's Oregon win—as low as 15 percent in a Harris poll. His negative numbers (that is, those polled who said they disliked Goldwater and his policies) had jumped to an astonishing 51 percent during the Oregon primary.[26] But Clif White and his people were still working quietly behind the scenes, racking up delegates at state conventions and state caucuses throughout the nation. By early May, just before the Oregon vote, *Newsweek* recorded that Goldwater may have accumulated as many as 451 delegates out of the 655 needed to nominate. An article in the *Saturday Evening Post* estimated that he had as many as 550 delegates. Goldwater himself believed he had over 500 delegates.[27] Before California, White and his people had collected delegates in Oklahoma, Nebraska, Indiana, Illinois, Kansas, Idaho, Iowa, the Dakotas, Washington, Texas, New Jersey, Kentucky, and Missouri.[28] Despite all the claims in the press that Goldwater and Rockefeller would slug it out in California for the GOP nomination, the race was essentially over well before California—or even before Oregon. Goldwater, however, believed he had to win in California in order to sew up the nomination. He also felt he needed to show party regulars that he could attract voters, something that he had yet to do. Thus he put all he had into the state. At the same time, Rockefeller thought that if he could destroy Goldwater in California he could win the nomination as the only other choice available. He would succeed in destroying Goldwater—but he would never get close to the nomination.[29]

Just after the Oregon primary, when it became apparent that Goldwater was on his way to the nomination, General Lucius Clay, a one-time Eisenhower supporter and Republican moderate, lamented over Goldwater's imminent nomination and the lack of a moderate candidate in the Republican field. The problem was, he said, that "nobody made a move. Not Bill [Scranton], or the others, nor [Eisenhower]. The sheer lack of anybody doing anything has got us where we are. It's a good lesson on how not to select a President."[30] For General Clay, the lack of moderate enthusiasm had turned the nomination over to Goldwater by default. Immediately, a flag went up. Goldwater was headed for the nomination and the moderates had no candidate. Rockefeller still breathed life, but even a victory in California and its eighty-six delegate votes would not put him over the 200-delegate mark. GOP moderates feared the worst. If Goldwater wins, said Nixon operative Tom Kuchel, "then the death knell of the two-party system would have been sounded, and the Republican Party would go the way of the Know-Nothings, the Copperheads and the Whigs."[31] George Romney called Goldwater's seemingly imminent nomination a "suicidal destruction of the Republican Party."[32] Again, the moderates looked to their leader, Eisenhower. And again, Eisenhower refused to endorse a candidate, so no one stepped forward. In an article in the *New York Herald-Tribune* in late May, Ike described to his party the kind of candidate he wanted, but went no further. He called for an "ideal" candidate, one who would, he said, support the 1956 and 1960 GOP platforms, support the United Nations and back the administration's Civil Rights Bill, then before Congress.[33] The "ideal" Eisenhower candidate certainly seemed to rule out Goldwater. With no specific endorsement attached to Ike's statement, Rockefeller acted quickly to step into the breach. Campaigning in San Diego, he said that he was Ike's "ideal" candidate, that he agreed with all of Eisenhower's pronouncements, and called Eisenhower's statement an all-out endorsement of his candidacy. Goldwater, he added, "is outside the framework of responsible Republicanism which has been defined by President Eisenhower." But when Ike did not respond, it became clear that the general did not have Rockefeller in mind and the issue dropped.[34]

If not Rockefeller, then who? Most observers saw Pennsylvania governor William Scranton as the candidate closer to Eisenhower and his policies than any other Republican in the field. If there was an Establishment candidate in the 1964 Republican campaign, Scranton was it. A modest millionaire, he had gone to the right schools and was connected to the right people. He could count among his supporters some of the cream of the Northeastern Establishment: Henry Luce, the denizen of the Establishment and chairman of *Time* Incorporated; Herbert Brownell, Thomas Dewey's political chief of staff; William S. Paley of CBS; the *New York Herald-Tribune*'s Walter Thayer; George Humphrey, Ike's treasury secretary; William Beverly Humphrey, president of Campbell's Soup; Walter Annenberg, owner of the *Philadelphia Inquirer*; Thomas Gates, Eisenhower's secretary of defense and now president of Morgan Guaranty Trust; and Tom McCabe, president of Scott Paper. For many of these Establishment types, Scranton was just the man to fill Eisenhower's shoes. And in mid-December it appeared that Eisenhower would weigh in and endorse Scranton. The general had lunch with the governor in Harrisburg and clearly encouraged Scranton to make a run. Ike's encouragement, however, was apparently not enough for Scranton. Supporters would plan through the spring of 1964, but without the general's endorsement, Scranton refused to take the plunge and announce his candidacy. Finally, in late April, with no signs of life (or a forthcoming endorsement from Eisenhower), Scranton announced that he was pulling out of the campaign—although he had actually never officially entered.[35] There were rumors that Eisenhower had tried to persuade Scranton to stay, or at least "keep the door ajar," as *Newsweek* reported it. And several times after that, possibly in response to Ike's suggestions, Scranton announced that he would accept from his party what he called "a sincere and honest draft," the exact words that Eisenhower had used in 1948 when he was first testing the waters for a presidential run. As the California primary got under way, however, Scranton remained quiet in Harrisburg, possibly waiting patiently for Eisenhower to tap him as the stop-Goldwater candidate, the man who would unite the party with the general's support. It did not come.[36]

* * *

The Wisconsin primary had turned George Wallace into a candidate, and he immediately began looking around for another primary to enter, one that

138

would again shake the eyeteeth of the nation. He settled quickly on Indiana, a state with many of the same features as Wisconsin—and a state that was, in fact, considerably more conservative. Northwest Indiana, the region often described as the East Chicago–Gary corridor, had many of the same characteristics as the Milwaukee Southside, but it was much larger. Stocked with the descendants of Eastern Europeans, now mostly steelworkers, the region had become a hotbed of racial strife because black neighborhoods, particularly in and around Gary, had begun to encroach on white areas. Here, in the spring of 1964, the region had not yet erupted into race riots, but tensions were high and the region would explode several times over the next three years. From the standpoint of race relations, the East Chicago–Gary corridor was considerably hotter than the Milwaukee Southside.

In 1964, Indiana had sent to Washington a fairly liberal delegation. Senator Birch Bayh had, in fact, fallen in right behind the Kennedys. He was young and good-looking, a Kennedy type from the Midwest. Some even said he had vigor. The state's other senator, Vance Hartke, was an old-line Democrat middle-of-the-roader. The state's governor, Mathew Welsh, pretty much fit the same mold. All three were LBJ operatives in early 1964, and all three adamantly opposed Wallace's run in their state. When the Civil Rights Bill came up for a vote in the House, all of Indiana's House members supported it.

Despite this liberal persona, down-state Indiana voters were some of the most conservative in the nation. Between 1896 and 1960, Indiana had gone for Democratic presidential candidates only three times.[37] Wisconsin's Joe McCarthy may have held the nation's attention during the red scare of the early 1950s, but it was men from Indiana who were often behind him, particularly Republican congressman William Jenner and the state's Republican senator in those years, Homer Capehart. Anti-communism had gripped the state in the early 1950s, just as old-line midwestern isolationism had defined the state's attitude toward the nation's foreign affairs before Pearl Harbor. Much of this conservatism had its roots in states' rights—a phrase usually identified with the South and not batted around often in Indiana. But the people of the Hoosier state had, through their history, opposed the encroachment of the federal government on their affairs, and the southern part of the state had maintained cultural ties to the Upper South. In addition, the Klan had always been strong in Indiana. In fact, in the 1960s there were, by some accounts, more Klan members in Indiana than in any state outside the Deep South, and there is some evidence that Wallace mistakenly believed that Indiana was the birthplace of the modern Klan. The John Birch Society was also strong in Indiana, particularly at the local political level. Robert Welch had begun organizing the society in Indianapolis, and large Birch Society billboards, with "Impeach Earl Warren" on one side and "Get the U.S. out of the U.N." on the other, dotted the state's highways well into the 1970s. Indiana had also made itself an example of southern-style states' rights by refusing large amounts of federal funds in the 1950s under the assumption that the money would be tied to federal control of various aspects of the state's business. In doing so Indiana had, as many Hoosiers saw it, succeeded in avoiding a pact with the devils in Washington. In addition, large numbers of southerners had migrated to Indiana during and after the war in search of high-paying factory jobs in the state's industries, which had grown rapidly as the Chicago–Detroit–Cleveland industrial complex expanded out into what became medium-sized industrial towns in northern Indiana, Ohio, and Illinois. Dallas Sells, the Indiana state president of the AFL-CIO, said that Wallace made a smart decision to run in Indiana. It is, he said, "the only [southern] state north of the Mason-Dixon Line."[38]

Mathew Welsh, the state's Democratic governor, had observed the Wisconsin debacle and had come to realize that Wallace would be a formidable candidate in Indiana. If Wallace ran unopposed, of course, he would take the state's fifty-one delegates. So Welsh decided to enter the primary as a favorite son committed to President Johnson.[39] Having learned from Wisconsin, Welsh also wisely shied away from predicting how many votes Wallace would take, although the state Democratic committee chairman, Manfred Core, gave Wallace exactly what he wanted by predicting that the Alabama governor would get only "a minimum" of votes. Of course, anything above that "minimum" would be a Wallace victory, and Wallace predicted "I'll win this race in Indiana by getting any sizable vote at all." The Alabama governor tried several times to lure the Indiana governor into a debate, but Welsh always refused, claiming, "you can't escape the stench when you fight a skunk."[40]

Wallace's big showing in Wisconsin seemed to awaken the White House. Johnson wanted desperately to remain above the fray and stay out of the primary campaigns, so he quietly poured money and administrative assistance into Welsh's campaign in Indiana. Later in April he had his photograph taken with Welsh, and then he sent Ted Kennedy to Indiana to campaign. Finally, two weeks before the election, Johnson himself, against his own better judgment, showed up campaigning in Indiana. The trip was billed as a presidential examination of economically depressed areas of the Midwest, and Johnson avoided being a partisan politician as much as possible while at the same time trying to show the party flag for Welsh.[41]

Just as Johnson saw something that needed attention in Wallace's candidacy, so Barry Goldwater was awakened. And for Goldwater, Wallace's successes seemed to speak directly to him. "There is something to this term backlash," Goldwater said in a news conference. "The people of the North and West, while they are eager for the Negro to have all his rights [they] don't want their [own] property rights tampered with. The people feel they should have the right to say who lives near them."[42] Goldwater must have been asking himself if there was a relationship between the backlash and his own conservatism. And, of course, could he harness this backlash into his conservative coalition—without incurring the racist baggage that obviously went along with it?

If Welsh wanted to hold Wallace to a percentage lower than he achieved in Wisconsin, he succeeded. Collecting just over 170,000 votes, Wallace racked up just 30 percent of the vote against Welsh's 368,400 votes and 64 percent.[43] Both men, of course, declared victory. Wallace still had no delegates, but he did have a message and he did have momentum. He began eying other primaries, particularly Ohio, a state that contained many of the same ethnic and economic demographics as Wisconsin and Indiana. His workers, however, failed to fulfill the requirements to get on the primary ballot before the deadline. Then someone mentioned to Wallace that qualifying for the Maryland primary was a simple process, that many of the regions in and around Baltimore had the same characteristics as South Milwaukee and East Chicago–Gary and were on the verge of severe racial tensions. Lastly, Maryland had just passed a law forbidding race discrimination in all public places. Again, it sounded like Wallace country.

The routine was familiar. Democratic senator Daniel Brewster of Maryland would run in the primary carrying the banner of the Johnson administration. In most such situations it would be the state's governor who would run as a favorite son, but Maryland's governor, J. Millard Tawes, had just pushed an unpopular tax hike through his state legislature, and he was not as popular as Brewster with labor and blacks, groups that were at the foundation of the Democratic party's power in Maryland. But Brewster, unlike Welsh in Indiana, stumbled into several public statements about Wallace's candidacy that only made it easier for the Alabama governor to claim victory no matter how the election went. He called Wallace's campaign a "joke," and insisted that after the election the Alabama governor would be little more than a forgotten extremist. Then, on the *Today* show, Brewster promised he would carry Maryland "by an overwhelming majority." Tawes chimed in, insisting that Wallace "won't get a vote of any significance," and that Brewster

George Wallace's run in the Democratic primaries in Wisconsin, Maryland, and Indiana showed that there were many northern white conservatives who shared the values of southern whites. (*Alabama Department of Archives and History*)

would "slaughter" the Alabama governor.[44] About all Wallace had to do to claim victory was show up.

The climax of Wallace's Maryland campaign was a fiery speech he gave to two thousand supporters in strife-torn Cambridge, a small conservative town on the eastern shore of Chesapeake Bay. Cambridge was segregated, but its black population had protested for years, and then in the summer of 1963 riots broke out in the town. Since then, for nearly a year, Cambridge had been under a proclamation of martial law. To add to the mix, a public accommodations law was being debated among the town's leaders. It was into this charged atmosphere that George Wallace took his campaign for the presidency in the summer of 1964. Wallace's speech to the wholly white audience in Cambridge lasted fifty-five minutes and was interrupted by applause at least thirty-five times. But as Wallace spoke, a crowd of black protesters began making their way from the Negro Elks Hall toward Wallace's campaign event in the white section of town. Wallace completed his speech before there was any confrontation and was whisked away, back to Baltimore and safety. But in the streets of Cambridge that night, and for several nights after, 400 National Guardsman, 50 state patrolman, and a local police force clashed with rioters.[45]

Wallace's campaign had brought age-old conflicts to the surface, and this awakened Maryland voters. The state's 1964 primary drew the largest primary turnout in Maryland's history. And for Wallace, it was his biggest victory. Brewster received almost 266,000 votes and 53 percent of the total. Wallace could have declared victory with 150,000 votes; he received over 214,000 and nearly 43 percent of the vote, while carrying fifteen of the state's twenty-three counties. Non-black ethnic neighborhoods in Baltimore that had gone overwhelmingly for Kennedy in 1960 fell in behind the white voters in South Milwaukee and East Chicago–Gary, pulling the lever for Wallace in big numbers. In the evening hours of election day, Wallace allowed himself to get caught up in the excitement of the moment and actually declared victory. However, when the final votes from Baltimore County were counted (where the black vote was heavier than at any other time in Maryland's history) Wallace was counted out. As always, though, it was expectations that won the day, and Wallace, for the third time in just seven weeks, exceeded all expectations. On the day after the election the *Baltimore Sun*, in its report of the election statistics, seemed to dwell on one point more than any other: Wallace had won a clear majority of white votes. Whatever advantage that victory gave to Wallace was spoiled when reporters overheard him comment, "If it hadn't been for the nigger bloc vote, we'd have won it all."[46]

* * *

The *Saturday Evening Post* called the 1964 California primary "the most dramatic presidential primary in recent history." It was dramatic to be sure, but not decisive. Goldwater had a substantial delegate lead. If he did not already have enough delegates to defeat Rockefeller at the convention, he was very close. His delegate count was probably even strong enough to defeat an Eisenhower-mounted stop-Goldwater movement. The same *Saturday Evening Post* article added, "About a month ago many called California the Last Chance for Goldwater. They did some math and now see it as the Last Chance to Stop Goldwater."[47] It was not even that. But Goldwater had not yet proven himself a vote-getter. He had lost in New Hampshire and again in Oregon; now he set out to win in California at all costs. For Rockefeller, a victory in California was the only chance to show that he was a stronger candidate than Goldwater, and possibly become the leader of a movement that would stop Goldwater at the convention and nominate Rockefeller as the leader of the GOP moderate majority.

Thus the California Republican primary became a fairly bitter contest. The campaign offices of both candidates received bomb threats throughout the campaign. Rockefeller supporters were often threatened with physical violence and forced to use body guards and private police. Goldwater reported telephone threats on his life. Rockefeller headquarters in Los Angeles received repeated telephone threats, bomb threats, and constant calls in which the caller would yell "nigger-lover," and then hang up. Each side sent pickets and hecklers to the other candidate's rallies and speeches. Rockefeller supporters would heckle Goldwater and often carry huge signs calling Goldwater a fascist and a racist. Goldwater supporters, in turn, handed out pamphlets describing Rockefeller as a socialist and a Kremlin dupe. The Goldwater campaign even targeted Rockefeller's personal life with literature that asked, "Do you want a leader or a lover in the White House?"[48] In early May, the Republicans in the California legislature drafted an appeal for peace, claiming that the campaign had "crossed the narrow line between healthy controversy and destructive charges."[49] Possibly because of all the mudslinging, a Harris poll showed that a solid 50 percent of California's Republicans did not like either candidate. Thirty-six percent said they objected to Rockefeller's private life, and 40 percent saw Goldwater as an extremist.[50]

The process of getting on the California ballot revealed a great deal about the progress and direction of the campaign. Thirteen thousand signatures were required to get on the ballot, and the first candidate to meet that re-

Rockefeller's last stand in 1964 was the California primary. Goldwater, however, controlled the populace south around Los Angeles and took the primary. *(Rockefeller Archive Center)*

quirement was awarded the top spot on the ballot. Lodge's people simply could not muster the volunteers and campaign workers to meet the deadline, and that left him off the ballot and out of the campaign. Rockefeller had to pay his petitioners to get enough bodies to collect the signatures needed to meet the deadline. Over a three-week period, his petitioners collected 22,000 signatures, 22 percent of which were invalid. That nevertheless got his name on the ballot. Goldwater's volunteers (none were paid) hit the ground running at dawn on the first day allowed by law and collected 36,000 signatures before noon.[51] Indeed, Goldwater's chief advantage going into the California primary may have been his army of enthusiastic supporters, campaign workers, and volunteers.

California became a two-man race that highlighted the debilitating split in the Republican party between the Goldwaterites on the right and Rockefeller and the Eastern Establishment on the left. Each candidate represented a minority wing of the party, which left the vast majority of moderate Republicans dangling in the middle without a candidate. This was not a point lost on either Rockefeller or Goldwater, and both candidates worked hard in California to moderate their stances and move to the center in hopes of picking up moderate votes. For Rockefeller this was a simple process of avoiding liberal issues such as equal housing, a particularly volatile topic in California. For Goldwater, a move to the center should have meant, at the very least, avoiding the caustic statements that had gotten him into such trouble in New Hampshire. Throughout California, Goldwater called for a "sound Social Security System," and "peace through strength," a peace achieved "without war." His campaign literature described him as "a true family man."[52] But Goldwater still could not avoid belligerent statements, statements that gave Rockefeller more ammunition to fire at Goldwater's campaign. Goldwater would win in California, but he would be bludgeoned and bloodied so badly by Rockefeller, and so open to criticism by the Democrats, that he would not be able to rise to the November campaign. Again, it was Rockefeller, more than anyone, who destroyed the Goldwater campaign in 1964.

At the same time, Goldwater could have stopped the flood of criticism by containing his comments. In early May he made what was clearly a joke, but the joke showed up first in the press and then in Rockefeller campaign literature. When asked by a reporter about the administration's objective of going to the moon within the decade, Goldwater said, "I don't want to hit the moon. I want to lob one into the men's room of the Kremlin and make sure I hit it."[53] As Goldwater later wrote, "Boy did I pay for that offhand quip!"[54] Just two weeks later, when asked how he would deal with the growing war in Vietnam,

Goldwater replied, "I'd drop a low-yield atomic bomb on Chinese supply lines in North Vietnam, or maybe shell'em with the Seventh Fleet."[55] Then on *Issues and Answers,* just nine days before the primary, ABC correspondent Howard K. Smith asked Goldwater how he might deal with the problem of Chinese supply routes into South Vietnam. His response was that "defoliation of the forest by low-yield atomic weapons could well be done."[56] Before the program aired, UPI picked up the story and beamed it around the world. Goldwater had advocated using nuclear weapons in Vietnam. One of Goldwater's advisors in California later called this a "bomb" dropped right on the senator's campaign, and Goldwater was again convinced by his people to stop speaking off-the-cuff.[57] *Newsweek* reported that Goldwater was "still his own worst enemy," and then on June 12, *Time* published a sort of retrospective on Goldwaterisms including his statement that "I think brinkmanship is a pretty good word," and "I always favored withdrawing recognition from Russia."[58] Within a week, Rockefeller's staff had mailed fliers to every registered Republican in California that said, "Who do you want in the room with the H-BOMB?" and told voters to "Reject Extremism." The flier concluded: "The very life of your Republican Party—and, perhaps, our nation's—is up to you."[59] Both statements were used over and over by Rockefeller to show that Goldwater was inexperienced, foolish, and reckless.

If Goldwater was not an extremist, then he certainly harbored extremists, and that gave the Rockefeller camp even more ammunition to destroy the Goldwater campaign. In the 1948 election, third-party candidate Henry Wallace had refused to disavow support of the Communist party. By the end of the campaign, the Democratic opposition had convinced the American people that Wallace was a communist. Much was the fate of Barry Goldwater in 1964. The John Birch Society openly supported Goldwater throughout the 1964 election. Its centers of strength were in the South, the Midwest, and the Far West, regions where Goldwater found most of his support. The JBS, which never reached strength much above about 60,000 members, was just one small part of a larger group that emerged on the radical right in the early 1960s. They were vehemently anti-communist, disgusted with what they considered the communist infiltration of the U.S. government at all levels and in both parties. They found communists in the nation's schools, the National Council of Churches, the U.S. military, most of the world governments, the United Nations, and even the Boy Scouts. The organization's founder and spirit was Robert Welch, a Connecticut candy salesman whose writings, rantings, and political activities seemed to offend nearly every important leader on the right except Goldwater. In his *The Politician* (*Time* called it his *Mein Kampf*), Welsh made the amazing statement that Dwight Eisenhower was either a "stooge" of the Soviets, or "a conscious, articulate instrument of the Soviet conspiracy. . . ."[60] Goldwater disagreed with this statement and told Welch so, but when Goldwater refused again and again to condemn Welch and the JBS, such statements hung around his neck and he found himself in the horrible position of defending the Birchers.[61] Goldwater had himself spoken out often against Eisenhower. In late 1963 he had said in regard to rumors that Milton Eisenhower, Dwight's brother, might be considering a run for the Republican nomination, "One Eisenhower in a decade is enough."[62] Interestingly, however, Welch was never quite satisfied with Goldwater's conservatism. In his *Blue Book*, Welch characterized Goldwater: "I think he is still not aware of the nature and totality of the forces at work."[63]

Others on the right had come to realize the damage that such right-wing activity and statements could do to the overall conservative movement. Bill Buckley and Bill Rusher met with a group of conservative leaders in Palm Beach, Florida, in the early 1960s and decided to reject Welch and his group primarily because they believed that the liberal press would use the John Birch Society to demonize the conservative movement. The result was several *National Review* articles written in 1961 and 1962 by Buckley and Rusher condemning the JBS.[64] At the time, Goldwater agreed. In a letter to the *National Review*, he described Welch as "far removed from reality and common sense," and *Newsweek* quoted Goldwater as asking for Welch's resignation from the JBS.[65] But Goldwater made it clear that his objections were with Welch and his statements and not with what he called "the fine, responsible people who are members" of the John Birch Society. "[A]s long as they are exercising their constitutional rights," Goldwater said in a press conference in New Hampshire, "I don't believe they are extremists."[66] The JBS, he said, had "no more political effect than the American Legion, the Episcopal Church or any other organization."[67] Then, just a month before the California primary, he told the press that he did not "consider the John Birch Society, as a group, to be extremist."[68] Goldwater never seemed to realize that as long as the JBS continued to support his candidacy and as long as he refused to disavow their support, he would have to answer for Welch's public and written statements; and the press and his opponents would, as Buckley and Rusher had feared, demonize the conservative movement and the Goldwater candidacy. There was no easier way for Nelson Rockefeller, and later Lyndon Johnson, to place the radical label on Goldwater than to point to his association with the John Birch Society. Add to that Goldwater's own statements about lobbing H-bombs into Kremlin washrooms and at Chinese coastal cities, and it was not difficult for his opposition to get away with calling him a radical. It was not long before the press agreed, and then finally much of the American public. Later in his life Goldwater defended his decision not to disavow JBS support. "I disagreed with some of their statements but refused to engage in any wholesale condemnation of them. The last thing conservatives needed," he wrote, "was to begin a factional war by reading small minorities or individuals out of our ranks."[69] It did not seem to occur to him that by accepting the JBS he, in fact, alienated large groups of moderates.

Rockefeller had ranted against the perils of the John Birch Society inside the Republican party since at least the summer of 1963, when he complained that "the Birchers and others of the radical right lunatic fringe" are "on a determined and ruthless effort to take over the [Republican] party, its platform and its candidates on their own terms."[70] In the New Hampshire primary he tried to pin the Bircher label on Goldwater, but the John Birch Society was not much of a factor in New Hampshire politics and few listened. But in California the situation was different. The JBS was strong, with some 300 local chapters in the state, and in open full force behind Goldwater. In early 1964, the JBS rose to control the California Republican Association and the organization endorsed Goldwater. The United Republicans of California and the California Young Republicans both had ties to the JBS and they both endorsed Goldwater.[71] In addition, Goldwater himself had joined several JBS-sponsored organizations with centers in California, including the American Committee for Aid to Katanga Freedom Fighters and the Committee Against Summit Entanglements.[72] And his own campaign manager, Dennis Kitchel, had only recently resigned from the John Birch Society.[73] In California, Rockefeller had very little difficulty associating Goldwater with the JBS and extremism in general.

Goldwater may also have been reluctant to condemn the JBS because of the problems Nixon had with the issue. Nixon had decided to denounce the Birchers in his 1962 run for California governor, and some analysts concluded it was this decision that led to Nixon's poorer-than-expected showing in southern California—and finally his loss to Democrat Pat Brown.[74] Goldwater knew he needed the conservative vote in southern California to carry the primary, and he may have realized that denouncing the JBS might bring him the same fate that Nixon suffered just two years earlier. In the 1964 primary Rockefeller was never able to pin the extremist label on Goldwater in southern California, despite his considerable efforts, and Goldwater took southern California and won the primary. For that reason it may have been wise for Goldwater not to denounce the JBS in California.

However, in the general election his JBS association—an association made clear to voters and the press in California by Rockefeller—would lead to further accusations of extremism by the Johnson campaign and the press, and severely damage Goldwater's national campaign. By November, the relationship between Goldwater and the Birchers allowed the Democrats (and in many cases the press) to blur the lines between Goldwater conservatism and organizations on the far right like the John Birch Society.

When Rockefeller decided to run for president in late 1963 he knew that his wife, Happy, was pregnant and that she would give birth right in the middle of the California primary. Certainly he did not foresee that such an event in his personal life would have such a disastrous effect on his political life.

Rockefeller's divorce and remarriage were simply more than some voters could handle in the mid-1960s, and the issue had hurt his campaign from its beginning. It was a constant question, a constant diversion, and a constant source of attack and criticism. In the last days of May, less than a week before the California primary election, sixteen Protestant ministers met in Los Angeles and asked Rockefeller to withdraw from the campaign because, as they said, he was unable to control his home life. On May 30, a Saturday, Happy Rockefeller gave birth to Nelson A. Rockefeller, Jr., giving the Protestant ministers a topic for their next day's sermons. Just six days before, Goldwater had trailed Rockefeller by nine points in the polls. That Sunday, Goldwater moved up nearly even with Rockefeller.[75]

Two days before the primary vote, Goldwater began a last-second television and newspaper advertising blitz that focused on the Los Angeles region, in addition to unleashing some 40,000 door-to-door campaign volunteers who blanketed the state. Four full-page ads came out in L.A. newspapers the day before the election, and Goldwater appeared on several half-hour TV commercials. Rockefeller's campaign in the last days was considerably weaker. The governor's advisors had concluded early in the campaign that media saturation would draw attention to Rockefeller's personal wealth and hurt the campaign. Consequently, they responded with smaller ads and fewer television commercials than Goldwater.[76]

Goldwater's people tried to keep their candidate out of the hands of the press in the California primary by scheduling large speaking events and fewer press conferences. These rallies were often large enough to demand press coverage, and Goldwater's advisors quickly realized that Hollywood celebrities brought more and better coverage from the press.[77] In addition, Goldwater's rugged western macho persona sold well among California vot-

Rockefeller courted black votes as much as possible. *(Rockefeller Archive Center)*

ers, so his staff arranged for their candidate to be accompanied on stage by Hollywood's leading men, the strong male figures of the period. Among those who appeared with Goldwater in California were Robert Stack, Robert Montgomery, Clint Walker, Efrem Zimbalist, Jr., Rock Hudson, John Wayne, and Ronald Reagan.[78] Wayne and Reagan worked the hardest on Goldwater's behalf, often doing televised campaign commercials and voice-overs for the senator. Wayne was still at the top of the movie game, but Reagan was at the end of a nearly thirty-year career in movies. By the mid-1960s, he was known to most Americans as the host of *General Electric Theater* or *Death Valley Days*, but to some political watchers like Lou Cannon, it was clear that Reagan was moving toward a future in politics—although few at the time took him seriously.[79] Reagan traveled throughout southern California making speeches on Goldwater's behalf. It was his first plunge into politics, and it was during Goldwater's campaign in the California primary that Reagan found his second calling.

Goldwater won the California primary by less than 60,000 votes—"by a whisker," as William Rusher called it. The final tally was 1.09 million to 1.03 million.[80] Goldwater rallied the vast majority of the votes in southern California—more specifically in the white, upper- and middle-income suburbs in Los Angeles, Orange, and San Diego counties. In that area—more or less south of Bakersfield—he won in all categories of age, sex, class, education, and income. *Newsweek* called the region "the denizens of southern California's cloud-cuckoo-land, with its fast turnover of the rootless and misplaced. This is where retired officers demand that Chief Justice Earl Warren be hanged, where city fathers rule against a public celebration of United Nations Day, and where fluoridation and mental-health clinics are attacked as tools of Communism. This is the Goldwater land primeval. . . ."[81] Rockefeller took, generally, the rest of the state, including the areas around San Francisco. In fact, he won forty-five out of fifty-eight counties statewide. But the thirteen counties that Goldwater took in the south were the state's most populous; and in Los Angeles County, where over 40 percent of California Republicans resided, he won by nearly 160,000 votes.[82]

Rockefeller may have lost his lead at the last minute because of his son's birth and with that the reemergence of perceived problems in his personal life. But he lost the election because California conservatives saw him as the personification of the welfare state—something that many upper- and middle-income whites had come to despise in the mid-1960s. Statistics do not show if race was an issue, but certainly Goldwater's opposition to the Civil Rights Act was consistent with his anti-statism and opposition to "welfarism" and the welfare state. Also, Goldwater was much better organized in California than Rockefeller. Goldwater's people had begun organizing as early as September 1963. They had fifty campaign offices in Los Angeles County alone, and at least one office in each of the other fifty-seven counties. Rockefeller's advantage had been money. He spent at least $2.4 million, probably the most spent in a state primary election up to that time.[83]

Time called the California primary "the moderates' Waterloo."[84] *Newsweek* counted 670 convention delegates now controlled by Goldwater; the Associated Press gave Goldwater 694 delegates. He needed only 655 to win the GOP nomination.[85] Goldwater, *Newsweek* reported, would take the nomination unopposed.[86] But the wounds the California campaign inflicted on the Republican party, and Goldwater, were potentially fatal. After California, the Republicans could have closed ranks, called for an end to the bickering, and emerged united (at least in appearance) for the general election. However, they refused. In fact, the wounds grew deeper and the blood continued to flow. Within days of the primary election, prominent Republicans began to complain about the outcome and about the apparent nomination of Goldwater. George Romney, possibly the fastest rising Republican star, wrote in a press release that if Goldwater's "views are in fact as clearly in variance with the nation's needs and the Republican party's needs, and if his views deviate as indicated from the heritage of our party, I will do everything within my power to keep him from becoming the party's presidential candidate."[87] Romney toyed with declaring his nomination, but he fell back on a pledge he made to the people of Michigan to complete his term as governor. Oregon governor Mark Hatfield told Romney that the opportunity had passed: "George, you're six months too late. If you can't add, I'll add it for you. Goldwater's got it."[88] Walter Lippmann, something of a spokesman for the Northeastern Establishment, was equally disgusted. He wrote in *Newsweek*, "[W]hat is afoot is not a normal attempt to nominate a Republican candidate for President. It is a determined attempt to take over an old party by men bent on ruling it in order to make it into a quite new and radically different party."[89] Even Nixon complained: "Looking to the future of the party," he said, "it would be a tragedy if Senator Goldwater's views as previously stated were not challenged—and repudiated."[90]

The problem for the moderates was no different than it had been a year before. They still had no candidate, and again they looked to Eisenhower. Finally, the general stepped out of the shadows and quietly convinced William Scranton to run. Even then he refused to endorse Scranton openly. "He never said that he would support me and come out and declare himself,"

Scranton told reporters, "but he made it very clear that he wanted me to run."[91] Ike and Scranton met on June 6. The next day, Scranton flew to Cleveland to attend the National Governor's Conference. When he arrived, he received a message to call Eisenhower. According to *Time*, Ike pulled back completely from the endorsement, insisting that he had not, as had been reported in the media, "encouraged" Scranton to run, and simply blamed the entire "misunderstanding" on "getting old." He insisted he would not get involved with a "cabal" to stop Goldwater.[92] Scranton had prepared to announce his candidacy that afternoon on *Face the Nation*, but the telephone call from Ike had apparently so upset him that he "hemmed, hawed and hedged," as *Time* put it, for half an hour. He even managed to add that he would not work to defeat Goldwater.[93] After the interview, Rockefeller was asked what he thought of a possible Scranton candidacy. "Did you see him on television?" was his response.[94] Five days later, in Baltimore, Scranton finally announced that he would make the run, about a week after Goldwater's California win and about a month before the convention. He said his campaign would offer "a real choice," not an "echo of fear and reaction."[95] With that, he headed off on a whirlwind tour of the state legislatures that had not yet declared delegation loyalty in hopes of grabbing enough delegates to go to the convention with some strength. In the process he lambasted Goldwater, picking up where Rockefeller had left off. Like Rockefeller, he saw that his only chance to beat Goldwater was to label him an extremist.

* * *

Over the next two months George Wallace continued to keep his name in the news by maintaining an active speaking schedule and by resting as much as possible on the laurels of his three primary "victories." But as the major party conventions approached, several things became clear. First, despite his shaking up the political status quo in three states, Wallace had collected no delegates. Second, the Republicans looked increasingly as though they would nominate Barry Goldwater, whose message on the constitutionality of the Civil Rights Act was identical to his own. And third, getting on the ballots in the individual states as a third-party candidate was, by the summer of 1964, nearly impossible. Consequently, Wallace found his campaign for the presidency winding down fairly quickly after the Maryland primary.

Wallace had, however, come up with a plan that might throw the election into the House of Representatives where, in the age-old southern dream, the South might wield its power as kingmaker in exchange for being allowed to continue its way of life through racial segregation. The plan had been concocted the summer before in Montgomery, just days before Wallace's inaugural speech, by a group of the nation's most notorious southern white supremacists, all with close ties to the White Citizens' Council movement. Of the seven men present at this quiet meeting, the most important were John Synon and Roy V. Harris, both publishers (Synon in Virginia and Harris in Georgia) of right-wing white supremacist diatribes. Others in attendance included Mississippi governor Ross Barnett, and Louisiana's most notorious leaders against civil rights and federal authority, Leander Perez and Willie Rainach.[96]

The plan was that in each of up to seven Deep South states a slate of electors would be pledged to pro-segregation favorite sons rather than to the major party candidates. The objective was to deprive the major-party nominees of a majority of electors. "If as many as six states," Wallace explained to a constituent, "chose to withhold their electoral votes in November, there is an excellent chance that these votes will constitute the balance of power and will place those of us in the great Southern region of this country . . . in a position to determine who will be President of the United States." His reasoning was sound, but only if Wallace could convince the other southern states to go along. "With the exception of the Roosevelt years and [1916] the withholding of 56 electoral votes would have accomplished our purpose in each and every election during the past fifty years," Wallace explained further.[97] The problem was that the other southern states refused to fall in line. Only Mississippi and Louisiana agreed to allow an undeclared slate of delegates to appear on the November ballot—but then only as a third choice to the two primary party candidates. Wallace's Alabama was the only southern state with a singular undeclared Democratic party slate on the ballot—and then the state went for Goldwater. The plan seemed to hurt Wallace in his home state. Both of Alabama's senators openly opposed the scheme, and constituents complained bitterly that Wallace had taken away their right to vote directly for the Democratic candidate, Lyndon Johnson. Wallace never again proposed the plan.[98]

By early July it was clear that Wallace's star had faded. In an almost desperate lunge, he apparently approached Goldwater (through an emissary) just before the Republican convention met in San Francisco and made himself available as Goldwater's running mate. By then, however, it was fairly clear that Goldwater would do well in the South on his own, and he had already been marked a racist by civil rights groups for voting against passage of the Civil Rights Act. The last thing Goldwater needed was George Wallace attached to his ticket.[99]

The governor's withdrawal from the campaign was hardly news by July 19 when he used an appearance on *Face the Nation* to call it quits.[100] A month before, in Baton Rouge, he told a crowd of supporters what he had learned from the campaign: "I come here tonight," he began, "to tell you that there are Southerners all over this nation! From the rock-ribbed patriotism of old New England, to the sturdy natives of the great Mid-West, to the descendants of the Far West flaming spirit of pioneer freedom. . . . [I]f nothing more, my campaigns in the North have convinced me that there are Southerners in every state of the Union. . . . Being a Southerner is no longer geographic. It's a philosophy and an attitude."[101]

Immediately, there was a shift (most apparent in the South) from Wallace to Goldwater. "Democrats for Goldwater" was formed in Mississippi the next day. Marvin Griffin, Georgia's ex-governor who had been instrumental in organizing Wallace support in Georgia, immediately announced for Goldwater. So did Louisiana governor John McKithen. The Alabama GOP chairman said, "Obviously we are thrilled that Governor Wallace is withdrawing. He . . . has practically the same views on everything that our presidential candidate has." Eugene Patterson, writing for the *Atlanta Constitution*, said, "Governor George Wallace's withdrawal from the presidential race will be a major gain for Sen. Goldwater in the South." And a Gallup poll estimated that Wallace's withdrawal from the campaign would aid Goldwater's numbers by as much as twelve percentage points.[102]

Daniel Brewster, Lyndon Johnson's stand-in in the Maryland primary, said during the campaign that Wallace was "sort of like a skyrocket. He's going up with a burst of speed and a lot of noise and light, and he's going to fall back down and be forgotten."[103] Wallace's campaign was very much a flash in 1964, but like many aspects of the 1964 election, George Wallace was at the very beginnings of his impact on American politics. Later in his life he made a simple observation that goes a long way toward explaining his impact: "[Ronald] Reagan ran on everything I ran on. He even used some of the phrases I used."[104] Reagan and his supporters might be more willing to trace Reagan's political philosophy back to Goldwater than to Wallace, but in 1964 the messages from the right were all similar. Wallace may have had a hidden agenda that revolved around race and the perceived need for the South to continue its segregationist ways, but he spoke about the problems of big government and a growing federal authority at the expense of the states that might mean a federal intrusion in local businesses and schools. He focused on the growing fears that surrounded court-ordered busing and the perceived breakdown in law and order in the nation's cities. While he was running his primary campaigns in the spring of 1964, the Supreme Court handed down several decisions that outlawed school prayer in the nation's public schools. Wallace quickly picked up on the matter and added it to his list of issues, and soon school prayer was added to the growing list of conservative issues that Goldwater began discussing in his campaign speeches.[105]

George Wallace found the backlash. He identified it and located it outside the South. It was primarily a backlash against the civil rights movement and the Civil Rights Act then before Congress, but it was also a backlash against American liberalism and the problems that conservative Americans believed liberalism had caused, including everything from social permissiveness and lawlessness in the streets to the abuses of big government. Goldwater, of course, was on much the same wavelength. Just after the Wisconsin primary, *Newsweek* seemed to see something in the future of 1964 politics: Wallace "demonstrated that there is a counter-revolutionary minority in the North. . . . [C]ould that minority be converted into a majority by a man free of Wallace's red-neck-rousing reputation?"[106]

It is too simple to say that Wallace found the backlash and handed it over to Goldwater. Both men were tapping into it at about the same time, making many of the same points, and discovering the support that would eventually become the conservative movement that would reach its apex in the 1980s. It is clear, however, that when Wallace left the field, his support—those most hostile to civil rights—went directly into the Goldwater camp. That support was, of course, more than just the South and roughly 30 percent of the electorate in Wisconsin, Indiana, and Maryland. Wallace had become a national figure with a message designed for a national audience.

In November, the backlash turned out to be more anticipation than reality. At least statistically, it had little impact on the election. But clearly it existed as a powerful force both in the South and the North, a force that Richard Nixon and later Ronald Reagan would attract and court. Wallace's candidacy in 1964 made that apparent.

* * *

It was in the midst of the primary season that the Civil Rights Act jumped to center stage and was finally voted on in Congress. The progress and final outcome of that bill had a major impact on the election for both the Republicans and the Democrats.

In the 1960 election, 85 percent of the nation's African Americans had voted for John Kennedy. In the summer of 1963, 89 percent said they would do the same in the 1964 election.[107] When Lyndon Johnson ascended to the presidency in November, those numbers may have changed somewhat, but clearly Barry Goldwater found no political strength in supporting civil rights issues. At the same time, the debate over the Civil Rights Act, and the urban riots that broke out in the summer of 1963 and then again in the summer of 1964, produced a significant backlash against the entire civil rights movement. Goldwater may not have been a racist, but by the spring of 1964 he had intentionally placed himself in a position to receive the support of white racists. Statements such as "I would bend every muscle to see that the South has a voice in everything that affects the life of the South" were directed at those in the South who wanted to maintain control of their states' segregated social system, but such statements were also directed at the general public, at anyone who had come to believe that the federal government might gain the power to force racial equality on all aspects of the nation's society, from education to housing.[108] To all of these conservatives there was one common denominator. The civil rights movement, they believed, was moving too fast, and the Civil Rights Act, then being debated before Congress, was the manifestation of the movement. It was also, many conservatives believed, the source of the power that Washington would ultimately wield over the nation on behalf of the nation's African-American population.

The Civil Rights Bill that was reported out of the House Judiciary Committee on January 31, 1964, was considerably stronger than the bill sent to Capitol Hill by the Kennedy administration just a year before. President Johnson approved. The new bill gave the federal government the power to intervene in cases where civil rights were violated or threatened, and it established an Equal Employment Opportunity Commission to monitor and enforce hiring practices. Much of the credit for guiding the bill through the House went to Republican minority leader Charles Halleck of Indiana, who built a successful coalition of moderate Republicans and northern liberals in support of the bill. Groups such as the liberal Americans for Democratic Action wanted an even stronger bill, but Johnson told those on the left that he wanted the bill passed "without a word or a comma changed," and the Civil Rights Act passed the House on February 10 by a vote of 290 to 130. It was sent on to the Senate just as the Republicans were finishing their fight in the New Hampshire primary.[109]

Southerners in the Senate, led by Georgia senator Richard Russell, threatened a filibuster, and for many on the left like Joseph Rauh of the ADA, it was only a matter of "whether the Senate filibuster could defeat the House-passed bill or gut it. . . ."[110] Hubert Humphrey led the Senate Democrats in favor of the bill. His strategy was to build a two-thirds majority coalition that would include Democrats outside the South and moderate-to-liberal Republicans, enough to evoke cloture and kill the filibuster. The question, of course, was how much compromising would be necessary to build that two-thirds coalition.

Humphrey had the reputation as the primary civil rights leader in the Senate. Only sixteen years earlier, at the Democratic National Convention in Philadelphia, Humphrey had called for a strong civil rights plank in the Democratic party platform at the expense, he said, of states' rights. In a rousing speech that catapulted him from mayor of Minneapolis to the Senate, he upset Democratic party politics: "To those who say that this civil rights program is an infringement of states' rights, the time has arrived in America for the Democratic party to get out of the shadow of states' rights and walk forthrightly into the sunshine of human rights."[111] That was 1948. In 1964, as Humphrey conspired to push the Civil Rights Bill past a southern filibuster, he was again forcing Democrats to chose between civil rights and states' rights, between northern black votes and the votes of southern whites. It was Humphrey, more than anyone else, who facilitated that political realignment.

One powerful aspect of a Senate filibuster threat is that the procedure bottles up all other legislation—it stops dead the progress of the administration's agenda, both foreign and domestic. For that reason, at least in part, all three post-war administrations had backed down when threatened with a Senate filibuster over the question of civil rights. Johnson, however, made it clear that he would not be intimidated by that strategy. He took that threat away almost immediately when he told the Senate leadership that he had no concern for any other bills until the Civil Rights Bill was passed and ready for his signature.[112]

In March, liberal Democrats, led by Majority Leader Mike Mansfield, succeeded in bypassing the southern-dominated Senate Judiciary Committee by having the bill placed directly on the Senate calendar. When Senator Russell objected, the Senate overruled his objection and the filibuster began. As the debate rolled into April and then May it became apparent that Humphrey was winning the battle. Polls showed increasing support for the bill, and senators reported the effects of several mail-in campaigns that favored passage. In April, *Newsweek* reported that Humphrey was only five or six votes short of the sixty-seven he needed to shut down the debate.[113]

Humphrey and others had concluded that the key to passing the bill was to get Senate Minority Leader Everett Dirksen on board. Dirksen, an Illinois Republican, had a history of voting a fairly moderate line on civil rights issues, but he continued to claim that the 1964 Civil Rights Bill was unconstitutional because he believed it impinged on the rights of the states and thus expanded federal authority beyond the boundaries of the Constitution.[114] But Dirksen had also come to realize that the coalition between Republicans and conservative Democrats that had stood against civil rights legislation and domestic liberalism since the war now threatened to mark the Republican party as the party of racism—at a time when various aspects of the civil rights movement were gaining wide support among the nation's moderates. Parts of the Civil Rights Act were unpopular with certain national groups for a number of reasons, but a majority of Americans outside the South had come to believe in the need for voting rights for African Americans, along with equal justice and equal opportunity under the law. Dirksen, as early as the summer of 1963, had realized that large numbers of congressional Republicans would join with the southern Democrats to oppose the bill. Many of these Republicans, like Dirksen himself, opposed the bill on constitutional principles, but Dirksen saw that the Democrats would use the debate to brand the Republicans as racists—right in the midst of the 1964 presidential campaign. In his notebooks, Dirksen asked the question that he believed Democrats were asking themselves as the election approached: "What can be done to smear the Republican Party?" The answer, he believed, was to force congressional Republicans to vote against the civil rights bill, and thus mark the party as the party of racism. He would not allow it to happen, he continued. "In a paraphrase of one of your leaders long ago," Dirksen wrote, "you shall not press a false crown of thorns upon us; you shall not crucify us upon a cross of color."[115] At the same time, he saw the bill as divisive within his own party, capable of splitting the GOP even further between the conservatives and moderates, between those who saw the bill as unconstitutional and those who had come to support civil rights—or at least various aspects of it. Thus his strategy was to force as much compromise as possible on the bill, while bringing an end to the debates (no matter what was gained or lost) before the Republican convention convened in mid-July.[116]

The debate opened in the Senate in early March. On March 8, Humphrey was confident enough to announce on *Meet the Press* that he believed Dirksen would support the bill.[117] In April, Dirksen offered a series of compromise amendments, but Humphrey refused to negotiate. Finally in May, Humphrey and Dirksen began talks. The pressure on Humphrey to hold the line on the bill was great, but he was willing to accept some compromises because he needed Dirksen's support to round up the votes necessary to evoke cloture. The liberal ADA urged Humphrey to resist all compromises, and Walter Reuther of the United Auto Workers wrote Humphrey that it was "both unwise and unnecessary . . . that concessions be made to Senator Dirksen in order to purchase his vote for cloture. We firmly believe," Reuther continued on behalf of the UAW, "that the compelling urgency of this great moral issue of civil rights will persuade Senator Dirksen to vote for cloture in June whether his proposed amendments are adopted or not."[118] Others like Joseph Rauh feared that concessions to Dirksen would further fuel the new black militancy that had taken root in the civil rights movement; and that would, in turn, feed the rapidly growing white backlash—all to the detriment of the Democrats in November.[119] But Humphrey came to realize that some compromise would be necessary if he was to get Dirksen on board, and he continued to believe that Dirksen held the key to ending the debates. From the standpoint of Democratic party campaign strategy, Humphrey also realized that with Dirksen's support the bill would receive a wider national acceptance, and in that way the entire episode would further isolate Barry Goldwater and the Republican right. With the GOP leadership in line behind the bill, Goldwater would be forced to carry the banner of racism— whether he wanted it or not.

The price for Dirksen's vote was minimal, nothing close to a watering down of the final bill. In the fair employment and public accommodations sections, Dirksen insisted on removing the attorney general's power to initiate court action in individual cases of discrimination. However, Dirksen agreed that the attorney general would retain the right to intervene in ongoing suits where a "pattern or practice" of discrimination was apparent. Dirksen also demanded that those discriminated against in public accommodations and employment must first seek remedy in state courts and agencies before the federal government could step in. These were hardly major demands. As Rauh later wrote, concessions had been made, "but the basic structure of the House-passed bill remained intact."[120]

On May 26, the bill, now carrying the stamp of both liberal Democrats and moderate Republicans, was introduced into the Senate. After some last-minute wrangling, the cloture vote was taken on Wednesday June 10, and, for the first time in the nation's history, the Senate evoked cloture against a civil rights filibuster. Quoting Victor Hugo, Dirksen told Congress "Stronger than all the armies is an idea whose time has come." Then he added, "the time has come for equality of opportunity in sharing in government, in education, and in employment. It will not be stayed or denied. It is here."[121] Nine days later, the Senate passed the bill seventy-three to twenty-seven. Johnson signed the Civil Rights Act of 1964 on July 2, 1964.

Only Goldwater and five fellow Republicans stood with the South.[122] Goldwater also voted down the line with southerners on a series of amendments designed to weaken the bill, and then, just days after his California victory, he responded to the Senate's impending cloture vote by delivering a bitter speech on the Senate floor. He had shown the speech to Eisenhower just days before and the general tried to convince him to tone down some of the language. Dirksen even tried to talk him out of delivering the speech altogether. Goldwater, nevertheless, charged ahead. *Newsweek* called his speech eight minutes of "droning." He "surprised no one," the article continued, "by announcing how he would vote. But he astonished everyone by the depth and harshness of his position." He called the Civil Rights Bill "the hallmark of the police state and a landmark in the destruction of a free society." The Senate, he said, was "once considered the greatest deliberative body on earth," but is now guilty of "political demagoguery" and "sledgehammer politics"; then he stormed out of the chamber. Dirksen, speaking later, pointed to Goldwater's empty seat and said, "Utter all the extreme opinions that you will, it will not be denied."[123]

Goldwater's speech had, however, fooled few. He may have believed it, but as the election approached it became obvious that his states' rights statements were directed at the South and the votes of white southerners. "Goldwater's vote against the civil rights bill," wrote *Newsweek*, "was eminently consistent with his strategy of concentrating on the South—and benefiting from the 'white backlash' elsewhere in the U.S."[124] The words may have been "states' rights," but to anyone who wanted to listen carefully, they were the words of a candidate who was willing to allow southerners the freedom to maintain their segregated social system.

Goldwater's reaction to the Civil Rights Act did what Humphrey had hoped. It further isolated Goldwater, while adding to his reputation as an extremist—a reputation that had, by the summer of 1964, come to dominate his campaign. He would win the South in November, but by then the white South had become the white racist South to many northern moderates. As Goldwater headed toward the Republican National Convention in San Francisco, he was already destroyed by the moderate wing of his own party—along with his own misstatements, misdeeds, and poorly perceived and initiated planning. Following the vote on the Civil Rights Bill, he suffered another drop in the polls. A Gallup poll in July showed that Republicans had turned against their leading candidate. An incredible 60 percent (to 34 percent) of Republicans polled said they would rather have Scranton as their candidate.[125] Nevertheless, by the summer of 1964 it was clear that Goldwater would receive his party's nomination. But he was both crippled and vulnerable. He would never be able to rise to the fight.

7

Guillotine: The Jacobins
Remove the Ancien Régime

The Republican National Convention, held in San Francisco's Cow Palace, promised to be a wild affair. The Democrats, most believed, would do little more than crown their king. The Republicans, however, were sure to stage a good fight. Most believed that the Goldwaterites on the right were sure to be challenged by a powerful stop-Goldwater faction from among the moderates. The press, some 5,400 reporters and behind-the-scene-workers, came prepared, as Theodore White wrote, "to report Armageddon."[1]

The press planned to cover the convention in a big way—bigger than ever before. Four years earlier, the 1960 campaign had drawn a far larger audience than any of the three networks had predicted, and that was their cue to take future conventions into America's living rooms. For the most of four days during the third week in July there was nothing else to watch on American television. At the same time, news reporting had reached something of a crescendo by 1964. No longer a fifteen-minute televised radio report, network television news had become an evening event and the newsmen themselves had reached the level of national celebrities. With that came intense competition between the three networks. ABC, NBC, and CBS ran major advertising campaigns on their own network stations and in the print media, each promising better coverage than the others. CBS initiated something of a coup at the 1964 Republican convention with its Minicam Mark II, developed just for the event. This monstrous, though portable, camera allowed cameramen, for the first time, to roam the convention floor without trailing cumbersome wire cables. They did, however, have to carry a large (and heavy) backpack apparatus with a long whip-wire antenna attached. One requirement for the job was a strong back. ABC News unveiled its own surprise when it announced that Eisenhower, the general himself, would do political commentary from the ABC booth during the convention.[2]

The Republicans' choice of San Francisco was a good one for Goldwater and his supporters. Goldwater's influence in the party had caused a power shift from the northeastern moderates to the western conservatives, and in 1964 San Francisco was the only major western city capable of hosting a party the size of the Republican National Convention. California was also a hotbed of Goldwater conservatism, and although most of that support had come from the southern part of the state, the short drive from the south to the Bay Area promised that the Cow Palace galleries would be filled with rabid Goldwater supporters.

The Bay Area also had its well-established and well-heeled Republican genteel side, that region of the city surrounding Nob Hill. The center of that culture (both socially and geographically) was the Pacific Union Club, which welcomed only those with the right money and the right politics. Once, when Harry Truman was staying at the nearby Fairmont Hotel, the Pacific Union Club closed its curtains lest its members accidentally lay eyes on the unworthy Truman as he took his daily walks in the neighborhood.[3] The Fairmont, owned by San Francisco real estate mogul and longtime Adlai Stevenson supporter Benjamin Swig, was a notorious haunt for Democrats as they passed through San Francisco. So, the Republicans in 1964 (not wanting to sleep where Democrats had slept) stayed at the nearby Mark Hopkins and the St. Francis hotels. They drew the press, the pickets, the presupposed intrigue.[4]

Despite all the anticipation, press coverage, and advanced technical innovations, the 1964 Republican National Convention was generally dull—at least as far as the question of who would snag the nomination. There was something of an expectation in the press (and most likely, the nation) that somehow the moderates in the party would rally at the last minute by combining their forces and steal the nomination away from Goldwater and conservatives. Such a political coup, however, was never in the cards. Goldwater arrived with more than enough delegates to win the nomination. Although they were a minority within the party, the conservatives made up at least a two-thirds majority of the delegates in San Francisco, along with dominance in the galleries. In addition, the well-oiled conservative machine had gained control of the party apparatus along with nearly every aspect of the convention agenda. Goldwater's nomination was never remotely threatened. The Republican convention, as it turned out, was as much a coronation as the Democratic convention six weeks later.

The only real surprise of the Republican convention was that it served to further divide the party rather than—what most party conventions do—bring the rebellious wings back into the fold and unite the whole. Groups representing and leading both wings of the party arrived in San Francisco in the first week of July hating each other for past indiscretions and statements. They left a week later with their hatred ratcheted up a few notches and the moderates prepared to vote for Johnson or sit out the election. It was one of the most contentious political conventions of the century. It was also a lesson for Republicans on the need for party unity—or at least the need to project an image of party unity.

If there was ever any hope for a moderate surge, that hope enveloped William Scranton. He had entered the race just five weeks before the convention, mostly in response to Goldwater's vote on the Civil Rights Act—and with Eisenhower's urging, but without the general's endorsement. He seemed to feel a need to take up the moderate cause because no one else would. "I felt very strongly," he said on *Meet the Press*, "that it was necessary that someone take up the cudgel, and so I did it."[5] Rockefeller lined up behind him, even to the point of encouraging the other moderates to join in, and handing over his campaign staff and his list of financial donors. Lodge, who had finally returned from Saigon, also supported Scranton. Tom Dewey endorsed him; and Milton Eisenhower, the general's brother, announced his support.[6] But despite the impressive line-up of moderates, Scranton simply had no chance of collecting enough delegates to win the nomination. There was, however, a remote possibility of winning the nomination beyond the basic strategy of accumulating pre-convention delegates. One such possibility was that Goldwater might stumble (as he often threatened to do) by saying something or doing something that would render him unelectable; or Ike might decide to step out of the shadows of statesmanship and into the sunshine of politics again and endorse Scranton. Under those circumstances the party moderates might rally; the favorite sons might throw their support. With these possibilities in mind, Scranton's convention strategy was to keep Goldwater from going over the top on the first ballot. Then, Scranton and his people hoped, with the delegates free to vote as they wished, the moderates would abandon Goldwater, and Scranton would win the nomination on the second ballot.[7] This was barely a hope worth hoping. The press, however, looking for any possible drama to rationalize their extensive coverage of the events, played the scenario for all it was worth. To Americans watching their TV screens, Scranton had a chance.

Eisenhower was the key. If he would step forward in the name of "Modern

Republicanism" and endorse Scranton, the winds might change in San Francisco. It had always been a common assumption among many political observers that Eisenhower had never really wanted to be president, that he had threatened to run in 1948 and then finally ran in 1952 for no other reason than to keep Robert Taft out of the White House and the far right out of power. And now, in 1964, with Goldwater on the verge of the nomination, the moderates hoped, even expected, that he would enter the mix, rally moderate support, and endorse Scranton. There was great speculation in the press when the general arrived in San Francisco on Friday before the convention opened on Monday. However, on each day of the convention he was asked to give his preferences, and each time he refused to endorse anyone or even so much as give Scranton and the moderates encouragement.[8] When the convention ended, he finally admitted to the press that Goldwater's nomination was a disappointment.[9]

In the five weeks before the convention, Scranton had mounted a fairly aggressive campaign. He attacked Goldwater, making the point over and over that his nomination would not only mean defeat for the Republicans in November, but ruin for the party. In late June he told an audience in Topeka that a Goldwater candidacy would allow the Democrats to "accuse us . . . of an irresponsible defense policy that would turn over the decision to use nuclear weapons to field commanders. Suppose," he added, "they can accuse us of trying to destroy the Social Security system? Suppose they show that when the chips are down, Republicans won't stand for equal rights for all Americans?"[10] Then just four days later he said, "I reject the echo we have thus far been handed, the echo of fear and of reaction, the echo from the never-never land that put our Nation on the road backward to a lesser place in the world of freemen."[11] As the convention approached, Scranton's attacks on Goldwater became even harsher, with the result that his campaign continued to drive a wedge deeper and deeper between the two wings of the party. In late June, before the Florida delegation, he compared Goldwater to "the gunslinging marshall of the frontier town." He added that Goldwater "reduces the complexities of foreign policy to simple emotional terms that have wide appeal. . . ."[12] And in the days just before the convention Scranton said that Republicans should "avoid at all costs falling into the trap of clasping to our bosom those who use the phrase 'states' rights' only as a cloak to deny Negroes . . . their human and civil rights." Then he accused Goldwater of hoping to gain votes in the South as a result of the "racial unrest in the nation."[13] Finally, at the San Francisco airport he told reporters that he had come to the city to keep the GOP from becoming "another name for some ultra-rightest society."[14] Every such comment divided the party's conservatives and moderates even further.

Scranton's five-week campaign rallied the moderates, giving the Pennsylvania governor a 62 to 38 percent lead over Goldwater in the days just before the convention.[15] But it was all too little too late, as Scranton was continually reminded. On a campaign stop in Illinois, Governor Nelson Howarth asked Scranton: "Why didn't you come in April, when the prevailing wind was out of the East, instead of July when a hot wind is blowing from the Southwest?"[16] Scranton simply did not have the delegate support. About all he succeeded in doing was further alienating the conservatives and splitting the party even worse. Every bit of that, of course, played directly into the hands of the Democrats, who were more than willing to feed on the quarreling Republicans.

The first thing that hit the candidates and delegates when they arrived in San Francisco was an interview Goldwater had given to the German magazine *Der Spiegel* just a week before. Quotes from the article had appeared in the *New York Times* on July 11, the Saturday before the convention opened on Monday. Goldwater, Clif White recalled, "suffered from one of his now infrequent lapses of shooting from the hip."[17] Asked if he would consider Scranton as a running mate, Goldwater told *Der Spiegel* that he had "completely ruled that out. At one time," he continued, "there was a strong possibility for it. But when he has turned to attacking personally a man that I always thought he considered a friend—well, the old *Et Tu, Brutus*."[18] Nevertheless, for the remainder of the week the national press continued to speculate that Goldwater would choose Scranton as his running mate in an attempt to shore up the party's differences and leave San Francisco united—at least to some degree.

Goldwater also told *Der Spiegel* that he did not believe he could defeat Johnson. "If you asked that question as of now—no. I don't think any Republican can as of now. . . ." It was, of course, an accurate analysis of the campaign at that point, and he added that he expected the situation to change before November. "But come Election Day, there's going to be another horse race, I believe."[19] Nevertheless the statement was fodder for the moderate opposition. Scranton, Rockefeller, and any number of other observers and players had been arguing since the California primary that Goldwater could not beat Johnson. Now Goldwater, it seemed, agreed. Scranton weighed in just a few days before the convention began: "How could the delegates nominate someone who says he can't win?"[20] Goldwater also said in the *Der Spiegel* article that he believed NATO commanders should be given the authority to use nuclear weapons without consulting the president. Then he added that defoliation in Vietnam using low-yield nuclear bombs might be a good idea. Scranton responded by telling the press that Goldwater has decided "to defoliate the Republican Party."[21]

The *Der Spiegel* article seemed to damage Goldwater further when CBS correspondent Daniel Schorr, reporting from Germany on July 11, insisted there was a relationship between Goldwater and what he called "right-wing elements" in Germany. Goldwater had mentioned in the *Der Spiegel* interview that he planned to visit a friend in Germany after the convention, and Schorr seemed to reason that the friend was somehow Nazi-connected. Schorr wrote that the Germans were "fascinated by the forthcoming Goldwater visit to Bavaria and, of all places Berchtesgaden, the former Hitler lair."[22] There was no basis for the statements, but the message was clear: Goldwater, the grandson of a Jew, had ties to German Nazis and admired Hitler. Scranton's people distributed copies of Schorr's broadcast among the convention delegates. The entire incident infuriated Goldwater and the conservatives.

Thus the blood was very bad when these two men arrived at the Mark Hopkins Hotel on July 9. Scranton's advisors and aides moved to the twelfth floor; Goldwater's crew occupied the two floors just above that. Scranton stayed in the Royal Suite on the sixteenth floor, and Goldwater was in the Presidential Suite one floor up. Each warring side employed guards to keep the other side off their floors. Each side spied on the other throughout the convention, and Goldwater's people later bragged that they had successfully jammed their enemy's walkie-talkies.[23]

Everyone seemed poised for the first shots to be fired at the meeting of the party Platform Committee at the St. Francis Hotel on Thursday and Friday before the convention officially began on Monday. It was, wrote Theodore White, "the first skirmishing ground where the opposing armies might clash."[24] But, as with most of the week, nothing of much significance happened. Goldwater controlled the one hundred or so delegates on the Platform Committee who sat quietly while Rockefeller, then Scranton, then Romney spoke, all three asking for moderation on civil rights and the repudiation of extremism. Rockefeller told the committee that the GOP would lose in November if it sought to serve only "the narrow interests of a minority within a minority." And Lodge added, "we can never countenance such things as a trigger-happy foreign policy which would negate everything we stand for and destroy everything we hope for—including life itself." Romney insisted that the party "unequivocally repudiate extremism of the right and the left and reject their efforts to infiltrate or attach themselves to our party or its candidates." These three attacks from the moderates seemed to signal that there would be no unity in San Francisco. The conservative-dominated Platform Committee responded with little more than cold stares. The words of Rockefeller, Lodge, and Romney, as Theodore White colorfully recorded, fell on the ears of the committee "with the near soundless thud of a cracked egg dropping in sawdust." Then on Friday, White continued, when Goldwater addressed the same group, they "roared with excitement and delight."[25]

Goldwater came to the platform committee meeting in a conciliatory mood. He told the committee that he would endorse any document they produced. Then, in a question-and-answer session following his address, he clearly hoped to soften his stance on civil rights by promising to uphold the Civil Rights Act if he became president: "[T]he legislative branch has spoken for the majority of the . . . American people," he said, "and while I didn't agree and I represented the minority, I stand with the majority." He explained his stance by comparing the situation to Harry Truman's veto of the Taft–Hartley Act in 1947. Truman, he said, went on to invoke the law six times through the remainder of his presidency.[26] While trying to soften his image in one area, however, he hardened it in another by reiterating his insistence that the Supreme Allied Commander in Europe should have the authority to use nuclear weapons without consulting the president.[27]

The Platform Committee produced a platform over the weekend. It was heavily Goldwater influenced, with plenty of anti-communism, states' rights advocacy, and requisite political platitudes. The platform of four years earlier, influenced of course by Eisenhower, Nixon, and the Republican moderates, had called for a commitment to social welfare programs, federal aid to education, and negotiations with the Soviets. All of that was eliminated here. It did call for "vigorous enforcement" of existing civil rights statutes, and the "full implementation and faithful execution" of the Civil Rights Act of 1964, possibly in response to Goldwater's promise the Friday before, but it specifically opposed what was identified as "inverse discrimination." On foreign policy issues, the platform pledged that Republicans in office would achieve military supremacy, seek the "eventual liberation" of communist nations, and promote a Cuban government in exile.[28] On Monday, Eisenhower announced that he approved of the platform. That seemed to be an official stamp of approval, and the press speculated that it was the first step toward a reconciliation between the two warring party wings. Rockefeller, however, complained bitterly that the platform did not disavow extremism and that it lacked support for civil rights.[29]

On Sunday about 40,000 African Americans marched in San Francisco in opposition to the Republican party and to Goldwater's votes against the Civil Rights Act. The most active organizer of the march was Congress of Racial Equality (CORE); but the most important spokesman was Jackie Robinson. Robinson was a life-long Republican who had supported Eisenhower through the fifties and was now a supporter of Rockefeller. He could not, he said, see how any African American could support Goldwater. Throughout the convention, small numbers of CORE demonstrators continued to picket the Mark Hopkins Hotel and the Cow Palace. They had no impact on the proceedings, and the press (with the exception of interviews with Robinson) paid little attention to African American protest activity during the week.[30]

On Sunday evening, the Scranton camp dropped a bomb that made unity in San Francisco impossible. Most likely on Scranton's orders, a Scranton aide wrote a four-page letter to Goldwater challenging him to a debate on the floor of the convention. Then the aide (described later as overzealous, tired, and inexperienced) added to the letter a whole series of vitriolic attacks on Goldwater. Scranton was not beyond making such attacks, and most likely he approved adding some statements of criticism to the letter. It seems certain, however, that Scranton had not read the letter before it surfaced on one of the Goldwater floors in the Mark Hopkins at about 7:00 P.M. By the next morning it had stirred the mix. The letter began by accusing Goldwater of assuming that his nomination was a foregone conclusion: "With open contempt for the dignity, integrity and common sense of the convention, your managers say in effect that the delegates are little more than a flock of chickens whose necks will be wrung at will." The letter continued, "You have too often casually prescribed nuclear war as a solution to a troubled world. You have too often allowed radical extremists to use you. You have too often stood for irresponsibility in the serious question of racial holocaust. . . ." Then, it was added: "Goldwaterism has come to stand for nuclear irresponsibility. Goldwaterism has come to stand for keeping the name of Eisenhower out of our platform. Goldwaterism has come to stand for law and order in maintaining racial peace. In short," the letter concluded, "Goldwaterism has come to stand for a whole crazy-quilt collection of absurd and dangerous positions that would be soundly repudiated by the American people in November."[31] Goldwater's people responded by sending a copy of the letter to every delegate and alternate in San Francisco with a note attached from Goldwater: "I am attaching a copy of a letter I received from Governor Scranton. I consider it an insult to every Republican in San Francisco."[32]

The next morning when the press confronted Scranton with the story, he responded by saying he had not seen the letter, but that he would take "full responsibility for it."[33] Through to the end of July, he continued to insist that he had not written the letter, that he considered it too strongly worded, but that because it came from his staff he would take responsibility. In an interview with CBS News later in the week, Scranton responded to Walter Cronkite's question, "did you write the letter?" "Well, Walter," Scranton said, "this rumor has been running around, and it is true I did not. . . . But," he added, "that doesn't mean that I don't take the full responsibility for it. I most certainly do." He then told Cronkite that he had not seen the letter before it was sent out.[34]

The *New York Times* argued the next day that the letter was a plan by Scranton to ensure that he would not be drafted as Goldwater's running mate.[35] David Reinhard has written in his *Republican Right Since 1945* that the letter was an attempt by Scranton to make Goldwater so mad that he would agree to a debate.[36] M. Stanton Evans argued that Scranton wrote the letter as a way of destroying Goldwater's chances of winning in November.[37] And Theodore White wrote that Scranton used the letter to go down in flames, "to go down bloody on the floor, in defeat."[38] More likely, however, it was only as it seemed: the work of an overzealous aide. Even Goldwater did not believe that Scranton had written the letter.[39]

Goldwater's people somehow seemed to feel bested by the event and on Tuesday they released their own scathing attack on Scranton, calling him a "reluctant Republican," a "recalcitrant candidate," and accusing him of being satisfactory to the liberal Americans for Democratic Action and voting a liberal line during his two years in Congress.[40] The exchange undoubtedly pushed the wedge deeper, and it made the wounds much harder to heal.

If Scranton was still being considered as Goldwater's vice presidential candidate, that option was at once gone. A Goldwater–Scranton ticket might have pulled the party together, given it some balance that might have satisfied many of the moderates.[41] The letter also served to negate much of the moral strength of the moderate cause at the convention, and it made Scranton look like a desperate mudslinger. Most importantly, however, there were only three men who could unite the Republicans in San Francisco. Scranton was one. After the "Scranton Letter," as the press began calling it, that opportunity was gone. As Goldwater speechwriter Karl Hess later wrote, "Scranton's role as a possible bridge between disparate elements of the party sailed right out of the window. . . ."[42] Rockefeller had begun the process in the spring of attacking Goldwater, alienating the right, and driving a wedge between the two wings of the party. The deeper the wedge was driven, the more difficult it was to reconcile, compromise, and unite the party for the November elec-

Without an Eisenhower endorsement, Scranton was a relunctant candidate who was unable to mount and effective stop-Goldwater drive near the end of the '64 campaign. *(Penn State Special Collections Library, Warren Scranton papers, 1933-2005)*

tion against Johnson. The Scranton Letter, in July, finished the process. The response of Goldwater and his followers was to close ranks even further, and harden their position. The moderates would have no place at the convention, on the ticket, or in the campaign, and that assured Goldwater's defeat in November.

The convention plodded along until Tuesday, July 14, Bastille Day. The press, still anticipating a slugfest, dubbed Goldwater's people the "Cactus Jacobins," apparently ready to revolt and guillotine the key members of the party's ancien régime.[43] As the party's eastern moderates spoke to the delegates that evening, each with a minority report that encouraged moderation in some form, Goldwater's Cactus Jacobins cut them down one by one.

The first to speak was Eisenhower, the voice of "Modern Republicanism," the primary representative of the Republican Eastern Establishment in power the decade before. But Eisenhower knew better than to stick his neck out before these right-wing conservatives. So, he played to them. He attacked the press, the "sensation-seeking columnists and commentators who couldn't care less about the good of our party." The convention exploded, as Theodore White wrote, "in applause, shouts, boos, catcalls, horns, klaxons and glory."[44] The delegates (and then the gallery) turned, almost in unison, and directed their rancor toward the press tables and television booths above the convention floor. Another observer recalled that "The delegates stood on their chairs, shouting, raving, shaking their fists and cursing the reporters in the press section."[45] Eisenhower then turned his attention toward a topic that would become part of the conservative mantra for the rest of the century. "[L]et us not," he said, "be guilty of maudlin sympathy for the criminal who, roaming the streets with switchblade knives and illegal firearms seeking a helpless prey, suddenly becomes upon apprehension a poor, underprivileged person who counts upon the compassion of our society and the laxness or weaknesses of too many courts to forgive his offense."[46] They could have been words from the mouth of George Wallace. The backlash had found a political party. The convention hall exploded.

During the demonstration that followed, newsman John Chancellor was arrested (for refusing to end an interview and clear an aisle) and carried out of the convention hall in full view of television cameras. It was, undoubtedly, one of the most entertaining events of both conventions—available to all Americans live on television. Whether or not the incident was a manifestation of the delegates' belligerence toward the press was never entirely clear, but it certainly appeared that way to the nation's TV viewers. As Chancellor was being carried off in a horizontal position by two officers (and as David

The three Republican party nominees between 1952 and 1964 meet in a hallway outside the main hall at the Cow Palace in San Francisco. Eisenhower refused to endorse a moderate candidate, paving the way for Goldwater's nomination in 1964. (*Eisenhower Library*)

Brinkley laughed in the broadcast booth), he said in a shaky voice, "This is John Chancellor, somewhere in custody."[47]

Melvin Laird, the Platform Committee Chairman, followed Eisenhower. He read every boring word of the 8,500-word platform document. Next on the agenda were the minority reports to the platform, and Scranton was to address the delegates first. He apparently knew better than to stand before such a group, and he sent his aide Huge Scott to deliver the plank. It called for the repudiation of extremism and mentioned by name the John Birch Society, the communists, and the Klan.[48] Scott's words were barely noticed by the delegates, but when Rockefeller rose and bounded toward the podium to defend the plank, the crowd began to boo. According to Theodore White, who apparently anticipated what was about to happen and was sitting in the Goldwater gallery, the boos grew to a "billowing of howling," and then into an explosion, cow bells, horns, a base drum beat, and then the crowd pulled together into a chant: "WE WANT BARRY! WE WANT BARRY! WE WANT BARRY!" At the podium, before them for the first time, recorded White, "was the face of the enemy. . . . [T]his was the man who had savaged Barry from New Hampshire to California all through the spring. This was the man who called them kooks, and now, like kooks, they responded to prove his point."[49] Clif White, who was operating a fairly sophisticated communications system from a van behind the convention hall, saw immediately what damage such an incident might cause and quickly contacted delegation leaders through thirty telephones he had hooked up on the convention floor and demanded that the booing be stopped immediately. Theodore White, who had moved from the galleries to (what he called) the safety of the convention floor, noticed an immediate silence among the delegates, no doubt as a result of Clif White's orders. But the galleries did not stop. They went on, Theodore White wrote, "hating and screaming and reveling in their own frenzy."[50]

As television cameras switched back and forth between Rockefeller (at the podium and unable to speak because of the noise) and the wild antics in the galleries, it became apparent that Rockefeller was enjoying himself, in fact, wallowing in the moment. He stood there, smirking, unflinching, clearly provoking the enemy. The more the galleries raged, the cooler he got. The TV cameras flipped from the frantic galleries, to Rockefeller, and then, occasionally, to a sobbing Happy Rockefeller in the stands, and then back to the smirking Rocky at the podium. He tried to speak, but each time he was drowned out by the screams from the galleries and the incessant pounding of a bass drum. Then he said, "It is essential that this convention repudiate here and now any doctrinaire militant minority, whether Communist, Ku Klux Klan, or Bircher." The crowd drowned him out again. "This is still a free country," he said, clearly trying to make the point that he should be allowed to speak. The crowd got louder. "These things," he yelled into the microphone, "have no place in America. But I can personally testify to their existence." He continued, referring to the California primary. "And so can countless others who have also experienced anonymous midnight and early morning telephone calls, unsigned threatening letters, smear and hate literature, strong-arm and goon tactics, bomb threats and bombings, infiltration and take-over of established political organizations by Communist and Nazi methods." This brought on a thunderous roar from the Goldwater people in the galleries who, it seemed, were trying to drown out Rockefeller so that the nation would not hear his words. "Some of you don't like to hear it," he added one more shot, "but it's the truth."[51] The hate and the fury of the Goldwaterites flooded into the nation's living rooms and, as Theodore White reported, "pressed on the viewers that indelible impression of savagery which no Goldwater leader or wordsmith could later erase."[52] Television had become a powerful medium and a major factor in the nation's politics; and to many Americans, the images before them were the faces of genuine radicalism. Clif White believed that Goldwater lost "hundreds of thousands, perhaps millions" of votes as a result of that incident.[53]

The delegates then voted down Scott's plank condemning extremism with a thunderous "no."[54] Rockefeller and many of his supporters left the hall in protest. George Romney followed Rockefeller to the podium. He proposed a softer anti-extremist plank, one that did not identify offending organizations. "Unlike the Ramblers I used to sell," he said, "the Republicans must have a big wheelbase and a big body."[55] The delegates did not agree, and shouted down his plank as well. Then Jacob Javits, the moderate Republican senator from New York, was booed down. "It chilled me with the thought," he later wrote, "that I might be seeing the beginnings of an American totalitarianism."[56] A civil rights plank and a nuclear weapons control plank were both voted down by the same substantial margins.[57] "The Cow Palace was no place for Republican moderation," Time reported.[58] And Ben Bradlee, who was covering the convention for Newsweek, believed that "The liberal wing of the GOP was dying before our eyes."[59] Finally, at 12:36 Wednesday morning the platform was accepted with no significant changes. Later in the day Goldwater told the press that he thought it reflected the party's new "conservative majority."[60]

On that day, Wednesday, Goldwater was nominated on the first ballot by the substantial vote of 833 to Scranton's 214. Rockefeller got 114 votes and Romney got 41. Scranton immediately came to the podium and asked the delegates to support Goldwater. It was probably the only serious stab at unity during the entire convention, and, like Scranton's own candidacy, it was too little, too late. To most of Goldwater's people, as Clif White wrote, "The harm was already done."[61] In fact, as Scranton spoke, some of his supporters were stalking out of the hall.

That evening, Goldwater announced his choice for running mate, William Miller of New York. The choice of Miller has always been debated. He was a seven-term congressman, a northeastern Catholic, and the chairman of the Republican National Committee (RNC). Often described as dapper or cocky, he wore homburgs and used a cigarette holder. *Time* called him "an acid-tongued orator." He was a strong debater, something of a hatchet man. At first glance this seems a logical balance for Goldwater, the philosopher king leader of a movement, a southwestern Protestant. But Miller was at least as conservative as Goldwater. He was probably best known within the Republican party as a primary leader in opposition to the Eisenhower administration and Modern Republicanism. Miller was not a compromise candidate, not at all the hand of reconciliation extended to the northeastern moderate wing of the party. Goldwater may have been looking for nothing other than geographic balance, or for a running mate who could take the low road and attack the administration while he campaigned on the issues and tried to sell his conservative philosophy to the nation's voters. Whatever Goldwater had in mind in choosing Miller, it led party moderates to take the decision as just another snub, or that Goldwater had become so embittered by the moderate challenge that he was beyond compromise, beyond naming a wound-healing moderate to the ticket—that he was going to go it alone. To make the decision even more insulting, Goldwater did not even consult the party leadership before deciding. Eisenhower and Nixon, among others, felt snubbed.[62] The Miller decision further alienated moderates, whether Goldwater intended to or not.

Miller was also a bad choice because he was generally an unknown. A month after the convention, an RNC poll showed that 72 percent of the American people classified themselves as "don't know" when it came to recognizing Miller's name, and 64 percent of Republicans said the same thing.[63] Two years after the election, Miller appeared on Johnny Carson's *Tonight Show*. No one in Carson's television audience could identify the one-time vice presidential candidate.

If it was not yet apparent to party moderates where they stood among the

Goldwater speaking to the faithful at the Cow Palace in San Francisco at the Republican National Convention. *(Arizona Historical Foundation)*

The 1964 Republican ticket. *(Arizona Historical Foundation)*

new party leadership, Goldwater took care of that with his acceptance speech on Thursday evening. Here Goldwater had one last chance to bind the party together, to talk of unity, reconciliation, and the healing of old wounds. Instead he chose to give nothing to the moderates. As in the case of the Miller decision, Barry made it clear that he was going to go it alone.

The speech was written some two weeks before the convention, primarily by Karl Hess and Bill Baroody, with some help from Harry Jaffa. It was a good speech, powerful. Goldwater attacked the policies of the Johnson administration, both foreign and domestic, without any severe harshness. He talked of violence in the streets and "aimlessness among our youth." He commended the successes of the Eisenhower administration, criticized communism, and blasted Johnson for having no plans for victory in Vietnam. He talked of the need for peace rather than war, obviously to counter the charges of warmongering. The speech had almost no reference to party unity, and except for that, it would probably not have been noticed in America's political history. But near the end of the speech, Goldwater made certain that the nation would remember what he had to say that summer evening in San Francisco: "Anyone who joins us in all sincerity, we welcome. Those who do not care for our cause, we don't expect to enter our ranks, in any case. And let our Republicanism, so focused and so dedicated, not be made fuzzy and futile by unthinking and stupid labels." Then he lit up the hall: "I would remind you that extremism in the defense of liberty is no vice! And let me remind you also that moderation in the pursuit of justice is no virtue!"[64] By that statement, extremism was the victor and moderation the vanquished. The statement hung over Goldwater like a dark cloud for the remainder of the campaign, and some would say, for the rest of his life. No matter how he (or his supporters) tried to explain what he meant, it was always understood by most Americans as an acceptance of extremists within his campaign and a rejection of the moderates.

The most immediate responses came from the moderates. New York senator Kenneth Keating walked out of the convention hall in response to the statement and the next day told a reporter from *Time* that because of Goldwater's statement he might vote for Johnson.[65] Manhattan congressman John V. Lindsay said much the same thing.[66] Republican congressmen Salvio Conte of Massachusetts and James Fulton of Pennsylvania said they would not support Goldwater.[67] Rockefeller expressed "amazement and shock" at the statement, and called the speech "dangerous, irresponsible and frightening." Eisenhower responded to the speech by saying he would not campaign for Goldwater—at least until Goldwater explained his "confusing" remarks.[68] Then, on Sunday, he told an ABC News commentator that he believed "the whole American system refutes that idea and that concept."[69] Lodge told *Time* that "A group has taken over [at the San Francisco convention] that doesn't understand the modern world."[70] Jacob Javits warned of "ominous indications" in Goldwater's speech.[71] And Nixon, who in front of national cameras pointedly refused to applaud during the last portion of Goldwater's speech, recalled later that if Goldwater "ever had a chance to win the presidency he lost it that night with that speech. . . . I felt almost physically sick as I sat there."[72] In a post-convention letter, Nixon chastised Goldwater, telling him that "in using these phrases you were, in effect, approving political recklessness and unlawful activity in achieving the goals of freedom and justice."[73]

Criticism from other areas seemed unrelenting. The *Saturday Evening Post* possibly hit the hardest. "That statement deserves to be the 'Rum, Romanism and Rebellion' of this election, and Barry Goldwater deserves to be defeated for it alone, no matter how much he tries to clown it away. He knows what he meant by it. . . ."[74] *Time* called the Goldwater people "Luddites," and insisted that the conservative cause was "a matter of principle, not politics."[75] Columnist Richard Rovere wrote that the conservatives in San Francisco were "as hard as nails. The spirit of compromise and accommodation was wholly alien to them." They aimed, he added, at "a total ideological victory and the total destruction of their critics. . . . They wished to punish as well as to prevail."[76] Joseph Alsop, following the convention, called Goldwater supporters "fanatics"; and Walter Lippmann, something of an icon of the northeastern moderate wing of the Republican party, wrote that Goldwater was "gambling recklessly on racism and jingoism." An editorial in the *New York Post* complained, "the Birchers and racists have never before enjoyed so big a night under such respectable auspices." And Drew Pearson wrote "the smell of fascism has been in the air at this convention."[77]

At the White House, Lyndon Johnson watched parts of the convention with Clark Clifford, who later recalled, "I remember from a political standpoint I got a great lift" from the convention "because you could just see the Goldwater forces running roughshod over all opposition. You could sense the disenchantment of the Rockefeller group as a result of the manner in which the convention delegates treated Governor Rockefeller. . . . This was a most humiliating experience for a prominent Republican to endure at his own convention. So you could get the feeling that the Republican party was splitting badly."[78]

So it was that the 1964 Republican National Convention adjourned with the party deeply divided and in disarray. The conservative minority was in control of the party apparatus for the first time since the end of the war, and the moderate majority was rejected and purged. There seemed to be very little chance for a November victory, and in that sense Goldwater became a sacrificial lamb. He had allowed himself to be drafted, to become the leader of a cause that had no real hope for victory. The only real objectives of the conservatives were to win control of the party, to purge the moderates of their leadership positions, and possibly build for the future. Winning the November election was never a reasonable objective. Goldwater was sacrificed on the alter of conservatism.

The moderates were successfully purged from the party in 1964, but this did not lead to mass defections of northeastern moderates from the Republican to the Democratic party. Certainly, many moderate Republicans voted for Johnson in November, but they did not leave the party in any great numbers. The significance of the events is not that the conservative minority cut itself away from its moderate base; it is that the 1964 Republican convention marked a power shift within the party. It was the end of the reign of the Dewey–Rockefeller moderate northeastern wing of the party that had dominated the Republican power structure since the early 1930s under Landon, Willkie, Dewey, and Ike. And it was the beginning of the rise in the party of the conservative West, which had forged a coalition with the Midwest conservatives and now the South. The conservatives would continue to control the party throughout the remainder of the century, even finally controlling the White House during Reagan's two terms. Almost thirty years later, Goldwater saw it just that way: "We knew that the only thing we could accomplish would be moving the Republican headquarters from New York to the West Coast, and we did that. We got it away from the money."[79]

The moderates never again enjoyed party control. Rockefeller ran for president again in 1968, continued on as New York's governor into the early 1970s, and became President Gerald Ford's vice president. He continued, through the 1970s, to be the leader of the party's northeastern moderate wing, but it had diminished in power considerably and Rockefeller remained something of a pariah among his own party's leadership, now focused in the West. William Scranton never again ran for elected office. John Lindsay became a Democrat, and mayor of New York City until the early 1970s. Jacob Javits stayed in the Senate until 1981, but like Rockefeller he was never a major party operative again outside of his own region. Kenneth Keating was defeated by Robert Kennedy in the 1964 senatorial election and never again held elective office. They were the vanquished, on the backside of a political power shift inside the Republican party.

Immediately following the convention, riots broke out in the east, first in New York City and then in upstate cities and New Jersey. They fed the backlash and made it appear, if only momentarily, that Goldwater might ride the backlash to victory. On July 29, the nation's black leaders issued a "moratorium" on demonstrations until after the election. On July 27, just one week after the convention closed, *The Killers*, a made-for-TV movie, was shown on NBC. It was Ronald Reagan's last film appearance before he began making his way into politics.[80]

8

LBJ's "Bobby Problem" and the Humphrey String-along

President Johnson's biggest problem as the conventions approached in the summer of 1964 was Robert Kennedy, the "Bobby problem," as the president and his aides called it. Kennedy had made it clear, several times, that he wanted the vice presidency—or at least he wanted the courtesy of being asked. At times Bobby even seemed to be running for the position. Johnson, however, remained adamant. He would not accept Kennedy as his running mate. He would not, as he told several advisors, leave a historical legacy of a lame duck president sandwiched between the two Kennedy brothers. The problem was, of course, how to keep Kennedy off the ticket without offending the Kennedy family and their supporters, by this time a prominent leadership contingency and a powerful component inside the Democratic party. Johnson could not, Ken O'Donnell recalled later, "just dump him like anybody else can be dumped."[1] "[T]he problem remained," Clark Clifford also recalled, "how to eliminate Bobby Kennedy as a possible running mate with a minimum of public outcry?"[2]

Bobby (along with most of the Kennedy family members) believed that it was his responsibility to carry on his brother's legacy. In the several months following Dallas, Bobby was clearly undecided about how best to accomplish that purpose, but accepting the party's nomination for vice president was definitely on his short list. The Kennedy family wanted it. The press considered it something of a foregone conclusion. And, of course, Kennedy supporters in the Democratic party wanted an LBJ–RFK ticket in November, a perpetuation of the Boston–Austin axis that had been successful in 1960. There was a great deal of pressure on Bobby to accept the roll as vice presidential candidate in 1964, even to push for it if Johnson resisted.

However, from Johnson's viewpoint, and from a purely political angle,

Bobby was the wrong man. Despite Johnson's almost desperate attempts to dispel the image, he was still widely perceived among voters as a conservative southerner, the balancing act to the 1960 ticket. Johnson was able to alter that image somewhat during the summer of 1964 and as the election approached, but to a large number of Americans, while he may have been willing to carry on the Kennedy agenda, he nevertheless remained a southern conservative. If the Republicans nominated a moderate, particularly Rockefeller, Scranton, or Romney, many believed that Johnson might actually have been vulnerable from the left. Both Rockefeller and Romney had strong liberal records that were, in many areas, more liberal than Johnson's own record. This was particularly true of Rockefeller, whose strong record on civil rights together with his support from organized labor might well have pulled blacks and labor away from Johnson in November. The greatest fear of the Democratic party leadership was a Rockefeller-led ticket with Romney, Scranton, or Lodge in the number-two spot. Romney had support from big business along with a midwestern appeal; Scranton had support from northeastern businessmen; and Lodge was big in the Northeast, in addition to his extensive foreign policy experience and his great name. If the Republicans could keep its emerging right wing in line while successfully depicting Johnson as a conservative southerner with weak ties to blacks, labor, and business, a moderate Republican ticket might be formidable in November, easily capable of holding the national center and giving the Democrats a run. Both Kennedy and Johnson were, of course, acutely aware of all this, and both knew that adding the Kennedy name to the 1964 ticket would deflect this Republican strategy. But Johnson, instead of courting Kennedy, worked to scrap his own image as a southern conservative and reinvent himself as a national liberal. By mid-July, Johnson had generally succeeded in this by pushing through Congress a strong liberal agenda. As the conventions convened Johnson had, on his own, shored up his liberal voting base. For that, he no longer needed Kennedy. That same month, the Republicans rejected the Rockefeller–Romney–Scranton moderate wing of its party and nominated Goldwater, virtually abandoning the national political center. Polls then showed that Johnson no longer needed Kennedy to win.[3] He could name just about anyone. In fact, by then it was clear that Kennedy might well be a detriment to the ticket. Goldwater's candidacy would send moderate Republicans scampering for a new home in November. The only reason Johnson might not pick up huge numbers of moderate Republican votes was if he frightened them off by choosing Kennedy as his running mate. Northeastern moderates who were tied to big business, for instance, feared Kennedy. The

185

Kennedy image had become tied to a social agenda that Republican moderates could accept, even support, but it had also come to mean anti-business—and Bobby carried the anti-business image even more so than his older brother. *Time* reported that Kennedy represented government intervention, anti-trust action, grand jury investigations, "and the heavy hand of Government in the U.S. Steel confrontations of 1962."[4] In addition, Bobby Kennedy was not at all popular in the South, the only region where Johnson was expected to have trouble, and he held no real appeal in the Border States or the West. In the summer of 1964, Johnson was not prepared to concede the South, or the deep pockets of big business, to the Republicans. He also wanted his own legacy, not one tied to the Kennedy family.

In March, a few Kennedy favorites in New Hampshire announced that they were organizing a Kennedy-for-vice-president write-in campaign. Few paid attention until the state's Democratic governor, John King, jumped on the bandwagon and the movement began snowballing. There were no official Democratic candidates on the New Hampshire ballot in 1964, so both Kennedy and Johnson were write-in candidates at the voters' discretion. A Kennedy victory would have placed Johnson in a very embarrassing position. Johnson quickly jumped to the conclusion that Kennedy (and Kennedy operatives) had designed the entire write-in campaign for just that purpose. "If they want to push Bobby Kennedy down my throat for Vice President," LBJ told a Texas friend, "I'll tell them to nominate him for president and leave me out of it."[5] Kennedy worsened the situation by sending a family politico, Paul Corbin, to New Hampshire for reasons that are not entirely clear. However, if Kennedy intended to annoy Johnson, it worked. The president was furious. He saw Corbin's undisclosed activities in New Hampshire as Kennedy's first move to take the vice presidency, or even the presidency, for himself. Following a cabinet meeting in early March, Johnson growled at Kennedy to get Corbin out of New Hampshire.[6] Kennedy then, on the eve of the primary, issued a statement that the choice for vice president "should be made by the Democratic convention in August, guided by the wishes of President Johnson."[7] The final tally in New Hampshire gave Johnson a slim victory of 29,317 votes for president to Kennedy's 25,094 votes for vice president, five times as many votes as Humphrey, the second-place challenger. The difference in votes between the president and his attorney general was not much, *Time* reported, "but it drew a sigh of relief that could be heard right in the White House Oval office."[8]

As is often the case in such political situations, Kennedy's denial fanned the flames of his candidacy. A Gallup poll in mid-March noted that 37 percent of the nation's Democrats wanted Kennedy as vice president, well beyond several other aspirants.[9] Kennedy-for-vice-president movements sprang up in several states around the country, most notably in Wisconsin to coincide with the April 7 primary there, but also in New York, New Jersey, California, and elsewhere.[10] Johnson became exasperated. He later told his biographer, Doris Kearns, "Every day as soon as I opened the paper or turned on the television there was something about Bobby Kennedy; there was some person or group talking about what a great Vice President he'd make. . . . It just didn't seem fair."[11]

Johnson, however, was not yet ready to dump Kennedy. In fact, he realized that he might need him to win in November if the Republicans chose a moderate. Through the early months of 1964 Rockefeller remained the Republican party favorite, high in the polls, a strong candidate. Johnson was still laboring under the southern conservative image that would be difficult to shake before November, particularly against the likes of Rockefeller. So Johnson waited and surveyed the field of other possible running mates.

Just after the New Hampshire primary the president began tossing out names of possible running mates—names other than Kennedy—with the obvious intention of making it clear that Bobby was not the only candidate under consideration. This tried and true political strategy was also intended to placate certain groups and national regions by recognizing one of their own. At the same time, Johnson seemed especially insecure in making this decision and may possibly have suggested several names simply in hopes of receiving feedback from advisors, the press, and even the public. Most likely for all these reasons, Johnson spoke privately and publicly of at least a dozen possible running mates other than Kennedy throughout the spring and summer of 1964.

The first name to come up was Sargent Shriver. As early as two weeks following Dallas, Bill Moyers had suggested to Johnson that Shriver might be a good candidate, and then leaked the idea to the press. Shriver was a Catholic, a voting group that had been felt in the 1960 election; and he was a Kennedy—or at least he was married to one. Robert Kennedy was probably correct when he told an interviewer in May 1964 that Johnson, in considering Shriver, thought he "could get a Kennedy without having a bad Kennedy."[12] The Kennedy family, however, vetoed the idea. In addition, Shriver had no political experience, no standing with party regulars, and he was barely a blip in the national polls.[13] Johnson would have to look elsewhere. In April, he offered the job to his secretary of defense, Robert McNamara, another member of the Kennedy camp.[14] McNamara, in his

memoirs, wrote that he turned down the job partly because he lacked political experience and partly because he did not trust Johnson to keep his
word: "[K]nowing Johnson as I did," McNamara recalled, "I knew that if I
answered yes, he might later reconsider and withdraw the invitation."[15] He
was probably right. McNamara's primary attribute was that he was close to
the Kennedys, yet not so close that Johnson would appear to be using a
Kennedy to get elected. But McNamara was a Republican, and Johnson
was desperate to shore up his liberal support within the Democratic party.
Running with a Republican would do nothing to accomplish that. It also
meant that McNamara had no standing with party regulars. And, like Shriver,
McNamara had no political experience. Johnson, however, continued to
talk openly and privately about the possibility of McNamara as his running
mate as late as July.[16] Another name that Johnson floated often was that of
Minnesota senator Eugene McCarthy. Unlike Shriver and McNamara,
McCarthy was an experienced politician with a strong liberal record in the
Senate. He was also a Catholic and had appeal in the Midwest, an area
where Johnson believed he would need help in November. Possibly of no
small significance, Lady Bird Johnson apparently approved of McCarthy
as her husband's running mate.[17] Other names bandied about for apparent
political effect included Mayor Robert Wagner of New York and Governor
Pat Brown of California. To appease the South, Johnson spoke occasionally of Georgia governor Carl Sanders. To appease the Jews, he threw out
the name of Connecticut senator Abraham Ribicoff. For the Italians he spoke
of John Pastore, senator from Rhode Island. Then just before the convention, Johnson pulled Connecticut senator Thomas Dodd up from nowhere
and tried to convince the press that he was being seriously considered.[18]
The charades continued right up to the convention. "President Johnson,
selecting a running mate," commented an editor in *The Saturday Review*
on the president's apparent wavering, "is like a lady selecting a hat in
Neiman-Marcus. It must look right in Dallas and in New York."[19]

But in true Johnson form, the president was doing more posturing than
wavering, trying to satisfy certain groups, build a consensus among party
officials and his advisors and aides. For most Johnson insiders, however,
the choice was always Hubert Humphrey. Humphrey probably jumped into
the lead among the other candidates as early as April, when Johnson pulled
together a group of his top aides and advisors and asked them to vote on
their choice for the second spot. Only White House aide Walter Jenkins,
who wanted McCarthy, kept the vote from being unanimous for Humphrey.
From that point on, Johnson may have toyed with the possibility of other

candidates, throwing names here and there to keep the press and the American people guessing about his decision, but all evidence points to Humphrey as an early choice.[20]

* * *

Bobby seemed to want to take himself out of contention for the vice presidential nomination when, on June 11, he sent the president a personal message offering to replace the retiring Henry Cabot Lodge as the American ambassador to Vietnam. Why Kennedy would be interested in such a position at this point in his career is difficult to determine. Clark Clifford, who knew both Kennedy and Johnson well, chalked it up to Kennedy's continued depression and confusion following his brother's death.[21] Kennedy may also have wanted simply to get away from the hot lights of Washington where he was under constant scrutiny from the press and the American people, and under what must have been extreme pressure to carry on the Kennedy legacy. A year or so in Saigon might have eased that pressure considerably, while giving him the foreign policy experience he desperately needed if he decided to run for the presidency in the future—something every political observer assumed he would do. Johnson, however, wisely refused to take responsibility for Kennedy's safety in a war zone and rejected the appeal. He was also concerned that the press might accuse him of banishing a political rival to the other side of the planet. The president never took the request seriously.[22]

Immediately following his request to go to Saigon, Kennedy announced that he would travel to Berlin to attend the dedication of John Kennedy Platz. The president asked him to delay his plans until after the Civil Rights Act passed. The bill passed the Senate on June 18 and Kennedy left the agonies of Washington behind and headed for Germany to bask in his brother's light. By then, however, Kennedy had added Warsaw and Cracow, Poland, to his itinerary, a move that rankled Johnson because such a trip, even without official presidential approval, immediately became a state visit by a representative of the U.S. government at the highest level—a state visit to a communist country. Johnson was not prepared to accept the diplomatic ramifications of such a visit. In addition, he was concerned that a trip honoring John Kennedy's foreign policy achievements would give Bobby a great deal of positive press and raise his popularity just weeks before the convention. He may also have feared that by going to Poland, Bobby was courting the Polish-American vote. At the same time, he did not feel he could tell

Kennedy not to make the trip.[23] Despite Johnson's apprehensions and concerns, Bobby went anyway.

He was received as a celebrity, even a hero. Some reports estimated that 250,000 Germans lined the streets of Berlin to see him, and as many as 80,000 packed the square where he spoke. In Cracow and Warsaw he drew huge crowds, mostly students and other young people, to hear the brother of John Kennedy speak. "I'm not running for president," he told a large crowd of admiring Poles, "but if I were, I wish you could all come to the United States and vote." The press at home speculated that if he decided to run for president (now or later) he would wrap up the Polish-American and Eastern European vote in the midwestern urban areas.[24]

Kennedy's trip was of little consequence to Democratic party politics. But just before he left, in the first week of June, Goldwater won the Republican primary in California and sewed up his party's nomination. Ten days after the primary, on June 12, Goldwater voted against the Civil Rights Act on the Senate floor. If Johnson still harbored any thoughts of offering Kennedy the number two position on the ticket, he certainly abandoned them here. Johnson had often said, in private to his aides, that he had no desire to run with Kennedy, but if that was the price of victory in November he would accept Bobby as his running mate. Now, with Goldwater on his way to the Republican nomination (and with his own approval ratings hovering around 75 percent), Johnson simply had no use for Kennedy. He did not need the Kennedy clout in the Northeast, with liberals, with labor, or with African Americans. In fact, with Goldwater as his opponent, Johnson might easily pick up large numbers of voters among several groups that traditionally voted Republican, such as businessmen, Republican moderates, and independents—groups that were generally repelled by Kennedy. By the time Kennedy returned from Europe the political dynamic in Washington had changed considerably. Johnson had gone from a willingness to accept Kennedy if necessary to a need to dump him out of the lineup quickly but gently.

Not surprisingly, Kennedy hit on the same conclusion and began considering his future outside the Johnson administration. One evening in mid-July Bobby summoned his closest aides to his home in Washington. Those in attendance made up a laundry list of Kennedy family operatives, including Kenneth O'Donnell, Larry O'Brien, Fred Dutton, Stephen Smith, and brother Teddy, among others. Bobby announced that he would not seek the vice presidential nomination and, instead, would run for the Senate in New York. His opponent would be Republican incumbent Kenneth Keating, a man he believed he could beat. Teddy and Smith wanted Bobby to announce his intentions at once and begin campaigning. O'Donnell suggested he wait long enough for party liberals to pressure Johnson into naming Humphrey as his running mate. Kennedy agreed.[25]

In the meantime, however, Johnson prepared to ease Kennedy out—as gently as possible. On Monday, July 27, he telephoned Kennedy and arranged for a Friday afternoon meeting at the White House.[26] "He's going to tell me I'm not going to be the Vice President," Kennedy told an aide. "I wondered when he'd get around to it."[27] He was right. Johnson hoped to convince Kennedy to withdraw from the race, to make an announcement that he would not accept the party's nomination for vice president. For Johnson, however, this was clearly going to be a touchy situation. Johnson was "fearful of what Bobby's reaction would be," Larry O'Brien recalled, "and what he might undertake as a result of that meeting."[28] So Johnson called in two of his closest political advisors, Clark Clifford and James Rowe. They produced what Clifford later called a "talking paper," a carefully worded statement that the president would use to deliver the bad news to Kennedy on Friday.[29] By all accounts, the meeting was tense. Johnson, instead of paraphrasing Clifford and Rowe, took a safer route. "I literally read it to him," he later recalled.[30] Kennedy listened quietly while Johnson explained the politics of November 1964 as channeled through Clifford and Rowe. "Goldwater's strength," Johnson began, "will be in the South, the Southwest and possibly in the Middle West; also it is my belief that the Border States will be of unusual importance in this particular election. If Goldwater runs a strong race, it is entirely possible that the outcome of the election could rest in the Middle West. I believe strongly that the Democratic ticket must be constituted so as to have as much appeal as possible in the Middle West and the Border States; also it should be so constituted as to create as little an adverse reaction as possible upon the Southern States. These are the considerations that have led me to the conclusion that it would be unwise for our party in this election to select you as the vice presidential nominee." He concluded by offering Kennedy any position he wanted in the administration, and then he asked him to assist in the campaign. According to Johnson, Kennedy's only response was, "Mr. President, I could have been of help to you."[31]

Johnson's analysis of the political situation in late July 1964 was correct. Goldwater's strengths were in the South, the Border States, the Southwest, and potentially parts of the Midwest. Yet Kennedy's analysis was correct as well. His name was anathema to most conservative groups and he was extremely weak in the South, but overall Kennedy-as-vice-president would have been a popular addition to the Democratic ticket in November. None of that, however, mattered in late July. Johnson simply did not want to run with Kennedy. He knew that with Bobby on the ticket he would never be perceived as winning on his own, and that with Kennedy as his vice president his administration would never be his own. As Johnson had said, he would take Kennedy as his running mate if he needed that strategy to win in November, but Goldwater's nomination sealed Kennedy's fate. Johnson could win without him.

Johnson had intended that one result of the meeting was that Bobby would announce that he would not be a candidate. But Kennedy seemed unwilling to give Johnson that satisfaction. He said nothing. His reasoning, as it appeared in *Time* that next week, may have been simply that "After all . . . he had not announced his candidacy, so why should he withdraw?"[32] For whatever reason, Kennedy kept silent, and his silence kept the heat on Johnson. The president had to do something to remove Kennedy from the vice presidential picture. He asked Kenny O'Donnell to ask Kennedy to withdraw his name. O'Donnell refused. Finally a reluctant McGeorge Bundy, Johnson's national security advisor and a holdover from the Kennedy administration, agreed to deliver the message. Bobby still did not respond, insisting to Bundy that such a message must come from the president himself.[33]

Johnson was again stuck in a corner. Again he called on Clifford for advice. Clifford came up with the thinly veiled ruse of eliminating all cabinet members from consideration, and thereby eliminating Bobby. "It might not fool anyone," Clifford later recalled. It was simply "a ploy that made life easier for everyone involved."[34] Clifford was correct. No one was fooled. "All of Washington guffawed at the clumsiness and transparency of the ploy," wrote political pundits Rowland Evans and Robert Novak. "[E]very politician and newsman in the country knew Johnson was aiming only at Bobby Kennedy. . . ."[35] It may have been clumsy, but it worked. The next day, Johnson told an aide, "Now that damn albatross is off my neck."[36] Bobby's response to an aide was that he was at once "miffed, disappointed and relieved."[37] He also felt a bit guilty. In telegrams to the other cabinet members who were purged along with him, he joked, "Sorry I took so many of you nice fellows over the side with me."[38]

With that, Johnson's "Bobby problem" should have ended. But that evening, Johnson, who was apparently unable to restrain his gloating personality, called three prominent journalists to the Oval Office and told them of his summit with Kennedy. "When I got him in the Oval Office," Johnson crowed, "and told him it would be 'inadvisable' for him to be on the ticket as the Vice President-nominee, his face changed and he started to swallow. He looked sick. His adam's apple bounded up and down like a yo-yo." Within days the story had run through Washington like small-town gossip. Kennedy stormed Johnson's office and confronted the president about the story. Johnson denied it. Kennedy apparently replied by calling him a liar.[39] In the meantime, Kennedy's people released their own account of the events of late July, which in turn made Johnson furious.[40] Johnson may have succeeded in removing the albatross from around his neck, but the means to that end only worsened an already bad relationship with Kennedy.

In what may have been an attempt to mend those fences, Johnson immediately issued a press release explaining further why Kennedy would be an unacceptable vice presidential candidate: "[T]he Goldwater nomination and the resulting situation in the South and in the border states makes it clear that the President cannot chose the Attorney General for this job." Johnson went on to invite Kennedy to be his campaign chairman: "[T]he President would like to draft him for this service." The press release concluded with a job offer: "It goes without saying that after the campaign the President would hope very much that the Attorney General would accept a most senior post in the new Administration."[41] There is no record that Kennedy responded to these offers. Most likely, Johnson knew he would not.

* * *

Just a week after Johnson eliminated his cabinet from vice presidential contention and three weeks before the Democratic convention convened in Atlantic City, the nation's eyes turned to the festering problem in Vietnam. The incidents that occurred there on August 1 and 4 could not have been more advantageous for Johnson-the-candidate. In just three months before the general election he was able to show the American people that he could stand strong against what was perceived as North Vietnamese communist aggressions, while at the same time show that he was prudent, that he would not drag the nation precipitously into a land war in Asia. With Goldwater being portrayed in the press as a warmonger, an itchy finger on the buttons of war, the incidents of early August 1964 were a stroke of luck for the president's campaign.

On August 1 the U.S. destroyer *Maddox* was engaged in electronic espionage in the Tonkin Gulf off the coast of North Vietnam when it was attacked by North Vietnamese torpedo boats. On the night of August 4, the *Maddox* returned to the area, this time accompanied by the destroyer *Turner Joy*. Both boats claimed to have come under attack that night, but recent accounts have raised doubts as to whether that attack actually occurred.[42] Johnson responded by ordering a retaliatory attack on North Vietnamese torpedo boat bases and nearby oil tanks. He then spoke to the American people in a televised address explaining his actions, actions that were firm but limited. "Repeated acts of violence against the armed forces of the United States must be met not only with alert defense, but with positive reply. That action is now in execution against gunboats and certain support facilities in North Vietnam which have been used in these hostile operations. . . . The determination of all to carry out our full commitment to the people and to the government of South Vietnam will be redoubled by this outrage. Yet our response, for the present, will be limited and fitting." He would, he said, seek a congressional resolution allowing him to "take all necessary measures to repel any armed attacks against the forces of the United States."[43] On August 5, the Senate voted ninety-eight to two in favor of the Tonkin Gulf Resolution. The House vote the same day was unanimous. Johnson's approval ratings jumped. A Gallup poll reported that a convincing 85 percent of those polled endorsed the action.[44] A combination of luck and political shrewdness had allowed Johnson to forge a bipartisan consensus on a primary foreign policy issue just three months before the election.

Johnson had been running as the peace candidate against Goldwater's hawkishness. But that strategy had left him open to charges of weakness and timidity in the face of North Vietnamese aggressions. The Tonkin Gulf Incident and the following resolution allowed Johnson to show his strength— that he could be aggressive if necessary. It also allowed him to show restraint by not escalating the situation further. The spin from the administration was that the actions taken were in the name of peace, not war. A White House press release said "firmness in the right is indispensable today for peace. That firmness will always be measured. Its mission is peace."[45]

The Tonkin Gulf Incident was so advantageous to Johnson's campaign that there has been speculation that it was planned in advance, that the incident was an intentional provocation designed to give Johnson the opportunity to quiet Goldwater's accusations of timidity in Vietnam. George Ball, assistant secretary of state at the time and the primary dissenting voice in the administration's involvement in Vietnam, has been the primary source for this argument. Ball told an interviewer in the late 1970s that "the sending of a destroyer [to] the Tonkin Gulf was primarily for provocation. . . . [T]here was a feeling that if the destroyer got into some trouble, that [it] would provide the provocation we needed."[46] However, most other administration operatives have argued against Ball's analysis. William Bundy, Johnson's assistant secretary for East Asian affairs, told the same interviewers that there was no such plan. "[A]s a matter of fact, it didn't fit our plans at all. . . . [N]obody would have planned this, nobody did plan it. It was totally unexpected and the [administration's] response was entirely on the level."[47] Robert McNamara has argued in his memoirs that such "charges are unfounded."[48] And Bill Moyers, one of Johnson's closest aides, told an interviewer in 1993 that Johnson "did not want to set up a situation [in August 1964] that would force him to take irretrievable steps. It was not a set up."[49] Nevertheless, the situation fell directly into Johnson's hands at a most opportune moment.

Just after the Tonkin Gulf Incident Johnson contacted Goldwater by telephone and briefed him on the situation. Goldwater immediately endorsed Johnson's actions. "You've got a good statement, Mr. President," Goldwater replied. "I don't know what else you can do. I'm sure you'll find everybody behind you. Like always," he added, "Americans will stick together." Johnson responded that he hoped Goldwater would agree that bombing was necessary. "You go right ahead," Goldwater responded, despite the fact that he had absolutely no independent knowledge of the situation that had led to the reprisals.[50] Armed with the approval of the opposition leadership, Johnson announced Goldwater's me-too opinion during his August 4 speech on national television: "[J]ust a few minutes ago I was able to reach Senator Goldwater, and I am glad to say that he has expressed his support of the statement."[51] That same day, Goldwater announced his support for Johnson's actions: "We cannot allow the American flag to be shot at anywhere on earth if we are to retain our respect and prestige."[52] The next day he added, "I am sure that every American will subscribe to the actions outlined in the President's statement. I believe it is the only thing he can do under the circumstances."[53] Goldwater's responses were undoubtedly influenced by Republican support in Congress for Johnson's actions and by popular support in the polls. He may also have honored the long-time axiom that in times of international crisis the nation's political parties must present a unified front, that a divided nation implies a weak nation and strengthens America's enemies. Nevertheless, when Goldwater agreed with Johnson over the Tonkin Gulf Incident and Resolution, he removed Vietnam from the campaign. Johnson had been vulnerable on Vietnam. Many in Johnson's own party had been warning him at least since spring that the situation there was deteriorating rapidly and that if it was not resolved quickly, the Republicans would hit hard on the issue in November.[54] But when Goldwater agreed with Johnson on the Tonkin Gulf Incident, their differences on the issue dissolved and

Vietnam was taken out of the political mix. Johnson became the undeniable leader of American foreign policy with almost no dissent from the Republicans, and the entire situation made him a much more appealing candidate.[55]

Goldwater managed to make the situation even worse. At a press conference in Hershey, Pennsylvania, where the Republican bigwigs were trying to heal their wounds after the convention, Goldwater criticized the president for authorizing the use of nuclear weapons in the Vietnam. Secretary of Defense McNamara, who had spent much of the year slapping down similar Goldwater accusations, issued a statement that Johnson had given no such order, and that "Senator Goldwater's interpretation is both unjustified and irresponsible."[56] As the general election approached, Goldwater abandoned his silence on Vietnam and occasionally brought up the issue, but his attacks were never specific and had no impact on events. In October, attempting to bring Eisenhower into the campaign, Goldwater announced that if he were elected he would send Eisenhower to Saigon.[57] But that notion apparently had little appeal to voters—or to Ike.

By the summer of 1964, Johnson and his advisors had come to the conclusion that after the election they would have to escalate the war in Vietnam, or lose it.[58] But the Tonkin Gulf Incident had placed Johnson in such an irresistibly favorable political position that throughout the remainder of the campaign he made promise after promise that the United States would not become further involved in Vietnam. "We don't want our American boys to do the fighting for Asian boys," he told a crowd in Oklahoma.[59] Then in Kentucky two weeks later he said, if "you seek no larger war, and you don't want to pull out and run home, the only thing you can do is what we are doing."[60] In New Hampshire, he added, "We are not going north and we are not going south."[61] Johnson buried Goldwater on the Vietnam issue. He had proven himself willing to stand up to the communists when necessary, yet he had come away from the events as the peace candidate in the face of both communist aggression and Goldwater's warmongering. After the election, however, Johnson paid an extreme price in national credibility when the bombing of North Vietnam began. In many ways, then, Johnson's handling of the Vietnam issue in the campaign of 1964 contributed greatly to his landslide, but also paved the way to his downfall in March 1968.

* * *

With Kennedy out of the vice presidential picture, the flood gates for the job immediately flew open—or at least it appeared that way when several potential candidates made it clear that they wanted the job. "To put it coldly and bluntly," Clark Clifford recalled, "it was well known that President Johnson had had a serious coronary attack years before, so I think the job was eagerly sought."[62] But for those who really had their fingers on the pulse of Democratic party politics in 1964 there was really only one possibility. When Adlai Stevenson first heard Johnson's announcement eliminating his cabinet from consideration, he reportedly jumped up and said, "This means Humphrey."[63] Larry O'Brien agreed: "I had little or no question about who was going to be on that ticket for a long period of time. . . . When the President asked me what my view was, I told him without equivocation, Hubert Humphrey."[64] Jack Valenti later recalled, "I don't believe any of the staff ever really thought [LBJ] was going to chose anybody but Humphrey."[65] As soon as Kennedy was eliminated, *Time* declared that Humphrey was "the odds-on bet."[66]

By the first days of August it was fairly clear that Johnson would win the election no matter whom he chose as his running mate, but it was Humphrey who had the attributes Johnson needed. Humphrey was a northerner and a liberal, which countered Johnson's southern conservative image. He had what *Newsweek* called "an intellectual bent," which most likely was intended to mean that he did not measure up to the intellectual image of the Kennedys, but that intellectuals generally liked him. That countered Johnson's corn pone image. In addition, Humphrey was popular in the Midwest, a region that Johnson believed would be an election-night battleground, and in the industrial Northeast where he thought he had little appeal.[67] He was popular with African Americans because of his work on the Civil Rights Act; and organized labor liked him—more even than they liked Kennedy. Even the Kennedy family supported Humphrey now that Bobby was headed for the New York Senate race.[68] Humphrey also had name recognition and press exposure. Since his defeat in 1960 when the Kennedy family's deep pockets bowled over his candidacy in the Democratic primaries, Humphrey had been majority whip in the Senate, in effect the number two position behind Majority Leader Mike Mansfield. Mansfield was a fairly colorless figure, which allowed Humphrey's star to remain one of the brightest inside the Democratic party structure. Humphrey's only real detriment was that he was weak in the South. But by August 1964 the South had become, for Johnson, a political write-off. Goldwater's states' rights stand and his vote against the Civil Rights Act would mean overwhelming support there. Humphrey was the right man.

Humphrey had been pining openly for the job ever since Dallas. Even at John Kennedy's funeral he discussed the possibility with several party leaders. He was never shy about wanting the job or even letting people know he wanted it; in fact, he was always blunt. He told his closest advisors in a meeting in early 1964, "I want to become president, and the only way I can is to become vice president." His advisors, however, often counseled him against it. Marvin Rosenberg recalled, "We said he'd lose his freedom. We said Johnson would cut his balls off."[69]

As early as January, Johnson began sending signals to Humphrey (through Humphrey's 1960 campaign manager James Rowe) that once Kennedy was removed he would be the choice. Humphrey responded by campaigning for the job through February, first in New York, then in New Jersey, California, Oregon, and Florida.[70] By mid-summer, Humphrey was clearly the front-runner. On July 30, just after Kennedy was dumped out of contention with the rest of the president's cabinet, Humphrey let the president know he wanted the job. "I want to come right to the point," he told Johnson during a telephone conversation that left nothing to the president's imagination. "If your judgment leads you to select me, I can assure you—unqualifiedly, personally, and with all the sincerity in my heart—complete loyalty. . . . And that goes for everything," he added. "All the way. The way you want it. Right to the end of the line."[71] Clearly, Humphrey wanted the job.

But it was not in Johnson's character to make it that easy. He would not give Humphrey the satisfaction of an early announcement. In fact, he seemed more interested in watching poor Hubert jump through hoops to curry his favor. In addition, he certainly was not going to give the press anything to print except to speculate on his decision-making processes. In short, Johnson, facing a fairly boring convention, turned the vice presidential decision into political drama. Whom would he chose? "I was involved in that," Valenti recalled later in an interview. "I think the President wanted to play a little game with the press at that time, and he always likes surprises, never liked to tip his hand, and I think this was part of the theatrics."[72]

As the convention approached in the last days of August, Johnson seemed to do all he could to focus the attention away from Humphrey. On August 22, two days before the convention opened in Atlantic City, the president sent aides to sound out Senate majority leader Mike Mansfield. The press immediately began speculating that Johnson disliked Mansfield and planned to kick him upstairs to the vice presidency, leaving the Senate's majority leadership to Humphrey, a stronger presidential ally. All this made a big splash in the press, something Johnson clearly wanted. And it worried Humphrey. "Nobody has to woo me," he told reporters. "I'm old reliable, available Hubert."[73] Mansfield, however, wanted nothing to do with the offer and pronounced it "nonsense."[74] The Mansfield speculation ended quickly.

Minnesota senator Eugene McCarthy was another name being bandied about by the press as Johnson's potential running mate, and McCarthy had made it clear he wanted the job by setting up campaign headquarters in Atlantic City and engaging in the process of rounding up support for his candidacy. Humphrey had done the same. In fact, the press had noted that Humphrey had ordered 8,000 "LBJ–HHH" lapel pins.[75] Reporters considered it presumptuous. On Monday the 24th, the day the convention opened, Johnson had sent word to Humphrey that he would be the choice. Humphrey was, however, sworn to secrecy. The president was so adamant he even insisted Humphrey could not even tell his wife, Muriel.[76]

Johnson, however, wanted to milk as much publicity from the press as possible. He announced that he would fly both Humphrey and McCarthy to Washington on Wednesday for a discussion, presumably to aid in his decision. McCarthy, however, had either gotten the word that Humphrey was the choice, or had simply become tired of being used as a presidential pawn. On Monday evening he told his aides he was withdrawing his name from consideration. Johnson, trying to keep up the charade, asked McCarthy to keep his decision quiet, but McCarthy made it public the next morning.[77] Not surprisingly, McCarthy felt used by the president, and the two men never again got along well. Within four years they would become bitter political enemies.

McCarthy's abrupt withdrawal meant Johnson needed a stand-in. He found one in Connecticut senator Thomas Dodd. Johnson, in his memoirs, insisted that Dodd had support from various factions in the party because he was a conservative northeasterner, attributes that would be valuable against Goldwater.[78] But most likely, Johnson dragged Dodd into the mix at the last minute because he was a willing participant. As Valenti recalled, "Dodd was up for reelection in Connecticut. The exposure wouldn't hurt him. . . ."[79] Probably to Johnson's delight (and certainly to Humphrey's frustration), Dodd's name swirled in the press for the next two days.

On Wednesday, August 26, two days into the convention program, Johnson summoned both Humphrey and Dodd to the White House. He would keep the dance going for just a few more hours. The nation waited. Both Humphrey and Dodd knew the decision had been made. Dodd was certainly under no illusion that he would be chosen; he was there only to enhance his position with Connecticut voters. Humphrey, of course, had known for two days that he had been tapped, but he never quite trusted Johnson. "I had begun to feel

199

as secure as one could in dealing with Lyndon Johnson," Humphrey later wrote.[80] So, to keep Johnson happy and the press in suspense, the ruse continued. Johnson even made both men wait in a car in front of the White House. Humphrey slept. Johnson called in Dodd first, and told him what everyone already knew, that Humphrey was the choice. "Dodd thought it was wonderful," Valenti recalled.[81] Then Johnson spoke with Humphrey, grilling him on loyalty to the office. "He knew Hubert wanted it so bad," O'Donnell recalled, "and, God, he gave him an awful tough time."[82] Humphrey responded with all the correct answers. Then Johnson called Humphrey's wife. "We're going to nominate your boy tonight," he bellowed over the telephone to Muriel.[83] The two then strolled outside to announce the decision to waiting reporters. As Humphrey later wrote, "Johnson had drained every bit of juice out of the nomination." From there they flew to the coronation in Atlantic City. For Goldwater, Johnson's decision to name Humphrey destroyed "the myth that the Johnson Administration is conservative." I want to "thank Lyndon," he added, "for drawing the differences between us so sharply."[84] It was probably just what Johnson wanted to hear.

9

The King Is Dead.
Long Live the King

The Democratic National Convention was to be the coronation of Lyndon Johnson, the beginning of his administration. "He orchestrated the whole [thing]," Ken O'Donnell recalled, "and that was his total consumption."[1] The last four Democratic party conventions had revealed gaping party splits and resulted in agonizing floor fights. Johnson would make certain that at his convention there would be no floor fights, no walkouts, no last-minute scrambling for votes, nothing that would embarrass him or put a damper on the happy event. And just to make sure there were no surprises, that the convention ran smoothly, that no rival or group of rivals was planning a coup or even a disruption, he dispatched a platoon of undercover FBI agents to infiltrate organizations and groups with questionable motives and to tap the phones of potential spoilers. All indicators pointed up. Polls said that the president could not lose in November, and that he was even cutting deeply into the Republican electorate.[2] Then, to add to the excitement, August 27, the last day of the convention, was his birthday. He would be fifty-six.

The convention did not go quite as smoothly as the president wanted. The first problem was that Atlantic City was simply not up to hosting a national convention. "Of Atlantic City it may be written," Theodore White complained, "better it shouldn't have happened."[3] White arrived in Atlantic City to research the sequel to his Pulitzer Prize–winning *The Making of the President—1960*, and he hated the place. To him, the town was little more than "a strung-out Angkor Wat entwined in salt-water taffy . . . [a city] trying to recapture some of its lost glamour." The event, he added, "was to be a marker on the road back." White went on to recount the experiences of various newsmen who had to endure everything from broken showers to door knobs coming off in their hands.[4] Why Atlantic City? It had, of course, been John

Kennedy's choice. He had wanted a West Coast convention, possibly San Francisco, but when the dates did not fit well with the schedule at the Cow Palace, the president began looking at Chicago. The city fathers there, however, could not raise the necessary $625,000 to host the event. The decision then slipped to Miami, the next choice on the short list. Miami wanted the convention and the city raised the money necessary to host it, but Kennedy aides feared protests by Cuban nationals who had flocked to the city. With few places to turn, New Jersey Democrats promised to raise the money and the decision went to Atlantic City by default. It was not the best choice. Atlantic City in 1964 had passed its heyday.[5]

Larry O'Brien described the convention as "about as placid as a Democratic convention could be." However, the appearance of the Mississippi Freedom Democratic Party (MFDP), a racially integrated organization claiming the seats of the all-white Mississippi delegation, not only brought some drama to the convention, it became a watershed event in the civil rights movement. It was also a major point of demarcation on the long journey that had resulted in the continuing weakness of southern influence in the Democratic party.

As early as 1948 it had become clear that the party was simply not big enough for both southern white segregationists and African Americans. By that year party operatives came to realize that blacks in northern cities could help deliver the states with the biggest electoral votes. From a purely political standpoint, supporting civil rights could win elections. Much of the white South, of course, became alienated from the party as the Democratic leadership continued to support civil rights initiatives, but to most party insiders and strategists it was a good trade. By 1964, however, civil rights had become more than just a political issue. It was a moral one as well. The vast majority of white Americans outside the South supported civil rights, or at least some degree or aspect of it. Certainly, many whites in the mid-1960s continued to fear black encroachment into white neighborhoods, schools, and the workplace, and that was evident in the growing backlash. However, the prevailing wisdom was that, if nothing else, African Americans should not be denied their rights as American citizens, and that if racial equality did not come immediately, it would come soon. This growing attitude among the general population, and within the Democratic party specifically, served to weaken the position of the white South even further. By 1964 the Democrats had fully embraced civil rights as both a moral issue and a political expedient. White southerners were given the choice of either joining in the moral and political victories, or going elsewhere. In 1964, some would stay in the party. Others would cross over to the Republicans to join many of their brethren who had begun the journey in 1948.

While America watched as its northern cities erupted in racial violence in the summer of 1964, African Americans in the South were quietly changing the nature of southern society, and along with it the nature of southern politics. As early as 1961, workers from the Student Non-violent Coordinating Committee (SNCC) began infiltrating Mississippi, the undeniable cornerstone of southern white racism. Many of SNCC's activities revolved around direct action, such as marching, protesting, boycotting, conducting sit-ins and bus rides, all of which had caused a huge outbreak of violence throughout Mississippi, something the Kennedy administration believed it could not tolerate. At the administration's behest, SNCC, in 1963, began focusing its energies on registering black voters in the state. This fit with the Kennedy administration's philosophy at the time (and also the conventional wisdom of many white liberals) that if African Americans in the South could get the power of the vote, the nation's racial ills would be greatly diminished. The administration believed as well that if SNCC's energies could be directed toward voter registration and away from direct action that the tense situation in Mississippi might be relaxed a bit and the violence would subside. The Kennedys also hoped that voting African Americans would vote Democratic and that this would, over time, finally moderate the segregationist agenda of southerners in Congress.

By the fall of 1963, SNCC's voter registration drive had evolved into a strategy that included a mock election. Blacks in Mississippi were kept from the polls primarily through intimidation, but also through a series of locally sponsored hurdles that made registering and voting extremely difficult. In turn, Mississippi whites often argued that African Americans had no real desire to vote. SNCC leaders intended to show through a mock election that black Mississippians would, in fact, vote in great numbers if given the opportunity. Thus in October 1963 some 70,000 black voters in Mississippi swarmed to extra-legal makeshift polls and cast their votes for the NAACP nominee for governor, Aaron Henry. It was an amazingly successful protest against the denial of equal political rights.[6]

To many in SNCC the election's success had come as a result of the organizational skills of several dozen white Yale and Stanford students who took two weeks off from classes to aid in the effort. Hoping to build on that success, the SNCC leadership decided to invite hundreds of white college students to Mississippi during the next summer, the summer of 1964, to aid the organization in a statewide voting rights drive. It would be called the Freedom Summer, and the plan was that the white students would bring press coverage, federal protection, and badly needed funding from white northerners.

Instead, the Freedom Summer of 1964 brought on further violence. In June, three volunteers were murdered near Meridian, Mississippi. During the remainder of the summer, white terrorists killed three more workers, assaulted another eighty, shot thirty, and burned some thirty-five churches in the state. These events, along with what many black leaders considered the unwillingness of the federal government to aid the civil rights movement and protect its workers and volunteers in the South, pushed many African Americans away from the nonviolent philosophy of Martin Luther King, Jr., and toward the radical self-help philosophy of Black Nationalism. As the civil rights movement grew ever more radical through 1964, the white backlash against it grew nearly directly in response.[7]

A second outgrowth of the fall 1963 mock elections was the establishment of the MFDP in April of 1964. The actions of the MFDP would give the Democratic convention in Atlantic City its only real drama. In addition, the manner in which the party would treat the MFDP in Atlantic City (together with the events surrounding the Mississippi Freedom Summer) served to further radicalize the civil rights movement by turning many of its leaders against the forces of moderation, compromise, and gradualism.

By most accounts, the radicalism that would emerge inside SNCC and other parts of the civil rights movement had its beginnings sometime in late 1963 or early 1964 when several SNCC leaders voiced their opinions that the Mississippi Freedom Summer should be a black-dominated movement, and that it should not depend on assistance from northern white students. Others inside the movement, however—most notably Fannie Lou Hamer— argued that SNCC (along with the entire movement itself) should be an integrated movement. "If we're trying to break down this barrier of segregation," Hamer said in a now-famous statement at a SNCC staff meeting in Greenville, Mississippi, "we can't segregate ourselves."[8] For the remainder of the summer Hamer's opinion would prevail.

As early as mid-January 1964 there was talk within SNCC of forming an organization to challenge the all-white Mississippi delegation to the Democratic national convention.[9] From those early conversations the MFDP was formed on April 26, 1964, in Jackson, by some three hundred disfranchised Mississippians. Among the early leaders were Robert Moses and Hamer.[10] It was Hamer, however, who would catch the national eye in Atlantic City. She was the wife of a desperately poor sharecropper who supplemented the family's income by working as a timekeeper on a cotton plantation in Ruralville, Mississippi. At the other end of the MFDP spectrum was Moses, a SNCC leader of such renown that Allen Matusow has called him "legendary."[11] A product of Harlem, Harvard educated, and a seasoned civil rights worker, Moses had suffered his share of beatings at the hands of Mississippi police and civilians. Although quiet and reserved (he found little dignity in speaking from the pulpit) he was possibly the most respected leader of SNCC and an important figure in the MFDP. He was also, by the spring of 1964, beginning to doubt the effectiveness of an integrated civil rights movement.

The MFDP believed it was strong enough—as exhibited by the numbers racked up in the mock election in October—to challenge the all-white Mississippi Democratic party. At first, the MFDP tried to participate in the state party conventions. When that access was denied, the MFDP decided it would challenge the all-white Democratic party regulars. The plan was simple. Following the rules of the Democratic National Committee, the MFDP would, through a series of statewide caucuses, choose an integrated delegation of forty-four delegates and twenty-two alternates to the party's convention in Atlantic City. They would then challenge the credentials of the state's party regulars on the grounds that the regulars had been elected through a process that excluded Mississippi's African Americans. In addition, most of the all-white delegates had refused to declare their loyalty for Johnson. The MFDP intended to arrive in Atlantic City as the only delegation from Mississippi prepared to support the president. That alone, they believed, would win them recognition.[12]

Johnson quickly saw the problems of such a convention challenge. Even though Goldwater would certainly carry several southern states in November as a result of his vote against the Civil Rights Act, the president hoped to hold on to southern moderates and carry as much of the South as possible in the general election. However, even the slightest support for the MFDP at the Democratic convention would certainly spin the Mississippi delegation into revolt, and Johnson feared that if Mississippi walked out of the convention much of the rest of the South might follow. Such an en masse southern revolt in Atlantic City might then push the entire South into the Republican column in the general election. At the same time, the president wanted African American support in November, and to deny the MFDP at the convention would certainly alienate black voters nationwide. Then there was the perpetual burden carried by every Democratic president since Roosevelt. Johnson needed support from powerful southern congressmen and senators to pass his legislative agenda. He could not afford to alienate the Harry Byrds, the Richard Russells, and the Allen Ellenders of Capitol Hill if he wanted to pass his Great Society programs—and be remembered as a great president. Although Johnson hoped he would not have to confront this problem—and he sincerely supported civil rights for African Americans—he knew exactly where he stood here: he needed to mollify the rebellious southerners. He would sacrifice moral principle for party unity—and worry about the consequences later.

The fear of an MFDP disruption at the convention was only part of Johnson's problems with the black community in the summer of 1964. Johnson worried that riots in Philadelphia, Chicago, New York, and in several New Jersey cities might do more harm to his nomination in Atlantic City than any contested delegation from Mississippi. The great fear among the Democrats, of course, was that these riots would produce a backlash of alarm in the white community that would push moderate Democrats to vote for Goldwater. Democratic party strategists who feared this most had begun calling the riots "Goldwater rallies," because as they raged Goldwater support appeared to rise. In addition, if riots erupted during the convention and into the campaign, Johnson and his strategists feared that the president might be (at best) embarrassed by the events, or (at worst) hurt badly in the election.

Consequently, in late July, a month before the convention, Johnson moved to quiet the riots and demonstrations by convincing the most conservative members of the civil rights movement to call for a moratorium on all direct action until after the election. This was not the first time the president had made such an attempt to moderate civil rights activism. Following the Civil Rights Act signing ceremony early in July, Johnson had tried to convince King, Roy Wilkins of the NAACP, the Urban League's Whitney Young, and a few other black leaders that the new law no longer made protests and demonstrations necessary, that further direct action might, in fact, prove to be detrimental to the civil rights movement. The black leaders mostly deflected Johnson's requests as pre-election political maneuvering designed to keep the movement quiet in order to pacify the South.[13] But on July 18 the situation changed. A major riot broke out in New York when an off-duty city policeman shot a fifteen-year-old African-American boy in Harlem. That was followed by what appeared to be a spread of the violence to Brooklyn and then the next week to Rochester.[14] By the end of the month, Johnson was genuinely afraid that the riots would spread further. And, of course, there were always political consequences and concerns. On July 16 Goldwater had received the Republican nomination and it was clear that the backlash, apparently growing with the severity of the riots, was solidifying behind his candidacy. In addition, three civil rights workers in Mississippi were missing. The nation was tense.

On July 24, just days after Goldwater's nomination and at Goldwater's request, the senator and the president met at the White House for a discussion of the riots. Johnson's advisors expected Goldwater to use the event to his own political advantage, and the president's guard was up in anticipation of a possible blind-side attack. But Goldwater, much to the president's surprise, was more interested in the nation's welfare than in the politics of the situation. The cities, he told Johnson, "are just tinder boxes, and I'll be darned if I will have my grandchildren accuse their grandfather of setting fire to it [sic]."[15] He then agreed to exclude the civil rights issue from his campaign. The two men issued a statement: "The President met with Senator Goldwater and reviewed the steps he has taken to avoid the incitement of racial statements. Senator Goldwater expressed his position, which was that racial tensions should be avoided. Both agreed on this position."[16] With that, one of the most volatile issues before the nation was removed from the campaign. Johnson was vulnerable on the issue, and if handled properly, it might well have aided Goldwater's campaign. The president surely breathed a great sigh of relief. Generally, Goldwater held to his civil rights pledge throughout the campaign, although as the campaign progressed into September and October he began using Wallace-like racially charged code words and phrases.

Possibly even more surprising was a second agreement that Goldwater made, one that was not released to the public. He agreed—apparently on his own initiative—not to attack the president's policies on Vietnam, effectively removing that issue, as well, from the campaign. This promise, both men agreed, was in the Cold War spirit of a united foreign policy in the face of a national enemy. Johnson, not surprisingly, was grateful to Goldwater for his willingness to eliminate yet another issue that might have damaged his campaign. Here again, Goldwater agreed to avoid an area where Johnson was vulnerable—and becoming increasingly vulnerable—in the late months of 1964. Just a week later the Tonkin Gulf Incident awakened the nation to the situation in Vietnam and Goldwater (then publicly) agreed to follow the president's lead on Vietnam.[17] In the last weeks of the campaign, Goldwater finally began to attack the administration's Vietnam policies, but because of the late date the attacks had little impact.

Despite Goldwater's unilateral pledge on civil rights, Johnson still believed that the situation was volatile both in the political arena and in the streets. Luther Hodges, Johnson's secretary of labor, told the president that he was afraid that the nation's workers might support Goldwater in November because they feared losing their jobs to blacks.[18] By mid-summer, polls began to show the effect of the riots on Johnson's support. A Harris poll in mid-July revealed that 31 percent of Democrats and 51 percent of Republicans believed that the civil rights movement was advancing too fast.[19] In the northeastern urban areas, the president's approval ratings had dropped almost ten points from a high of 74 percent. The drop only meant that LBJ's majority was less impressive than it had been, but for Johnson, who was looking for a landslide to pale all other landslides, this was a drop that deserved attention. In addition, the president had promised in several campaign speeches that he would preserve the nation's "domestic tranquility." The riots threatened to undermine that promise.[20]

Johnson responded to the problem by pressuring the nation's civil rights leaders to stop all direct action until after the election. In July, NAACP president Roy Wilkins (apparently acting at the president's request) sent a two-page telegram to the nation's black leaders calling for a moratorium on all civil rights activity, warning that any additional demonstrations might further damage Johnson's candidacy.[21] Wilkins had never been a fan of direct action, particularly when it led to violence. He believed in the long-held NAACP strategy of litigation and lobbying, and he thought that the Civil Rights Bill, which had passed Congress just a month before, was the answer to most of the problems faced by the nation's African Americans. He had refused to support SNCC's Mississippi Summer Project, and he believed that the urban riots served to aid Goldwater's campaign and damage the civil rights cause. Wilkins's telegram asked that the nation's civil rights leaders attend a meeting at the Roosevelt Hotel in New York on July 29.

For most in attendance at the Roosevelt Hotel meeting it must have seemed like déjà vu. This was essentially the same group, meeting in the same place, that had planned the March on Washington the year before. Those in attendance included King from the Southern Christian Leadership Conference, A. Philip Randolph of the Brotherhood of Sleeping Car Porters and the March on Washington Movement, Bayard Rustin, John Lewis of SNCC, James Farmer of CORE, and a few others. "I assumed," Farmer recalled, "that [the meeting] was at the request of the White House," and that the purpose of the meeting was the concern "that further demonstrations might generate more backlash and help elect Goldwater."[22]

The group split over the issue of calling a moratorium, a split that was indicative of the movement itself that was beginning to divide between the conservative nonviolent elements and a growing radical wing. John Lewis wrote later, "the alignments were predictable." Those supporting the morato-

Johnson feared a white backlash at the polls and tried desperately to convince Martin Luther King, Jr. and other civil rights leaders to moderate direct action during the campaign. King quietly acquiesced, alienating many radicals in the movement. *(Johnson Library)*

rium included Randolph, Rustin, Wilkins, and Young. King, "which surprised me," Lewis continued, fell in with the conservatives.[23] Lewis opposed the moratorium, arguing that demonstrations would not necessarily aid the Goldwater campaign, and that surrendering the right to protest, even for a short time, would undermine the movement, while opening it to criticism as a tool of the Democratic administration. Farmer supported Lewis: "I thought it would be a disaster," he recalled, "if we issued a public statement saying, 'We're going to stop demonstrations,' and the demonstrations continued, as they were bound to do. . . . The kids in the streets . . . would laugh at us."[24] "So Farmer and I stood at that meeting against the moratorium," John Lewis later recalled, "a thorn in the flesh of the American body politic. . . ."[25] Despite the objections from Lewis and Farmer, the moratorium was issued. The statement, appearing in the nation's leading newspapers the next day, urged "a broad curtailment, if not total moratorium of all mass marches, picketing and demonstrations until after election day. . . ."[26]

This ideological split, all too apparent at the Roosevelt Hotel meeting, was widening significantly inside the civil rights movement through the summer of 1964. Most discussions of this split have revolved around differences between the younger leaders and followers inside SNCC and CORE who found only shallow victories in nonviolent activism, and the older leaders and their followers who rallied around King and his church-based movement anchored in the rural South. In the summer of 1964, however, these two groups were developing divergent paths because the movement's conservatives were willing to follow the lead of the Johnson administration, to ally themselves with white liberalism, while leaders like Lewis and Moses believed the movement should seek its goals outside of politics. The Roosevelt Hotel meeting further split the two groups. But it was the events that surrounded the Democratic convention of 1964 that more than anything opened a wide gulf in the civil rights movement, placing SNCC and CORE directly on a path to radicalism and separatism in the years that followed.

Possibly because of the moratorium, possibly for other reasons, the cities quieted and memories of the summer riots faded quickly. As the election approached, and most civil rights activism ended, Johnson was no longer the focus of a white backlash—and that added to the president's appeal. He had been vulnerable on civil rights, and vulnerable to a backlash against civil rights activism, the violent street riots, and the fears that many came to associate with the Civil Rights Act. When the riots stopped the backlash waned. In fact, the Johnson's campaign advisors had planned a series of ads focusing on civil rights issues, but when the riots ended, white fears were gener-

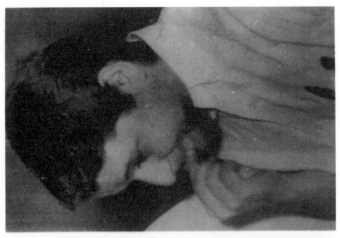

The murders of civil rights workers Michael Schwerner, James Chaney, and Andrew Goodman near Philadelphia, Mississippi in the summer of 1964 radicalized large segments of the civil rights movement as the election approached later that year. *(Ronnie Moore Collection, Amistad Research Center at Tulane University, New Orleans)*

ally eased and the administration canceled the ads.[27] Johnson, then, shifted from fearing a backlash to touting what he called a growing "frontlash" of moderate Republicans who, he believed, were coming to his side because of his support for civil rights and other issues. "If you really care about lashes," the president told reporters later in the summer, "let's get into this frontlash." It is, he added, "two to three times larger than the backlash."[28] It sounded like campaign spin, but it was prophecy.

On June 21 three civil rights workers, Mickey Schwerner, Andy Goodman, and James Chaney, had disappeared near Meridian, Mississippi. Three days later Schwerner's burned-out blue Ford station wagon was found in the nearby Bogue Chitto Swamp, leading most southern project workers to believe that the three men had been murdered. The events struck fear into the entire summer project. The bodies of the three volunteers were finally found in August in shallow graves in Neshoba County, clearly the victims of murder and racial injustice. As tragic as it was, the incident played well into Johnson's campaign. Despite the president's strong push for civil rights legislation, he was still perceived in some liberal circles as a southerner who might be willing to pass civil rights legislation in exchange for black votes, but who, in deference to his southern brethren, would not move quickly to enforce civil rights laws. The murders in Mississippi gave Johnson the opportunity to show that he was more than just rhetoric, that he would act when necessary. Also, the incident showed the extreme brutality of racism in the South, a brutality that might not be altogether clear to many whites in the North. If this brutality could be exhibited to the American people through the media, if those southern whites who so violently opposed civil rights could be pegged as ignorant right-wing Klan-type radicals, opposition to the civil rights movement—the white backlash, particularly in the North—might diminish further. Thus Johnson acted decisively. He flooded central Mississippi with FBI agents and federal marshals. The press followed. The murders of the three civil rights workers in Mississippi became one of the biggest stories of 1964, and the president-as-civil-rights-activist came away as the savior of civility over ignorance and brutality.

The moratorium on direct action intentionally stalled the civil rights movement, which in turn quieted the backlash against it. The deaths of the civil rights workers in Mississippi made those who opposed civil rights appear to support the brutality of.racism. And that further quieted the backlash. As the Democratic convention approached, race was no longer a serious issue. George Wallace's virulent campaign against the Civil Rights Bill and in support of states' rights was just a memory. Goldwater continued to pump the issue, but with little effect outside the South. The MFDP would raise the issue again at the convention, and the president himself would make a surprising civil rights speech in New Orleans, a speech that would be one of his finest moments. But generally, by August, civil rights had waned as a campaign issue.

The MFDP challenge, however, continued to worry Johnson. He was a coalition-maker, a politician whose greatest abilities had been to bring people together. He wanted to win the November election in a landslide, not so much because he was a vain man, but because a landslide would mean he had built a national coalition, brought the nation's groups and regions together, appealed to members of both parties, to blacks and whites, northerners and southerners, liberals and conservatives alike—the way, in fact, Roosevelt had done in 1936. Goldwater's candidacy made that even more possible by alienating moderate Republicans. The MFDP challenge, however, threatened to destroy Johnson's intentions by splitting the party (as it had so often been split in the past) between the North and the South, over the party's greatest burden, the race issue. It also threatened to alienate the white South, possibly sending that entire region spiraling out of control into the Republican camp; and if (as a result of the MFDP clash) race became a primary campaign issue, Johnson stood to lose a great deal of support from those who felt threatened by the civil rights movement and the Civil Rights Act. Certainly, many of those votes were headed in Goldwater's direction anyway, but if race became a campaign issue, those numbers would undoubtedly rise significantly. "I have a desire to unite the people," Johnson told George Reedy right in the midst of the MFDP fight in Atlantic City, "and the South is against me and the north is against me. And the Negroes are against me."[29] The MFDP challenge worried him. Thus, throughout most of August he spent much of his energy and time trying to defuse the problem. He used extreme political leverage; he used illegal FBI surveillance. And he used Hubert Humphrey.

In the first week of August, in a telephone conversation with Walter Reuther of the United Auto Workers union, Johnson explained his dilemma: "The only thing that can really screw us good is to seat that group of challengers from Mississippi. . . . [T]here's not a damn vote that we get by seating these folks." Johnson's fear was that by seating the MFDP delegates he might, he said, "run off fourteen border states like Oklahoma and like Kentucky." Then he hinted at a compromise: "I'll guarantee the Freedom delegation," he told Reuther, that "somebody representing views like [theirs] will be seated four years from now."[30]

Armed only with this simple promise, Johnson sent Hubert Humphrey to forge a compromise with the MFDP—but most importantly to do everything possible to head off a floor fight over the issue of race.[31] In these weeks prior to the convention, the negotiations were carried out, primarily, between Humphrey and MFDP representatives, particularly Joseph Rauh. Rauh was a well-known high-powered Washington lawyer who had spent much of his life as a legal advisor to the labor and civil rights movements, and an occasional advisor to Democratic presidents and candidates. Through the summer of 1964, Rauh and a large staff had spent time in Mississippi compiling evidence and framing legal briefs to document the legitimacy of the MFDP—and the illegitimacy of the Mississippi regulars. Immediately after the MFDP was formed, SNCC leaders knew that if their plan was to succeed they would need the experience and abilities of Joseph Rauh.[32] White, bow-tied, and bespectacled, Rauh hardly looked the part of a sixties civil rights leader. He was, however, a party insider, a liberal, a lawyer with experience and knowledge of the party structure, rules, and personalities. But Rauh, as the MFDP members would later discover, carried with him loyalties that conflicted with the goals of the MFDP. He had been a Humphrey supporter since at least 1948, and he badly wanted the Minnesota senator to be Lyndon Johnson's vice president. Johnson knew it; Humphrey knew it. The MFDP, however, never quite realized the conflict.

As the intentions of the MFDP grew more threatening, the president made it clear to all involved in the negotiations (to his aides and even to the press) that if Humphrey failed to solve the MFDP challenge he would not be considered for the vice presidency. "Johnson let the MFDP delegation know," John Lewis recalled, "that if we wanted Hubert Humphrey to be his vice presidential choice, which most of us did, the MFDP had better accept this compromise, or Johnson would select someone far less sympathetic to the cause of civil rights as a running mate."[33] This pushed several groups to pressure the MFDP and their supporters to accept a compromise—in essence to go along with Johnson's dictates in exchange for Humphrey's nomination as vice president. Humphrey, then, armed with the threat of his own demise (and thus with the threat of someone other than himself on the ticket) went to his liberal friends and they in turn put pressure on the MFDP and their liberal supporters.

Thus, it was Humphrey who offered the White House compromise to the MFDP—through Rauh. It was simple. The MFDP delegates would be seated as "guests," with all the floor privileges of delegates except the right to vote. Added to the compromise was a promise by the party that the Mississippi delegation would be desegregated in the future. In the meantime, the all-white Mississippi delegation would be seated with all its voting privileges.

Not surprisingly, the members of the MFDP saw this as no compromise at all. They rejected it outright and planned to take their challenge to Atlantic City. Humphrey and Rauh, however, were still very much in the mix (and unknown to the MFDP) working generally on the same side.[34]

The MFDP delegation boarded buses at Tougaloo College in Jackson and headed northeast toward New Jersey. Many had never been outside their home state of Mississippi. They arrived in Atlantic City on August 21, a Friday. They had brought with them, towed behind one of the buses, a replica of Mickey Schwerner's burned-out Ford station wagon. They intended to put the car on exhibit at (or near) the convention hall as a symbol of violence and brutality in Mississippi.

The delegation checked into the rundown blacks-only Gem Hotel on Pacific Avenue, about a mile from the convention hall, and set up their center of operations at the Union Baptist Temple. By Sunday, the day before the convention was to begin, the delegation, along with dozens of supporters, began congregating outside the convention hall. "I doubt [Atlantic City] had ever seen that many black people collected on its sidewalks at one time," John Lewis recalled. "[D]ozens of black men and women talking and laughing and hugging outside the city's civic center. . . ."[35] The pre-convention events had produced no excitement for the some 5,500 newsmen and their accompanying technicians. So the arrival of the MFDP, the only entity capable of producing news, was covered with great interest by the press.

At just about the same moment that the MFDP arrived in Atlantic City, George Wallace arrived. He denounced the Democrats as radicals who "would sell the birthright of our nation" to install "an alien philosophy of government." He called for a repeal of the Civil Rights Act, and then insisted that he was not finished with national politics, that he would be a contender in 1968.[36] Wallace, however, drew little attention. By then, the press considered his springtime flash-in-the-pan primary run of little significance. Other southern governors, however, were getting attention. John McKithen of Louisiana had just resigned as the head of the Louisiana delegation to the convention and was threatening to lead a walkout of the southern states if the MFDP was seated instead of the Mississippi regulars. Disruption in the proceedings of one sort or another seemed imminent. Johnson continued to worry.

The number of FBI agents that Johnson sent to monitor the situation might best gauge the importance the president placed on these events. In what was apparently the first use of such agents at a national convention Johnson, through his aide Walter Jenkins, asked FBI chief J. Edgar Hoover to send agents to Atlantic City to keep the MFDP under surveillance and report back to the White House. Hoover, who had always been convinced that the civil rights movement was riddled with communists, was more than willing to comply. Some fifty agents and informants under the command of the bureau's domestic surveillance chief, Cartha "Deke" DeLoach, infiltrated MFDP meetings and bugged the rooms and telephones of the primary MFDP members and supporters. Throughout the convention they maintained surveillance of the convention hall floor by flashing phony NBC press badges—with NBC News complicit in the entire operation. Johnson would monitor events closely. DeLoach later called all this pre-Watergate spooking "a serious breach of the law."[37]

The decision to seat either the Mississippi all-white regulars or the MFDP was left up to the party's 108-member Credentials Committee. That committee met on the afternoon of Saturday, August 22, to hear both sides. The party rules stated that if as few as 10 percent (eleven members) of the Credentials Committee supported the MFDP the dispute could be taken to the convention floor. At that point, if eight or more states requested it, the dispute would be voted on by the entire Democratic party delegation; a roll-call vote would decide which delegation should be seated. That was the MFDP strategy. If it got that far, Lewis recalled, "our people would be voted in by a landslide."[38] The MFDP, however, still had no idea what was going on behind the scenes.

"We have only an hour to tell you a story of tragedy and terror in Mississippi," Rauh began his arguments before the committee. And his arguments were simple. He told the committee that the MFDP was the only Democratic party in Mississippi that was open to all Mississippi residents of voting age. It also supported the national party platform, pledged its support to Lyndon Johnson, and promised to work for the president's reelection in Mississippi. The all-white Mississippi regulars in turn agreed that they had denied black participation in their organization, but insisted that they, and not the MFDP, represented the majority of voting Democrats in Mississippi. That, of course, was probably true, since most African Americans in Mississippi could not register. The regulars also insisted that they would not support the national platform and refused to support Lyndon Johnson. In fact, they openly pledged their support to Goldwater.[39] Not surprisingly, the members of the MFDP were confident that they would be seated over the white delegation.

Rauh announced that he would call three witnesses before the Credentials Committee. The first two, Aaron Henry and Edwin King, had run for governor and lieutenant governor in the MFDP's mock elections in October the year before. The third speaker was Fannie Lou Hamer, then the vice chair of

216

SNCC. Hamer was one of the most spectacular figures to come out of the civil rights movement. Most of the movement's leaders were religious types like Martin Luther King or Fred Shuttlesworth, well spoken or well educated or both. Other leaders like Whitney Young or Roy Wilkins were organization leaders, comfortable in the highest circles of the nation's business or government, even society. But Fannie Lou Hamer was at the very grassroots of the movement. She had very little education. She was the youngest of twenty children. A large woman, she was in her mid-forties, although she looked much older. For attempting to register to vote, she had been fired from her job and evicted from her home of eighteen years. In 1961 she was sterilized, without her knowledge, following a minor surgical procedure. She suffered chronic back pain and walked with a limp, conditions resulting primarily from polio and malnutrition she had suffered as a child.[40] Since her eviction, she had been a SNCC organizer in Mississippi and a founder of the MFDP. Her story riveted America.

The pain in her face was apparent. She told the national television audience of how she was kicked off her land in 1962 for attempting to register to vote. "I had to leave that same night," she told the committee. She told of her arrest by a Mississippi state policeman in 1963 in Winona while returning from a voter registration workshop. In jail, she was beaten savagely, first by the white police officers and then by black prisoners who beat her with blackjacks to avoid being beaten themselves. "The first Negro began to beat, and I was beat until he was exhausted." Then "the State Highway Patrolman ordered the second Negro to take the blackjack. The second Negro began to beat. . . . I began to scream, and one white man got up and began to beat me on my head and tell me to 'hush.' . . . All this," she added, "on account we want to register, to become first-class citizens, and if the Freedom Democratic Party is not seated now, I question America. . . ."[41] In the eight minutes during which she spoke she exposed the horror and brutality of Mississippi to a nation that knew little of race relations in the rural South, of the way blacks were treated in Mississippi when they tried to do nothing more than exercise their rights as Americans. Other witnesses followed, including Rita Schwerner, whose husband had been killed in Mississippi. Then Roy Wilkins and Martin Luther King spoke in favor of seating the MFDP. The nation, however, remembered Hamer's speech.

In his concluding statement, Rauh had the opportunity to appeal to the national conscience, but instead he sought acceptance from the only man who really counted that day. "Are you going to throw out of here the people who want to work for Lyndon Johnson, who are willing to be beaten and shot and thrown in jail to work for Lyndon Johnson? Are we the oppressor or the oppressed?"[42]

The electricity of Hamer's speech reached the White House in an instant; the FBI was doing its job of keeping the president informed of any breaking news regarding the MFDP challenge. Johnson was in the process of hosting the nation's Democratic governors in the Oval Office—a sort of send-off to Atlantic City. When the event got under way he implied to the press that he might be ready to name his running mate, and that provoked an impromptu press conference that was clearly designed to preempt Hamer's emotional testimony. But instead of addressing the question of his running mate, the president refused questions on the point and used the moment to send his regards to Texas governor John Connally, who was still recovering from the gunshot wound he suffered in Dallas in November. The lead story on the evening news reports, however, was Fannie Lou Hamer and the brutality in Mississippi, not Johnson's obvious attempt to quiet her testimony.[43]

Hamer's statement as Johnson saw it threatened to split the party North and South. It gave the MFDP such moral strength that the president was certain that a floor vote on the MFDP challenge would win. The result of that, he believed, was that he could lose as many as fifteen southern and border states to Goldwater in November. Despite that, Johnson continued to cling to his original offer of little more than floor privileges and a promise of a desegregated Mississippi delegation in 1968. The MFDP continued to reject the compromise, hoping that their moral position would win the day.

On Monday, August 24, Johnson consulted with Richard Russell, the senator from Georgia and longtime Johnson friend and confidant. Russell, like most southern senators and congressmen, had stayed away from the convention. There was always the fear among southern legislators in the Democratic party that their state delegation might walk out of the convention over the race issue and they would have to chose between that decision and the national party. It was not a good position to be in, particularly when the party's presidential candidate was a sure winner in November. Johnson's comments to Russell included both the president's concerns about the MFDP and his yearlong fears about Bobby Kennedy's motives. In addition, Martin Luther King had tried several times, through statements in the press, to draw Johnson into the Mississippi credentials controversy by insisting that he support the seating of the MFDP. "It would be so much better if I'd stay out of the convention if I could," he told Russell. However, he knew that if he threw his support to the regulars he would be marked as a racist, a supporter of the Mississippi System of race prejudice, disenfranchisement, and brutality. And that, he believed, was the trap that some of his enemies were trying to set for him. "I don't think there's any question what Martin Luther King and that group wants me to be in a position of giving them an excuse to say that I have turned on the Negro." Then he reverted again to his deep-seated fear that Bobby Kennedy wanted to take over the convention and win the nomination for himself. Kennedy, he told Russell, is "trying to get me in every way he can. And I think this is Bobby's trap. . . . Yeah," he added a moment later, "I think that's Bobby's strategy. . . . He told me, when he left me with a sneer on his face, 'I think I would have been able to help you a lot.' And I think he wants to prove that. . . ."[44] Johnson expressed his two fears of the moment: that the MFDP challenge would divide the party and that Kennedy would be swept into the nomination ahead of a flood of sympathy for his dead brother. To head off the latter, Johnson had already arranged to postpone a JFK tribute until after the close of convention business. He had also sent orders to DeLoach and his FBI spooks to begin surveillance of the Kennedy family.

That next day, Monday, Humphrey met with members of the MFDP at a room in the Pageant Motel and again offered the challengers much the same compromise, which included seating the regulars with voting privileges, giving the MFDP delegates nonvoting seats, and promising that there would be no segregated delegations in the future. The only thing added was that the Mississippi regulars were to pledge their support to the Democratic party candidate—and to the party's civil rights platform. The same oath would be demanded of the Alabama delegation.[45]

Later that day, Johnson called in Walter Reuther to negotiate a peace between the two sides with the primary objective of keeping the challenge off the floor.[46] Reuther's presence, of course, seemed to imply that Johnson was unhappy with Humphrey's progress and that Humphrey might have lost the president's favor. The result was that liberals involved in the negotiations (most of whom wanted Humphrey to be named vice president) began pushing the MFDP to accept some sort of compromise under the assumption that a compromise acceptable to the president would resolve the issue and keep Humphrey in the running for the vice presidential nomination.

The convention opened that evening with a keynote address by John Pastore, "the short, scrappy Senator from Rhode Island," as Mike Wallace had called him in a CBS interview.[47] Johnson chose Pastore because he was a passionate speaker. He fit the bill—and excited the delegates. His job, of course, was to attack the opponent. "Six weeks ago," Pastore told the delegates, "despite the efforts of responsible members of the opposition, reactionaries and extremists captured the Republican Party—lock, stock, and barrel."[48] Pastore did his job. He excited the faithful. But as he spoke, the convention's important events were taking place behind the scenes.

After an all-night marathon brainstorm, Reuther, Humphrey, and Jenkins finally decided on a plan regarding the MFDP challenge. It had become clear to everyone involved that the MFDP ranks were split, that it had its own internal troubles. There was one faction, led by Moses, that wanted only total victory. They would settle for nothing less than full voting rights and an expulsion of the regulars—even at the price of party unity. Reuther, Humphrey, and the others concluded that any attempt to satisfy this group would alienate the southern delegations and split the convention wide open. That, of course, was what the president wanted to avoid at all costs. Their plan, then, became to play to the moderates inside the MFDP and hope that others, like Martin Luther King and Wilkins, would fall in line. They also made it clear to Rauh that if their plan failed, Humphrey would not get the vice presidential nomination.[49]

In an attempt to break the deadlock, the administration's negotiators decided to offer the MFDP two "at-large" seats with full voting privileges. The seats were to be filled by Ed King and Aaron Henry. The remainder of the delegation would be seated, but as "nonvoting delegates." In addition, the Mississippi regulars would be required to take an oath to support the ticket before they could take their seats and vote.[50] To most observers, this was more than generous. Rowland Evans and Robert Novak, writing for the *New York Herald-Tribune*, called it "a magnanimous compromise," a deal "that was far better than they had a right to expect. . . ."[51] Anthony Lewis of the *New York Times* called the compromise "a long step toward ending racism in Southern Democratic politics."[52] Theodore White called it "a true triumph." Reuther then turned his big guns on Martin Luther King. Reuther's United Auto Workers had gone a long way toward supporting the civil rights movement, particularly King's victory in Birmingham the year before. "[Y]our funding is on the line," Reuther told King sharply. "The labor movement gave . . . the SCLC $176,000, and they won't give them any more if they [won't] go along."[53] Reuther then called Rauh and insisted he accept the offer. The Credentials Committee voted. The compromise passed.

"That's when the pressure started," Rauh recalled in an interview. "[T]hat's when the president really started to put the pressure on me to give up, to stop it. . . ." It was, he added, "the greatest aggregation of power that I'd ever seen in action. . . . You had the whole Democratic political machine, the President, the whole White House, the whole labor movement, all trying to stop a few little Mississippi Negroes and me from making a little stink at the Democratic Convention."[54]

The word spread through the MFDP delegation like wildfire. The MFDP members themselves were, at that moment, locked in a discussion with Minnesota attorney general Walter Mondale, who they thought spoke for the administration. When the compromise was pushed through the Credentials Committee (without the MFDP present) they felt betrayed, cheated. Under Moses's leadership, the MFDP, in a unanimous vote, immediately rejected the compromise. Moses called it a "back-of-the-bus" deal.[55] Wilkins called the MFDP "ignorant." Most MFDP members, like Moses, rejected the plan because it was clearly just a token pitch intended to salve the civil rights activists. Other MFDP members, however, rejected it for other reasons. James Farmer of CORE hated the insistence of Humphrey and others that Aaron Henry and Ed King had been chosen as the at-large delegates. "[T]hat smacked of an attempt to pick our leaders," he said later. "If they had said to the [MFDP] 'Pick two of your members and we will seat them,' but to say, 'We'll be glad to seat these two,' was bound to go down the wrong way. . . . [T]here had been too much of a tradition of the establishment picking our leaders," Farmer recalled, "and saying 'We'll pat this one on the head and oppose the others.'"[56]

From the other side of the compromise, the southern leadership threatened to bolt the convention because the challengers had been given concessions—no matter how small or insignificant. Mississippi and Alabama were sure to leave. Mississippi's governor Paul Johnson went on national television and claimed Mississippi's ground. Because of Reconstruction, he said, "We have definitely owed a deep debt of loyalty to the Democratic party. As of tonight, my friends, I say that we have now paid that debt in full." Then he added, "Since Mississippi was readmitted to the Union . . . we have never voted the Republican ticket. . . ."[57] The threat was clear. Such statements probably did not surprise Johnson, but he was truly rankled when he heard that Georgia and Texas were threatening to follow Mississippi's lead.[58] He complained to Texas governor John Connally that he was tired of the issue: "nigger, nigger, nigger," he said. "I'm just harassed to death. . . . Mississippi's seated," referring to the regulars. "She gets every damned vote she's entitled to. She oughtn't be seated," he added. "She wouldn't let those nigras vote. And that's not right. . . . Now she says, 'I'm gonna be a goddman dog in a manger.'"[59] Johnson was despondent over the issue. Both sides had demanded war and total victory. Attempts at compromise had simply alienated them both.

The pressure of the events pushed Johnson over the edge. He prepared a

221

statement, to be read the next day at the convention, announcing his resignation as president. The whole situation had simply been too much for him. He read the statement to George Reedy: "The times require leadership about which there is no doubt and a voice that men of all parties and sections and color can follow. I've learned, after trying very hard, that I am not that voice or that leader. Therefore," he concluded, "I suggest that the representatives . . . do their duty, and that no consideration be given to me because I am absolutely unavailable. . . ."[60] He continued to Reedy: "I just don't want these decisions I'm being required to make. I don't want the conniving that's required. . . . I'm absolutely positive that I cannot lead the South and the North. . . . And I don't want to lead the nation without my own state and without my own section. I am very convinced that the Negroes will not listen to me. They're not going to follow a white Southerner. And I think the stakes are too big to try to compromise."[61] Later that day he told Walter Jenkins much the same thing. "I don't think a white Southerner is the man to unite this nation in this hour. I don't know who is, and I don't even want that responsibility. I've had doubts about whether a man born where I was born, raised like I was raised, could ever satisfy the Northern Jews, Catholics, and union people."[62]

Jenkins and Reedy both tried to convince Johnson that to withdraw from the campaign now would only hand the election to Goldwater. Johnson disagreed, arguing that a Democrat could still win. But clearly the possibility of a Goldwater win gave him pause. Then Lady Bird weighed in. In a letter marked "personal," and headed "Beloved," she told her husband that he was brave, "as brave a man as Harry Truman—or FDR—or Lincoln. . . . You have been strong, patient, determined beyond any words of mine to express. I honor you for it," she added. "So does your country." And then she let him know where she stood. "To step out now would be wrong for our country. . . . Your friends would be frozen in embarrassed silence and your enemies jeering."[63] Johnson eased out of his depression. By later that afternoon, Tuesday, he was telling Reuther how great the Democratic party was because it had taken the time to listen to the Mississippi challengers. As "[l]ong as the downtrodden and the bended know that they can come to us and be heard. And that's what we're doing. We're hearing 'em. . . ."[64]

The MFDP, led now by Moses, tried to rally their forces and produce enough votes before the Credentials Committee to send the question of replacing the Mississippi regulars to the floor. But it was too late. The liberals had abandoned them and accepted the compromise, so had the primary black leadership, including M.L. King, Wilkins, Bayard Rustin, MFDP chairman Aaron Henry, James Farmer, and Andrew Young. Liberal support from

New York, California, and Michigan, their real trump cards, evaporated instantly. The vast majority of the MFDP—those who insisted on holding hard for recognition, and their supporters—felt betrayed by the moderate black leadership and their liberal allies.

On the other side, all but two of the Mississippi regular delegation headed home. The two who remained signed their loyalty oaths. A small group of Alabama delegates also signed.[65]

That evening, with one slam of the gavel, John Pastore announced the approval of the compromise amid only a few dissenting groans from the convention floor. Rauh approached the podium, tears in his eyes, and, in protest of the decision, returned the two at-large delegate credentials issued to Aaron Henry and Edwin King. The MFDP responded to their defeat by protesting, by staging what the press called in sixties terminology a "walk-in." Using credentials of supporters from Michigan, Colorado, and Oregon, they invaded the convention hall, occupied the empty seats of the gone-home Mississippi delegates, and generally disrupted the convention for some three hours.[66]

At a meeting of the MFDP delegates the next day, Hamer and Aaron Henry got into an argument that summed up much of the feeling within the MFDP. Henry had hoped to convince the delegates to return to the convention hall and insist that discussions be reopened to consider a second compromise giving the Mississippi regulars and the MFDP a full twenty-four votes each. Hamer, enraged by now at the prospect of any compromise, and possibly realizing that such a plan would never be considered, responded to Henry's suggestion. "Why you going to compromise for twenty-four votes, Dr. Henry? You know good and well that we won't have but two. If you go out there . . . and say that . . . you stay there, don't you come home. You better stay in that convention hall then the balance of your life, 'cause if you come out I'm gon' cut your throat." The delegation entered the hall that evening. Henry was to announce the MFDP's decision. "No compromise," he said quickly, and handed the microphone to Hamer. She said, "We didn't come all this way for no two seats."[67]

The MFDP challenge had a major impact on the civil rights movement and on American politics. For Theodore White, it was an "episode [that] marked the end of a chapter in politics." He admitted that he knew little of what the future held, "But the chapter that had begun with Hubert Humphrey's advocacy of a strong civil-rights plank in the Party platform in 1948 and a walkout from the Democratic Party of four Southern states was over."[68] His reference was to the Democratic party's adoption, in 1948, of a strong civil rights plank (proposed on the floor of the convention by then Minneapolis mayor Hubert Humphrey) followed by a southern walk-out and the third party "Dixiecrat" presidential candidacy of Strom Thurmond. White's point was that the South's grip on the Democratic party began to loosen in 1948. Prior to that election, the South had maintained a near-veto on the presidential nomination. Following 1948 the party began to see the importance of the civil rights movement—both from the practical, vote-getting standpoint and from the basic moral standpoint. Truman's victory in 1948 showed the political significance of the northern, urban, African-American vote in delivering states with large electoral numbers—electoral numbers that were far more significant than the electoral numbers that the southern states could deliver. In that election, Truman won California, Illinois, and Ohio; and without the black vote in Los Angeles, Chicago, and the Ohio urban areas he would probably have lost all three states and a total of seventy-eight electoral votes. Thurmond won only thirty-nine electoral votes in the South. The message was clear. Throughout the 1950s and early 1960s it became increasingly apparent that civil rights was an extremely volatile issue and that the Democratic party's big tent was simply not big enough to accommodate both southern white racists and African-American voters. Add to that a very clear moral issue that became apparent to northern whites as a result of the civil rights movement in the South and its coverage on national television, and by 1964 the Democrats had made a choice. The South would change or leave.[69] Theodore White saw it at the Democratic convention in 1964. He reported that New York, California, Illinois, Ohio, and Michigan (all states with large urban African-American populations) came to Atlantic City with black delegates who "sat so casually, in such old-shoe companionship with white politicians with whom they had worked for years, that their presence was too commonplace for any commentator to note or record." In addition, he noted, Tennessee, North Carolina and Georgia also had black delegates. By 1964 the Democrats had embraced civil rights at the expense of the white South. "Mississippi and Alabama, as they walked out," White concluded, "were the last of a rear-guard action that had for sixteen years been in retreat; not even South Carolina or Virginia or Arkansas followed them."[70]

It was, of course, this decision to embrace the civil rights movement (which reached its fruition in 1964) that brought on a white backlash against the party—a backlash that had always been apparent in the South, but because of George Wallace's candidacy in 1964 was uncovered in regions outside of the South as well. However, when the votes were counted in November 1964 it was clear that the impact of the white backlash was minimal, most likely because of Goldwater's weak campaign. Four years later, however, Richard Nixon would rally what he called the "Silent Majority" and they would have an impact on the electorate and damage the Democrats. Some have argued that this backlash was still identifiable in the 1980s as the "Alienated Voters" and "Reagan Democrats."[71] The MFDP challenge was a watershed in the civil rights movement and in the modern development of the Democratic party. It was also a watershed on the long road that has turned white southerners from Democrats into Republicans—the party that after 1964 began to accept conservative southern Democrats with open arms and talk of states' rights.

The 1964 election may have gone a long way toward bringing African Americans into the Democratic party, but it also went a long way toward dividing the civil rights movement. The MFDP delegates and many of their supporters in Atlantic City and around the nation felt betrayed by the compromise offered by the party. They felt betrayed by the Johnson administration, the liberal establishment, and by black moderates like Martin Luther King, Wilkins, and the others who accepted the compromise and counseled the MFDP delegates to do the same. The result was a clearly identifiable break between the radicals within the movement and the moderates; between those who came to believe that the movement must not rely on white liberal leadership and those who wanted to work within the system; between those who were moving rapidly toward black nationalism and those who saw the movement as an integrated movement steeped in the southern church and the strategy of nonviolence. It was a break that had been coming within the movement for a long time. Some have argued that it was the manifestation of natural divisions within the black community that have always existed.

The changes came first to SNCC, a group that was already, in some ways, on the road to radicalism. "Things could never be the same," Cleveland Sellers of SNCC wrote after the Atlantic City challenge. "Never again were we lulled into believing that our task was exposing injustices so that the 'good' people of America could eliminate them. We left Atlantic City with the knowledge that the movement had turned into something else. After Atlantic City our movement was not for civil rights, but for liberation."[72] For Stokely Carmichael, who would be elected to head SNCC just a few months after the convention, the MFDP experience showed "not merely that the national conscience was generally unreliable but that, very specifically, black people in Mississippi and throughout this country could not rely on their so-called allies."[73] John Lewis recalled the anger among the MFDP supporters after Atlantic City: "Anyone who trusted the white man at this point, who believed

225

we could work together, was a fool, a Tom." Many within SNCC and within the civil rights movement, Lewis recalled further, "were ready now to play by a different set of rules, their own rules. 'Fuck it.' You heard that phrase over and over among SNCC members that month. 'We played by the rules and look what it got us. So fuck the rules.'" For Robert Moses, it was the last straw, "a cruel lesson . . . from which he never recovered," Lewis wrote in his memoirs. Moses vowed never to speak to a white man again, changed his name, and moved to Africa.[74]

Despite the radicalization of portions of the civil rights movement (at least due in part to the incidents at Atlantic City in 1964) the MFDP challenge had an extremely important and positive impact on the Democratic party and the future of the civil rights movement. The party kept its promise. Never again, after 1964, were there all-white delegations at the party conventions. Atlantic City had been, as Theodore White had predicted, the last gasp of southern racism as a political force within the Democratic party structure. The MFDP challenge also went a long way toward exposing to white America the powerlessness of black Mississippians together with the raw brutality of white racism in Mississippi. It also made it clear to white northerners that blacks in Mississippi wanted to vote, that they were not being allowed to vote, and that the primary method of keeping black Mississippians away from the polls was simple intimidation and brutality. All of this was instrumental in the passage of the Voting Rights Act of 1965. The MFDP left Atlantic City disenchanted, even angry. But their efforts had not been in vain.

The MFDP lost its challenge, but the administration gained considerably. Johnson had averted any significant southern revolt that might have split the party and damaged his campaign by fueling the backlash that he believed might grow to engulf the entire South—and conceivably other regions of the nation. The compromise also quieted what was believed by the Democrats to be the most radical elements inside the civil rights movement. It was also a victory for the liberals, particularly those liberals who wanted Humphrey to be Johnson's vice president. The president's hidden hand made sure that the liberals would push the MFDP into a compromise in order to save their favorite son—in fact, abandon the MFDP to make Humphrey vice president. Joseph Rauh did his job by facilitating the entire operation. He was certainly upset that the MFDP refused to accept the compromise, but he had made certain that Humphrey emerged from the event with solid liberal support for the vice presidency. "That you ultimately resolved the Mississippi problem fairly to all concerned," Rauh wrote his friend Humphrey a few days after the convention, "was evidence of your brilliance and strength."[75]

* * *

By Wednesday, the third day of the convention, the MFDP controversy had been largely settled. The way was now clear for Lyndon Johnson's nomination. The MFDP challenge had angered him, brought him to the edge of despair just the day before, but by Wednesday the president, still in Washington and still keeping private counsel on his vice presidential choice, was back in control of events and his own emotions. This was, after all, his convention. He had planned nearly every second of it well in advance, and now, with his hand hidden primarily behind Bill Moyers, he micromanaged every nuance of the events. He chose the convention theme song, "Hello Lyndon," and the convention motto, "Let Us Continue." He designed the convention rostrum with its two forty-foot portraits of himself that towered above significantly smaller portraits of the great liberal monarchs who had gone before him: FDR, Truman, and JFK. He also chose those who would nominate him—twice; first: California governor Pat Brown, then his good friend Texas governor John Connally—the other man who was shot in Dallas. He would accept his party's nomination the next day, August 27, on his fifty-sixth birthday.[76]

The party had, for the last four conventions, either split wide open or wallowed in divisive floor fights over aspects of the platform. Not in 1964. By the time the platform reached the Platform Committee it had already been written, largely by Frederick Dutton, the assistant secretary of state for congressional relations, and Moyers, and approved by Johnson weeks before. Just as the president wanted, the platform attacked the Klan, the John Birch Society, and the Communist Party, all by name. No one missed the point. The GOP had refused to confront extremism, and Johnson wanted the nation to know that it was the Republicans—and not the Democrats—who believed that extremism was not a vice. The platform also contained a strong civil rights plank. The southerners who might have objected to it had left. There were no objections. The platform was passed out of Congressman Carl Albert's Platform Committee and passed on the floor without so much as a whimper.

Back at the White House, the president teased reporters about his decision to choose a vice presidential candidate. In an impromptu press conference on the White House lawn he told the press corps that he had invited Hubert Humphrey to Washington to discuss the decision. That was, of course, if Hubert was not too busy, "if he can come down."[77] Johnson continued to drag the story out as far as possible.

By that time, Humphrey had known for two days that he was LBJ's choice—and Johnson had probably known for months. Having milked the decision process for all he could, Johnson and Humphrey announced to the press that afternoon that it would be Humphrey. Immediately, Johnson realized that he did not want the delegates in Atlantic City to hear his decision from the press, so he told his staff that he would fly to Atlantic City. Most of his aides did not want him to go. Reedy was afraid the president might be accused of hogging the limelight; but as Johnson saw it, that was the purpose of the convention.[78] That evening, with Humphrey at his side, Johnson finally let go of his last card and made the announcement that everyone had been waiting for. "This is not a sectional choice," he told the delegates, knowing that only the South would object. "This is not merely the way to balance the ticket," he said, in reference to the reason that he, for the most part, had been placed on the ticket in 1960. "This is simply the best man in America for the job."[79] But, of course, Humphrey did balance the ticket. Johnson needed Humphrey's northern, African-American, midwestern, labor appeal. Humphrey was very much a part of Johnson's consensus building, of his desire to be president of all the people.

The South did object, although that response was no surprise. James J. Kilpatrick, writing for the Richmond *News Leader*, complained that Humphrey had been a co-founder of the liberal Americans for Democratic Action in the late 1940s. The ADA, Kilpatrick wrote, "In the demonology of Dixie . . . has larger horns than CORE." Kilpatrick also recalled, as did many other southerners, the role Humphrey played in forcing a civil rights plank into the 1948 Democratic party platform, "when his razor tongue slashed at Southern delegations." Then he quoted from Humphrey's famous speech before the 1948 convention. " 'The time has arrived to get out of the shadows of States' rights.' " He went on to complain of Humphrey's role in passing the Civil Rights Act earlier that year. "He whipped the Southern senators. And he got his bill. . . . In the whole of the Convention Hall," Kilpactrick concluded, "Lyndon Johnson could not have chosen one man less palatable to the South."[80] Johnson still hoped he could pull the South into line before November, but the South, for the Democrats, simply did not carry the electoral weight it once did. Johnson needed support from other areas and other groups.

* * *

In mid-July Robert Kennedy had decided to run in the New York Senate race against Kenneth Keating, a one-term incumbent Republican with strong moderate leanings toward the Dewey–Rockefeller wing of the party. It seemed that after eight months of misdirection, indecision, and instability, Kennedy had finally found his place. Through August, Kennedy and his people surveyed the New York race, working to line up the state's party bosses, collect polling data, and influence the press. The key to New York boiled down to New York City mayor Robert Wagner, who clearly resented the Kennedy family's intrusion into his political world. Finally, after a great deal of pressure and wrangling, Wagner came around and endorsed Kennedy on August 22. Kennedy immediately leased a house on Long Island to establish residence, and three days later, the day after the convention opened its doors in Atlantic City, he announced his candidacy from the steps of Gracie Mansion. With Wagner at his side, Kennedy said that the president would help with his campaign.[81] Hoping to draw attention to the carpetbagger issue, that Kennedy was not a New Yorker, Keating announced the same day that he would not be a candidate from Massachusetts. He also announced he would not endorse Barry Goldwater.[82]

* * *

Newsweek called Thursday, August 27, coronation day.[83] Johnson and Humphrey had been nominated the day before, and the nominations had closed immediately. There would be no challengers to the ticket. Only at that moment was Johnson willing to give Robert Kennedy the podium. He had worried, nearly beyond any reason, that Kennedy might somehow entice the delegates in Atlantic City, through a tearful recollection of his dead brother, to take the nomination away. In fact, Kennedy had had a short film prepared about his brother's time in office to be shown at the convention, entitled *A Thousand Days*. Johnson feared it, feared the power it might have over the convention. The film had been scheduled by the Arrangements Committee to be shown on Monday, the convention's opening day. But Johnson stepped in and had the film rescheduled until after his nomination. Could such a film have carried the day and hoisted Kennedy to the nomination over a sitting president? Clark Clifford thought so. I "recall very clearly," he told an interviewer five years later, "the President's wisdom in getting that particular problem settled and disposed of before the convention because the convention could have run away at that time and have nominated Robert Kennedy because of the emotional reaction with reference to his brother."[84] A reporter at *Newsweek*, recording the events as they happened, agreed. "Had the original schedule held fast, the impact on the convention might well have posed

229

an unbeatable challenge."[85] Roland Evans and Robert Novak, in their biography of Johnson written just a year after the convention, also agreed. The president's changing of the film date "might have been necessary to head off [a] revolt on the boardwalk at Atlantic City."[86] Possibly with good reason, Johnson believed that Kennedy could have snatched the nomination had he wanted it.

Senator Henry "Scoop" Jackson was scheduled to introduce Kennedy. He motioned Kennedy up to the podium from a runway below the seats. One of Kennedy's aides in the Justice Department, John Seigenthaler, was with Kennedy as he approached the microphone. The moment the crowd caught a glimpse of Bobby, Seigenthaler recalled, "it just hit. I mean it really hit. . . . The roar, the applause, the tears, It just went on and on." Each time Kennedy raised his hands to bring it to an end, "it reached a new intensity." "Let it go on," Jackson whispered to Kennedy. "Let them just do it, Bob. Let them get it out of their system."[87] Depending on the source, the ovation lasted anywhere from thirteen to twenty-two minutes.[88] It was by any account a tremendous cathartic release of sympathy, support, and emotion.

When the crowd finally calmed, Kennedy made the most memorable speech of the convention, his voice often wavering but always strong. Near the end of the speech he quoted a passage from *Romeo and Juliet* given to him by Jackie:

> When he shall die
> Take him and cut him out in little stars
> And he will make the face of heaven so fine
> That all the world will be in love with night
> And pay no worship to the garish sun.[89]

It was a tearful moment. But to anyone paying attention the symbolism was clear. Johnson understood it. He knew he was being likened to a "garish sun" being outshined by "little stars." And he did not like it.[90]

The film *A Thousand Days* followed Kennedy's speech. Not only had Johnson arranged for the film to follow his nomination on the last day of the convention, he had also stepped in and pressured the company that made the film, Wolper Productions, to cut out all images of Bobby.[91] The film was moving; the delegates in some sense seemed to be saying goodbye. "The memorial film itself," Evans and Novak wrote, "evoked an unrestrained weeping seldom seen on the floor of any National Convention."[92] At the very end of the film Richard Burton's deep voice resonated through the conven-

The 1964 Democratic ticket. *(Johnson Library)*

tion center: "Ask every person if he's heard the story, and tell it strong and clear if he has not, that once there was a fleeting wisp of glory . . . called Camelot." "It was plain," *Newsweek* reported, "that many had come to believe it."[93]

Following the film, the president and Lady Bird entered the hall to a standing ovation from the delegates. Just a few months before, America had been forced to face the shock of the dour Lyndon Johnson following the glamorous Jack Kennedy in the White House. Many of the delegates, having just seen *A Thousand Days*, must have experienced those same feelings again as Johnson and his wife moved slowly toward the presidential box. Moments later, the president gave his acceptance speech. Written by his new speechwriter, John Steinbeck, it was not the rousing speech it probably should have been. It was, in fact, probably one of the worst speeches of Johnson's political career.[94] But it carried an important message. He made it clear that he was done with Kennedy's work and that now he was prepared to do his own. "I ask the American people for a mandate," he said, "not just to keep things going. I ask the American people for a mandate to begin." Then he ended his speech with the phrase, "Let us be on our way."

One theme in the speech was unity—as it is the theme of most such convention speeches. But for Johnson, unity and consensus building was his life's theme. He wanted desperately to pull all parts of the nation together. It was, in fact, his ideal, his dream. "I am determined," he said, "in all the time that is mine to use all the talents that I have for bringing this great, lovable land, this great Nation of ours, together—together in greater unity in pursuit of this common purpose. I truly believe that we someday will see an America that knows no North or South, no East or West—an America that is undivided by creed or color, and untorn by suspicion or strife."[95] Theodore White wrote that "All Lyndon Johnson's life and political art had been spent in trying to reconcile differences, to bind and hold them together and, out of them, to make law. . . ." Now, he added, this was "to become the campaign program, the campaign theme." Possibly because there was nothing new about a politician talking about unity, the press had little to say about Johnson's theme. White, however, went on to call it "one of Johnson's greatest triumphs."[96]

It was Humphrey who went on the attack and brought the convention to its feet. He made it clear to the Democrats before him, and to the nation, that Barry Goldwater was outside the mainstream of American politics. Humphrey recounted policy after policy that had received bipartisan support in Congress and in the nation, but had been opposed by Goldwater. The list included the nuclear test ban treaty, the tax cut, the civil rights bill, the establishment of an arms control and disarmament agency, the National Defense Education Act, emergency funding for the United Nations, and on and on. Humphrey then followed each example by the refrain, "But not Senator Goldwater," and the Democrats went wild. Over and over he brought the crowd up, as they shouted in unison, "But not Barry Goldwater." "Yes, yes my fellow Americans," Humphrey continued, "it is a fact that [Barry Goldwater] is not in the mainstream of his party. In fact he has not even touched the shore. . . . I say to those responsible and forward-looking Republicans—and there are thousands of them—we welcome you to the banner of Lyndon B. Johnson; we welcome your support. Yes, we extend the hand of fellowship."[97] It was Humphrey's rousing invitation to moderate Republicans that was the true capstone of the convention—and the central theme of the Democratic campaign.

Following the speeches a birthday party was held for the president in the convention ballroom above the convention hall. The partygoers paid a thousand dollars each to attend the event. The cake was a giant red, white, and blue map of the United States, and various groups of ethnic singers sang "Happy Birthday." The party then ooed and ahed at the three tons of fireworks exploded from the Atlantic City beach. The entire event was televised.[98] Afterward the president said, "I've been going to conventions since 1928, and this is the best of all."[99] Theodore White gushed, "Big Daddy had had the biggest birthday party in the biggest and best country in the world."[100]

10

Goldwater and Johnson in
a Cause Predetermined

By the time the conventions ended and the general campaign began, most of the drama and excitement of the 1964 campaign was over. The polls had shown for months that Goldwater stood no significant chance of defeating Johnson in the general election. For Goldwater, the objective became little more than to try and avoid being embarrassed in November, to avoid dragging down other Republican candidates, and to, somehow, give some legitimacy to the conservative message so the party could build on it for the future. For Johnson the objective became to push for as big a victory as possible, a huge mandate, so that he could fulfill his greatest desire: to be the president of all the people—or at least as many of the people as possible.

Just about everything was on the president's side. The economy was strong. The nation had enjoyed over forty consecutive months of economic growth under the Kennedy–Johnson administration and all economic indicators pointed to continued growth. The gross national product was up; consumer spending was up; business profits were up; and unemployment was down, below 5 percent in the summer just before the election. The Democrats could take credit for the creation of some 4 million jobs since Kennedy's inauguration.[1] There was also a sense of action in Washington. Johnson, it seemed, was fulfilling the great promises Kennedy had made at his inauguration, doing what JFK had said he would do. Just since Dallas, Johnson had built a powerful consensus on Capitol Hill and pushed through Congress the Civil Rights Act, the Wilderness Preservation Act, and the War on Poverty's Economic Opportunities Act with its Head Start, VISTA, Job Corps, and Community Action programs. He had also passed a tax cut and slashed the budget, initiatives that boosted the economy and won the hearts of much of big business. In addition, African Americans were in line;

labor was in line. And from a regional standpoint, the president looked strong in every part of the country except the deepest of the Deep South and parts of the Far West. Johnson worried about the South, he worried about California—and the possibility of losing his home state of Texas kept him up nights. But beyond that, the president was solid.

Johnson's greatest strengths were in domestic affairs. He had dealt very little with foreign policy. But through 1964, as the election approached and with the election in mind, he had achieved his foreign policy objectives—as limited as they were. He had shown strength in dealing with Vietnam while at the same time showing restraint. The message was clear: if need be, he would stand up to communism with necessary force, but he would not send American boys to war unless it was absolutely necessary. It was a stance that America seemed to like, particularly as the election approached and Goldwater (no matter how hard he tried to dispel the image) was perceived as an impulsive warmonger. At the same time, the Soviets and the Chinese were both deeply involved in their own internal problems and in a growing conflict with each other. Their power may not have diminished, but their aggressions had. Thus, with the exception of the events in Southeast Asia, which appeared to be of only minor consequence, all seemed right with the world. As the election approached, Johnson could take credit for a nation that was generally at peace, its interventions justified and controlled, its conflicts considerably less tense than during the anxious Kennedy years.

The polls reflected the nation's satisfaction with the administration and its dissatisfaction with Goldwater. Before the Republican convention in mid-July (while the Republican candidates slashed at each other), Johnson's advantage over Goldwater was extremely high, with 76 percent of those polled supporting the president and only 24 percent supporting Goldwater, then the presumed Republican nominee.[2] "I feel sure," Ken O'Donnell told Walter Jenkins, "we'll see a more normal balance in the spring and summer."[3] But Goldwater never really recovered from those terrible early deficits. His post-convention surge only jumped his numbers to a paltry 36 percent approval rating to Johnson's almost insurmountable 64 percent.[4] Right in the midst of the Republican campaign, Gallup gave Johnson a whopping edge of 77 percent to Goldwater's barely measurable 20 percent.[5] By late August, *Newsweek* gave Goldwater a bit of a push, but only to 29 percent against the president's 65 percent.[6]

Time broke the numbers down by regions, giving Johnson a commanding lead in every part of the nation except the South. In the Northeast, Kennedy country, his approval rating topped an amazing 70 percent. In the Midwest it

235

was 59 percent; and in the West, perceived as Goldwater country, the president had a 62 percent approval rating to Goldwater's 33 percent. In the South, Goldwater was ahead 51 percent to 40 percent.[7] Johnson had been showing remarkable strength in the polls since the early summer. Among the White House staff, however, the election was not counted as a certain Johnson victory until late September when the polls still had not changed and it was clear that Goldwater's campaign was in disarray and going nowhere. Not surprisingly, the campaign of 1964 (between the conventions and the election) was of little interest to the American people. It was often pushed off the front pages of the *New York Times* and was seldom the lead story on the nightly news.

Johnson, however, was not satisfied with only winning. He wanted a landslide, a mandate from the people to carry on his policies. This meant that he address every problem, try to pacify every voting bloc, shake every hand. He refused even to concede Arizona. He considered his biggest problem to be the white backlash, and it burdened him. The Civil Rights Act had alienated the South, something that Johnson, of course, had expected. He saw that the civil rights movement was powerful, with a great deal of national support, and that it was bound to succeed by bringing an end to de jure segregation in the South. It was the race issue, Johnson believed, that had handicapped the South, his own region—both economically and politically—since the Civil War. He believed that the Civil Rights Act would go a long way toward releasing the South from that burden and would allow the region to join the rest of the nation as an equal. Many white southerners, however, disagreed and chose to fight the bill and oppose the administration on the issue. In addition, the backlash turned out to go beyond the Deep South. As George Wallace dragged the issue north, and as Goldwater picked it up when Wallace dropped out of the race, it became apparent that large numbers of northerners also opposed the Civil Rights Act and were prepared to vote for Goldwater. To make matters worse, riots broke out in several east coast cities between the conventions in the summer of 1964, and that added fuel to the backlash. Johnson lamented the backlash, the recalcitrant South, and those northerners who opposed the Civil Rights Act and his administration. He also believed that Goldwater was fanning the flames. "It's to his advantage to encourage this backlash," the president told John Connally in July.[8] Johnson's constant defense against the backlash was the "frontlash," those voters who now supported him (presumably moderates from the Republican party) because they believed in the policies of his administration—or disliked the policies of Goldwater. When the votes were counted, the backlash had little impact on the election. Johnson's frontlash was real, even substantial.

One potential problem that Johnson faced was apathy. There was a fear among his staff that campaign workers, anticipating an easy Johnson victory, would not put out a necessary get-out-the-vote effort. "One of our great problems," Ken O'Donnell told the president, "unquestionably is a sense of overconfidence, which leads to apathy in the field."[9] There was also a fear that voters would not bother to vote because the pollsters had already called the election for Johnson, "a la Dewey in 1948," White House aide Henry Wilson told his boss Larry O'Brien in the summer.[10] It may have been this fear of apathy among workers and voters that finally sent Johnson out onto the campaign trail in September, to rally the faithful and bring in the landslide he so wanted.

* * *

The tone inside the Republican party following the clash of philosophies in San Francisco immediately turned from division to unity—or at least an attempt at unity. In the days following the convention, Goldwater called an organizational meeting of the Republican National Committee and promised that he had not intended to purge the party of moderates and that he would do all he could to heal the wounds he had opened in San Francisco. He then turned to seeking the approval, and ultimately the endorsement, of the only man who could pull the divided party back together, Dwight D. Eisenhower.

In the first days of August, Goldwater called on Ike at Gettysburg. The two men had not gotten along well over the last ten years, mostly because of Goldwater's actions and utterances. In 1953, Goldwater had voted with GOP conservatives against the confirmation of Charles Bohlen, Eisenhower's choice as ambassador to the Soviet Union. Four years later, Goldwater had infuriated Eisenhower by voting with southern conservatives to weaken the administration's civil rights bill. That same year Goldwater decided to break with Eisenhtower, and in a speech on the Senate floor went so far as to accuse the administration of "aped New Deal antics."[11] Then a year later, in 1958, Goldwater led the charge by the Republican right in demanding the resignation of Eisenhower's chief of staff and most trusted aide, Sherman Adams, for influence peddling.[12] The Adams incident was not only embarrassing for the Eisenhower administration just before the 1958 congressional elections (in which the Republicans were beaten badly), but it continued the process of dividing the party between the right and the Eisenhower moder-

237

ates, a division that the GOP was still grappling with in 1964. Consequently, when these two men met in Gettysburg on August 1964 they both called themselves Republicans, but they were not political allies. One was the founder of modern Republicanism; the other had spent his political life spurning it.

Goldwater emerged from the Gettysburg meeting speaking in decidedly moderate tones. He may well have realized that to rally moderate support he would have to present himself to Eisenhower as a moderate, or at least more moderate than the "extremism is no vice" candidate in San Francisco. Or Goldwater's moderation may have come at Ike's insistence, the price Goldwater had to pay for the general's endorsement. Nevertheless, the meeting was something of a turning point in Goldwater's stance, and Ike came away a Goldwater supporter, or at least, as he told a friend, he believed the candidate's image was much worse than the candidate himself.[13]

Another outcome of the meeting was an announcement by Goldwater, again possibly at Ike's insistence, that the prominent Republican party leaders would meet, resolve their differences, and heal their wounds. The meeting was to take place on August 12 in Hershey, Pennsylvania, just down the road from Gettysburg and outside of Harrisburg—in William Scranton's backyard. The objective of the meeting would be to tone down Goldwater's extremist image. The irony of the occasion was that several of those in attendance were the very ones who had shackled Goldwater with just that image. Now he would have to win their support—the support of men whose political philosophy he despised, politicians he had fought and insulted (and been insulted by) for several months.

Ike, as the unifying force, attended, and the event was hosted by Scranton. Some thirty other GOP governors and gubernatorial candidates from around the country also attended, but it was the party leadership (Nixon, Romney, Rockefeller, Miller, Eisenhower, and Scranton) who met behind closed doors for nearly three hours and tried desperately to hash out their differences. Just to make sure that everyone understood where the meeting was headed, Eisenhower oversaw the writing of the speech Goldwater delivered to the group, even assigning his own speechwriters, Bryce Harlow and Ed McCabe, to the job.[14] Under the general's direction there would be no surprise statements condoning extremism on any level. Then, in his opening statement, Eisenhower said, "I have read the statement [Goldwater] is going to make. I respect it and admire it. And because of this," he added, "I am going to make a definite statement . . . that I will not only support the ticket and the program, but will urge all other Republicans to do so."[15] He went on to call for party unity, observing that there are differences among the party's leadership, but, he said, "let's bring them out and see whether there isn't an honest answer that all of us can support, and do it with enthusiasm and with all the might and energy which the Good Lord gave us."[16] Nixon then added that "everyone in this room" will be able to support Goldwater's statement.[17] What followed was the new, moderate Goldwater, ready to conciliate, compromise, even apologize.

He began his speech by addressing the problem that had haunted him since he began campaigning: "[T]he number one problem facing the Republican Party [is the belief] . . . that the election of a Republican President in November will somehow lead to war." He then argued that his election would, in fact, "mean an immediate return to the proven policy of peace through strength which was the hallmark of the Eisenhower era." He went on to promise that he would not name a Secretary of Defense or a Secretary of State, "or other national security posts until I have first discussed my plans . . . with General Eisenhower, Dick Nixon, and other experienced leaders seasoned in world affairs. . . ." He then added that he supported the United Nations, wanted to strengthen it, and even make use of it. This was clearly intended as a direct rejection of the John Birch Society position, expressed in its slogan "Get the U.S. out of the U.N."

He then turned to social programs. At several points during the primaries he had called for a "restructure" of Social Security by making it voluntary. He had also threatened to dismantle a number of programs designed to aid the poor and the elderly. In Hershey he backpedaled. He promised that as president he would "undertake to help people with those tasks they cannot adequately perform for themselves." Then he added, "let me repeat, for perhaps the millionth time—lest there be any doubt in anyone's mind—that I support the Social Security system and I want to see it strengthened. . . . [E]very American," he continued, "will be assured of a compassionate and understanding approach by the Federal government to the human problems growing out of automation, rising costs, incidents of catastrophic illness, unemployment, and cost of education, and the like."

On civil rights, he pledged, "in the literal words of the President's oath of office, 'faithful execution' of the 1964 Civil Rights Law and all other civil rights laws. . . . I will," he added, "use the great moral influence of the Presidency to promote the prompt and peaceful observance of civil rights laws." Then, believing that he would clear up all the talk of extremism, he said, "Let me reiterate what I have said over and over and over in this campaign: I seek the support of no extremists, of the left or the right."[18]

Following the speeches of others in attendance, the discussion fell to the question of civil rights and the backlash. Romney, particularly, feared that the Republican party was about to become the party of racism. "[A]s far as I can determine," he told his fellow Republicans, "people are concerned about whether this is a racist campaign. . . ." He continued, adding his fear that the GOP will be seen by voters as the heir to Wallace's racism, that Goldwater's states' rights advocacy will be misperceived as racism.[19] Then Romney caught a glimpse of a problem that Democrats had faced for decades: "And I don't know how you pick up on this other vote and at the same time retain the Negro. . . ."[20] To satisfy Romney, Goldwater simply promised to leave the question alone, the same promise he had made to Johnson just two weeks before. "I will promise you with every degree of seriousness and strength that I have that I will never talk about racism. I don't even intend to talk about civil rights." Eisenhower added, "I don't know anything about this backlash; I would never mention it. I would say, this is something we will have no part of."[21]

Time magazine reported that the meeting was "remarkable."[22] David Brinkley said on NBC News, "Eisenhower joined the team wholeheartedly, Rockefeller's enthusiasm was not excessive, other Republicans either joined in or said nothing, Goldwater became more of a moderate and the whole thing smacked of the sweet smell of moderation." Ike apparently got caught up in sixties jargon and called it a "love-fest."[23] The Republicans seemed united.

But they were not. At best it was a veneer of harmony. The two sides had simply been fighting in the trenches for too long. Just to make sure that everyone understood the obvious, Goldwater, near the end of the meeting, let go one jab to the enemy's face. He was the candidate of the party, he told them, and they—the moderates sitting before him—were not. "I think it's time," he said, "that [you] decide that you've got a candidate for the President and Vice President." Then he added, "You might not like us, but you're stuck with us, and we are Republicans. . . ."[24] After the meeting, Eisenhower told Nixon, "You know, before we had this meeting, I thought that Goldwater was just stubborn. Now I'm convinced that he is just plain dumb."[25]

The Hershey meeting was only partially successful. Goldwater most likely assembled the meeting and moderated his stance as a condition of Eisenhower's public endorsement. He got that. "I am right on his team," Ike told *Time*.[26] But certainly part of that deal was support from the other moderates. Scranton and Nixon supported the ticket, even campaigned for Goldwater—undoubtedly at Ike's urging. But Rockefeller and Romney did not. The meeting was also designed to dispel Goldwater's extremist image, an image certainly created by the candidate's own words and actions, but reinforced over and over again by Rockefeller, Scranton, and the moderates throughout the entire year. That failed. The extremist image was indelible, about to be picked up and amplified by the Democrats with a vengeance that the Republican moderates had never approached or imagined. A few statements of moderation at Hershey could not change that.

* * *

Following what was much closer to a real "love-fest" in Atlantic City, Lyndon Johnson, clearly riding a wave that marked a high point in his manic personality, rounded up his aides, his biggest supporters, the press, and his new vice presidential candidate and headed for his ranch just east of Fredericksburg in the Texas hill country. Many on board Air Force One that evening had no advanced notice of the trip, including Humphrey; "our own plans a matter of indifference," he recalled.[27] At the airport, several supporters were on hand to see the Johnsons off and to offer congratulations. One was Katherine Graham, owner of the *Washington Post*. According to Humphrey, she was standing on the other side of a fence from Johnson. He "reached over," Humphrey wrote in his memoirs, "and literally lifted her off her feet. . . . 'On the plane, Katie,'" he told her, "'we're going to Texas and we want you with us.'" Humphrey recalled that Graham protested, insisting that she had to return to Washington that evening and that she had no luggage. "Her protests were muted in the bear hug and, moments later, she like the rest of us, was on the way to the ranch."[28]

Johnson apparently wanted to show the press that he and Hubert were more than just political allies, so he planned that the two would go horseback riding. Johnson insisted that Humphrey look the part, so he provided Humphrey with a Texas rancher's outfit—which did not fit. "The pants were huge," Humphrey recalled, "so big that I thought I could put both my legs in one pant leg and still dance a polka. The jacket draped like a tent over a shirt whose neck was several sizes too large. I looked ridiculous and I felt ridiculous as I smiled wanly from under a cowboy hat that was made for his head and clearly not for mine."[29]

The next step was actually to ride a horse. "Hubert, get on that horse," Johnson told Humphrey, "we're going for a ride." Humphrey knew nothing of horseback riding, and Johnson had provided him a horse that was much too big and spirited—possibly intending to see how Humphrey would handle himself under such conditions. "There seemed to be an acre of cameramen

The victorious Democratic ticket. (*Johnson Library*)

and reporters grinning and clicking as the horse sort of reared," Humphrey recalled, "leaving me filled with fear and clutching that horse like a tiny child on his first merry-go-round ride, hanging on for dear life."[30] Humphrey was clearly humiliated by the incident, although most press photos of the events showed Humphrey in a good light.[31] Nicholas Katzenbach said later that the situation was "almost like Johnson holding Humphrey up by the ears the way he did his beagle."[32] Several months earlier, Johnson had pulled one of his beagles up off the ground by its ears to the delight of the White House press corps and the disgust of animal rights activists.

* * *

The Johnson campaign, at first glance, appeared to be unfocused and disorganized. Just before Atlantic City, John Connally had told Johnson that the best campaign was no campaign, that he should not travel, should not confront Goldwater, that he should simply let the nation know that he was taking care of the peoples' business. Connally even suggested a front-porch, William McKinley–type campaign. The president had, said Connally, already won the election. "Why bother?" was the reasoning. During a press conference at the White House, Johnson was asked about the coming campaign. He responded, pointing to the Rose Garden: "That's where I'm going to run my campaign from this fall."[33] As late as September 5 he was still telling the press that he would make "as many appearances as we think we can without neglecting the interests of the nation."[34] Throughout most of September, that was the president's campaign style.

Similar advice was coming from Johnson's advisors. Jack Valenti, who carried on as a sort of campaign coordinator in the absence of any appointed director, told Johnson that "the President stays above the battle. He is President and acts like one." The strategy should be, he added, "to treat Goldwater not as an equal, who has credentials to be President, but as a radical, a preposterous candidate. . . ."[35] Even as late as October 2, just a month before the election, *Time* complained that the campaign was boring, primarily because Johnson refused to engage Goldwater on any level.[36]

One problem for Johnson in this noncampaign strategy was the continual call by the press for debates. The 1960 Nixon–Kennedy debates had already reached the level of legend in American politics, and there was some national interest that debates of that type should become a regular part of the election process. The president, however, had no intention of giving Goldwater equal time by appearing with him on national television, where Johnson would

243

have nothing to gain and everything to lose. Goldwater, of course, would have nothing to lose and everything to gain by going on the attack. In addition, the lessons of the Kennedy–Nixon debates must surely have been apparent to Johnson: he was not about to match debating skills and physical appearances with the handsome, telegenic Goldwater. One way to make it difficult, if not impossible, to have debates was to change the law. Section 315 of the Communications Act allowed debates only if all candidates were given equal television time. In 1964 there were at least six other candidates running for president, representing parties ranging from Prohibition to Socialist. In 1960, to allow for the Nixon–Kennedy debates, Section 315 was waved through an act of Congress. In August 1964, Congress was debating an act that would permanently eliminate Article 315, paving the way for debates every four years between the candidates of the two major parties. However, on direct orders from the White House that act was killed, making debates legal if only all candidates participated. There was, however, one more loophole in the bill. If the cost of airing the campaign would be split by the two major parties, the minor candidates could be excluded. Dean Burch, head of the Republican National Committee, offered to pay his half. John M. Bailey, chairman of the Democratic National Committee, did not respond to the offer.[37] Thus Johnson succeeded in making debates almost impossible, or at least undesirable. The press continued to ask the president, "Will you debate Goldwater?" And Johnson continually had to duck the question. It is difficult to imagine, however, that any member of the press ever seriously considered the possibility that the president would agree to debate Goldwater. Goldwater, at the same time, refused to push the issue. On the *Jack Paar Show* he actually let the president off the hook. It is "kind of dangerous," he said, "to subject the president of the United States to questioning. . . . [H]e might just slip and say something inadvertently that . . . could change the course of history."[38] There would be no debates in 1964.

Johnson's front-porch campaign began to worry some of the president's aides and supporters. "I am quite concerned," the postmaster general told Valenti in late August, "by what appears to be relatively little organized Johnson for President activity."[39] Stating similar fears, a Johnson supporter in Texas wrote to the White House, "[W]here is the Democratic campaign? Where are the bumper stickers and the paraphernalia? Are the Democrats organized? . . . There is," he added, "a fear of a Dewey-like complacency. . . ."[40] The administration may have appeared complacent, but Johnson's lead was enormous, a lead that even a Truman-like surge at the end by Goldwater could never overcome. So, until late September, Johnson intended to take the high road and campaign by being president. During the summer, however, a campaign had been coming together. Both organization and strategy existed, but it was all very loosely structured. There was, for instance, no campaign manager, "unless," Valenti recalled, "it would be President Johnson himself."[41] That, generally, characterized the campaign. Johnson made all the decisions at the top, with advice, as always, from as many sources as possible. Among the president's aides, Valenti and Moyers had the most influence and the most power among those involved directly in the campaign. Walter Jenkins, Johnson's most trusted aide, was certainly closer to Johnson and had more influence over his decisions than others, but Jenkins's primary role in the administration was to control White House affairs, thus he was not as directly involved in the campaign as Valenti and Moyers. Ken O'Donnell handled scheduling for the president. Larry O'Brien worked with the local and state party organizations. There was a speechwriting team, an advance team, position papers were drawn up regularly, radio and television time was purchased early.[42] Everything was being done. There was even a group, known as the Five O'clock Club, that worked behind the scenes with direct permission from the president to sabotage Goldwater's campaign through such means as sending anti-Goldwater letters to the editors of newspapers throughout the country, printing and distributing anti-Goldwater literature, and even planting spies among Goldwater's closest advisors.[43] The campaign simply gave the appearance of complacency and chaos because the president was not out on the hustings, shaking hands, whistlestopping through the nation, attacking his opponent. "The wonder of the Johnson campaign," Jack Valenti recalled, "is that it worked so well. . . ."[44]

Johnson also refused to bring the Democratic National Committee into the campaign. Most likely, Johnson wanted to keep his campaign management close, with the power under his direct control. He may also have feared that working within the DNC might have exacerbated his own poor image as a party wheeler-dealer, an image that Johnson and his people expected the Republicans to exploit. Hubert Humphrey, however, insisted that Johnson, despite his reputation to the contrary, did not work well within the Democratic party structure, that it was within the party that Johnson had suffered his greatest political defeats and made his worst political enemies. Humphrey also argued that Johnson's great desire to be president of all the people also meant that he wanted to be a president who transcended the confines of the national political party structure. Johnson shunned the DNC because he refused to be just the president of the Democrats. Not unlike the way he perceived his model, Franklin Roosevelt, Johnson expected to be a true national president.[45]

There was also a Johnson campaign strategy—in fact, possibly one of the most effective campaign strategies since Truman defeated Dewey. It was, however, much less complicated. "Our overriding issue in 1964 was very simple," Larry O'Brien recalled. "In one word, Goldwater."[46] "Right now," Valenti wrote to Moyers, "the biggest asset we have is Goldwater's alleged instability in [relation to] atom and hydrogen bombs. . . . 'A-Bomb Barry'— 'wagons in a circle.' . . we need to whack at him EVERY day with gags and humor that deny him any right to be called sane or stable."[47] Then to the president, Valenti expanded his ideas. "Our main strength," he wrote Johnson, "lies not so much in the FOR Johnson but in the AGAINST Goldwater. . . . Therefore, we ought to treat Goldwater . . . as a radical, a preposterous candidate who would ruin this country and our future. . . . We must make him ridiculous and a little scary: trigger-happy, a bomb thrower, a radical, absurd to be President . . . [who] will sell TVA [Tennessee Valley Authority], cancel Social Security, abolish the government, stir trouble in NATO, be the herald of World War III." We must, he added, "Keep fear of Goldwater as unstable, impulsive, reckless in [the] public's mind. This is our strongest asset."[48] Thus, a strategy emerged. "We finally developed," Valenti later recalled in an interview, "that the big issue of the campaign was whose finger do you trust on the button and of course the idea that Goldwater was going to dismantle the great social gains that had been stretched over the years."[49]

This strategy did not, of course, originate with the Democrats. Goldwater and the Republicans largely created this situation. Goldwater had said several times in the New Hampshire primary campaign that Social Security should be voluntary. Rockefeller, and then Scranton, hit him hard on the point, and no matter what Goldwater had said otherwise the statement stuck to him. Over and over, he endorsed Social Security. But the damage was done. The finger-on-the-button issue had developed from Goldwater's statement that NATO commanders should have the authority to use nuclear weapons in the case of a Soviet attack and his insistence that the United States should strive to win the Cold War. Rockefeller, and then again Scranton, used those statements to create an image of Goldwater as a warmonger. Like the Social Security issue, Goldwater could not shake it, no matter how often he described himself as the peace candidate or tried to associate himself with the Eisenhower–Dulles foreign policy of peace through strength. By the time the Democrats sunk their teeth into these issues, the image was indelible in the American mind, put there by Goldwater's own statements and then reinforced and largely exaggerated by the Republican moderates. The Democrats, in their campaign against Goldwater, created nothing. "It wasn't something that we pushed on him," O'Brien defended the administration.[50]

The force of the administration's strategy was a series of television ads that changed the face of American politics by transforming campaign advertising. Prior to 1964, campaign ads were almost always positive and uplifting. The opposing candidate (or his policies) was rarely mentioned. Candidates were most often depicted speaking, campaigning, surrounded by supporters, or in the presence of a figure whose association would bring votes. If a candidate intended to attack his opponent, it was done in the press, never in advertising, and certainly not in television advertising. The process changed in 1964 when the Johnson administration produced the nation's first true attack ads. Possibly the most important legacy of these ads is that they used images, rather than language, to make their points. These ads remain one of the primary legacies of the 1964 presidential campaign.

It was Valenti, the Houston advertising executive, and Bill Moyers, the trained Baptist minister, who masterminded these commercials. They were produced by Doyle, Dane, Bernbach, a New York advertising agency that had made a name in the industry for producing evocative soft-sell ads for Volkswagen and Avis. The cost of the ads was about $3 million, a substantial sum for the time. The national television air time cost $1.7 million, and the time slots that the administration most often purchased followed NBC's *Today* show (directed at women viewers) and small-town national markets during and following the *Lawrence Welk Show*.[51]

The most famous of the Democratic party's 1964 campaign commercials was what has become known as the "Daisy Spot." It is, in fact, usually considered the most famous campaign commercial in history. The ad ran on September 7 during a commercial break in NBC's popular *Monday Night at the Movies*, and only once. It immediately became news and was shown nationwide as part of national news reports for several days afterward. The ad presented a sweet blond little girl (by some accounts Bill Moyers's own daughter) plucking peddles from a daisy and counting—cutely incorrectly—from one to ten. When she reached nine, a powerful male voice took over, counting backward to zero. The camera zoomed in to the little girl's right eye, followed by a flash and a rolling mushroom cloud. There was a pause while the cloud billowed. Then Lyndon Johnson spoke: "These are the stakes, to make a world in which all of God's children can live, or go into the dark. We must either love each other, or we must die." This was followed by a black screen and the voice-over: "Vote for President Johnson November 3rd. The stakes are too high to stay home." The spot produced such a stir (particularly thousands of phone calls to local stations) that Moyers jerked it immediately.[52] Dean Burch, chairman of the Republican National Committee, filed a formal complaint with the Fair Campaign Practices Committee, calling it "libel against the Republican nominee." And Everett Dirksen, clearly intending to represent the Republican party response, wrote an open letter to the vice president of the National Association of Broadcasters to complain that the ad "takes the level of political campaigning to a depth never before approached. . . ."[53] Most complaints to local stations focused on the jarring nature of the ad, but many complaints were directed at the use of such a small child to convey such a harsh message.[54] Immediately after the ad aired, Johnson phoned Moyers: "I guess it did what we Goddamned set out to do, didn't it?"[55]

Despite all the negative responses, Moyers realized that the attention the ad received made it a success, and that convinced him to continue with the television ad strategy. A few days later another ad appeared. This time a young girl, eating an ice cream cone, was on screen for the entire ad. A female voice-over asked:

> Do you know what people used to do? They used to explode atomic bombs in the air. Now children should have lots of vitamin A and calcium, but they shouldn't have strontium 90 or cesium 37. These things come from atomic bombs and they're radioactive. They can make you die. Do you know what people finally did? They got together and signed a Nuclear Test Ban Treaty and radioactive poison started to go away. But now there's a man who wants to be President of the United States and he doesn't like this treaty. He even voted against it. He wants to go on testing more bombs. His name is Barry Goldwater, and if he's elected they might start testing all over again.

As in the "Daisy Spot," the ad ended with a male voice: "Vote for President Johnson on November 3rd. The stakes are too high to stay home." *Time* magazine called this ad "vicious," and complained that it "depicted Goldwater as a man willing to sprinkle a girl's ice cream with cancer-causing strontium 90."[56] Another ad began with an image of an atomic blast and then a short voice-over: "On October 24, 1963, Barry Goldwater said of the atomic bomb, 'just another weapon.'" The voice then asks, "Merely another weapon?" That was followed by the same ending as all the ads: "Vote for President Johnson on November 3rd. The stakes are too high for you to stay home." Still another ad showed a pregnant woman and a young child walking. The voice-over explained that 108 nations had signed the Test Ban Treaty, and that the "Kennedy–Johnson administration joined with other nations in halting poi-

The "Daisy Spot" television commercial depicted a young girl counting the petals from a daisy. When she reached nine, a bold voice took over and counted back to zero. The screen went white, followed by a nuclear mushroom cloud. The message was clear: Goldwater was dangerous. The "Daisy Spot" changed the nature of campaign advertising. *(Johnson Library)*

sonous atomic tests in the atmosphere." Not all ads dealt with Goldwater and the nuclear button. Another spot showed a hand tearing up a Social Security card with the voice-over: "On at least seven occasions Senator Barry Goldwater said that he would change the present Social Security system. But even his running mate, William Miller, admits that Senator Goldwater's voluntary plan would destroy the Social Security system. President Johnson is working to strengthen Social Security. Vote for him on November 3rd." The press responded to this spot by digging up Goldwater quotes on Social Security from the New Hampshire primary and reminding readers that Goldwater had, in fact, said several times that he wanted to make Social Security voluntary. *Time* then quoted the president: "The majority said yes long ago to Social Security. The echo still says no."[57]

Other ads dragged out Goldwater's various musings before the press. At some point in Goldwater's past (possibly as early as the 1930s) Goldwater had voiced his frustrations with northeastern Republican moderates by saying that the nation would be better off if the eastern seaboard were simply sawed off and allowed to float out to sea. In an August 1963 interview in the *Saturday Evening Post*, Stewart Alsop resurrected the statement.[58] Throughout the month before the election, a television ad ran in the Northeast showing a map of the United States with a giant saw cutting the northeastern states away from the rest of the nation—and then the eastern seaboard sinking slowly into the ocean. The male voice-over asked, after quoting Goldwater's statement, "Can a man who makes statements like this be expected to serve all of the people justly and fairly?" The message was clear. Goldwater had no use for the Northeast.

The Glen Canyon Dam spot was a bit different than the others. It was designed to turn Goldwater into the most hated of all types of politicians—the hypocrite pork barrel politico, the elected official whose only purpose was to pump money into his own pet projects at the expense of everyone else. The spot began with a man sitting below the Glen Canyon Dam in Arizona. "This is Arizona," the man begins,

> Barry Goldwater's state. It's dry country out here. Water's priceless. That's why they're building this dam. It's a federal dam. Federal taxes built it. It was sponsored by Barry Goldwater. Now here's the funny part. Barry sponsored this federal dam for his state, but he wanted to sell the TVA dams in Tennessee. He voted against the Hell's Canyon Dam in Idaho, against the Hanford Atomic Power Project in Washington, against public works all over the country. In Barry's book this is creeping socialism, except when it creeps into Arizona.

The ad then ends with, "President Johnson is president of all the people. Vote for him on November 3rd."[59]

All these ads were successful because they conveyed a message effectively. The image that Rockefeller, Scranton, and the Republican moderates had reinforced about Goldwater was now placed on television by the Johnson advertising campaign and sent to every household in America. By election time it hardly mattered what Goldwater thought about nuclear arms or the future of Social Security, or how he would run the nation if elected. The image was stronger than the candidate. Never again would the American electoral process be quite the same.

All of this, of course, was aimed at what Johnson was calling the "frontlash," those moderates who saw Goldwater as a radical, possibly a racist, even dangerous. The intent was to push Goldwater so far to the right in the public mind, to make him so unpalatable to anyone with even moderate tendencies, that they would abandon the Republicans and vote for Johnson. It was the most basic of political tactics: hold the center by forcing the opposition to the fringes. It worked in 1964.

* * *

By the first of September Goldwater's own polling data showed his deficit to be insurmountable at about 27 percent to Johnson's 61 percent, and that he was losing in every national region except the South—and even there his lead was statistically insignificant. His polling data also showed that he was seriously off the mark in confronting issues. Civil rights was, by far, the most important issue to his constituents and he had pledged to avoid it. Some of the issues that he hit the hardest in his campaign speeches (particularly the corruption scandal involving Johnson protégé Bobby Baker, and a lack of morals in the White House, discussed below) barely showed up in the polling data as a national concern.[60] With defeat a near certainty, the Goldwater campaign shifted from a strategy of winning the election to salvaging the message—from a pragmatic political campaign to an ideological crusade. Goldwater hoped he could transcend his horrible image and get his conservative message across to the American people, in fact, educate them about his conservative philosophy. To that end he became a martyr to the cause. Following Hershey, he put all his efforts into explaining himself, trying to show that the poor image he was carrying was not the real Goldwater, that he was not an ogre who would destroy the world and starve the poor to feed the rich. A secondary strategy was to keep from being slaughtered by Johnson,

251

to keep the landslide to a minimum. If he could make a respectable showing, win states in the South and the West while maintaining control of the conservative Midwest and holding the line at 40 or 45 percent of the vote, the foundations for a future conservative movement would be set. He could at least show some strength.

On September 3, Goldwater kicked of his official campaign from the steps of the county courthouse in Prescott, Arizona. His speech was carried heavily in the press and he clearly hoped to use it to reverse misconceptions and confront his poor image. "We must," he said, "proceed with care in our task of cutting the government down to size. Honesty requires that we honor the commitments government has made to all areas of the economy. [We] shall never abandon the needy and the aged—we shall never forsake the helpless." The federal government, he concluded, "Must ease the distress from loss of jobs and income that . . . occasional rough spells [in the economy] may bring." He also promised "an administration that will keep the peace." He went on to add that he would bring an end to the draft; he attacked the federal bureaucracy, and then he spoke of lawlessness in the streets.[61]

Crime was a topic that Goldwater had been adding to his speeches since the convention, and despite his insistence that he would avoid the race issue in the campaign there is little question that he had picked up some of George Wallace's strategy of using code words that did not refer specifically to race or race issues, but that were definitely designed to appeal to the racism in the white mind—words that incited the backlash. Code words, of course, allow the speaker to deny racial intent. Just a week before the Prescott speech, Goldwater told a crowd of the need for increased law and order in the streets of the nation's cities. "I don't have to quote statistics for you to understand what I mean," he said. "You know. Every wife and mother—yes, every woman and girl—knows what I mean." Then in the Prescott speech he added, "our wives, all women, feel unsafe in our streets."[62] *Newsweek* certainly saw the statement as code: "The allusion to racial tensions was plain."[63] During an interview with Robert McNeil on NBC in mid-September, Goldwater denied that he had used code words in his speeches, insisting that there was no connection between the street riots and the civil rights movement.[64] But in his speeches he continued on with the message of crime in the streets, particularly when he spoke in the South and in northern urban areas where Wallace had been popular.

He was, however, never willing to take the race issue much beyond these few code words. In October, when the Democrats were pounding him with their advertising barrage, the Republican National Committee decided to fight back. The result was the RNC's own television attack spot that attempted to link Johnson to national moral decay. The ad filled the screen with shots of urban race riots, drug dealing, and crime. The voice-over asked: "What has happened to America? We have had the good sense to create lovely parks—but we're afraid to use them after dark. We built libraries and galleries to hold the world's greatest art treasures—and we permit the world's greatest collection of smut to be freely available. . . ." Then Goldwater, speaking to the camera, said, "The national morality, by example and by persuasion, should begin at the White House. . . . Now this is not the case today because our country has lacked leadership that treats public offices as a public trust." *Time* described the remainder of the ad as "striptease babes, wild Twisters [dancers], Negro riots. . . ." In March 1964 the press had run a story about Johnson, beer can in hand, driving his Lincoln Continental at breakneck speeds along Texas country roads. The Republican ad, *Time* continued, was "interlaced with shots of a black Lincoln Continental limousine careening madly along a country road, with beer cans being tossed out of the driver's window." Theodore White saw the ad and reported in his *Making of the President—1964*, "Naked-breasted women, beatniks at their revels, Negroes rioting and looting in the streets succeeded each other in a phantasmagoric film. . . ."[65] After NBC refused to run the spot, Goldwater finally intervened and, seeing too many black faces, pronounced the spot "racist" and demanded it be pulled. It never ran.[66] Most likely, Goldwater saw no reason to sink to the bottom in a losing effort. He continued on with his own television advertising strategy, which included buying thirty five-minute time slots in which he outlined his various positions. These slots were expensive. In fact, Goldwater spent 40 percent more on television advertising than Johnson.[67]

Following his first speeches of the official campaign, Goldwater left his home state for the friendly surroundings of Los Angeles. It was September 1964. At Dodger Stadium, before 53,000 fans, World War II hero Jimmie Doolittle introduced Goldwater as "the leader of the modern American Revolution."[68] Other speakers included ex-actor George Murphy, who was running neck-and-neck for the Senate against JFK's press secretary Pierre Salinger, and actor Ronald Reagan, the head of California's Goldwater campaign. Following advice from University of Chicago economist Milton Friedman, Goldwater emphasized the need to reduce taxes, and then he argued that such a reduction would fuel the economy, which would, in turn, allow for debt reduction, a balanced budget, and even increased military spending.[69] The press questioned the feasibility of such an economic philosophy that promised a tax cut while significantly increasing the military budget.

This set the stage for an important economic distinction between the Republicans and the Democrats after the 1964 election, with the Republicans insisting that Friedman's economic philosophy would work, while Democrats argued that it would plunge the nation too deeply into debt.[70] From there the Goldwater campaign stopped in Seattle, Minneapolis, and then upstate New York and Chicago. It was in Chicago where Goldwater, as he almost always did, attacked the excessive power of the executive branch of the federal government, but here he addressed a new issue, the excessive power of the judicial branch. The Supreme Court, he said, maintained an "obsessive concern for the rights of the criminal defendant." He also attacked the court's decision outlawing school prayer. To most Americans, Goldwater appeared to be tilting at windmills by this time in his campaign. He was, however, laying much of the groundwork for the future of American conservatism.

On September 15, Goldwater headed on a two-week tour through the friendly confines of the South. Large crowds of white southerners met him everywhere he went: 30,000 in Memphis, 24,000 in George Wallace's Montgomery, 27,000 in New Orleans.[71] In a major speech in Charlotte he called Humphrey a "socialistic radical," and referred to Johnson as the "interim president." Throughout his southern swing, Goldwater always hit hard at the power of the federal government at the expense of the states. It was this states' rights message that the southerners wanted to hear; and no one was under the illusion that states' rights meant anything in the South except the right of white southerners to perpetuate racial segregation. "Federal power," Goldwater said in Charlotte, "crushes the concurrent powers of the state in one field or another, until the states have no will, and finally no resources, moral or financial, of their own."[72] In Montgomery he called for a transfer of "decisions on domestic services to governors, legislatures, mayors, city councils, boards of education, and similar local agencies—where they belong."[73]

Goldwater's objective in the South was to push conservative white southern Democrats into the Republican party—not just for the 1964 election, but for the future of American conservatism. He concentrated his efforts on the Carolinas, Florida, Tennessee, Alabama, Georgia, and Louisiana, all regarded by Republican strategists as key conservative states. Only Texas and California were considered more important. He stayed away from Virginia because he believed that Senator Harry Byrd, a powerful conservative Democrat, would lead Virginians to vote against Johnson. And he refused to go to Mississippi because he feared that his appearance there might make worse the already tense racial situation in that state.

If Goldwater was going to succeed in winning over the white South for the Republicans he would need a southern leader, a symbol, who would change affiliation from Democrat to Republican, someone who could tell white southern conservatives that their interests, the interests of the South, and the interests of the Republican party were all three the same. That symbol, Goldwater hoped, would be South Carolina senator Strom Thurmond.

Southern conservatives had been disenchanted with the Democratic party at least since 1948 when conservative Democrats in several southern states left their party and formed the Dixiecrats. For some in the Dixiecrat party the issue was race, for others it was states' rights, and for still others the two issues were the same, since states' rights allowed the South to deal with race issues without federal interference. The 1948 Dixiecrat presidential candidate was Strom Thurmond, then the governor of South Carolina, and now, in 1964, that state's junior senator and a venerable symbol of southern states' rights, southern racism, and even white supremacy in opposition to the civil rights movement. Ever since the Civil Rights Act was passed, Goldwater had courted Thurmond, not just for an endorsement, but to make the big jump and change parties. The two men not only had a great deal in common politically, they were also good friends. Thurmond had never forgotten that Goldwater had aided the southern cause during the filibuster of the 1957 Civil Rights Act by taking the Senate floor long enough to give Thurmond a breather away from the podium. Then, when Johnson chose Humphrey—the very personification of post-war America liberalism and civil rights activism —Thurmond decided that the Democrats had lost their way. But more importantly, he decided that the Republican party was the way of the future for the South.[74]

On September 12, just three days before Goldwater left for his southern tour, Thurmond told Goldwater that he would make the switch. CBS News broke the story on September 15, and the next day Thurmond flew to South Carolina to explain his intentions to the people of his state, many of whom were ideologically split between their historical obligation to the Democratic party and the emerging conservative philosophy of Barry Goldwater and the Republicans. What he said (and even the party switch itself) all appeared at first to be little more than symbolic. It certainly would do little to help Goldwater's 1964 candidacy. But Thurmond said what so many southerners felt in 1964. It was, in fact, an old song. With a giant poster of Goldwater behind him, the senator from South Carolina told southerners that the "Democratic Party has abandoned the people." It is now, he said, "the party of minority groups, power-hungry union leaders, political bosses, and businessmen looking for government contracts and favors. . . ." The party, he added, "had

In 1964 South Carolina senator Strom Thurmond made the dramatic shift from southern conservative Democrat to Goldwater Republican. For white southern conservatives, Thurmond's change of party affiliation seemed to say that the Republicans would do more than the Democrats to protect southern values. *(Clemson University Libraries)*

encouraged lawlessness, civil unrest and mob actions." If the Democrats remain in power, "freedom as we know it in this country is doomed, and individuals will be destined to lives of regulation, control, coercion, intimidation and subservience to" Washington. He concluded by asserting that the "future of freedom and constitutional government is at stake, and this requires that I do everything in my power to help Barry Goldwater return our Nation to constitutional government. . . ."[75]

Thurmond's switch was important because he was an important southern leader—in many ways, himself a symbol of the white South. When Strom Thurmond became a Republican it was acceptable for others to follow his lead. In the month prior to election day, Thurmond made some twenty-nine appearances on Goldwater's behalf throughout the South. He led the way to an emerging Republican party in the South, the emergence of a two-party system in the region for the first time since the end of Reconstruction, and a realignment of southern politics that made the South an anchor of the Republican regional coalition that came to include the West and the Midwest. Strom Thurmond had led southern Democrats out of the Democratic party in 1948, and (with George Wallace's help) he led them into the Republican party in 1964.

Goldwater, during his southern tour, seemed to fall into something of a self-destructive mode, or at least the press saw it that way. In early September, he voted against Medicare in the Senate and then traveled to St. Petersburg later that month, in the very heart of one of the nation's largest retirement communities, and railed against the program. In Knoxville, where the TVA was a mainstay of the local economy, he proposed the sale of the TVA's power plants. In Memphis, the home of the Cotton Exchange, he made it clear that he wanted to bring an end to cotton subsidies. In West Virginia, where poverty was the highest in the country, he called the administration's War on Poverty a "hodgepodge of handouts" and a "phony, vote-getting scheme." Then, on September 19, he left the South for Fargo, North Dakota, and the National Plowing Contest, the most important political gathering of farmers in the Plains, and, before 75,000 farmers in a pouring rain, against the advice of those closest to him, he called farm price supports "absurd," and promised to end them.[76] For the press and other political observers, these statements were treated as little more than other "Goldwaterisms," more shooting from the hip from an undisciplined candidate. But they may have been more than that. Certainly, Goldwater had strong opinions, and he was not reticent about expressing them—even to people who did not want to hear them. That is, he believed what he said. But Goldwater also believed that

New Deal and Great Society liberalism had won elections since the 1930s by dispensing favors to certain groups and regions in exchange for votes and political power. To Goldwater, this was the height of hypocrisy. Most likely, he hoped that by going to these areas and denouncing these programs he could draw attention to what he believed was the hypocrisy of Democratic party politics. As with most of Goldwater's strategies in these months before the election, it failed, leaving voters scratching their heads and wondering why he would work so hard to lose so many votes. As with other Goldwater strategies at this time, however, it laid the groundwork for the future of American conservatism. Republicans in the future would argue against what they called the unsound liberal philosophy of tax and spend, spend and elect. This argument originated (at least in the speeches of a national political candidate) in 1964.

In an attempt to shore up his numbers a little, Goldwater, in late September, went to the font of modern Republicanism: Eisenhower. The plan was that Goldwater and Eisenhower would meet in front of national cameras in a bucolic setting near the general's home in Gettysburg. They would then, before the nation, discuss the issues. The men were supposed to have been relaxed, just talking about the campaign. But when the ad appeared, both men looked stiff and rehearsed. The only interesting statement that came out of the discussion was Ike's response to Goldwater's concern that voters thought he might start a nuclear war. "Tommyrot," he said.[77] It hardly countered the Johnson administration's devastating campaign ads.

* * *

Despite his image problem, Goldwater continued to push a hard-line foreign policy—a policy that left the nation uneasy in an uneasy time. His stance allowed Johnson to carry the banner of peace—mostly by default. The president continued preaching the wisdom of moderation in foreign affairs, highlighted by his firm but measured response against the North Vietnamese in the Tonkin Gulf along with his support of the Nuclear Test Ban Treaty. By a large margin, most Americans agreed with the president. In fact, in a late September Gallup poll only 2 percent of those polled described Johnson as reckless, while 24 percent were willing to use that word to describe Goldwater.[78] Goldwater, however, pushed on. He called Johnson "soft on communism," and said it was "silly" to think that the communist bloc was breaking up. He argued that it was wrong (as a result of the Cuban Missile Crisis) to agree not to invade Cuba; he called the Nuclear Test Ban Treaty a policy of appeasement; and he complained that selling wheat to the Soviets served to strengthen our enemy. Following a conservative policy that went all the way back to the immediate post-war years, Goldwater argued that the foreign policies of co-existence and containment were contradictory and inadequate objectives, and should be replaced with a foreign policy of buildup, rollback, and ultimately victory over the forces of communism. Then, in the midst of the campaign, he published the campaign volume *Where I Stand*, in which he reiterated all his earlier statements that NATO commanders should have authority over tactical nuclear weapons—despite the beating he was taking on the issue, an issue that he had raised.[79] Then, in his speeches, while continuing to insist that he was the peace candidate, Goldwater repeatedly called for a Cold War victory—without offering any explanation of how that victory was to be achieved or even what type of victory he had in mind. Such statements (despite his constant calls for peace) no doubt rankled the electorate.[80]

· Then, if anyone wondered about the need for cool heads during times of crisis, Hollywood released the summer blockbuster movie *Fail-Safe*. The plot revolved around an order given in error to the crew of an American aircraft to attack Moscow. A composed American president, played by Henry Fonda, went to great lengths to avoid a nuclear war with the Soviets, includ-ing, finally, incinerating New York City as a military balance to the destruc-tion of Moscow. The message was clear: despite the tragedy, cooler heads prevailed and the world was not destroyed in a nuclear holocaust. Americans must have asked how the itchy-fingered Goldwater might react in such a high-pressure situation. Moyers saw the movie's advantage. He sent a memo to the president: "It should have a pretty good impact on the campaign in our favor."[81]

By the first of October Goldwater's situation had not gotten any better. *Time* reported that his campaign organization was "sputtering," and "inef-fectual" in every region of the nation except southern California and parts of the Deep South. Looking at a thirty-point insurmountable deficit, Goldwater said, "We have only one direction to move in and that's up. We can't go any lower."[82] By then, possibly the most distressing aspect of the campaign were the jokes. A truly wonderful campaign slogan, "In your heart you know he's right," became "In your heart you know he's far right," "In your heart you know he might," "In your heart you know he's white," and "In your guts you know he's nuts." The jokes, of course, got more play than the slogan itself.[83] Also, everywhere placards called for "Goldwater in 1864," and "Back to the store in '64." Stand-up political comics joked that Goldwater's watch went "tock-tick" and that the Goldwater doll, when wound up, walked backwards. On the other side of the campaign, political jokes about Johnson were directed more at his Texas drawl and his crude manner than his political philosophy—all, certainly, to the president's advantage. As television matured in the mid-1960s, comedians began to take their political humor to shows like the *Tonight Show* and even the *Ed Sullivan Show*. The 1964 campaign was possibly the first time that political comedians—stand-ups like Mort Saul and Lenny Bruce—weighed in as a significant factor in a national election. Unfortunately for Goldwater, his conservatism was often their target.

Nor did Goldwater's image fare well in the national press. His seemingly open defiance of American public opinion (or at least the opinion of the eastern liberal-to-moderate press) mixed with a hard-line foreign policy did not attract much sympathy in the press. In addition, his poor image, manufactured by Republican moderates and now expanded beyond all imagination by the Democrats, was accepted (and even perpetuated) by the press. And as the press became more and more hostile, Goldwater and his people shut the press out more and more. By the end of the campaign, the press hated Goldwater and the feeling was mutual. Not surprisingly, Goldwater supporters (many new to the political game) came away from the election with a terribly bitter taste in their mouths, believing (with validity in many cases) that their candidate had been treated unfairly and that the press was itself the enemy, a tool of the liberal establishment. "To almost all Goldwater admirers," *Time* reported just before the Republican convention, "the press represents the 'Eastern establishment' that is out to get Barry. . . . [N]ewsmen are viewed as liberals who distort Goldwater's views and conspire against him. . . . [R]eporters often [meet] hostile airport crowds, with Goldwater partisans glaring at them and demanding: 'Why don't you tell the truth about Barry?'"[84] The hostilities between the press and Goldwater supporters seemed to grow throughout the summer and fall of 1964, and after the election Goldwater supporters never quite forgot how the press—as they saw it—sabotaged their candidate's campaign.[85]

Goldwater received considerably fewer newspaper endorsements than Johnson, but more importantly he also received fewer endorsements than Nixon had in 1960. This was a significant turnabout in the history of American journalism. Throughout the twentieth century, Republican owners have generally dominated the nation's print press, leading the vast majority of the nation's dailies to endorse Republican candidates in national elections. In Roosevelt's 1936 landslide victory, for example, the nation's newspapers overwhelmingly supported the Republican candidate Alf Landon. In 1964,

Johnson received the endorsement of 455 papers, with a combined daily circulation of 27.6 million readers, about 61 percent of the total national readership. Goldwater was endorsed by only 368 papers, about half the number that had endorsed Nixon, with a readership of only 9.7 million.[86] What is significant is that the press, after 1964, generally remained in this anti-Republican mode. Nixon was devastated by the press in the 1968 and 1972 elections.[87] Even Ronald Reagan, who possibly handled the press better than any president since Kennedy, warred with the press through much of the 1980s and often expressed his belief that newsmen were constantly waiting in ambush to destroy his presidency.[88] Whether it was the Nixon persona or the Goldwater image—or both—by the end of the 1960s the Republican party (particularly the Republican right) and the national media were at war. The way in which Goldwater supporters believed their man had been treated seems to have had a great deal to do with that conflict.

Of all the anti-Goldwater reports and stories in the press in the 1964 campaign, there was none that rankled Goldwater supporters more than an article that appeared in October in the not-so-aptly-titled *Fact* magazine under the headline, "1,189 Psychiatrists Say Goldwater Is Psychologically Unfit to Be President."[89] The magazine was not widely distributed, but *Fact*'s editor took out several ads in national newspapers promoting the story and the magazine. And not unlike the Johnson campaign's television spots, the *Fact* article generated its own news—adding further to Goldwater's already crumbling image. The article is still used by Goldwater supporters as the primary example of how their candidate was treated unfairly by the press, at least in part because the legitimate press printed the gist of the story (or more often than not, just the title of the article) without checking the story's accuracy.[90]

So, the question remains: was Goldwater treated unfairly by the press? The bad relationship was the result of several things. First, Goldwater's problems were much the result of his own doing. He did not know how to manage the press; he did not know how to talk to the press. His rash statements, his Goldwaterisms, were legendary, and certainly some reporters rushed to turn his misstatements into headlines. "Whatever the personal politics of the working press," *Time* reported, "Barry Goldwater creates many of his own problems. His statements are so imprecise that they lead to a wide variety of interpretations and misinterpretations. Seldom has a major political candidate in the U.S. found it so necessary to clarify or revise what he has said."[91] Theodore White, in his *Making of the President*, recounted one small incident to illustrate the plethora of misstatements Goldwater was capable of making and his general inability to understand that what he said in public would most likely be scrutinized and published the next day. During the New Hampshire primary, Goldwater visited a family at home in New Hampshire and (with the press looking on) said that he would abolish the electoral college, claimed that the United States had the lowest tariffs in the world, that the United States should have used nuclear weapons against North Vietnam ten years earlier, that the Great Depression had begun in Austria, that New York was the most racist state in the nation, and that the U.S. debt was over one trillion dollars—an amount, he added, equal to $20,000 per American family.[92] As ridiculous as these statements are, as vulnerable as Goldwater was in having made them, they were never reported in the press. In this and other instances, reporters not only did not try to destroy Goldwater, they often protected him from his own misstatements, giving him an opportunity to retract, restate, further explain himself—or (as in this case) they simply ignored him for his own good. Theodore White wrote that "when Goldwater would hang himself with some quick rejoinder, the reporters who had grown fond of him would laboriously quiz him again and again until they could find a few safe quotations that reflected what they decided he really thought. They were," he added, "protective of Goldwater in a way that those zealots who denounced the Eastern press could never imagine."[93] *Time* agreed, insisting that reporters not only treated Goldwater evenhandedly, but had, time and again, bailed him out of trouble of his own making: "Most reporters are personally fond of him; some have even helped him out when his tongue seemed about to get him into trouble." The *Time* article then recounted a press conference in San Diego when Goldwater told reporters that he would attack southern China with nuclear weapons. The reporters gave Goldwater the opportunity to rethink the statement: "[A]re you certain you want to say this?" Goldwater then retracted the statement and asked the reporters not to print it.[94] Similarly, correspondent Sam Donaldson recalled being told by one of Goldwater's people to "Write what he means, not what he says."[95] The *Fact* article aside, most reporters gave Goldwater more leeway than he possibly deserved as a candidate for the nation's highest office.

It is also important to see that a great deal of the negative reporting was often directed more at Goldwater's right-wing zealots than at Goldwater himself. This was particularly true during much of the convention reporting when the press, nearly unanimously, denounced all aspects of the Republican far right. Goldwater, however, was seldom the target of these attacks. When Drew Pearson wrote of "[t]he smell of fascism . . . in the air" at the Cow Palace in San Francisco, he was not writing about the candidate, but of his supporters in the galleries. The *New York Post* wrote that "the Birchers and racists have never before enjoyed . . . such respectable auspices." Theodore White wrote often of "the real kooks: the Birchers, zealots, fanatics and sectarian crusaders," who made up large parts of Goldwater's support, but he seldom had any serious criticism of Goldwater—the candidate or the man. And Joseph Alsop was not attacking Goldwater when he wrote that "Goldwater enthusiasts are genuine fanatics. . . ."[96] In most cases, the candidate was not the target.

In addition, much of the press had clearly come to believe the loathsome image that had been created not by the press, but by members of Goldwater's own party. As the nation's various newspapers and magazines stated their reasoning for not supporting Goldwater they often fell back on words like "warmonger" and "racist," and expressed their fear that he might start a war, sell the TVA, destroy Social Security, or end farm supports.[97] It was not the press, or even the Democrats, who helped to create this image. However, it is not surprising that the press, along with much of the rest of the nation, was willing to accept it.

There were other factors that made it appear to many of Goldwater's supporters that the press was unfair. Goldwater had succeeded in bringing large numbers of Americans into the political process. They were first-timers, and many were naive about the system. They followed Goldwater because they loved him; they were fanatical about him. When their candidate was attacked, it became a personal attack. Many of these people were unable to see it as part of the process, part of the give-and-take of a political campaign where candidates attack each other and the press relishes reporting the attacks. It is no wonder that by election time, Goldwater's supporters saw that their candidate's words had been twisted, that the Democrats had lied about him, and that the press (seemingly in collusion) had reported it all incorrectly. Added to this was the general perception among many conservatives that the national press was either strongly liberal or the voice of the Eastern Establishment Republican moderates, and thus ideologically anti-Goldwater. Thus it should not be surprising that Goldwater's supporters came away from the 1964 election with the feeling that the national media had treated their candidate unfairly. The message for many Goldwaterites was to learn from the experience and not let it happen again.

* * *

By the first of October it was clear that Goldwater's campaign was dead. He had lost control of his own image, the party had refused to unite behind him, and, finally, his campaign organization began to break down over who should bear the blame for what was quickly becoming a political fiasco that might possibly embarrass, even destroy, the Republican right. As with almost all of these problems, the blame must go back to Goldwater. As the campaign began to unravel it became clearer and clearer that he had done a poor job of choosing his closest advisors; over and over again he had bypassed the politically experienced for the company of loyal amateurs and the result had been poor management at all levels of the campaign. Possibly the best example is Clif White, the man who had planted and cultivated the draft-Goldwater movement from the very beginning, rounded up the delegates necessary to hand Goldwater the nomination in San Francisco, and then orchestrated the convention from the top down. Most in the party expected White to be rewarded by being named head of the Republican National Committee, a position that would have placed him near the top of the Goldwater campaign. Instead, Goldwater relegated White to the nearly powerless position of Coordinator of Field Operations, while Dean Burch, whose only qualification was that he had been Goldwater's legislative assistant in the Senate, was named to head the RNC. Up until the convention, White had been the chief grassroots organizer. After the convention, when local volunteers complained about communications, managerial, and morale problems, White could do little more than pass on the information.[98] Goldwater, however, later said that he chose Birch because of his loyalty, and that loyalty had been more important to him than experience.[99] Other competent people, like Draft-Goldwater Committee chair Peter O'Donnell and the women's director Ione Harrington, were pushed aside for politically inexperienced (though extremely loyal) characters like John Grenier, Karl Hess, and William Baroody, men who had almost no experience running a national political campaign. Stephen Shadegg, who had a great deal of talent and experience, sat out the campaign as the regional head of the western district with almost no influence on Goldwater. Campaign manager Denison Kitchel—supposedly the leader of the campaign—was a political novice who often looked to Clif White for advice, and not surprisingly, received much of the blame for the campaign's failure after November.[100]

It was, however, Goldwater's bypassing of White that had the most impact on the Republican campaign, and Goldwater came to realize it. He later wrote that he had favored White to head the RNC, but other advisors close to him, particularly Baroody, Kitchel, and Richard Kleindienst, disliked White's connections to wealthy northeastern conservatives, particularly those who were connected to the *National Review*, and insisted that White be exiled in favor of the Dean Burch. Goldwater relented. The result of this decision was a split in the already small conservative movement. Led by Baroody, "the

Arizona Mafia," as the group became known, shut the northeastern conservatives out of the campaign and Goldwater allowed himself to become isolated from what might have been (at the very least) an important source of money and political advice. Also, people like Bill Buckley, Bill Rusher, and Brent Bozell were never part of the campaign only because, it seems, they had never been close to Goldwater and were from the much-hated Northeast. Stephen Shadegg noticed the change in San Francisco. "Of all the men . . . now advising the Senator, there was not a single one from that early group [the draft-Goldwater group]. Kitchel, Baroody, [Karl] Hess, [Ed] McCabe and [Charles] Lichenstein had taken possession of the candidate."[101]

Certainly the Arizona Mafia pushed Goldwater into dumping White and isolating Buckley and the northeastern conservatives, but Goldwater himself had never liked that crowd and never trusted them. That he did not choose others to run his campaign should have been no surprise. William Rusher, who was, of course, on the receiving end of Goldwater's rejections, recalled later how he believed Goldwater saw the northeastern conservatives, many of whom, like Clif White, had been instrumental in drafting Goldwater in the first place: to Goldwater "[we were] simply a roving band of samurai who had attached themselves to him, drafted him into a presidential election he was probably going to lose, compelled him to give up a safe seat in the Senate he revered, and were obviously quite prepared to offer him up as a living sacrifice on the alter of [our] beloved conservatism."[102] Goldwater, in fact, not only rejected this group, he sent them off unceremoniously. We "were allowed to depart," Shedegg recalled, "without being told our services had been appreciated or asked by Kitchel, Burch, or the Senator himself to participate in the general campaign."[103] Later in life, Goldwater lamented the rejection of White and the isolation of the northeasterners. It "caused dismay among Buckley, Rusher, and others whose intelligence and active help would have been very valuable in the campaign. . . . Not selecting White," he added, "was a mistake. . . . Buckley, Rusher, and the others should have been aboard working with us."[104] In hindsight it may have been clear, but in 1964 Goldwater wanted nothing to do with the *National Review* crowd and the rejection damaged his already weak campaign.

For Goldwater, the campaign was a loss. In the final six weeks, he could only salvage his message and hope that the defeat was salvageable in the future. For Johnson, the plan was to win big, bring in a landslide, a mandate. He hoped to isolate and then crush the right, while emerging as the president of all the people—to do what Roosevelt had done. But for that, he would have to leave the Rose Garden and hit the hustings.

11

Home Stretch

On September 28, the president abandoned John Connally's cautious front-porch campaign strategy and launched himself into a forty-two–day, 60,000-mile campaign swing. He would deliver over two hundred speeches. There were those (inside and outside the White House) who encouraged Johnson to get on the campaign trail because they thought his noncampaign might actually cause him to lose the election, but more likely, as Jack Valenti recalled, it was "not so much because he thought he would lose but because he wanted to win by an enormous vote."[1] He ran, Ken O'Donnell remembered, "like he wanted to set the world's record."[2]

Johnson may have wanted the landslide, the mandate necessary to pass his domestic program after the election, but he also had that deep-seated need to be more than just the president of the nation's Democrats. He wanted to appeal to the public at large, to get the support of as many widely different constituencies as possible, to be a national candidate. "He wants to feel himself beloved by everyone," *Time* reported.[3] One key to that strategy was his frontlash. He wanted desperately to appeal to those voters who were traditionally Republican, to make it clear to Americans that the Democratic party was big enough (and conservative enough) to accommodate Republican moderates. By late September this strategy was already generally successful; Goldwater, at least in part through his own doing, was isolated on the far right. But the president set out to make perfectly clear to anyone who doubted it that he was in firm control of the national political center.

With that in mind, Johnson waded into the Northeast—not because it was Kennedy country and because he believed he needed northeastern liberal votes, but because it was the geographic center of the moderate wing of the Republican party, the group that had been drummed out of the GOP in San Francisco, voters without a home, the frontlash. In an amazing sweep, Johnson made thirty speeches in twenty-four hours in six states. And they responded.

Johnson was a master campaigner, and in many areas of the country he was mobbed by adoring fans and supporters. (*Johnson Library*)

Valenti recalled: "[T]he crowds that greeted the President in each of these [northeastern cities] were simply overwhelming. . . . We were mobbed. . . . When we saw these crowds [we] . . . knew something big was afoot. This was the first time we realized that we had a landslide in the making. . . ."[4]

Here was Johnson campaigning at his best. Wisely, he had avoided debates, not only because he wanted to deny Goldwater any legitimacy as a candidate, but because he was not good at them. He did not look good on camera, did not debate well, and his long southern drawl offended half the nation. To his credit, he understood and accepted these limitations. But Johnson could wade into a crowd like no other candidate. "The crowds nearly tore him apart," *Time* reported. "Everywhere he went, he halted his motorcade, made impromptu speeches through a hand-held bullhorn, bounded out of his car to press the outstretched hands of crushing mobs." Another observer, Eric F. Goldman, recorded much the same: "A few more blocks the limousine stopped again and out came Lyndon Johnson, pushing into the crowd, both arms working, until the worried Secret Service got him back in the car for another stretch of the journey." He was, Goldman recalled, "The Y.A. Tittle of handshaking."[5] At one point, "he was seen taking care of eight voters almost simultaneously, quickly squeezing with one of his hands some part of an available arm." Such intense campaigning caused the president's right hand to become swollen and even to bleed. To avoid further damage, he developed what Goldman called "The Touch, which seemed to leave the recipient almost as pleased."[6]

In Manchester, New Hampshire, Johnson spoke about Vietnam. His statements would haunt him in the years after the election as the United States became deeply involved in Southeast Asia. In keeping with his strategy of being cautious but firm in dealing with the situation in Vietnam, Johnson criticized Goldwater and "some of our people," meaning Goldwater's supporters, for suggesting "the possible wisdom of going north in Viet-Nam. . . . I want to be very cautious and careful," he added, "when I start dropping bombs around that are likely to involve American boys in a war in Asia with 700 million Chinese. So just for the moment I have not thought that we were ready for American boys to do the fighting for Asian boys. What I have been trying to do . . . [is] to get the boys in Viet-Nam to do their own fighting with our advice and with our equipment. . . . So we are not going north and drop bombs at this stage of the game, and we are not going south and run out and leave it for the Communists to take over."[7] Within days of this speech, Johnson approved American air strikes, to begin in December, along the Ho Chi Minh Trail infiltration routes in Laos and South Vietnam.

By March 1965 the air strikes had escalated into sustained bombing of North Vietnam.

The press made much of Johnson's visit to the bedside of Ted Kennedy, who was recuperating in a Boston hospital from a June airplane crash. However, it may have been more important that he was photographed with Dwight Eisenhower's younger brother Milton in Baltimore. Milton was the president of Johns Hopkins University, and although he was only the brother of the general, the message was clear. The frontlash was real. Moderate Republicans in the Northeast liked Lyndon.[8]

The northeastern trip seemed to stimulate Johnson, and his fears and insecurities vanished. "We kept up a drum fire of activity," Valenti recalled.[9] From the Northeast he swung into the Midwest and Upper South. In Des Moines, 200,000 came out to see him. In Peoria, 70,000; 250,000 in Louisville, 85,000 in Nashville, and 40,000 in Indianapolis.[10] Goldman wrote that after he left the gentile Northeast his manner became more homegrown, or "corn pone," as Johnson's style was often described. "Come on, folks," the president of the United States would yell into a bullhorn, "come on down to the speakin'. You don't have to dress. Just bring your children and dogs, anything you have with you. It won't take long. You'll be back in time to put the kids in bed."[11]

With Johnson finally on the stump and the campaign headed for a final push to election day, it would seem that the press would gear up to cover the fireworks. But the campaign was boring. It was also over, and the press had largely lost interest. Johnson did not feel compelled to address any issues or even answer GOP charges and accusations. He spent most of his time recounting his achievements and promising for the nation's future— but generally in vague terms. He spoke of prosperity, the need for labor and business to work together, the promise of an expanded economy, the need to aid the poor, to meet the needs of our growing country, and seldom bothered to mention Goldwater by name. "[I]t takes a man who loves his country," Johnson told the steelworkers in late September, "to build a house instead of a raving, ranting demagogue who wants to tear it down."[12] As the election got closer, Johnson's speeches grew more emphatic, more rousing. But they also grew more and more vague. "I am going to talk about the issues," the president told a crowd in Dayton in one of his most important campaign speeches, "and the only issue is responsibility versus irresponsibility. Peace or war, prosperity or recession." Then his attacks on Goldwater, whom he called "the opposition candidate," were always distorted, but devastating. Goldwater would, he claimed, "sell the TVA and make Social

269

Security voluntary, and wipe out our farm programs, and undermine collective bargaining, and get out of the United Nations, and break the Nuclear Test Ban Treaty, and play with atomic bombs when the stakes of life are high."[13] Yet he said little else. *Time* began to complain by early October that the campaign was dull, that the president was refusing to address the big questions, the important issues, particularly civil rights. Civil rights, *Time* complained, was "a significant issue" that has been "lost in an emotionally charged fog about 'law and order' and the 'white backlash.' . . . Instead of the usual election-year exchange of thrust and counterthrust, charge and countercharge . . . there is [instead] invective and counterinvective."[14] By the first week in October the campaign was bumped from the front page of most national dailies. "[R]eporters see little to bother them," *Time* concluded, "beyond reporting a clash of personalities."[15]

On September 28, the day Johnson waded into the frontlash of New England, Goldwater headed into the mostly friendly confines of the Midwest. He continued to push his themes of limited government, individual freedom, and peace. The crowds that greeted him were large, but it was clear that he was still being hounded by a poor image, that his messages on the nuclear issue and Social Security were not getting through. In the minds of most Americans, he later wrote, he was "the cowboy who shot from the hip, the Scrooge who would put the penniless on the street with no Social Security, the maniac who would blow us and our children into the next kingdom in a nuclear Armageddon."[16] In a speech in early October, he hoped to show his moderation on the Vietnam issue by saying that, if elected, he would send Eisenhower to Vietnam because he wanted "the very best and soundest advice available."[17] When Eisenhower, in 1952, pledged to go to Korea if elected, it had put the final nail in the coffin of Adlai Stevenson's campaign. Goldwater's statement had almost no impact. Even Ike did not respond.

Clearly, the Goldwater campaign was languishing. Morale among the candidate's advisors was low, and all agreed that the campaign needed a change in direction, a breakthrough that might awaken conservatives and get them out on election day. Polls showed that Johnson was vulnerable on the issue of crime, particularly among groups that had rallied to George Wallace's campaign earlier in the year, the backlash. Early in September Goldwater had hit the topic hard, saying in several speeches that "Our women, all women, feel unsafe in our streets."[18] But he had left the topic as he toured the South, possibly fearing charges of racism, and turned instead to counterpunching against all the accusations of warmongering. Now, with the election only a month away, he chose to revisit the crime issue. On

October 1, he used nearly the same phrase, "Our wives, all women, feel unsafe in the streets."[19] Then on October 16, at the Mormon Tabernacle in Salt Lake City, he said that "The moral fiber of the American people is beset by rot and decay." The problem, he concluded, was with Lyndon Johnson. "[I]mmorality always starts at the top."[20] But it was in Chicago, within earshot of the conservative white suburbs in northern Indiana and southern Wisconsin that had been good to George Wallace, where Goldwater really pulled out the stops and went for race. He called busing to achieve racial balance in schools "morally wrong" and a "hypothetical goal of perfect equality. . . ." Wallace, speaking in the same area of the country earlier in the year, had promised that the Civil Rights Act would cause the initiation of government-directed quotas to establish racial equality, a concept abhorrent to many in the working classes who feared for their jobs and their property values. Here Goldwater picked up where Wallace had left off. "One thing that will surely poison and embitter our relations with each other," he said, "is the idea that some predetermined bureaucratic schedule of equality—and worst of all, a schedule based on the concept of race—must be imposed. . . . That way lies destruction." Then he concluded: "No law can make one person like another if he doesn't want to."[21] He carried the topic to the other major cities of the Midwest, directing his words to the white suburbs and the working classes, people who believed that the civil rights movement was moving too fast, who feared that blacks would take their jobs, move into their neighborhoods and their schools, and demand more than they believed they deserved.

Then several times in speeches throughout the Midwest, Goldwater said that Johnson was soft on communism. The press criticized him harshly for using what *Time* characterized as "an old and ugly phrase." It "revives the memories of the McCarthy era, smacks not only of weak foreign policy but of treason within the highest circles of American Government." When Goldwater was asked why he chose to make the statement, he pointed his finger at Herbert Hoover and Nixon who, he said, had suggested it. Nixon immediately denied making any such suggestion to Goldwater. Such talk, *Time* continued, "presumably has great appeal to his diehard, ultraconservative admirers. But it is hard to see how it could be winning votes from among the moderate Republicans and the independents he so desperately needs." Concluding that Goldwater had nothing to gain by drawing out the "soft on communism issue," *Time* stated the obvious: "It almost seems that Goldwater . . . has given up all hope of election and has decided to go down fighting, along with his hardcore following."[22]

* * *

Johnson was popular. Polls showed, by the first of October, that he was out in front and pulling away from Goldwater in every region—except the South.[23] The passage of the Civil Rights Act and the choice of Humphrey had made him extremely unpopular in the South, a region he liked to call his own. He had been, of course, placed on the ticket in 1960 because of his popularity there, and now, four years later, he was in danger of losing the entire region to the Republicans. Valenti thought Johnson might carry Georgia or Louisiana, but the general consensus in the White House, he later recalled, was that "the South was going down the drain."[24] At the same time, Johnson did not feel he could campaign effectively in the South. The image on the evening news of the president of the United States being booed, heckled, and possibly even attacked would not be a good one—and he would likely not win many southern votes anyway. Then again, he felt badly about ignoring the South, and he knew southern Democrats felt abandoned. For there were, of course, still loyal Democrats there, voters who had not abandoned the party over the race issue, moderate whites of the New South, people who, in fact, might build a coalition with the growing number of black voters and take back the region for the Democrats. Possibly one of the most important political statistics of the 1964 election was that the number of black voters in the South had doubled since the 1960 election. The South was not as important as it had once been to the Democrats, but it was important enough that Johnson could not ignore it, not let it simply be picked off by the Republicans.

The plan then became for Lady Bird to make the trip—a classic whistlestop tour of the South. The president would meet her at two stops: one near the beginning of the tour in Raleigh, and another at the end in New Orleans. The trip would be one of the high points of the president's campaign.

Political reasons for the trip aside (most of which were not that strong), Lady Bird wanted to go. She wanted to be a part of the campaign, and what better way to do it than to head into the region of the nation where she was most comfortable. She had hatched the plan with her assistant Liz Carpenter during the convention, and then Carpenter approached several southern governors about the idea. The response was not good. The advice from the governors was to stay away, let the local Democratic candidates run their own races without the burden of the White House and the yoke of the administration's Civil Rights Act. They also feared for the First Lady's safety. But Lady Bird persisted. She passed over the objections of Ken O'Donnell and John Connally and took the idea directly to the president—who agreed.

It would give the South some necessary attention from the White House, without the president having to be subjected to abuse. The assumption was that southerners would not attack the First Lady.

She may also have felt a need to get involved because Peggy Goldwater had been so active on the campaign trail. No shrinking violet, Peggy maintained a full campaign schedule, independent of her husband's, throughout most of September and October.[25] She probably had little impact, however. *Time* wrote that she went through the campaign "smiling shyly when she is introduced and saying little or nothing." She received a lot of press coverage when she spoke on "Peggy Goldwater Day" in her hometown of Muncie, Indiana, even though she declined to say much to the crowd of well-wishers. "One speaker in the family is enough," she said. At a press conference in Columbus, Indiana, she insisted she would not talk about politics, and spent most of the time discussing her husband's favorite foods. The other candidates' wives apparently felt the pressure to get on to the campaign trail as well. Muriel Humphrey did a six-state Midwest tour during which, *Time* reported, she "gave warm little speeches." The same article relegated Miller's wife and two daughters to the level of "adornments."[26]

Lady Bird's foray into the South, however, had some significance in the campaign. If nothing else, it was the first time that a First Lady had campaigned on her own, and that alone demanded press attention. The train of nineteen cars, known as *The Lady Bird Special*, left Union Station in Washington on October 6. The trip was planned for four days, 1,682 miles, through eight states. The First Lady would deliver some forty-six speeches. Luci and Lynda accompanied their mother, along with a media entourage of nearly 150 reporters.

It may have been a surprise to some that Lady Bird was competent and capable. She stood only five feet four inches and weighed just 114 pounds, but she was a strong and confident woman who often showed that she was thicker skinned than her husband. George Reedy, a Johnson aide, had the utmost respect for her. "She's a woman of sense and sensitivity both," he said in an interview in the 1970s. "[S]he's very intuitive about people; she's not swept off her feet by flattery. She has a marvelous knack for saying the right thing at the right time. And," he added, "she has extraordinary good sense."[27]

She would need those characteristics. Through most of her tour Lady Bird was treated with the respect she deserved. She enjoyed small towns and small-town people, and every chance she got she altered the route to the very smallest of southern towns. The residents, excited to see the First Lady of the United States, responded by treating Lady Bird well. But when her tour took her to larger cities, the situation often grew nasty. Southern gentlemen proved to be considerably less respectful of the First Lady than the president expected.

Her first problem was that she was overtly snubbed by governors, congressmen, senators, and local political leaders—men who wanted to put a great deal of distance between their campaigns and the White House, between their campaigns and the Civil Rights Act. In Virginia, Senator Willis Robertson decided to go hunting in Montana rather than meet the First Lady. Senator Harry Byrd refused an invitation to ride in Lady Bird's motorcade, and Strom Thurmond refused to see her. Dan Moore, the Democratic nominee for governor in North Carolina, would not return her calls. Georgia senator Richard Russell, one of Johnson's oldest friends, refused to meet her. So did George Wallace and Louisiana governor John McKithen.[28] Each snub was a news story, and each snub branded the white South as racist.

At most stops, Lady Bird handed out copies of her recipe for pecan pie as if they were campaign fliers. The First Daughters spoke often. *Time* wrote that they "made girlish speeches punctuated with dimples and fond comments about 'Daddy.'"[29] The kindness and "girlish speeches," however, were never news, barely back-page coverage. But when Lady Bird was treated badly, snubbed by a local politician, or heckled and drowned out by rude Goldwater supporters, the story hit the front pages and was the lead on the six o'clock news. In Columbia, South Carolina, she was heckled and booed. Chants of "We Want Barry" at times drowned her out completely. At one point an angry Lynda grabbed the microphone from her mother and yelled at the top of her lungs: "I know these rude comments were not made by people from the good state of South Carolina but by the people from the state of confusion."[30] Finally, Lady Bird raised a gloved hand and said, "I respect your right to express your [opinion]. Now it is my turn to express mine." The crowd fell silent.[31] But six hours later in Charleston an angry crowd of Goldwater supporters refused to relent. Signs appeared in the crowd that said "Johnson's a Nigger Lover," and "Black Bird Go Home." When the First Lady tried to speak, the booing and chanting drowned her out. She raised her hand to quiet the crowd, as she had in Columbia, but the noise simply got louder. Louisiana congressman Hale Boggs, who was traveling with the First Lady, took the microphone and called the crowd "a Nazi gathering."[32] The press had its story. In Savannah, Lady Bird met much the same situation. Then, as the train headed into northern Florida there were a series of bomb scares and threats on the First Lady's life. From

In early October, Lady Bird embarked on a whistlestop tour of the South. Occasionally heckled by Goldwater-supporting crowds and generally ignored by southern politicians, the first lady conveyed the message to southern moderate Democrats that the administration had not abandoned them in favor of northeastern liberals. It was the first time in history that a first lady had gone on the campaign trail alone. *(Johnson Library)*

there she headed west to Mobile and finally ended her tour in New Orleans on October 9.

Lady Bird's trip into the South appeared to have had little impact. But it allowed the president to give some attention to the region and not ignore it, and to show those Democrats in the South who still supported the party that its leadership had not abandoned them to the Republicans. More importantly, however, Lady Bird's trip in her husband's name helped foster Lyndon Johnson's image as the moderate candidate, the candidate who most opposed the extremism of southern racism. By the mid-1960s the brutality and ruthlessness of southern racism was being reported regularly on the television news and in the national print media. White southern racism could no longer hide behind the cloak of paternalism and the old arguments that segregation was a natural system approved by both races in the South. The civil rights movement and the media coverage of it had broken down all those old myths. To a growing majority of white Americans outside the South, the image of southern racism as seen on TV consisted of fire hoses, attack dogs, the Klan, "whites only" signs, and the hateful slurs of race baiters like Bull Conner and Gerald L.K. Smith. This was the ugly face of racism that rose to attack Lady Bird Johnson in Columbia and Charleston. The perpetrators were on national television, and they carried "Goldwater for President" signs. All this played into Johnson's hands to appeal to a frontlash of moderates who opposed the extremist image of Barry Goldwater.

At 8:16 P.M. on October 9, the *Lady Bird Special* pulled into the New Orleans train station. Lyndon, who had just arrived from campaigning in Louisville, met her on the platform. "He greeted his wife with great warmth," Valenti recalled. "[H]e was very very proud of her because it was quite a successful trip." Later that evening at a party fund raiser at the Jung Hotel, Johnson had one of his finest hours. First he made the point that he had been making since the convention, that the battle was not that of party but of nation, that Lyndon Johnson was not the candidate of the Democrats, but the candidate of all America. "Our cause is no longer the cause of a party alone," he said. "Our cause is the cause of a great nation." He then added, "This year, as in no year before, you work not as partisans for party, but you work as Americans for America." From there he added his early recollections of Huey Long, always a popular Louisiana topic. Then Johnson tossed away his prepared speech and launched into a story about a senator from a southern state, "and I won't call the name of the State," he said. "[I]t wasn't Louisiana and it wasn't Texas." This anonymous senator, Johnson recalled, was speaking to Texas congressman (and LBJ mentor) Sam

Rayburn. He said: "I would like to go back [to my home state] and make one more Democratic speech," Johnson recalled. "The poor old State," he added, "they haven't heard a Democratic speech in 30 years. All they ever hear at election time is nigger, nigger, nigger."[33] There was an immediate hush over the crowd. Had the President of the United States, a southerner, actually used the word "nigger"—and in the South? Quickly, the president's point sunk in and a slow applause broke out, and then a five-minute standing ovation.[34] Southern politics, Johnson was saying (but the region's economic and social structure as well), had suffered enormously from the race issue. It was time to put that issue behind and become part of the nation. It was a strong statement, a courageous statement, an appeal to loyal Democrats in the South and moderates in the North.

* * *

As the campaign reached into its last weeks, Goldwater may have seemed a lonely figure fighting a personal campaign, but in fact he was not totally abandoned by his party's leadership. Scranton spoke on Goldwater's behalf several times, keeping mostly to his home state of Pennsylvania and parts of the Northeast. Even Eisenhower occasionally left his Gettysburg sanctuary to speak for the candidate. It was Nixon, however, more than any other Republican, who gave all he had for Goldwater.[35] During the last month of the campaign Nixon covered 25,000 miles, through 36 states, making some 136 speeches and giving over 100 press conferences. Later in his life, Nixon insisted he had worked so hard for Goldwater in order to head off the defection of Republican moderates to the Democrats, a political shift that, he believed, might ultimately destroy the future of the party.[36] However, he most likely was also laying the groundwork for his own candidacy in 1968. By October 1964 it was not difficult to see that the election was headed for a Democratic landslide in November, and that Goldwater, after a crushing defeat, would not be in any position to run again in four years or even keep control of the party apparatus. Rockefeller and Scranton had both damaged themselves badly by alienating the conservatives, and neither could look to 1968 with much hope of winning the nomination. Nixon might well have seen himself stepping into the breach, the only real candidate who had not managed to alienate either the right or the left. In 1968, after the defeats in the 1960 presidential campaign and 1962 California gubernatorial race had worn off the public mind, his party (and the nation) might just be ready for a new Nixon to make another run for the presidency. The new Nixon would be the unity candidate, possibly the only one who could bring the party back together and heal the wounds of 1964.[37]

In the midst of all this last-minute campaign activity a story broke that had the potential of derailing Johnson's campaign. Goldwater had attacked the administration for corruption and immorality in governing, and it seemed to play right into his hands when Johnson's closest aide, Walter Jenkins, was arrested in the basement of a Washington YMCA for "disorderly conduct." The press reports, which broke on October 17, revealed that Jenkins had been caught in a homosexual liaison with a sixty-year-old resident of Washington's Old Soldiers Home. In addition, the Johnson administration had tried to cover it up. Goldwater, it seemed, had been handed his October Surprise, one of those last-minute events that can stir the emotions of voters and turn a losing campaign into a winner.

Jenkins had been at Johnson's side since 1939. He ran the White House; he even handled Johnson's personal financial affairs. Possibly his greatest asset in the months following Kennedy's assassination was that he was liked by the Kennedy people who stayed on in the White House and acted as a bridge between advisors like Bill Moyers and Jack Valenti on one side and Ken O'Brien and Lawrence O'Donnell on the other. Valenti later recalled, "Walter was the number one man. No one questioned this, no one debated it, and no one resented it."[38] Jenkins was married, Catholic, with six children (one named Lyndon), and he was extremely close to Lady Bird. LBJ had even built a house for Jenkins and his family on the Johnson ranch to keep him close by. As *Time* wrote, "Johnson's life became Jenkins' life."[39]

The event had occurred on October 7 in a pay toilet in the basement of the G Street YMCA, a place that *Time* described as a "spot reeking with disinfectant and stale cigars . . . a notorious hangout for deviants." Jenkins had just left a party given by *Newsweek*. "He had one or two high balls," *Time* reported, and told friends he was headed to his office at the White House to work. He was arrested by two undercover Washington police officers who observed the encounter through peepholes in a bathroom closet.[40] The "acts" of "disorderly conduct" were never described in the press or in police reports.

According to *Time*, which covered these events in minute detail, within two days of Jenkins's arrest members of the Republican Congressional Campaign Committee and the Republican National Committee had (anonymously) notified Washington's newspapers of the incident. On Wednesday, October 14, Jenkins heard that the word was out and called Johnson's close friend and advisor Abe Fortas. Fortas called in Clark Clifford and the cover-up began.[41] Fortas and Clifford went to the three Washington newspapers, the *Washington Star*, the *Washington Daily News*, and the *Washington Post* and asked the editors of each paper to suppress the story. All three agreed, as long as the story did not break elsewhere.[42]

From the other side, however, Dean Burch, the RNC chairman, had worked to see that the story broke in all three newspapers, and he expected that to happen on that same Wednesday. When the story did not appear in the afternoon editions, he broke the story himself in a statement that evening: "There is a report sweeping Washington that the White House is desperately trying to suppress a major news story affecting the national security." Two hours later, at 8:00 P.M., United Press International broke the story and it appeared in newspapers around the nation the next morning.[43]

Johnson was campaigning for Robert Kennedy in New York City and about to speak at the Al Smith Dinner at the Waldorf Astoria Grand Ballroom that Wednesday evening when he received a call from Fortas, who explained the situation.[44] *Time* reported that when the president's "time came to speak [at the Al Smith Dinner] he cut his talk in half, delivered it in a hoarse monotone. Lyndon Johnson looked for all the world as if he had just lost one of his best friends. In a sense he had."[45] Valenti recalled that "this must have been an absolute blow with an axe handle to his stomach. . . ."[46]

The next day, Jenkins resigned and was replaced by Moyers. Johnson issued a quiet statement praising Jenkins's "personal dedication, devotion, and tireless labor. . . ."[47] And the event ended. Goldwater refused to use it, despite insistence from his advisors that Johnson was vulnerable on the issues of corruption and immorality, and that Jenkins's apparent homosexual activity made him vulnerable to blackmail and thus a security risk. But Goldwater stood firm. He knew Jenkins, and as he later wrote, "It was a sad time for Jenkins' wife and children, and I was not about to add to their private sorrow."[48]

Despite the obvious political repercussions that such a scandal could have had just three weeks before election day, all this amounted to little. The story broke in the midst of a whole series of much more important news stories and was pushed off the front page of nearly every American daily. On the day the story broke, Soviet premier Nikita Khrushchev resigned and Leonid Brezhnev took power. Two days later, China exploded its first atomic bomb, and the Labor party won a victory in Britain. If that was not enough to smother the Jenkins story, the scandal hit the press right in the middle of an exciting World Series between the Cardinals and the Yankees. The weekly news magazines covered the story well, but when Goldwater refused to use the scandal, it was pushed well behind the other stories and barely caused a ripple in the polls.[49]

* * *

Beyond the presidential campaign, it was the New York Senate race that captured the most national attention. Robert Kennedy had announced his candidacy on August 25, but only after a great deal of backroom political wrangling. Certainly, Kennedy was a strong candidate, ranking well ahead of all other Democratic hopefuls in the early polls. He was undoubtedly the man most capable of beating Republican incumbent Kenneth Keating in the general election. Kennedy, however, could not win the support of the very powerful New York City mayor, Robert Wagner, Jr. Over the years, since becoming mayor in 1954, Wagner had wrested control of the state's Democratic party machinery from state bosses like Buffalo's Peter Crotty, Brooklyn's Stanley Steingut, Harlem's Adam Clayton Powell, and Charlie Buckley of the Bronx. By 1964, Wagner was the undisputed state party leader and he saw Kennedy's candidacy as a move that would diminish his control and cut into his power base statewide.[50] The Kennedy family, however, had a unique insight into New York State politics in Stephen Smith, the thirty-six-year-old husband of Bobby's sister Jean and the offspring of a wealthy Brooklyn Irish Catholic clan that had been the Kennedy family's eyes and ears in New York since the late 1940s. Smith had managed JFK's last Senate race and Ted Kennedy's 1962 Senate race, and now, in 1964, he would be Robert Kennedy's campaign manager. Through Smith's efforts, the various New York State Democratic party bosses were convinced to come to Kennedy's side. "Last week," *Time* reported in late August, "the walls came tumbling down—and there stood Bob Wagner." Alone, and being pushed hard by the president to fall in line, Wagner finally relented and threw his support to Kennedy.[51]

When Kennedy announced his candidacy he immediately jumped way ahead in the polls. At first look, Bobby seemed to pick up near where his brother left off. Huge crowds greeted him throughout the state. "[H]e has been mobbed wherever he has gone," *Time* reported. But *Time* also noted that the crowds were very young, in fact, by a large majority, too young to vote.[52] Kennedy had also never run for public office, and he was clearly not a polished campaigner. To most observers he never approached his brother's charisma or campaign abilities. New York's Jewish voters, for instance, had flocked to JFK in 1960 in numbers that exceeded 90 percent—despite a barrage of accusations from the Republicans that father Joe Kennedy had been soft on Hitler before the war. But in 1964, Bobby was never able to neutralize those same accusations and he never won much Jewish support. His almost amazing lack of his brother's campaign savvy became apparent when, while campaigning in an Italian neighborhood in New York City, he tried to dig into a pizza with a fork. The "incident" made national news.[53] Bobby's candidacy also sputtered with the New York press. A *Time* magazine survey of twelve state newspapers found nine in direct opposition, two neutral, and only one in support. The *New York Times*, which had supported JFK with enthusiasm in 1960, never came around to the younger Kennedy. "[A]pparently [Bobby Kennedy] needs New York," the *Times* reported, "but does New York need Bobby Kennedy?"[54] Then, to further punctuate the differences between Bobby and his older brother, a large group of very visible, New York–based celebrity types who had supported JFK in 1960 formed a political organization called Democrats for Keating and openly and loudly opposed Bobby's candidacy. Led by writers Gore Vidal and James Baldwin, actor Paul Newman, and historian Richard Hofstader, this group mounted a campaign that attacked Kennedy in the press for his role in advising and supporting Joseph McCarthy's anti-communist crusade in the early fifties.[55] All this hurt Kennedy's candidacy badly.

At the same time, Keating was no pushover. A veteran of twelve years in Congress and six in the Senate, he was considered by *Time* to be "a respected public servant with a record anybody but a reactionary can admire."[56] He was a Republican moderate who made it clear that he wanted nothing to do with Goldwater's right-wing beliefs, and had stated even before the Republican convention that he would support Lyndon Johnson for president rather than fall in line with his own party and its right-wing divergence.[57] In fact, as a New York Republican moderate, his own political philosophy was not that far from where Kennedy stood on most issues. "Each claims to be more liberal than the other," *Time* wrote, "yet both are moderates with similar positions. . . ."[58]

Keating also had the support of most of the state's newspapers. And he had received Rockefeller's endorsement. That meant more than just the good words of the state's powerful Republican governor; it also meant use of Rockefeller's statewide campaign network. Keating's campaign was managed by Herbert Brownell, one of the GOP's primary lights in the 1940s and 1950s. Brownell had managed Tom Dewey's two unsuccessful presidential bids in 1944 and 1948, then helped catapult Eisenhower into the presidency in 1952 and later served as Ike's attorney general in his first term. Keating might not have attracted the crowds or the press that Kennedy did, but he maintained a solid foundation of support. By early October, once the Kennedy celebrity had worn off, Keating began a slow and steady upward tick in the polls. On October 8, he had surpassed Kennedy by a 2 percent margin. What was important about that statistic was that Johnson was burying Goldwater in New York by a solid 20 percent margin.[59] The New York race, wrote *Time*, "will be decided not so much by Bobby's popularity as by the length of Lyndon's coattails."[60] Kennedy needed Lyndon Johnson.

Keating, however, had his own problems. His snubbing of Goldwater had offended New York's conservative party, and they split off to run their own candidate, Henry Paolucci, with the support of the state's conservatives led by the venerable Clare Booth Luce. All this placed Keating in a very bad position. He was losing votes to the Goldwaterites on the right, while he must have realized that if Kennedy attached himself to the Johnson juggernaut he would lose votes to the left as well.

As Keating's numbers improved, Kennedy became increasingly desperate to cling to Johnson's coattails. However, the last thing Kennedy wanted to do was to ask the president to help him win in New York. But by mid-October it was clear that Kennedy was on the road to defeat if he did not act quickly. Finally, at Stephen Smith's insistence, Kennedy asked the president to come to New York and campaign in his behalf.[61] Immediately, posters appeared throughout New York: "Get on the Johnson, Humphrey, Kennedy Team."[62]

Johnson was not particularly excited about Kennedy (and the Kennedy family) building a power base in New York, and he was no more excited about the power Bobby Kennedy would wield in the Senate.[63] But possibly for the sake of the party and the liberal seat the Democrats would gain in the Senate, Johnson weighed in and gave all he had to Kennedy's campaign. He went to New York on October 14 and, as the *New York Times* reported, "threw his arm, literally and figuratively, around . . . Robert F. Kennedy."[64] The two men barnstormed about the state hugging and complimenting each other. At the concluding rally at Madison Square Garden, Johnson called Kennedy his "old friend" and praised his "knowledge in the field of education, housing and slum clearance, [and] national defense. . . ." He will be, Johnson added, "one of the most valuable members of the entire Senate, and the people of New York and the Nation will be the gainers."[65] On October 31, the president made another appearance in New York. Humphrey also interrupted his own campaign three times to help Kennedy shore up his labor flanks. Kennedy and Keating headed into the election in a statistical dead heat.

Robert Kennedy's senatorial campaign in New York was never a sure thing. LBJ and RFK barely got along, but in mid-October Kennedy was forced to ask the popular president to campaign for him—to put him over the top against the Republican moderate Kenneth Keating. It worked. Johnson beseeched the New York crowds "ta vote fur ma boy." *(Johnson Library)*

* * *

In Texas, as in much of the rest of the nation, the politics of the future was taking hold. There, in Johnson's own backyard, a young Republican upstart named George Bush had abandoned all realms of moderation, taken up the mantle of Barry Goldwater and George Wallace, and was running for the Senate against the Texas liberal Democrat Ralph Yarborough. Bush was the son of a well-known moderate Republican senator from Connecticut, Prescott Bush, Jr. He had collected a distinguished war record as a navy pilot and then graduated from Yale in 1948. Immediately afterward, he left the northeastern patrician lifestyle for Texas to make his mark in the oil business. By the early 1960s he was chief executive officer of Zapata Off-Shore Oil Company, a wildly successful enterprise with fields in Midland and offices in Houston. In 1964 he decided to try his hand at politics.[66]

The Texas Democrats had always fought among themselves, and 1964 was no exception. The problem was—as it had been for sometime—that Yarborough and John Connally could not get along. Connally was running for reelection as governor in 1964, so he and Yarborough were able to stay out of each other's way. But the two men controlled large opposing political bases that left the Democrats in the state split. Johnson often played mediator between these two men and their factions, more often than not coming in on the side of his good friend and advisor Connally. It was in November 1963 that John Kennedy and Johnson had traveled to Dallas to try to mediate a compromise between these two warring factions in the Texas Democratic party. In 1964, Johnson stood to suffer a great humiliation if George Bush defeated Yarborough, joining Goldwaterite John Tower in an all-Republican Texas Senate team. "[I]t would be a blow to LBJ's personal vanity," *Time* reported.[67]

Bush's political roots were sunk deeply in his party's northeastern moderate wing, but in 1964 he saw that Yarborough was vulnerable because of his liberal voting record and his support of the Civil Rights Act. Taking a cue from George Wallace's primary campaign and Barry Goldwater's successes in the Republican party, Bush abandoned his moderation (along with his New England roots) and set out to attack Yarborough, a man whose record Bush called "ultra-liberal." His campaign was pure Texas. He traveled the state with a singing group called the Black Mountain Boys who sang again and again: "Sun is gonna shine in the Senate some day/George Bush gonna run them liberals away." He supported right-to-work laws, cuts in foreign

284

aid, and increased tariffs. He opposed the 1963 Nuclear Test Ban Treaty and the Civil Rights Act.[68] "The new civil rights act," he told four hundred all-white employees of the Ling-Temco-Vought Corporation in Grand Prairie, Texas, "was passed to protect 14 percent of the people. I'm worried about the other 86 percent."[69] *Time* called him "an attractive, articulate Goldwater Republican."[70] Lyndon Johnson's coattails were, however, too long for Bush to overcome. He lost the election to Yarborough.

* * *

A Senate seat up for grabs in California also drew a lot of national attention, and like the Texas election it was something of a portent for the future. Many Californians in 1964 were asking a simple question: Can an actor find success in politics?

The actor was George Murphy, the Broadway-to-Hollywood song and dance man who had hoofed it in pictures with Shirley Temple, Ginger Rogers, Judy Garland, Liz Taylor, and Lana Turner. Now, at age sixty-one, he was running as a Republican for the California Senate seat. Murphy had been the two-term president of the Screen Actors Guild, and he had helped Ronald Reagan, Adolphe Monjou, Eddie Arnold, Robert Montgomery, and others remove a significant communist element from that organization. Like Reagan, Murphy had dropped his Democratic party affiliation and become a Republican who now supported Goldwater. But Murphy worried that voters might not accept an actor as a legitimate politician. "I had this thing researched for months," Murphy told *Time*. "I wanted to learn if people would accept an actor running for office. And the word was that I had a pretty fair chance."[71]

The California Senate seat in question had become vacant when Clair Engle died of a brain tumor in July 1964. Engle had been a Democrat, and the Democrats scrambled to hold onto the seat. But, not unlike Texas, the Democratic party in California was split. The governor, Pat Brown, wanted to name state controller Alan Cranston to the seat. But Jesse "Big Daddy" Unruh, speaker of the California State Assembly and also a Democrat, wanted to name someone else—anyone, apparently, other than Cranston. Unruh finally settled on Pierre Salinger, John Kennedy's press secretary and one of a number of Kennedy people who simply could not go on under Johnson's leadership. Salinger beat Cranston in a statewide primary by a paltry 140,000 votes and that forced Brown to name him to fill Engle's seat. To most observers, Salinger was a shoe-in to beat Murphy in November.[72]

Salinger had every reason to believe he could win. He carried the Kennedy mystique, and he had been in the public eye as JFK's press secretary for three years. Engle's wife supported him, and even Jackie Kennedy put in a few good words.[73] His only real problem was that he was not a Californian, but polls showed that (not unlike Robert Kennedy in New York) he overcame that issue fairly easily and quickly. There was something about Pierre, however, that never seemed to click with Californians. "When Salinger speaks," *Time* wrote, "his lips move with the relish of a winetaster and his jowls quiver like jelly in a railroad dining car." Salinger and Murphy debated on television in October, and it was the actor who projected the best image. "[M]ost observers agreed," *Time* added, "that Murphy had projected himself as a real good guy. That should hardly have been surprising, since he has been playing that role professionally for all of his adult life." Salinger, *Time* concluded, "came across as a somewhat stuffy sort."[74]

In 1963 the California legislature had passed the Rumford Act, which outlawed discrimination in housing. In the 1964 election, Proposition 14 had been placed on the ballot by California Republicans to repeal the measure. Although both Salinger and Murphy tried to avoid the issue, it was generally known that Salinger supported the Rumford Act while Murphy supported Proposition 14. When the votes were counted it was clear that the issue had been important and that the backlash was strong in California. The proposition passed, and Salinger's upstate liberal support was not strong enough to stave off Murphy's conservative surge in the greater Los Angeles suburban regions downstate where the backlash was strongest. In addition, Murphy was wise enough to gauge the coming of Johnson's vote-getting strength in November and dropped much of his right-wing rhetoric for a softer line in the weeks before the election. The result was that significant moderate support shifted to Murphy and he won the election.[75]

* * *

On October 27, just a week before the election, Ronald Reagan spoke to a national audience on Goldwater's behalf and changed the face of conservatism in America. It was a spectacular speech. To William Rusher, it was from this speech that "In the last weeks of Barry Goldwater's doomed campaign—out of its very ashes, like a phoenix—arose his successor as leader of the conservative movement."[76]

Reagan's political life had had some odd twists and turns. He had supported Roosevelt throughout the 1930s and 1940s, and after the war he joined the Americans for Democratic Action, an organization of New Dealer types that pushed economic liberalism, but opposed communism—both international and domestic. He had openly supported the U.S.–Soviet post-war alliance, and had supported Hubert Humphrey for the Senate in 1948; he introduced Harry Truman at a Los Angeles rally during the 1948 presidential campaign, and in 1950 he worked for liberal Democrat Helen Gahagan Douglas in her unsuccessful campaign against Richard Nixon for the Senate. In 1947 Reagan took over as president of the Screen Actors Guild (SAG), a labor union designed to keep the powerful studios from exploiting actors. From that position, and later as a SAG board member, Reagan was instrumental in purging communists and communist-sponsored unions from Hollywood. By the early 1950s he had begun his celebrated shift to the right. He traveled the nation in the 1950s and early 1960s on behalf of General Electric, speaking mostly to business and civil groups on the successes and benefits of the American free market.

By the time of the 1964 election (actually before that) Reagan's movie career had mostly dried up. In 1962 he began introducing a weekly television western, "Death Valley Days," and he still made an occasional movie. But it was his speaking engagements that were beginning to define Reagan as a conservative. It was in these speeches on capitalist virtues (which were basically several variations on that theme) that he turned his attention to the issues that would later define him: the evils of communism, high taxes, and big government. These speaking engagements also helped Reagan develop an extremely effective speaking style that combined an immediate sense of urgency with a personable demeanor. By the early 1960s he was a rock-hard conservative, an ardent Republican, and an avid Goldwater supporter. In the 1964 campaign, Reagan co-chaired Californians for Goldwater–Miller.[77]

By the early 1960s, Reagan's speeches had coalesced to become what those around him liked to call "The Speech," a well-honed piece of material that had, over time, grown in intensity and length. In October 1964, Reagan delivered "The Speech" (adding statements of support for Goldwater) before a sympathetic crowd of Goldwater supporters at the University of Southern California. He then had copies distributed to California Goldwater campaign offices and to most state campaign offices for local release under local sponsorship.[78]

Reagan's speech came to the attention of Clif White, who immediately pushed Goldwater's advisors to broadcast it nationwide. Denison Kitchel and William Baroody, however, opposed the idea because they both thought it was too negative on Social Security. But Reagan, who wanted the speech broadcast, appealed directly to Goldwater, and Goldwater relented.[79]

Reagan's message was clear. The nation was in trouble. It was the fault of liberals, and Goldwater was the last best chance to save humanity from socialism and totalitarianism. One problem, he said, was taxes. "No nation in history has survived a tax burden that reached a third of its national income. Today thirty-seven cents out of every dollar earned in this country is the tax collector's share. . . ." Another problem, he said, was an imbalanced budget. "[O]ur government," he added, "continues to spend seventeen million dollars a day more than [it] takes in. We haven't balanced our budget twenty-eight out of the last thirty-four years. . . . [O]ur national debt is one and one-half times bigger than all the combined debts of all the nations of the world." He continued for thirty minutes. It was the Soviet Union, he said, that was behind the situation in Vietnam. This election would give the nation a choice, not between liberalism and conservatism, but between individual freedom and the "ant heap of totalitarianism." In closing, he said of the coming election, "You and I have a rendezvous with destiny. We'll preserve for our children this, the last best hope of man on earth, or we'll sentence them to take the last step into a thousand years of darkness."[80]

Reagan's speech raised more money for Goldwater's campaign than could be spent over the next week until the election.[81] It was such a success that Goldwater's people rushed to have it re-telecast on Saturday night, October 31.[82] William Rusher wrote later that it was just "one more reason to be grateful for 1964." Karl Hess called it "a superb show." And Stephen Shadegg wrote that it was "by far the most effective exposition of conservative concern for the future of the nation offered by anyone in the 1964 campaign."[83] There was a momentary sense among Goldwater's people that the campaign had been reinvigorated. But it had been lost, and not even a great speech from the Gipper could turn that around. For many inside the Goldwater campaign and in the conservative movement, Reagan's speech was possibly the last chance to articulate conservatism to the American people. The conservative message had somehow gotten lost in all the backpedaling and defensive actions of trying to counter the charges that Goldwater was a warmonger who would kill Social Security, farm subsidies, and the TVA. Here, now, finally, were the ideas American conservatives believed in, articulated brilliantly by an extremely appealing figure. Few may have recognized it at the time, but it was the passing of the baton from one leader in the conservative movement to another. Reagan later recalled, "I didn't know it then, but that speech was one of the most important milestones in my life—another one of those unexpected turns in the road that led me onto a path I never expected to take."[84]

In two years Reagan would be elected governor of California. By then he

In the last months of the campaign it was clear to many conservatives that
the baton of American conservatism was being passed from Barry Goldwater
to Ronald Reagan. Here Reagan speaks in Los Angeles on Goldwater's behalf. *(Reagan Library)*

was already the emerging leader of the conservative movement. Over the next ten years Reagan would become the undisputed leader of the Republican right, and the acknowledged disciple of Barry Goldwater and the conservative movement of the early 1960s.

* * *

In the two weeks before the election, Goldwater went through the motions of campaigning in a fog of defeat and demoralization. It was not, however, in his nature to let down his supporters, so he did what all candidates do: as the election approached, he pushed hard up until the end, appearing in Maryland, Pennsylvania, and New York, then Tennessee, Kentucky, and one last stop to visit StromThurmond in South Carolina. He hit the Midwest one last time, visiting Iowa, Wisconsin, Illinois, and Ohio; and then made one more sweep of the West: Wyoming, Nevada, Texas, and California. His last-minute message was a strong statement in support of Social Security, obviously in hopes of defusing that issue just as voters headed to the polls.[85]

Following his last big campaign speech in California, Goldwater headed off to Fredonia, Arizona, a small town north of the Grand Canyon where he had ended his Senate campaigns in the past. From there he flew to Phoenix and a reception for the press at the Camelback Hotel. In what some in the press saw as an omen of the campaign's outcome, the candidate and his wife had to stand in line at the Phoenix Country Day School for an hour and a half to vote.[86] At the press reception, Goldwater was exhausted and demoralized, unable even to eat. That evening, pushed for one last statement before the polls closed, Goldwater mused about what might have been. "We may not have spelled out the issues as well as we could," he said. "That was the point of it all—the point of the entire campaign. If only Jack Kennedy were here."[87]

Like Goldwater, Johnson hit the hustings hard in the last weeks before the November 3 election day. And like Goldwater he probably did it because it was expected of him as a candidate and because the engagements had been scheduled far in advance. It was a rigorous schedule, four or five major speeches each day, with a focus on the Midwest, California, and Florida. As usual, he said very little about Goldwater, sticking instead to touting his own accomplishments, tying his presidency to John Kennedy, promoting Democratic candidates, and making it clear that he supported and admired Republican moderates—living and dead from the first Roosevelt to Ike. One of his favorite points was to claim that as senator he had voted with President Eisenhower 96 percent of the time, while "another man who was in that same Senate," meaning Goldwater, of course, "voted against Eisenhower 76 percent of the time."[88] At one point, clearly speaking off the cuff, Johnson reminded an audience in Los Angeles of Goldwater's statement that he would "lob one into the men's room in the Kremlin," and occasionally he asked his listeners "to decide which man's thumb you want close to that button," but generally he stayed away from such direct references to Goldwater and instead spoke of his handling of the Tonkin Gulf Incident and his role in the Cuban Missile Crisis.[89] Both incidences, as Johnson portrayed them, were firm but prudent responses that had assured U.S. integrity abroad without starting a war. The message was, of course, that Goldwater's handling of such incidents might well have led directly to a nuclear holocaust.

Johnson ended his campaign in Houston, accompanied only by his family and advisor (and Houston resident) Jack Valenti. The rest of his staff remained in Washington. By late October the situation in Vietnam had become so tenuous, and the government in Saigon so weak, that the campaign had taken a back seat to the administration's foreign policy initiatives. The election had been a sure thing for at least a month, and many of Johnson's people had been turned away from the campaign and redirected to deal with other issues, particularly Vietnam. Few had the time to go to Texas with the president to celebrate. From Houston Johnson flew to Austin, where he had dinner at the Driskill Hotel. In the Jim Hogg Room he "watched the returns come in rather impassively," according to Valenti, with about twenty of his friends.[90] Later in the evening he joined the faithful on the grounds of the state capitol. "All of these years," he told his friends and supporters, "have been in preparation for this responsibility."[91] That evening, in a televised address, he explained how the nation had come out of the depression. "I watched," he said, "and sometimes I helped a little, as America forged, in the bitterness of common disaster, a new partnership between Government and business and farmers and workers. And I watched, and sometimes I helped, as a compassionate Nation built new protection for the helpless and the needy. Those measures have endured these 30 years. . . . I ask each of you to pause for a moment tonight in your homes . . . and ask yourself if these principles have not enlarged your freedom, enriched your life, and strengthened your confidence in your children's future. It is hard to believe," he added, "that we should now be asked to throw them all away." He went on to complain that the Republicans intended "to shatter the tested foundation of our economy. And it will bring disaster." On foreign policy, he said, "We are told to regard as fruitless the search for lasting agreements, such as the test ban treaty. We are attacked for our restraint in the use of our mighty power. We are told to ignore . . . the great dream of the United Nations. We are told that tactical nuclear weapons are simply a new kind of conventional explosive. If these views prevail . . . I have no doubt that our hopes for peace and the cause of freedom will be in serious peril."[92]

At about 1:40 A.M., Johnson made a victory speech at the Austin Municipal Auditorium. The facility was adorned with red, white, and blue bunting; a presidential seal was affixed to the podium. On November 22, 1963, John Kennedy had been scheduled to speak at the same auditorium. Never used, all the patriotic and presidential adornments had been boxed since that date, brought out now for Johnson's benefit. He called his victory a "mandate for unity," introduced his family, and then boarded a helicopter for his ranch in the hill country.[93] The victory, and the presidency, was now his own.

The campaigns did not serve the American voter well. Goldwater spent so much time on the defensive that his campaign never really got to the starting line. He found himself engulfed in the futile process of trying to repair his loathsome image, while at the same time trying to deflect the accusations placed on him by members of his own party. Partly because of his own rash statements, partly because of his inept campaign, and partly because of the White House smear campaign that capitalized on every weakness, Goldwater was never able to get across to the American people even the basics of his own political philosophy. At the same time, Johnson maintained such a strong lead throughout the campaign that he never saw a need to confront Goldwater, debate him, or even address the issues with much aggression. His campaign centered around a series of attack ads that were designed to do little more than solidify Goldwater's image as a warmonger and an opponent of established social and economic programs. Johnson's people made sure that the American voters saw only the radical Goldwater, a candidate who was not equal to the president—or to the presidency. Johnson's strategy was successful.

12

Analysis

On the day after the election, James Reston of the *New York Times* wrote that "Barry Goldwater not only lost the presidential election yesterday but the conservative cause as well. He has wrecked his party for a long time to come and is not even likely to control the wreckage."[1] Such were the pundits' post-mortems of the Republican debacle and the Democratic landslide. The editors of *Time* wrote that "the humiliation of [the Republican] defeat was so complete that they will not have another shot at party domination for some time to come." And in the same issue, "Whatever the mechanics of change to come, one thing is certain: Barry Goldwater and his type of conservatism have had their moment in the sun."[2] The pundits were wrong. They were wrong because they based their analysis on the assumption that Barry Goldwater created the conservative movement. Thus, they concluded, when he was removed from the scene in mortifying defeat, the movement would die with him. In fact, the conservative movement, growing rapidly under its own power, had created Barry Goldwater and drafted him as its leader. The 1964 election was barely a pause in the growth of American conservatism. Goldwater had helped define it; he had given it direction, realigned its voting base, and uncovered its leaders. The campaign had also given to the movement's generals and soldiers some much needed political experience— a sort of baptism by fire. After 1964 Goldwater stepped aside, happy to accept the role of the movement's founder and prophet. But the movement itself continued on, growing by leaps and bounds.

Goldwater's campaign also redefined the Republican party for the remainder of the twentieth century—and probably well beyond that. The conservatives had taken control by purging the northeastern moderates—the political power structure that had wrested control of the party in election after election since the 1930s. Before Goldwater, the Republicans had found their center in the Northeast, among the Wall Street establishment moderates and liberals. Midwestern conservatives, the Taftites, were allies, but when it came to naming presidential candidates they were always second best, pushed to the sidelines by the moderates. The midwestern conservatives continually charged the moderates with "me-tooism" and often vied for power within the GOP, but they were never strong enough to take control of the party. After Goldwater, the Republican power base shifted to the West, the land of rugged individualism and its modern interpretation of right-wing conservatism. Goldwater and his westerners maintained the alliance with the midwestern conservatives, brought in the South, and rejected the northeastern moderates and liberals. In 1964 that coalition was considerably less than a majority. But by 1980, this conservative coalition had built a political majority that coalesced around Ronald Reagan, Goldwater's heir apparent to the conservative mantle. Modern conservatism—Reagan conservatism—was born in Barry Goldwater and his 1964 campaign.

By contrast, many saw Johnson's landslide victory as the beginning of something almost epochal. It was, first of all, the culmination of the Kennedy dream of a better America, a nation both prosperous and at peace. There were few proponents who were more star struck by that notion than Theodore White. In his reportage on the 1964 campaign, White saw Johnson's victory as a fulfillment of that dream, a fulfillment of biblical proportions: "It was as if Kennedy, a younger Moses, had led an elder Joshua to the height of Mount Nebo and there shown him the promised land which he himself would never enter but which Joshua must make his own. For Johnson's must be the design that will organize the place in civilization that John F. Kennedy cleared."[3] Also, Johnson's victory (over the forces of conservatism) seemed to signal for many Americans the beginning of a new era. Again, White was caught up in the prospect: "For Americans live today on the threshold of the greatest hope in the whole story of the human race, in what may be the opening chapter of the post-industrial era. No capital in the world is more exciting than Washington in our time, more full of fancies and dreams and perplexities. For the first time in civilization, man's mastery over things is sufficient to provide food for all, comfort for all, housing for all, even leisure for all."[4]

There was something about the 1960s that evoked great promise. Possibly it was the appearance of forward movement and the promises of the Kennedy administration. Possibly it was the advances of the civil rights movement, the promises of new technology, the hope of economic equality. Whatever it was, by 1968 it was mostly dead. The Great Society, the great hope that Theodore White saw as the legacy of the Kennedy administration and the beginning of a new era, became an unfulfilled promise, a tragic disappointment. Underfunded and often poorly planned, most of Johnson's Great Society programs fell short of even minimal expectations. And, of course, it was Lyndon Johnson (and not the supposedly warmongering Barry Goldwater) who took the nation to war after the election. The Vietnam War tore at the nation's fabric and sapped the financial resources needed to make the Great Society programs work. By 1968, New Deal–style liberalism, from which the Great Society had grown, had fallen into disrepute—a dying economic and political philosophy—and Johnson himself was gone. Instead of a new beginning, the Great Society became the last gasp of New Deal–style, broad-sweeping, liberal, social legislation.

So it was that the election of 1964 was not as it seemed. It was not the death of American conservatism, and it was not the birth of some new liberal epoch. It was in many ways, the opposite of both.

* * *

Goldwater's concession speech in the Peace Pipe Room at the Camelback Inn in Phoenix was a moving, even wrenching, scene. Just before he spoke, he gave his daughter, Peggy, a statue of a crying clown. The sign around the clown's neck read, "I voted for Barry." Several Goldwater supporters in the crowd were crying, and Vic Gold, the candidate's assistant press secretary, recalled that he "felt like I was there when Lee said farewell to the troops." Goldwater spoke of the need to keep the conservative movement alive. "[I]t's not an effort we can drop now," he said.[5] Some one thousand miles away in Austin, Johnson, in his acceptance speech, acknowledged the mandate he had just received and talked of unity. "Our nation," he said, "should forget [its] petty differences and stand united before all the world."[6] For America, there was a winner and a loser, both anticipated. The only surprise was the size of Johnson's victory.

It was staggering. His 61 percent margin and his 15 million vote plurality were the largest in American history. His Electoral College total of 486 to Goldwater's 52 was second only to Roosevelt's historic trouncing of Alf Landon in 1936.[7] That victory had solidified the New Deal and kept Democrats in the White House for another eighteen years and in control of Congress for much of that time. Johnson made a clean sweep of every national region except the South, and even there (including all the states of the old Confederacy) he won a majority of the votes. Even in the Midwest, the Far West, and the Border States, areas where Goldwater's strength was thought to be formidable, Johnson took huge majorities. He was the first Democrat ever to carry Vermont; the first to carry Maine since 1912. He was the first southern president since Wilson, but he received 90 percent of the black vote, 20 percent more than Kennedy had received four years earlier.[8] If there was any question where black voters stood, it was answered here unequivocally.

Not surprisingly, the Johnson juggernaut carried with it very long coattails. Senate Democrats gained two seats for an increase in voting strength to sixty-eight. In the House, where they had hoped to gain something over twenty seats, the gain was, in fact, a whopping thirty-eight seats for a commanding majority of 295 to the Republicans' 140.[9] The gain, Larry O'Brien recalled, "provided us with an opportunity to move more aggressively. . . . [T]he road was just made much smoother, and Lyndon Johnson seized that opportunity. The net result was the Great Society programs"[10] *Time* called it "an ideological shift," and "the most liberal [Congress] since the early days of President Roosevelt."[11] Johnson had not only been handed a mandate from the people, he now had a commanding majority in Congress. The vote appeared to be a clear and overwhelming endorsement of the Great Society, the War on Poverty, and the president's hold-the-line policy in Vietnam. The heart of the nation, it seemed, was now Johnson's to lose.

Goldwater's fifty-two electoral votes came from the Deep South states of Alabama, Georgia, Louisiana, Mississippi, and South Carolina, and from his own state of Arizona. Of the 435 congressional districts in the nation, Goldwater carried only 60. Possibly the ultimate rejection was that Goldwater ran far behind his party. "[T]he most fascinating facet of the election," *Time* observed the morning after, "was the amazing amount of ticket splitting, as voters chose LBJ—and then skipped down the ballot to vote for deserving Republican candidates."[12] In California, for instance, Johnson won by a convincing 1.2 million votes, but George Murphy beat Pierre Salinger. In Michigan, Johnson won handily, but so did George Romney. John J. Williams of Delaware, Roman Huruska of Nebraska, Hugh Scott of Pennsylvania, and Winston Prouty of Vermont, all Republicans, won in states that Johnson carried by big majorities. Other Republican gubernatorial candidates ran well ahead of the Republican national ticket, including William Avery in Kansas, Niles Boe in South Dakota, Tim Bacock in Montana, Warren Knowles in Wisconsin, Daniel Evans in Washington, John Volpe in Massachusetts, and John Chafee in Rhode Island. It did not escape most observers that many of these candidates could be counted as moderates.[13] At the same time, Johnson's coattails brought down Republican bright lights Charles Percy of Illinois and Robert Taft, Jr., of Ohio, both perceived as future presidential timber.

Just about everything Goldwater had hoped for failed to materialize. His biggest disappointment was the perceived northern backlash. What had appeared to be a tidal wave of political dissent in the spring had evaporated by November. In fact, in the areas where George Wallace had kicked up the most ruckus, Goldwater scored no better than Republicans had scored in past elections. Johnson won big victories in Philadelphia, where some of the largest and most destructive summer riots had occurred. He also drew strong majorities in the white neighborhoods in and around Baltimore, Milwaukee, Detroit, Los Angeles, and Chicago, regions that had responded well to Wallace's campaign. He even carried Indianapolis, Gary, and Columbus, Ohio, all hotbeds of pro-Wallace activity.[14] At the same time, Johnson's frontlash was clear and present. Strongholds of moderate Republicanism flooded into Johnson's column. Possibly Johnson's greatest personal victory (and the most revealing aspect of the frontlash) was the support he received from Wall Street. Historically supportive of the GOP (particularly GOP moderates like Willkie, Dewey, and Ike) the nation's leaders in business and industry threw their money and support to Johnson in 1964. And the reason was clear: The Democrats had stimulated sales, fueled profits, and lowered corporate taxes.[15]

But Johnson's mandate was fleeting. Between the 1964 election and March 1968 (when Johnson announced that he would not run for reelection) Johnson's 1964 landslide mandate disintegrated. In the 1966 congressional elections the Republicans came roaring back with the greatest GOP gains in twenty years by adding forty-seven House seats and three Senate seats, bringing to an end the brief period of liberal dominance in Congress. The elections that year showed the resiliency of the conservative movement, an ability to reorganize and bounce back just two years after the 1964 debacle. In addition, by November 1967 Johnson's approval rating had dropped to a paltry 41 percent in a Gallup poll.[16] Then, in early March 1968, the president was embarrassed by Eugene McCarthy's strong showing in the New Hampshire primary and Bobby Kennedy's imminent run for the Democratic nomination. Finally, when Larry O'Brien told him later that month that he would lose to McCarthy in the Wisconsin primary, the president decided that the run was over and announced to the nation on March 28 that he would not seek reelection. The 1964 mandate, one of the largest in American history, had deserted Johnson and the Democrats in less than four years.

The reasons seem apparent. The Vietnam quagmire is important in understanding this change in the national feeling toward Johnson. His war policies had become unpopular with a large and increasingly vocal sector of the population. The rise of the Democratic left was also important in building opposition to Johnson's administration. Yet it might have been that the 1964 mandate (as clear as it seemed) was not a mandate at all, that it was more a vote against Goldwater and his policies (or perceived policies) than a vote for Johnson and his policies. It would not be surprising, then, as Johnson began to spell out the specifics of his liberal Great Society programs that the 1964 consensus (made up of both moderate Republicans and conservative Democrats) collapsed, and opposition to his programs formed. The evidence of the anti-Goldwater vote in 1964 is, of course, in the massive ticket splitting by Republican voters who were willing to accept other Republicans—even conservative Republicans like Murphy in California—but not Goldwater.

There is nothing more tragic in American politics than a misperceived mandate, a mistaken assumption about why voters voted as they did. In 1946, the Republicans were swept into power in the first congressional election since Roosevelt's death. It was a mandate, they believed, to sweep out the New Deal. The voters, however, had mostly been upset with Truman's postwar reconversion policies. The misperceived mandate was a major factor in Truman's 1948 victory when he came out four-square for New Deal programs, and voters, unwilling to abandon the New Deal, responded by voting Democratic. In 1964 Johnson believed that the landslide he received was a mandate in support of his Great Society programs and his policies in Vietnam. In fact, Johnson had succeeded during the 1964 campaign in demonizing Goldwater, which produced a huge split-ticket, anti-Goldwater vote that went to Johnson. Not surprisingly, when the president took his new political allies into battle, they balked. They refused to fight.

* * *

If there was any particular issue that turned the election it was the fear of a "trigger happy" president. Goldwater simply could not spin this issue. Of course, he had no one to blame but himself. He had made the statements that grew into the issue. Then Rockefeller picked it up and used it against Goldwater—to the greatest effect in the California Republican primary. Scranton, in his brief campaign, piled on the accusations and exaggerations where Rockefeller left off. By the time the general election campaign began, American voters had already been introduced to the "trigger happy" candidate, and it took little for Johnson to use it to destroy Goldwater's campaign. "Rockefeller and Scranton had drawn up the indictment," conservative writer M. Stanton Evans has written, "Lyndon Johnson was the prosecutor. Goldwater was cast as the defendant."[17]

To combat the issue, Goldwater went on television several times, nearly begging voters to understand that he would not take the nation into a nuclear war. However, while Goldwater was trying to get that message across to the nation he was also saying in speech after speech that he believed the United States should strive to achieve victory in the Cold War, a message that most American voters saw as much too aggressive in a time of international uncertainty. The Cuban Missile Crisis in October 1962 was still fresh in the American mind. For the first time the possibility of a nuclear attack on the United States was real, and it frightened many Americans into supporting a more conciliatory relationship with the Soviets.[18] Goldwater's antagonistic words alarmed voters, while Johnson's firm but measured response in Vietnam seemed safe, less likely to bring war. At the same time, the international situation appeared to be extremely unstable in 1964. A shakeup at the Kremlin, just days before the election, resulted in Khrushchev being ousted and replaced by Leonid Brezhnev and Aleksei Kosygin, two unknowns to American voters. At almost that same moment, the Chinese detonated their first atomic bomb and Xhou Enlai, the Chinese foreign minister, visited Moscow. The mid-1960s were precarious times, and voters clearly saw Lyndon Johnson as the safer candidate, the antidote to Goldwater's warmongering.

There were, of course, other issues (Social Security, Medicare, civil rights, crime), but no matter what the issue, Johnson was able to attach to Goldwater a negative image and Goldwater was unable to transcend that image—no matter how hard he tried. Possibly it was only because of his contradictory statements on all sorts of issues, possibly it was because of his right-wing radical support, but Goldwater was not, to the American people, a believable candidate. They did not believe he was sincere when he said he would not start a nuclear war because he had said he would use nuclear weapons in some situations. They did not believe him when he said he would not destroy Social Security because he had said he would consider making the program voluntary. Would he sell TVA? He had said he would. Why should voters believe him when, later, he said he would not?

All this leads to the conclusion that Goldwater was not a very good candidate. By most accounts he did not want to run for president.[19] He would have gladly stayed in the Senate representing his state, the place where he always seemed to believe he belonged. He did not have the temperament of a national candidate. He hated the long campaigning, the crowds, and the contentiousness of the fight. He even hated shaking hands. His wife Peggy hated campaigning even more than he did. He had no real understanding of image, a factor that had become extremely important as television became more and more a part of national campaigns. He harbored, in fact, an almost naive notion that the campaign would turn on the issues, that he could convince (even educate) the American people that his ideas were correct—and they would come to him on election day. Goldwater's chief speechwriter, Stephen Hess, wrote in his memoirs, "If you were to direct a petition to heaven, asking angelic dispatch of the ideal candidate for the American Presidency, the odds are 100–1 that the return mail would not bring you Barry Goldwater."[20]

The 1964 election is a good example of the strength of the American political center. With their liberal and conservative bases generally intact, the two parties, every four years, jockey to control the center. Most often, the center splits in some way. Good examples are the elections of 1960 and 1968. The result is possibly the most effective criticism of the American political system: that the candidates and their platforms are seldom distinctive. But in 1964 the conservatives and Goldwater said they intended to offer "a choice, not a echo," to give the American voter an ideological alternative to the Democrats rather than just an organizational alternative. In embracing that strategy, Goldwater not only lost the center, he abandoned it. Johnson, with his liberal base stable (mostly because of the Kennedy association, the Civil Rights Act, and the War on Poverty), was able to control the center with little difficulty. The result, then, was a landslide.

* * *

Almost immediately after the votes were counted, Republican fingers began to wag and point. Goldwater, speaking the day after the election, insisted that he had made no mistakes in the campaign. The blame, instead, should be directed at two groups that he insisted had worked against him by destroying his image and exaggerating his statements: the press and the moderates in his own party. The working press, he said, had treated him fairly, but the national columnists and television commentators had not. "I think these people should frankly hang their heads in shame," he said. *Newsweek* speculated that "these people" in Goldwater's statement meant specifically Rosco Drummond, Eric Severeid, James Reston, David Brinkley, Walter Lippmann, Howard K. Smith, Drew Pearson, and Marquis Childs. "I've never seen or heard in my life," Goldwater continued, "such vitriolic, biased attacks on one man as has been directed at me. . . . I have never in my life seen such inflammatory language as has been used by some men who know better . . . who should have enough decency, common ordinary manners about them. . . . I think these people . . . have made the fourth estate a rather sad, sorry mess."[21]

Redirecting his attack toward his party's moderates, he said, "You cannot in this game of politics fight your own party. It just doesn't work."[22] That seemed to echo what he had said just days before the election, a statement that stuck in the craws of Republican moderates: "Rockefeller and Scranton have done me more damage than the Democrats ever could."[23] Generally, his analysis of the press and the moderates was correct, but Goldwater was never able to see that he gave his enemies the ammunition they needed to destroy his campaign.

Nixon immediately blamed Rockefeller, calling him a "spoiled sport" and the party's "principal divider." Rockefeller responded from his vacation home in Spain, calling Nixon's statement a "peevish post-election utterance." Then he added, "We don't have a Republican Party right now. We have 50 Republican parties."[24] Nixon weighed in again with a call for an end to the bickering, but his statement did nothing to heal wounds. The party, he said, should be big enough for both conservatives and moderates, but not for the "'nut' left or the 'nut' right." Possibly with an eye on the 1968 nomination, he then classified himself: "I'm perhaps at dead center."[25] George Romney emerged from the election unscathed by the Democratic landslide and immediately became the leader in the press for the 1968 Republican nomination. He called for a broadening of the party, and immediately began organizing a group of seventeen Republican governors and other party leaders for the purpose of taking back the party structure for the moderates. They called for the immediate resignation of RNC chairman Dean Burch.[26]

The conservatives responded in a somewhat bitter defense. Ronald Reagan, already on the fast track to Republican party stardom, responded to the moderates: "We don't intend to turn the Republican Party over to the traitors in the battle just ended."[27] Kitchel insisted that the fight had just begun: "We may have to wait four years, but we're going to get this government back where it belongs." And John Tower told the press that a moderate would likely have lost all fifty states instead of just forty-four.[28]

Ike, whose refusal to endorse a moderate candidate had kept the road clear for Goldwater's nomination, said that the party must find "methods for correcting the false image of Republicanism . . . as a political doctrine primarily for the rich and privileged." Scranton saw other problems: "The truth is that the general impression now is that our party is . . . anti-ethnic. This has got to be eradicated very quickly."[29] Only Dean Burch, the head of the RNC, seemed to be calling for unity. In a press release on the day of the election, he pleaded with the party leadership: "[A] minority party cannot afford the luxury of disunity. . . . The wounds of the primaries and the conventions must be given an opportunity to heal completely."[30]

301

It was Burch, however, who became the immediate focus of the power struggle within the Republican party when several powerful moderates, led by Idaho's governor Robert Smile, began a call for his resignation. At the January Republican governors' conference in Denver the moderates voted unanimously to replace Burch with Ohio state party chairman Ray C. Bliss, a moderate. Burch resigned in April. Then in the House, Republican moderates pushed out their minority leader, Indiana conservative Charles Halleck, and replaced him with Michigan moderate Gerald Ford. The ousters of Burch and Halleck seemed to be a post-election inevitability—the retaking of the party by the moderates, and thus, it seemed, the death of the conservatives.[31]

* * *

In New York, Bobby Kennedy rode Johnson's coattails to victory over Kenneth Keating. He won by over 700,000 votes, a comfortable victory, but ran far behind Johnson in the state. Johnson won by a whopping 2.7 million votes, the greatest majority victory in any state in any American election.[32] The *New York Times* wrote that Kennedy won because of his campaign organization, the black vote, and Johnson's two visits to the state.[33] Of those, it had been Johnson's campaigning in New York, more than anything else, that pulled Kennedy over the top. With Kennedy dropping in the polls in late September, Johnson waded into New York on Bobby's behalf, asking New Yorkers to "vote fur ma boy." Kennedy grabbed at Johnson's coattails and won. At the victory celebration at the Statler Hotel in New York, Kennedy, always the reluctant politician, told the crowd, "If my brother was alive I wouldn't be here. I'd rather have it that way."[34] Then, he marched through a long list of supporters, aides, and workers, thanking each.

He did not thank Johnson. It would be one snub among many. Jack Valenti recalled later that the president never forgot it.[35] Undoubtedly, the event increased the split between the two men that had begun at the 1960 Democratic convention and ended only with Bobby's death in 1968.

In the California senate race, the Republican George Murphy beat Pierre Salinger, making it clear that an actor could be elected to office in California. Murphy, a strong conservative in the Goldwater tradition, had anticipated Goldwater's imminent defeat and distanced himself from him in the last weeks of the campaign. At the same time, Murphy hung close to Proposition 14, a referendum that would repeal the Rumford Fair Housing Act.

Salinger opposed the proposition, and thus supported Rumford. The Rumford Act was designed to end all discrimination in housing in California, and to many Californians such a notion cut into everything from property values to personal preferences. Proposition 14 passed by a two-to-one margin, Rumford was repealed, and Murphy was elected. Murphy's victory, along with Goldwater's statewide organization of conservatives and the animosity toward Rumford, all laid the groundwork for Ronald Reagan's election as California's governor two years later.[36] In the last month before the election, Murphy's campaign received an infusion of cash from Walt Disney allowing him to run a last-minute media blitz that apparently put him over the top. The press could not resist the obvious. Murphy had come in on Mary Poppins's coattails.[37]

* * *

For many of those who analyzed the political events in 1964, the conservatives had had their place in the sun and it was now time to step aside and hand the Republican party back to the moderates. Writing in the September 1964 issue of *Life* magazine, Stewart Alsop concluded that Goldwater would lose the election, then some two months away. However, he said, it was the margin of defeat that would determine the future of the Republican party: "If Goldwater runs a respectable race . . . then the Goldwaterites will almost certainly keep their tight grip on the party power structure, and Goldwater himself could well be the candidate again in 1968. But if Goldwater loses in a landslide," Alsop wrote, "then it is absolutely predictable that the moderates of the 'Hated Eastern Establishment' will stage a counterrevolution, and it is highly probable that it will succeed, with the nomination in 1968 of William Scranton or someone like him."[38] After the election, many in the party leadership insisted that the conservatives step aside. They had lost. "This Goldwater ideology, the thing he called conservatism, was beaten," outgoing Kansas governor John Anderson said immediately after the election. "These Goldwater people have got to roll over. They're beaten," he added.[39] Alsop's prophecy came true and Anderson's demands were heeded, if only temporarily. The conservatives, however, continued to maintain control of many state Republican party organizations, mostly as a result of Clif White's skills and efforts that had begun at least a year before the 1964 election. This conservative grassroots network had produced real power within the Republican party. It was not enough power to elect Goldwater, but it was enough to get him nominated amid the divided moderates. And after the election, although there was an immediate coup by the moderates, the conservatives remained the strongest wing within the party. As the Republicans began to put the 1964 defeat behind them and look to the 1968 campaign, it was Nixon and not the Scranton–Romney–Rockefeller moderates who emerged as the front-runner, and it was his conservative support that kept him out in front of the moderate candidates right up to the convention.

Nixon had flirted with the moderates during the 1964 campaign, running early as an Eisenhower moderate and finally criticizing Goldwater's convention speech. But after the convention he campaigned tirelessly for Goldwater, and following the election he attacked the moderates. He said that Goldwater had conducted a "very courageous campaign," and he called for an end to "kicking Goldwater" by party members.[40] Not surprisingly, Goldwater took note of Nixon's support among all the attacks and party treason, and in January 1965 he announced that Nixon was his man for 1968. Nixon may not have been as conservative on most issues as Goldwater and his 1964 followers, but he was conservative enough—and he would keep the nomination away from the Scranton–Romney–Rockefeller moderates. Nixon knew where the power was, and as long as he continued to emphasize conservative domestic themes and maintain his commitment to free South Vietnam, he knew he would receive conservative support. "They don't like me," he said, "but they tolerate me."[41] Thus Nixon became the conservative candidate as the 1968 campaign approached—with the support of such Goldwater conservatives as John Ashbrook, William F. Buckley, Strom Thurmond, and John Tower.[42]

It was the 1966 congressional elections that seemed to turn the corner for the conservatives. The Republicans took back forty-seven seats in the House and three in the Senate, and many of those were conservative victories. Conservative writer M. Stanton Evans wrote in 1968 that "Goldwater may have lost in '64, but he delivered the goods in 1966."[43] And David Reinhard wrote in his the *Republican Right Since 1945* that "The year 1966—and not 1964— would . . . become the key year in the post–World War II history of the Republican Right."[44]

Of all the 1966 victories, it was Ronald Reagan's win in the California governor's race that excited most party conservatives. Considering the extreme enmity that conservatives (particularly California conservatives) had for Republican moderates, their excitement was more directed at Reagan's victory over Republican moderate George Christopher in the California party primary than Reagan's victory over Democrat Pat Brown in the general election. Nevertheless, Reagan seemed poised to pick up the conservative gauntlet and run for president in 1968—with the full support of the Goldwater conservatives. The day after the 1964 election, a group of Goldwater conservatives meeting in Michigan formed "Republicans for Reagan" with the intention of pushing their man for the 1968 Republican nomination.[45] For many in the Goldwater camp, Reagan was the new conservative light. Henry Salvatori, a multi-millionaire California oil man who began his support for Reagan immediately after the 1964 election, said: "We realized that Reagan gave the Goldwater speech better than Goldwater. He seemed steadier, less likely to fly off the handle than Goldwater. He had more self-control, he could say the same things but in a more gentle way."[46] Reagan himself was to have said of the 1964 campaign: "The message was right. Only the messenger was wrong." But Goldwater continued to control the direction of conservatism as the 1968 election approached and he had never been impressed with Reagan. When he threw his support to Nixon, the conservative army followed. Reagan continued to pursue the nomination right up to the Miami convention in the summer of 1968, but Nixon's solid conservative support from Goldwater and his followers (along with Strom Thurmond's ability to hold the South for Nixon) left Reagan out of the running and Nixon won the nomination on the first ballot. When Nixon resigned in 1974, the conservative mantle fell, uncontested, to Reagan.

The 1964 election brought the South firmly into the Republican party for the first time. Goldwater took the Deep South states of Louisiana, Mississippi, Alabama, Georgia, and South Carolina. The press, though, was not impressed. "In the end," editors at *Time* wrote, "all that Goldwater and his devoted band of active amateurs got out of their many months of hard work was the distinction of upsetting the voting patterns in the South to carry five states. And he triumphed in those states mostly on the voters' belief that he would slow the Negro revolution—a stance which now seems to have little future in American politics."[47] However, in just four years the South (except Texas and Maryland) went for either George Wallace or Nixon, with Wallace carrying the Deep South (mostly those states Goldwater carried in 1964) and Nixon carrying the Border States (mostly those southern states that Goldwater did not win). In 1972, Nixon swept the entire region. This process of the South moving into the Republican party had been going on at least since the end of World War II. Some analysts have found its origins as early as 1928 when the Republican Herbert Hoover took the Upper South, Texas, and Florida away from the northeastern liberal Democrat Al Smith. But in the post-war period the question revolved around civil rights for African Americans and the Democratic party's continued and growing support of that movement. As Democrats began to see the advantage of the northern urban black vote they chose to embrace civil rights and exchange African-American votes for southern white votes. The prize, Democrats hoped, would be the many electoral votes of California, Illinois, Michigan, Ohio, and Pennsylvania, states where large numbers of African Americans had migrated during the twentieth century. If that gain was at the expense of the few electoral votes from a small number of states in the Deep South, then it was a good trade, particularly if they could keep control of the Upper South and the Border States. That philosophy worked for Truman in 1948 when he gave up the Deep South to Thurmond and the Dixiecrats but won in California, Ohio, and Illinois primarily because of the large numbers of black votes from the big cities in those states. In the three elections between 1952 and 1960 the Democrats (Adlai Stevenson and John Kennedy) tried to walk the line between civil rights and states' rights, by keeping a states' rights plank in the party platform, and that was enough to keep most of the South in line while still pulling in most black voters. But in 1964 that all changed. Johnson's sponsorship of the Civil Rights Act pushed white southerners away from the Democratic party. The Republicans, particularly conservative Republicans, saw this as an opportunity to bring the South into the Republican fold and build a powerful conservative coalition of the nation's most conservative regions—the South, the Midwest, and the West. Only 26 percent of Americans in 1964 called themselves Republicans, while 48 percent went on record as Democrats.[48] To add the South to a Midwest–West coalition, Republican strategists believed, would almost certainly push those numbers up even with the Democrats. To win the South, however, Republicans would have to do what northern Democrats had done for years, embrace states' rights while disavowing (or ignoring) southern racism in order not to offend northern moderates. George Wallace's run in early 1964 simply amplified this situation. He made his point loud and clear to southerners that the Democratic party was no longer the party of the white South, that the Democrats no longer had southern interests at heart, that they had abandoned states' rights for civil rights. Then, when he left the campaign and handed his arguments over to Goldwater, Wallace made it just as clear to white southerners that their future was with the Republicans. Although Wallace never in his life left the Democratic party for the Republican, he did more to bring the Republican party to the South than any other politician—except possibly Strom Thurmond or Richard Nixon. After 1964, if it was not true that the Republican party swept the South, it was certainly true that the two-party system had finally returned to the region at all electoral levels.

Goldwater set the platform for the future of the Republican party. He moved it away from the post-war role of being little more than a minority party of loyal opposition, the anti–New Deal party. He also took the party away from the northeastern moderate leadership, the party wing most noted for what Robert Taft had called "me-tooism," the willingness to accept the popular Democratic-sponsored social programs in an attempt to control the national political center. With the exception of Ike's popularity and successes in the 1950s, that political philosophy and strategy had been a dismal failure. Goldwater headed in new directions, away from the moderates, and toward a different philosophy and a different strategy. And that changed the nature of the Republican party after 1964. His coalition included the West, the Midwest, and the white South. He appealed to traditional conservatives, but he also appealed to the group that was being called the "white backlash" in the 1960s, the group Nixon would refer to as the "silent majority" in the 1970s and that others would later call the "disaffected voters" and even "Reagan Democrats" in the 1980s. Most opposed big government and its impositions on state and local affairs: others in northern cities feared street crime and the encroachment of African Americans into neighborhoods, jobs, and school districts. Goldwater's coalition was weak in 1964, but within four years it became the dominant wing of the Republican party and strong enough to be a major factor in Nixon's win.

The Democrats were about to embark on possibly their darkest time since World War II. Even the Eisenhower years did not present as much pain for the Democrats as the era between 1964 and 1992. Even though they maintained solid majorities in Congress until the 1980s, their presidential candidates were weak in the face of growing conservative insurgency in the Republican party on one hand and the growth of the left within the Democratic party on the other. Johnson's New Deal–style domestic program faltered and his Vietnam policy failed. By 1972 the Democrats had relinquished the political center to the Republicans, and by 1980 the conservatives had found their stride, solidified and marketed their philosophy, and discovered their candidate in Ronald Reagan. Much of this change turned on the election of 1964.

Appendix

The Johnson Landslide

	Percentage of vote	
	Johnson	Goldwater
National	61.3	38.7
Sex		
Women	63	38
Men	60	40
Race		
White	59	41
Nonwhite	94	6
Education		
College	52	48
High school	62	38
Grade school	66	34
Occupation		
Professional and business	54	46
White collar	57	43
Manual	71	29
Member of labor union	73	27
Age		
Under 30	64	36
30–49	63	37
50+	59	41
Religion		
Protestant	55	45
Catholic	76	24
Party affiliation		
Republicans	20	80
Democrats	87	13
Independents	56	44
Region		
East	68	32
Midwest	61	39
South	52	48
West	60	40

Source: Nelson W. Polsby and Aaron Wildavsky, *Presidential Elections: Strategies and Structures of American Politics*, 10th ed. (New York: Chatham House, 2000).

1964 Vote for President

	Thousands of votes			Percentage		
	Democrat	Republican	Total	Democrat	Republican	Electors
Alabama	211	479	690		69.5	R- 10
Alaska	44	23	67	65.9	31.4	D- 3
Arizona	238	243	481	49.5	50.4	R- 5
Arkansas	314	243	560	56.1	43.4	D- 6
California	4,172	2,879	7,058	59.1	40.8	D- 40
Colorado	476	297	777	61.3	38.2	D- 6
Connecticut	826	391	1,219	67.8	32.1	D- 8
Delaware	123	78	201	60.9	38.8	D- 3
District of Columbia	170	29	199	85.5	14.5	D- 3
Florida	949	906	1,854	51.1	48.9	D- 14
Georgia	523	617	1,139	45.1	54.1	R- 12
Hawaii	163	44	207	78.8	21.1	D- 4
Idaho	149	144	292	50.9	49.1	D- 4
Illinois	2,797	1,906	4,703	59.5	40.5	D- 26
Indiana	1,171	911	2,092	56.0	43.6	D- 13
Iowa	733	449	1,185	61.9	37.9	D- 9
Kansas	464	387	858	54.1	45.1	D- 7
Kentucky	670	373	1,046	64.0	35.7	D- 9
Louisiana	387	509	896	43.2	56.8	R- 10
Maine	262	119	381	68.8	31.2	D- 4
Maryland	731	385	1,116	65.5	34.5	D- 10
Massachusetts	1,786	549	2,345	76.2	23.4	D- 14
Michigan	2,137	1,060	3,203	66.7	33.1	D- 21
Minnesota	991	560	1,554	63.8	36.0	D- 10
Mississippi	53	357	409	12.9	87.1	R- 7
Missouri	1,164	654	1,818	64.0	36.0	D- 12
Montana	164	113	279	58.9	40.6	D- 4

Nebraska	307	277	584	52.6	47.4	D- 5
Nevada	79	56	135	58.6	41.4	D- 3
New Hampshire	184	104	288	63.9	36.1	D- 4
New Jersey	1,868	964	2,848	65.6	33.9	D- 17
New Mexico	194	133	329	59.0	40.4	D- 4
New York	4,913	2,244	7,166	68.6	31.3	D- 43
North Carolina	800	625	1,425	56.2	43.8	D- 13
North Dakota	150	108	258	58.0	41.9	D- 4
Ohio	2,498	1,471	3,969	62.9	37.1	D- 26
Oklahoma	520	413	932	55.7	44.3	D- 8
Oregon	501	283	786	63.7	36.0	D- 6
Pennsylvania	3,131	1,674	4,823	64.9	34.7	D- 29
Rhode Island	315	75	390	80.9	19.1	D- 4
South Carolina	16	309	525	41.1	58.9	R- 8
South Dakota	163	130	293	55.6	44.4	D- 4
Tennessee	635	509	1,144	55.5	44.5	D- 11
Texas	1,663	959	2,627	63.3	36.5	D- 25
Utah	220	182	401	54.7	45.3	D- 4
Vermont	108	55	163	66.3	33.7	D- 3
Virginia	558	481	1,042	53.5	46.2	D- 12
Washington	780	470	1,258	62.0	37.4	D- 9
West Virginia	538	254	792	67.9	32.1	D- 7
Wisconsin	1,050	638	1,692	62.1	37.7	D- 12
Wyoming	81	62	143	56.6	43.4	D- 3
Totals	43,130	27,178	70,644	61.1	38.5	R- 52
						D-486

Notes

Abbreviations
(Used in Notes and Bibliography)

ADAH   Alabama Department of Archives and History
AHF   Arizona Historical Foundation
BMG   Barry M. Goldwater
DCC   Dirksen Congressional Center
DNC   Democratic National Committee
LBJ   Lyndon Baines Johnson
LBJL   Lyndon Baines Johnson Library
LBJLOHC Lyndon Baines Johnson Library Oral History Collection
LBJP   Lyndon Baines Johnson Papers
MFDP   Missisipi Freedom Democratic Party
MLK   Martin Luther King, Jr.
NAACP   National Association for the Advancement of Colored People
NAR   Nelson A. Rockefeller
RAC   Rockefeller Archive Center
RFA   Rockefeller Foundation Archives
RNC   Republican National Committee
SCLC   Southern Christian Leadership Conference
SNCC   Student Non-violent Coordinating Committee
UT   University of Texas

Introduction

1. "Barry Goldwater Campaign Speeches," (March 14, 1964), vol. 1 manuscript collection AHF. Goldwater made the statement at other times. See *Time*, October 18, 1963.

2. *Newsweek*, February 24, 1964.

Chapter 1. Conservatives in the "Modern" World of Eisenhower, and the Rise of Goldwater

1. Karl Hess, *In a Cause That Will Triumph: The Goldwater Campaign and the Future of Conservatism* (New York, 1967), 6.

2. M. Stanton Evans, *The Future of Conservatism: From Taft to Reagan and Beyond* (New York, 1968), 223.

3. Ibid., 258.

4. Lou Harris, *Is There a Republican Majority? Political Trends, 1952–1956* (New York, 1954), 204.

5. *New York Times*, July 11, 12, and 13, 1952.

6. *U.S. News & World Report*, April 3, 1955; Charles E. Bohlen, *Witness to History, 1929–1969* (New York, 1973), 309–36.

7. Quoted in William Manchester, *The Glory and the Dream: A Narrative History of America, 1932–1972* (Boston, 1973), I, 812.

8. Stephen Ambrose, *Eisenhower: Soldier and President* (New York, 1990), 307.

9. *Cong. Rec.*, 82d Cong., 1st sess., 6556–6603. McCarthy's entire argument against Marshall is in Joseph McCarthy, *America's Retreat from Victory: The Story of George Catlett Marshall* (New York, 1951).

10. Gallup poll quoted in Robert Griffith, *Politics of Fear: Joseph R. McCarthy and the Senate*, 2d ed. (Amherst, MA, 1987), 263.

11. Barry Goldwater, *With No Apologies: The Personal and Political Memoirs of United States Senator Barry M. Goldwater* (New York, 1979), 159. For more on the Goldwater–McCarthy relationship see Robert Alan Goldberg, *Barry Goldwater* (New Haven, CT, 1995), 106–7.

12. Griffin, *Politics of Fear*, 199–200.

13. *Cong. Rec.*, 83d Cong., 2d sess., 16005.

14. Quoted in Manchester, *The Glory and the Dream*, I, 813.

15. Ibid., I, 813. Eisenhower also failed to balance the budget in 1954.

16. *National Review*, June 27, 1956.

17. Quoted in Richard W. Reinhard, *The Republican Right Since 1945* (Lexington, KY, 1983), 124–25; and David Oshinsky, *A Conspiracy So Immense* (New York, 1983), 473–94.

18. Ambrose, *Eisenhower: Soldier and President*, 399; *Time*, September 19, 1964.

19. John Judis, *William F. Buckley, Jr.: Patron Saint of the Conservatives* (New York, 1988), 128–33: (December 31, 1954); *National Review*, November 5, 1955; *Cong. Rec.*, 83d Cong., 2d sess., 16030.

20. *Life*, September 3, 1956.

21. Quoted in Kurt Schuparra, *Triumph of the Right: The Rise of the California Conservative Movement, 1945–1966* (Armonk, NY, 1998), 25.

22. *New York Times*, November 7, 1956.

23. Quoted in Gary W. Reichard, *Politics as Usual: The Age of Truman and Eisenhower* (Arlington Heights, IL, 1988), 131.

24. Good examples are Arthur Larson, *A Republican Looks at His Party* (New York, 1956), and Emmet John Hughes, *The Ordeal of Power: A Political Memoir of the Eisenhower Years* (New York, 1963). Reinhard, *The Republican Right*, 139.

25. William A. Rusher, *Rise of the Right* (New York, 1984), 64–65. Rusher claims that the United States could have launched a satellite before the Soviets if Eisenhower had allowed the army to use the Jupiter rocket instead of the Vanguard.

26. Quoted in Ambrose, *Eisenhower: Soldier and President*, 334. See also *New York Times*, November 8, 1954.

27. This "rumor" is fairly well borne out in Rusher, *Rise of the Right*, 66. Knowland still got a divorce. He committed suicide in 1974. See Trotton Anderson, "The 1958 California Election," *Western Political Quarterly* 12 (March 1959): 276–300.

28. *New York Times*, November 6, 1968; Hess, *In a Cause*, 8–9. In 1964 the Republicans lost forty-eight seats in the House (but won back ten for a net loss of thirty-eight). In the same year the Republicans lost only three seats in the Senate. In 1958 nine Republican governorships were lost, to only three lost in 1964. In 1958, 686 Republican seats were lost in state senates and lower houses. In 1964 that number was 541.

29. *National Review*, November 12, 1958. The article was entitled "Coroner's Report." The Nixon quote is in Manchester, *Glory and the Dream*, II, 1034.

30. Goldwater voted with the administration 66 percent of the time through 1956. That number dropped to 52 percent by 1958. Goldberg, *Barry Goldwater*, 118.

31. *Cong. Rec.*, 86th Cong., 1st sess., 5258–65.

32. *Time*, June 23, 1961; *New Yorker*, April 7, 1957.

33. Jerome L. Himmelstein, *To the Right: The Transformation of American Conservatism* (Berkeley, CA, 1990), 66.

34. The group was known as The Committee of One Hundred and continued to exist up to the 1960 Republican convention. Goldberg, *Barry Goldwater*, 142; Lee Edwards, *Goldwater: The Man Who Made a Revolution* (Washington, DC, 1995), 105–6.

35. Barry Goldwater, *Why Not Victory? A Fresh Look at American Foreign Policy* (New York, 1962), 12–13. Clarence Manion, the dean of the Notre Dame Law School, convinced Goldwater to write *Conscience of a Conservative*. Bozell, as Goldwater stated later, "put the thing together." Goldwater interview with Robert Alan Goldberg, September 24, 1992.

36. Barry Goldwater, *Conscience of a Conservative* (Shepherdsville, KY, 1960), 23.

37. Ibid., 18.

38. Ibid., 20.

39. Ibid., 23.

40. Ibid., 50, 60–61.

41. Ibid., 25–26.

42. Ibid., 35.

43. Ibid., 92, 123, 125.

44. Ibid., 122.

45. Ibid., 125.

46. Barry Goldwater, "How to Win the Cold War," *New York Times Magazine*, September 17, 1961, 100.

47. Pat Buchanan, "The Voice in the Desert," Introduction to Goldwater, *Conscience of a Conservative* (Washington, DC, 1990), ix.

48. Edwards, *Goldwater*, 110. Edwards insists that *Conscience of a Conservative* is rivaled only by Thomas Paine's *Common Sense* as the most significant treatise in U.S. political history.

49. Richard Hofstader, *The Paranoid Style in American Politics, and Other Essays* (New York, 1967), 44.

50. See Goldwater on his relationship to Taft in *New York Times*, October 4, 1988. See also, Mary C. Brennan, *Turning Right in the Sixties: The Conservative Capture of the GOP* (Chapel Hill, NC, 1995), 31–33; Goldwater, *Conscience of a Conservative*, 79.

51. *Inquiry*, October 27, 1980; George Nash, *The Conservative Intellectual Movement Since 1945* (New York, 1976), 145; Rusher, *Rise of the Right*, 72–83; Lee Edwards, *The Conservative Revolution: The Movement That Remade America* (New York, 1999), 78–83.

52. *New York Times*, December 27, 1959.

53. Goldwater, *With No Apologies*, 110–11; David Halberstam, *The Fifties* (New York, 1993), 313.

54. Stephen C. Shadegg, *What Happened to Goldwater? The Inside Story of the 1964 Republican Campaign* (New York, 1965), 32; Theodore H. White, *The Making of the President—1960* (New York, 1961), 210–18; Rusher, *Rise of the Right*, 88; *National Review*, August 6, 1960; *Time*, August 1, 1960. For Nixon's account, see Richard M. Nixon, *Six Crises* (Garden City, NY, 1962), 314; Richard M. Nixon, *RN: The Memoirs of Richard Nixon* (New York, 1978), 215.

55. Barry Goldwater, *Goldwater* (New York, 1988), 256.

56. Quoted in Halberstam, *The Fifties*, 314.

57. *New York Times*, July 24, 1960; *Time*, August 1, 1960; *National Review*, August 6, 1960; T. White, *Making of the President—1960*, 112.

58. Goldwater, *With No Apologies*, 102.

59. *Time*, July 24, 1960, and June 23, 1961; *New York Times*, July 28, 1960; T. White, *Making of the President—1960*, 196–205.

60. Evans, *Future of Conservatism*, 227–29

61. *U.S. News & World Report*, November 21, 1960.

62. *Time*, July 24, 1964.

63. Phyllis Schafaly, *A Choice Not an Echo* (Alton, IL, 1964).

64. Rusher, *Rise of the Right*, 85.

Chapter 2. The Democrats Resurgent and the Rise of the Boston–Austin Axis

1. In 1948, the electoral votes of Alabama, Florida, Georgia, Louisiana, Mississippi and South Carolina totaled fifty-nine. Gary Donaldson, *Truman Defeats Dewey* (Lexington, KY, 1999), 190.

2. Ibid., 112–22, 215.

3. *New York Times*, July 27, 1952.

3. Ibid., July 27, 1952.

4. Steven M. Gillon, *Politics and Vision: The ADA and American Liberalism, 1947–1985* (New York, 1987), 84–85; John Frederick Martin, *Civil Rights and the Crisis of Liberalism: The Democratic Party, 1945–1976* (Boulder, CO, 1979), 96–100.

5. William C. Berman, *The Politics of Civil Rights in the Truman Administration* (Columbus, OH, 1970), 231.

6. William H. Chaffe, *Unfinished Journey: America Since World War II* (New York, 1993), 3d ed., 154–55.

7. *New York Times*, August 13, 1956. Humphrey helped push a strong civil rights plank into the Democratic party platform at the 1948 Democratic National Convention, prompting a walkout of southern delegates and the formation of the States' Rights Democrats. Humphrey was then the mayor of Minneapolis and running for the Senate. He won the election. See Donaldson, *Truman Defeats Dewey*, 163–66.

8. Joseph P. Lash, *Eleanor: The Years Alone* (New York, 1972), 241. Mrs. Roosevelt made additional such statements at the convention. See *New York Times*, August 3, 1956.

9. Stevenson made one major civil rights speech in Harlem on October 4. See John Bartlow Martin, *Adlai Stevenson and the World: The Life of Adlai E. Stevenson* (Garden City, NY, 1977), 361.

10. Kenneth O'Reilly, *Nixon's Piano: Presidents and Racial Politics from Washington to Clinton* (New York, 1995), 175.

11. Jack Valenti interview, LBJLOHC.

12. The other two senators were both from Tennessee: Albert Gore and Estes Kefauver.

13. Merle Miller, *Lyndon: An Oral Biography* (New York, 1980), 269.

14. Ibid., 268.

15. Ambrose, *Eisenhower*, 444.

16. Miller, *Lyndon*, 269–70.

17. Lyndon Baines Johnson, *The Vantage Point* (New York, 1971), 156; Miller, Lyndon, 273.

18. Hubert Humphrey interview, LBJLOHC.

19. Miller, *Lyndon*, 299.

20. Humphrey interview, LBJLOHC.

21. Democratic leader in the House, and fellow Texan Sam Rayburn also pushed Stevenson to choose Johnson as his vice presidential candidate. George Reedy interview, LBJLOHC; Arthur M. Schlesinger, Jr., *A Thousand Days* (Boston, 1965), 47–48.

22. *New York Times*, November 3, 1959.

23. John Connally, India Edwards, and Oscar Chapman headed an unauthorized campaign organization. Sam Rayburn had opened a twelve-room "Johnson for President" headquarters in Austin. See Reedy interview, LBJLOHC.

24. Reedy interview, LBJLOHC.

25. James Rowe interview, LBJLOHC.

26. In 1928, Alfred Smith chose Joseph T. Robinson of Arkansas (and lost much of the South anyway). In 1932, Roosevelt chose John Nance Garner of Texas. In 1944 he chose Harry S. Truman from Missouri (perceived as both a southerner and a midwesterner). In 1948 Truman chose Alben W. Barkley of Kentucky. In 1952 Stevenson chose John J. Sparkman of Alabama. In 1956 he chose (or the convention chose) Estes Kefauver of Tennessee.

27. *New York Times*, July 8 and 14, 1960; Reedy interview, LBJLOHC.

28. Guthman, *We Band of Brothers* (New York, 1971), 76. See also several quotes in Victor Lasky, *RFK: The Man and the Myth* (New York, 1968) 452–53, 470.

29. JFK had Addison's disease, which was once considered fatal but by 1960 was treatable, though not curable, with cortisone. Bobby Kennedy denied it the next day. See India Edwards, *Pulling No Punches: Memoirs of a Woman in Politics* (New York, 1977), 229; Miller, *Lyndon*, 317.

30. It turned out to be true. Had Kennedy lost just Texas and any two other southern states he would have lost the election. Louisiana congressman Hale Boggs was insistent in a 1965 interview that Kennedy had wanted Johnson all along. See Hale Boggs interview, LBJLOHC. Clark Clifford has written that Kennedy offered the vice presidency to Symington, but then backed away from the offer and chose Johnson. Clark Clifford, *Counsel to the President: A Memoir* (New York, 1991), 318; Nancy Dickerson, *Among Those Present: A Reporter's View of Twenty-five Years in Washington* (New York, 1976), 43.

31. Humphrey interview, LBJLOHC; Joseph Alsop, *I've Seen the Best of It* (New York, 1992), 425–28. See also Guthman, *We Band of Brothers*, 73.

32. Thomas P. O'Neill, *Man of the House* (New York, 1987), 93–95.

33. For RFK's interest in Jackson, see Guthman, *We Band of Brothers*, 75–80. Guthman was an advisor to Robert Kennedy and worked for him at the Los Angeles convention.

34. Boggs interview, LBJLOHC; Larry O'Brien interview, LBJLOHC.

35. Guthman, *We Band of Brothers*, 77. According to Guthman, RFK thought it "inconceivable" that LBJ would run with his brother.

36. Reedy interview, LBJLOHC.

37. Abe Fortas interview, LBJLOHC.

38. *New York Times*, November 6, 1960; Jan Jarboe Russell, *Lady Bird: A Biography of Mrs. Johnson* (New York, 1999), 207.

39. In reality, Johnson had moved through the crowd as slowly a possible, hoping to draw as much enmity as he could for the benefit of the press; and more than once he had to restrain Lady Bird from returning with a vengeance what he was being dealt.

40. Miller, *Lyndon*, 271; Irwin Unger and Debi Unger, *LBJ: A Life* (New York, 1999), 251–52.

41. Valenti interview, LBJLOHC.

42. Jeff Shesol, *Mutual Contempt: Lyndon Johnson, Robert Kennedy, and the Feud That Defined a Decade* (New York, 1997), 101–3; Robert Dallek, *Flawed Giant: Lyndon Johnson and His Times* (New York, 1998), 37.

43. Edwin O. Guthman and Jeffrey Shulman, eds., *Robert Kennedy: In His Own Words* (New York, 1988), 215.

44. Shesol, *Mutual Contempt*, 107; Kenneth P. O'Donnell and David F. Powers, *"Johnny, We Hardly Knew Ye": Memoirs of John Fitzgerald Kennedy* (Boston, 1972), 6.

45. Reedy interview, LBJLOHC.

46. Johnson, *Vantage Point*, 539.

47. See some examples in *U.S. News & World Report*, February 25, 1963; Gore Vidal, "The Best Man, 1968," *Esquire*, March 1963, 59.

48. He told Orville Freeman as much. See Freeman interview LBJLOHC. Bobby Baker, *Wheeling and Dealing: Confessions of a Capitol Hill Operator* (New York, 1978), 126.

49. Arthur M. Schlesinger, Jr., *Robert Kennedy and His Times* (New York, 1978), 414.

50. Baker was indicted in 1966, convicted a year later, and finally jailed for eighteen months in 1971.

51. *Time*, October 18, 1963.

52. LBJ made statements to this effect to journalist Helen Thomas; see Helen Thomas, *Dateline White House: A Warm and Revealing Account of America's Presidents from the Kennedys to the Fords* (New York, 1977), 121. See also, Schlesinger, *Robert Kennedy*, 414.

53. Miller, *Lyndon*, 384–85; 397–98.

54. See conversation between JFK and George Smathers recounted in O'Donnell and Powers, *"Johnny,"* 5.

55. Miller, *Lyndon*, 397. Hubert Humphrey generally agreed with this analysis, see ibid., 397.

56. Rowland Evans and Robert Novak, *Lyndon B. Johnson: The Exercise of Power* (New York, 1968), 905; Schlesinger, *Thousand Days*, 1018; Schlesinger, *Robert Kennedy*, 631; Jeff Schesol, *Mutual Contempt*, 110; O'Donnell and Powers, *"Johnny,"* 386–87; O'Brien interview, LBJLOHC.

57. Schlesinger, *Robert Kennedy*, 631–32. See Gallup polls cited here as well. See also Guthman and Schulman, *Robert Kennedy*, 388, 392.

58. Ibid., 392.

59. *Newsweek*, January 20, 1964.

60. Benjamin C. Bradlee, *Conversations with Kennedy* (New York, 1975), 232.

61. Roy Reed, "The Liberals Love Barry Goldwater Now," *New York Times Magazine*, April 7, 1974, 48.

62. Schlesinger, *Thousand Days*, 1018.

Chapter 3. Goldwater Ambivalence and the Decision to Run

1. *Newsweek* (November 14, 1964); Jules Wiltcover, *The Resurrection of Richard Nixon* (New York, 1970), passim. A year after the 1960 election, a survey in the *New York Times* showed that of the 1960 Republican convention delegates, nearly 50 percent expected Goldwater to be the GOP candidate in 1964. Nixon and Rockefeller made up the substance of the remaining 50 percent. *New York Times*, October 28, 1961.

2. Copy of the Sharon Statement is in Rusher, *Rise of the Right*, 89. Moderate Leonard Nadasdy won control of the Young Republicans in 1960. Rusher, Clifton White, and others in the conservative movement retook control of the organization in June 1963 with the election of David "Buz" Lukins. White, Rusher, and other conservatives had controlled the YR since the 1950s. Himmelstein, *To the*

Right, 66; Rusher, *Rise of the Right*, 98–99; John Andrew III, *The Other Side of the Sixties: Young Americans for Freedom and the Rise of Conservative Politics* (New Brunswick, NJ, 1997), 56–60.

3. M. Stanton Evans, *Revolt on Campus* (Chicago, 1963), 38.

4. Evans, *Future of Conservatism*, 112–13; *Time* reported that the YAF had grown from 100 to 23,000 members in one year. *Time*, June 23, 1961; Reinhard, *The Republican Right*, 172. Another active college conservative organization was the Intercollegiate Society of Individualists.

5. Nash, *Conservative Intellectual Movement*, 138, 276; Goldberg, *Goldwater*, 157.

6. Andrew, *Other Side of the Sixties*, 141–43. An excellent account of the March Madison Square Garden rally is in Rick Perlstein, *Before the Storm: Barry Goldwater and the Unmaking of the American Consensus* (New York, 2001), 164. *Time*, March 16, 1962.

7. *Time*, June 23, 1961.

8. Clifton White, *Suite 3505* (New York, 1967), 37–42; Rusher, *Rise of the Right*, 101–4; *Time*, July 17, 1964; Perlstein, *Before the Storm*, 172–73.

9. C. White, *Suite 3505*, 42–48. Goldwater insisted he knew nothing of this. See his recollections in Goldwater, *Goldwater*, 134.

10. C. White, *Suite 3505*, 49.

11. The Conservative party received nearly 150,000 votes. It was widely perceived that the New York Conservative party was the nucleus of a conservative third party movement. See Rusher, *Rise of the Right*, 97, 131. See also Daniel J. Mahoney, *Actions Speak Louder: The Story of the New York Conservative Party* (New York, 1968).

12. *Newsweek*, February 18, 1964; Goldwater, *With No Apologies*, 146.

13. *Why Not Victory?* was based in large part on a speech written by Brent Bozell. See Edwards, *Goldwater*, 116.

14. Goldwater, *Why Not Victory?* 154–55.

15. *U.S. News & World Report*, July 8, 1963; *National Review*, August 13, 1963; Andrew, *Other Side of the Sixties*, 175–76. Nelson Rockefeller was invited to speak at the Young Republican convention in San Francisco, but turned down the offer. For the invitation, see James B. Schryver to Rockefeller (March 6, 1963). For the rejection, see Robert B. Douglas to Schryver (March 26, 1963), NAR, RFA. Rockefeller was also asked to donate money to the Young Republicans. He refused that as well. Hinman to NAR (April 6, 1962), Politics–Hinman Files, 93/642, RFA, RAC.

16. *Newsweek*, July 15, 1963; Goldberg, *Goldwater*, 171.

17. Evans, *Future of Conservatism*, 122.

18. Stewart Alsop, "Can Goldwater Win?" *Saturday Evening Post*, September 24, 1963, 19.

19. Rusher, *Rise of the Right*, 147; William Rusher, "Crossroads for the GOP," *National Review*, February 1963, 109–12.

20. Goldberg, *Goldwater*, 149. The biographies are: Jack Bell, *Mr. Conservative: Barry Goldwater* (Garden City, NY, 1962); Stephen Shadegg, *Barry Goldwater: Freedom Is His Flight Plan* (New York, 1962); Edwin McDowell,

Barry Goldwater: Portrait of an Arizonan (Chicago, 1964); Schlafly, *A Choice, Not an Echo*, passim.

21. Stephen Shedegg and at least eight others wrote the articles. See *Time*, June 23, 1963. At the time, Shedegg was the chairman of the Arizona Republican party.

22. C. White, *Suite 3505*, 94, 100.

23. Ibid., 104–5.

24. Ibid., 106–7; *New York Herald-Tribune*, December 5, 1962; *New York Times*, December 4, 1962.

25. Ibid., 117.

26. Goldwater, *Goldwater*, 157.

27. Rusher, *Rise of the Right*, 142; C. White, *Suite 3505*, 121–22.

28. Ibid., 122. In his memoir, Goldwater complained that the primary reason he refused to work with White was that he was an intellectual, a Washington insider, and a political professional of the type Goldwater detested. He was, Goldwater wrote, a "pro, much more than a mere public relations man or college instructor in political science. He had been a GOP party worker since his twenties and was a very experienced technician." Goldwater, *Goldwater*, 156

29. Rusher, *Rise of the Right*, 109, 142.

30. Goldwater, *Goldwater*, 157. See also Transcript of Goldwater statement on NBC program *Campaign and the Candidates* (July 30, 1964) 3H515, Goldwater Collection, Center for American History, UT. Here Goldwater recalls, "When the Draft-Goldwater movement got started . . . I sort of laughed at it."

31. Rusher, *Rise of the Right*, 146. See also Himmelstein, *To the Right*, 68.

32. BMG to Kitchel (March 5, 1963), "W" Series, 13/21, Goldwater Papers, AHF; *Time*, July 17, 1964.

33. RNC Press Release "Dean Burch," n.d., "W" Series, Goldwater Papers, AHF. Shedegg, *What Happened to Goldwater?*, 87–90.

34. Rusher, *Rise of the Right*, 157; Hess, *In a Cause*, 28. Milton Friedman from the University of Chicago advised Goldwater on economic issues. The aide was Tony Smith, Goldwater's press secretary. Goldwater, *Goldwater*, 150, 156.

35. Rusher, "Crossroads for the GOP," 109–12; For Clif White's similar analysis, see C. White, *Suite 3505*, 98. These numbers were apparent to others outside the conservative movement. Stewart Alsop came up with much the same analysis a few months later. See Stewart Alsop, "Can Goldwater Win in 1964?" *Saturday Evening Post*, August 24, 1963, 24. This strategy is also spelled out in *Harpers*, May 1963.

36. *Newsweek*, June 1, 1964; Schuparra, *Triumph of the Right*, 88.

37. George Hinman to Rockefeller (June 16, 1962), Box 93/642, Politics–Hinman Files, RAF, RAC. See similar letters, Hinman to Rockefeller (August 10, 1962), Box 93/643, and (November 23, 1962) Box 93/644 in same. For a discussion of these breakfasts, see Michael Kramer and Sam Roberts, *"I Never Wanted to be Vice-President of Anything!" An Investigative Biography of Nelson Rockefeller* (New York, 1976), 266–69.

38. C. White, *Suite 3505*, 86–87; Perlstein, *Before the Storm*, 162.

39. Theodore H. White, *Making of the President—1964* (New York, 1965), 82.

40. *Newsweek*, July 15, 1963; Andrew, *Other Side of the Sixties*, 175–76.

41. *Life*, July 26, 1963. Rockefeller was on vacation when this statement was released to the press on July 14.

42. *Newsweek*, July 22, 1963; *Time*, July 22, 1963; *New York Times*, July 15, 1963.

43. Quoted in Goldberg, *Goldwater*, 173; *Newsweek*, July 22, 1963.

44. Evans, *Future of Conservatism*, 118–19.

45. *Time*, July 24, 1964.

46. Alsop, "Can Goldwater Win?" 22–23.

47. *Life*, July 12, 1963. See also *Washington Post*, July 22, 1963. Goldwater had been making such statements for some time. In 1961 he was quoted in the *New York Herald-Tribune*: "The Republican Party has not attracted Negro voters. It is time to admit we cannot get them . . . so let's quit trying specifically to get them." *New York Herald-Tribune*, February 28, 1961.

48. *New York Times*, June 23, 1962.

49. *Time*, August 28, 1964.

50. It was believed by some liberals that the idea of hiring quotas was begun, as one observer described it, by "a whispering campaign fostered by agents provocateurs from the Goldwater camp." See Herbert Harris, "Riddle of the Labor Vote," *Harpers*, October 1964, 45. Many of the organizations supporting Goldwater opposed labor unions. These organizations included the John Birch Society, Americans for Constitutional Action, Christian Crusade, Texans for America, The Minutemen, The National Right-to-Work Committee, and the National Association of Manufacturers. Labor leadership supported Johnson overwhelmingly. See Harris, "Riddle," 43.

51. I.F. Stone, "The Collected Works of Barry Goldwater," *New York Review of Books*, August 20, 1964, 3. For a broad-brush look at all these conservative groups, see Himmelstein, *To the Right*, 69–77; and Irving Crespi, "The Structural Basis for Right-wing Conservatism: The Goldwater Case," *Public Opinion Quarterly* (Winter 1965–1966): 540.

52. Norman Mailer, "In the Red Light: A History of the Republican Convention in 1964," *Esquire*, November 1964, 83. See also Seymour Lipset and William Schneider, *The Confidence Gap: Business, Labor, and Government in the Public Mind* (New York, 1983).

53. *Time*, July 24, 1964.

54. *Time*, October 8, 1963. Walter Lippmann, however, believed that Goldwater would not run because his "philosophy is radically opposed to the central traditions of the Republican Party." See *Time*, September 6, 1963.

55. Transcript of BMG statement on NBC program *Campaign and the Candidates* (July 30, 1964) 3H515, Goldwater Collection, Center for American History, UT. Copy also in Presidential Campaign Files, 11/1, Goldwater Papers, AHF.

56. See Schuparra, *Triumph of the Right*, 84.

57. Transcript of BMG statement on NBC program *Campaign and the Candidates* (July 30, 1964) 3H515, Goldwater Collection, Center for American History, UT.

58. *New York Times*, November 26, 1963; Goldwater, *Goldwater*, 149.

59. Rusher, *Rise of the Right*, 157–58, 179. See also Evans, *Future of Conservatism*, 126.

60. Transcript of BMG statement on NBC program *Campaign and the Can-*

didates, (July 30, 1964) 3H515, Goldwater Collection, Center for American History, UT.

61. *New York Times*, January 4, 1964; C. White, *Suite 3505*, 255; *Newsweek*, January 13, 1964; *U.S. News & World Report*, January 13, 1964. See also Richard G. Kleindienst, *Justice: The Memoirs of Attorney General Richard Kleindienst* (Ottawa, IL, 1985), 30–31.

62. Rusher, *Rise of the Right*, 170.

63. C. White, *Suite 3505*, 255; Hess, *In a Cause*, 184. Goldwater even replaced Ione Harrington, the leader of the woman's arm of the Draft-Goldwater Committee, with Ann Eve Johnson, the former national committeewoman from Arizona. See White, *Suite 3505*, 255. Kleindienst states in his memoirs that he had "far less ability and experience" than White. See Kleindienst, *Justice*, 33.

64. Rusher, *Rise of the Right*, 171.

65. Goldwater, *Goldwater*, 202.

66. *Newsweek*, February 3, 1964. Nixon made this type of statement often. See *Newsweek*, April 6, 1964.

67. The story that Eisenhower had encouraged Lodge to run broke on the front page of the *New York Times* on December 8, 1963. See also *Newsweek*, January 13, 1964.

68. *Newsweek*, March 16, and April 20, 1964; *Time*, March 6, 1964; Jon Margolis, *The Last Innocent Year: America in 1964, The Beginning of the Sixties* (New York, 1999), 152.

69. *Newsweek*, May 18, 1964.

70. *Newsweek*, January 20, 1964.

71. *Newsweek*, March 16, 1964. Eisenhower traveled to Harrisburg to encourage Scranton to run, but he refused to give him an endorsement. *Newsweek*, May 18, 1964. See also George D. Wolf, *William Warren Scranton: Pennsylvania Statesman* (University Park, PA, 1981), 91.

72. T. White, *The Making of the President—1964*, 84–85; *Newsweek*, January 13, 1964.

73. Herbert Parmet, *JFK: The Presidency of John F. Kennedy* (New York, 1983), 130, 272; Theodore C. Sorensen, *Kennedy* (New York, 1965), 754; Guthman and Shulman, *Robert Kennedy*, 76.

74. *Newsweek*, January 13, 1964.

75. Ibid., February 10 and 24, 1964.

Chapter 4. Early Republican Battlegrounds and the Rise of George Wallace

1. *Newsweek*, January 20 and February 24, 1964.

2. Ibid., February 24, 1964.

3. *Meet the Press* transcripts, Barry Goldwater (January 5, 1964), Box 218, Lawrence Spivak Papers, LC. Goldwater made the same statement on *Face the Nation*. See *Newsweek*, January 20, 1964.

4. Harris polls cited in *Newsweek*, February 24 and March 23, 1964. In November 1963, 62 percent of prospective voters in New Hampshire approved of Goldwater.

5. Goldwater, *Goldwater*, 202–3. Kleindienst, *Justice*, 34–35.

6. Rusher, *Rise of the Right*, 172.

7. *New York Times*, March 11, 1964; *Newsweek*, March 23, 1964. Later Goldwater recalled, "The New Hampshire primary was a lesson in how not to run a campaign." Goldwater, *Goldwater*, 202. On *Issues and Answers* in late May, he blamed it all on "over exposure, not to the people, but to the press. . . . We had too many press conferences. We were too available." *Issues and Answers* transcript (May 24, 1964), Press Campaign Material, 20/5, Goldwater Papers, AHF.

8. Transcript of Press Conference at Concord, New Hampshire (January 7, 1964), Goldwater Papers, "W" Series, 12/53, AHF. Here Goldwater says "I would like to suggest one change, that Social Security be voluntary, that if a person can provide better for himself let him do it. . . ." *New York Times*, March 2 and March 16, 1964; *New York Times Magazine*, November 24, 1963; *Newsweek*, January 20, 1964; *Time*, June 12, 1964. Here *Time* reiterates several quotes from the New Hampshire primary. Barry Goldwater Campaign Speeches (February 12, 1964), vol. 1, manuscript collection, AHF. In this speech, delivered at the Commonwealth Club in San Francisco, Goldwater compares the Soviets to the Nazis and calls for an immediate blockade of Cuba. See also, T. White, *Making of the President—1964*, 104–6.

9. *Time*, March 6, 1964. For Goldwater's explanation, see Goldwater, *Goldwater*, 203. At the time there were more senior citizens in New Hampshire, per capita, than in any other state in the nation.

10. *New York Times*, January 8, 1964. For Goldwater's explanation of this issue, see Robert Goldberg's interview with Goldwater (September 24, 1964). At a press conference in New Hampshire on January 7, Goldwater said, "I have said the Commanders should have the ability to use nuclear weapons. . . . That is my opinion." Transcript of Press Conference, Concord, New Hampshire (January 7, 1964), "W" Series, 12/53, Goldwater Papers, AHF. Goldwater had been saying this for some time. See *Washington Post*, October 25, 1963, and *New York Times*, November 24, 1963. On Goldwater's statement that the water at Guantánamo should be turned on by force, see *Newsweek*, February 24, 1964. See also T. White, *Making of the President—1964*, 104; and *Congressional Quarterly*, September 20, 1964, 1605

11. *Newsweek*, March 2, 1964. See also Hess, *In a Cause*, 56, 85.

12. *Newsweek*, January 13, 1964.

13. Ibid., February 10, 1964.

14. Goldberg, *Goldwater*, 184; *Time*, July 17, 1964. The comment was a clear reference to Rockefeller, who made a point of kissing babies, shaking as many hands as possible, and sampling ethnic cuisine whenever possible.

15. *Newsweek*, March 9, 1964.

16. Ibid., March 23, 1964.

17. Transcript of press conference, Concord, NH (January 7, 1964), "W" Series, 12/53, Goldwater Papers, AHF; *Time*, June 12, 1964; *Newsweek*, February 2, February 17, May 4, and May 20, 1964; T. White, *Making of the President—1964*, 103–4. The Goldwater campaign demanded a retraction of the headline and got it. The retraction, however, made little difference. See Kleindienst, *Justice*, 34; and *Congressional Quarterly*, September 20, 1964, 1605.

18. *Newsweek*, January 20, 1964.

19. T. White, *Making of the President—1964*, 106–7. Rockefeller did, in fact, have a research team whose job it was to compile information on all political opponents, particularly Goldwater. Rockefeller's director of Candidate Research was Graham Molitor. For examples of Molitor's work, see box 8/3–28, various dates, 1963–1964, Graham Molitor Papers, RFA, RAC.

20. *Newsweek*, November 6, 1964.

21. The reporter was Walter Means of the Associated Press. Hess, *In a Cause*, 26. Goldwater's people insisted that he use more prepared statements and fewer off-the-cuff statements. See Evans and Novak, "Goldwater's New Strategy," *New York Herald-Tribune*, May 20, 1964.

22. Goldwater, *Goldwater*, 157–58.

23. *Newsweek*, March 9, 1964; *Time*, March 6, 1964.

24. T. White, *Making of the President—1964*, 108–10. See also William J. Miller, *Henry Cabot Lodge* (New York, 1967), 358–59.

25. *Newsweek*, March 23, 1964.

26. Quoted in T. White, *Making of the President—1964*, 111.

27. *Newsweek*, April 13, 1964. For primary election results see *New York Times*, March 15, 1964. Miller, *Henry Cabot Lodge*, 358.

28. *Newsweek*, April 6, 1964.

29. *Newsweek*, February 10, 1964.

30. C. White, *Suite 3505*, 301–32. Goldwater's prediction of a 40 percent victory is in *New York Times*, March 7, 1964. Following the primary, Kitchel delcared a Goldwater victory. See Goldwater for President Press Release (March 11, 1964) "W" Series, 8/2, Goldwater Papers, AHF.

31. *Newsweek*, March 9, 1964.

32. *Newsweek*, February 24, 1964.

33. *Newsweek*, April 13, 1964.

34. Taylor Branch, *Pillar of Fire: America in the King Years, 1963–1965* (New York, 1998), 442.

35. *New York Post*, May 11, 1961.

36. *Public Papers of the Presidents, John F. Kennedy, 1963* (Washington, DC, 1964), 483–94 (hereinafter, *PP, JFK, 1963*); *New York Times*, February 29, 1963. Copy of White House Press Release (February 28, 1963) in Everet M. Dirksen Papers, Working Papers, f241, DCC.

37. Quoted in David Burner, *John F. Kennedy and a New Generation* (New York, 1988), 127.

38. *Time*, June 19, 1963; Carl M. Brauer, *John F. Kennedy and the Second Reconstruction* (New York, 1977), 267–70.

39. *PP, JFK, 1963*, 493.

40. John Lewis, *Walking with the Wind: A Memoir of the Movement* (New York, 1998), 205. Lewis, as the president of the SNCC, was present at the meeting. Arthur Schlesinger also attended the meeting. See Schlesinger, *A Thousand Days*, 968–70.

41. *New York Times*, March 2, 1963.

42. *Public Papers of the President, Lyndon B. Johnson, 1964* (Washington, DC,

1964–1971, 8–10 (hereinafter, PP, *LBJ, 1964*); *New York Times*, November 27, 1963.

43. *Newsweek*, February 24, 1964.

44. Goldwater, *Goldwater*, 219–220.

45. *New York Times*, February 15, 1964.

46. Quoted in McDowell, *Barry Goldwater*, 178.

47. Transcript in Alabama Governors' Speech Files, George Wallace, ADAH.

48. *Nation*, October 26, 1964.

49. Theodore White, *America in Search of Itself: The Making of the President, 1956–1980* (New York, 1982), 288; T. White, *Making of the President—1964*, 233; Theodore White, *The Making of the President—1972* (New York, 1973), 92.

50. Wallace always insisted he never made this statement, but, as Stephen Lesher has pointed out, the line "clung to Wallace like a sweat-soaked shirt throughout the rest of his career." See Lesher, *George Wallace: American Populist* (Reading, MA, 1994), 128–29. The story probably originated in Marshall Frady's, *Wallace* (New York, 1976), 127. See also Dan T. Carter, *From George Wallace to Newt Gingrich: Race in the Conservative Counterrevolution, 1963–1994* (Baton Rouge, LA, 1996), 2. Carter concluded that Wallace not only made the statement, but that he repeated it several times to friends and colleagues over several days. An aide's denial of the incident can be found in Sandra Baxley Taylor, *Me 'n' George: A Story of George Corley Wallace and His Number One Crony, Oscar Harper* (Mobile, AL, 1988), 28. On Wallace's stance against the 1957 Civil Rights Act, see *Birmingham News*, February 6, 1957. On the nature of his 1958 campaign, see Birmingham News, *Wallace: A Portrait of Power* (Birmingham, AL, 1998), 40.

51. Harold H. Martin, "George Wallace Shakes Up the Political Scene," *Saturday Evening Post*, May 9, 1964, 89.

52. *New York Times*, March 11, 1956; James Graham Cook, *The Segregationists* (New York, 1962), 140–44; Dan T. Carter, *The Politics of Rage: George Wallace, The Origins of the New Conservatism, and the Transformation of American Politics* (Baton Rouge, LA, 1995), 107.

53. Transcript of *Meet the Press* (June 2, 1963), Alabama Governors' Speech Files, George Wallace, ADAH. See also *Meet the Press* transcripts, George Wallace (June 2, 1963), Lawrence Spivak Papers, LC.

54. *New York Times*, June 12, 1963.

55. Carter, *From Wallace to Gingrich*, 6.

56. Wallace speech in Atlanta, Georgia (July 4, 1964), Alabama's Governors' Speech Files, George Wallace, ADAH.

57. Speech transcript (n.d., late March-to-early April, 1964?), Administrative Files, S67030, Wallace Papers, ADAH.

58. Donaldson, *Truman Defeats Dewey*, 184.

59. All examples from Wallace speeches delivered in the Wisconsin primary campaign in March 1964, Alabama Governors' Speech Files, George Wallace, ADAH.

60. Wallace to Lurline D. Youngblood (October 21, 1964), Administrative Files, SG22373, Wallace Papers, ADAH.

61. Ann Permaloff and Carl Grafton, *Political Power in Alabama: The More Things Change* (Athens, GA, 1995), 200; Carter, *Politics of Rage*, 196–99; *Birmingham News*, November 5, 1963; *Montgomery Advertiser*, November 6, 1963; Lescher, *Wallace*, 264.

62. *Montgomery Advertiser*, January 8–9, 1964. Wallace spoke to a crowd of 1,300 in Phoenix, Arizona. *Alabama Journal*, January 9, 1964.

Chapter 5. Lyndon Johnson and the Reins of Power

1. *Time*, October 4, 1963.

2. William Manchester, *Death of a President* (New York, 1967), 3; Arthur Schlesinger interview, Valenti interview, Reedy interview, all in LBJLOHC. See also, Shesol, *Mutual Contempt*, 113, 137.

3. Johnson had made a brief statement to the press at Andrews Air Force base on the night of the assassination.

4. *PP, LBJ, 1963–1964*, 9; *New York Times*, November 28, 1963. Sorensen later insisted that he wrote only about half of the speech. Humphrey always claimed credit for the line, "Let us continue." Miller, *Lyndon*, 434.

5. Manchester, *Death of a President*, 474.

6. Clifford, *Counsel to the President*, 390.

7. Ibid., 390.

8. Eric Goldman discussed Johnson's decisions to keep these men on in the new administration. See Eric F. Goldman, *The Tragedy of Lyndon Johnson* (New York, 1968), 93–94.

9. Kenneth O'Donnell interview, LBJLOHC.

10. Guthman, *We Band of Brothers*, 25.

11. Doris Kearns, *Lyndon Johnson and the American Dream* (New York, 1977), 170.

12. Goldman, *Tragedy of Lyndon Johnson*, 21.

13. Miller, *Lyndon*, 501.

14. Ibid., 502. For more on LBJ's insecure character, particularly his propensity to mimic leaders he admired, see Paul R. Henggeler, *In His Steps: Lyndon Johnson and the Kennedy Mystique* (Chicago, 1991), 125–28.

15. Clark Clifford interview, LBJLOHC.

16. Schlesinger, *Robert Kennedy*, 657.

17. The Martin interview was on May 14, 1964, and is in Guthman and Schulman, *Robert Kennedy*, 415, 417. See also, Shesol, *Mutual Contempt*, 171–72.

18. Dallek, *Flawed Giant*, 124.

19. O'Donnell interview, LBJLOHC; Guthman, *We Band of Brothers*, 269–70; Clifford, *Counsel to the President*, 396; Evans and Novak, *Lyndon Johnson*, 444; *Time*, August 7, 1964.

20. Guthman, *We Band of Brothers*, 279; Schlesinger, *Robert Kennedy*, 681. Ted Kennedy and brother-in-law Steve Smith were already pushing RFK to run for the Senate from New York. See Shesol, *Mutual Contempt*, 193.

21. George Gallup, *The Gallup Poll: Public Opinion, 1935–1971*, vol. 3, *1959–1971* (New York: 1972), *1860*, 1874–75.

22. Clifford interview, LBJLOHC.

23. Guthman, *We Band of Brothers*, 256. MacArthur died five weeks later.

24. O'Donnell interview, LBJLOHC.

25. Kearns, *Lyndon Johnson*, 199–200.

26. Clifford agreed with Johnson's analysis. "[T]here was no chance that a Johnson–Kennedy team could function effectively. . . . With Robert Kennedy as Vice President, President Johnson would be treated almost as a lame duck for the entire four years of his elected Presidency." Clifford, *Counsel to the President*, 396.

27. O'Donnell interview, LBJLOHC.

28. Guthman, *We Band of Brothers*, 269–70; Schlesinger, *Robert Kennedy*, 682.

29. Guthman, *We Band of Brothers*, 270. Others have disagreed. Robert Dallek has argued that RFK was "intentionally provoking" LBJ, "that his refusal to step down was a thorn in LBJ's side." Dallek, *Flawed Giant*, 141.

30. Guthman, *We Band of Brothers*, 271–72.

31. Ibid., 269.

32. Guthman and Schulman, *Robert Kennedy*, 414–15.

33. Guthman, *We Band of Brothers*, 269.

34. Schlesinger, *Robert Kennedy*, 682.

35. O'Donnell interview, LBJLOHC. Much of this advice was coming from Milton Gwirtzman. See ibid., 180, 193.

36. Clifford, *Counsel*, 395; Jack Valenti, *A Very Human President* (New York, 1975), 141.

37. Ben Bradlee, "What's Bobby Going to Do?" *Newsweek*, July 7, 1964, 24–26.

38. Johnson, *Vantage Point*, 39. Larry O'Brien did much of the congressional liaison work in his mourning coat.

39. Ibid., 40.

40. The bill, in its final form, was a $9.1 billion cut in individual income tax and a cut of $2.4 billion in corporate taxes. Two-thirds of these cuts would come in fiscal 1964, one-third in 1965.

41. Johnson, *Vantage Point*, 36.

42. Goldman, *Tragedy of Lyndon Johnson*, 77–78; Johnson, *Vantage Point*, 36–37.

43. *New York Times*, March 6, 1964.

44. *Newsweek*, April 6, 1964.

45. T. White, *Making of the President—1964*, 222–23.

46. Time, August 14, 1964.

47. T. White, *Making of the President—1964*, 224–25.

48. PP, LBJ, 1963–1964, 9; *New York Times*, November 27, 1963.

49. Kearns, *Lyndon Johnson*, 191.

50. Allen J. Matusow, *The Unraveling of America: A History of Liberalism in the 1960s* (New York, 1984), 95.

51. Goldman, *Tragedy of Lyndon Johnson*, 83.

52. Lady Bird Johnson, *Lady Bird Johnson: A White House Diary* (New York, 1970), 237.

53. Dirksen Notebooks, f205 (July 1963) Dirksen Papers, DCC. The editorials and cartoons most often appeared in the *New York Herald-Tribune*.

54. Ibid.

55. LBJ to Humphrey (May 13, 1964), telephone conversation #3445, LBJL.

56. Valenti interview, LBJLOHC.

57. Joseph L. Rauh, Jr., "The Role of the Leadership Conference on Civil Rights in the Civil Rights Struggle of 1963–1964," in Robert D. Loevy, ed., *The Civil Rights Act of 1964: The Passage of the Law That Ended Racial Segregation* (Albany, NY, 1997), 70. According to Rauh, p. 70, Walter Reuther and the UAW leadership opposed the amendments. As a result of the compromise, the attorney general can not initiate suits on behalf of aggrieved individuals, but the Justice Department can intervene in such suits. The attorney general can also intervene where there is deemed a "pattern or practice" of discrimination against a person or group.

58. Ibid., 71. For Humphrey's analysis of these negotiations and the importance of Dirksen, see Humphrey interview, LBJLOHC.

59. *Cong. Rec.*, 88th Cong., 2d sess. (June 19, 1964), 12866. Dirkson-typed copy in Dirksen Notebooks, f200 (June 1964), Dirksen Papers, DCC; *New York Times*, May 20, 1964. The quote was actually from Hugo's *Histoire d'un crime.*

60. *Time*, June 19, 1964. Byron C. Hulsey, *Everett Dirksen and His Presidents* (Lawrence, KS, 2000), 200–2. Since the beginning of the century there had been twenty-seven cloture votes; only five had received the two-thirds majority necessary to pass. This was the first time cloture had been invoked on a civil rights bill.

61. *New York Times*, February 15, 1964.

62. *Newsweek*, May 25, 1964.

63. *Cong. Rec.*, 88th Cong., 2d sess. (June 18, 1964), 14319.

64. See particularly Harris poll in *Newsweek*, July 13, 1964. See other polls in White House Press Release (July 20, 1964) WHCF: Aides-Moyers, LBJ Papers, LBJL.

65. *New York Times*, August 20, 1964. See a similar statement in Speech Transcript (September 3, 1964) 3H511, Goldwater Collection, Center for American History, UT.

66. "Peace Through Strength," *Vital Speeches of the Day*, XXX (October 1, 1964): 743–46. See a similar statement in Speech Transcript (September 10, 1964) 3H511, Goldwater Collection, Center for American History, UT.

67. Press Release (July 3, 1964), WHCF, Aides—Moyers, LBJ Papers, LBJL; *New York Times*, July 3, 1964.

68. Shesol, *Mutual Contempt*, 166; *New York Times*, July 3, 1964.

69. *Washington Post*, November 13, 1988.

70. *PP, LBJ, 1963–64*, 77, 112, 114, 247, 367.

71. See Leon Keyserline, "Poverty and the Nation's Economy," *Nation*, June 7, 1965, 615–17.

72. Dallek, *Flawed Giant*, 75.

73. *New York Times*, March 17, 1964.

74. *Time*, January 1, 1965; *Newsweek*, August 31, 1964. A good source on the Great Society is John A. Andrew III, *Lyndon Johnson and the Great Society* (Chicago, 1998). See particularly chapter 2 on the War on Poverty legislation and programs.

75. *PP, LBJ, 1963–64*, 704–7. For a discussion of the speech and the birth of the phrase "Great Society," see Richard N. Goodwin, *Remembering America: A Voice from the Sixties* (New York, 1988), 267–81; and Valenti interview, LBJLOHC.

76. Goodwin, *Remembering America*, 278. Goodwin was the primary writer of the speech.

77. *Time*, August 14, 1964.

78. White House Press Release (August 21, 1964), WHCF: Aides—Moyers, LBJ Papers, LBJL; *New York Times*, August 25, 1964; *Time*, January 1, 1965; *Newsweek*, August 31, 1964.

79. Jack Bell, *The Johnson Treatment: How Lyndon B. Johnson Took Over the Presidency and Made It His Own* (New York, 1965), 98. Andrew, *Lyndon Johnson and the Great Society*, 69–70. John Tower of Texas, a Goldwater supporter and member of the Senate Labor and Public Welfare Committee, also voted against the bill.

Chapter 6. Conservatism Triumphant: Wallace and Goldwater in the Primary Season

1. Taylor, *Me 'n' George*, 24–25.

2. Birmingham News, *Wallace: A Portrait*, 57–58.

3. Carter, *Politics of Race*, 202–3; *Alabama Journal*, March 5 and 19, 1964. The Republican slate was headed by Congressman John Byrnes (he had no opposition) and was committed to Goldwater. Republicans in the Wisconsin primary could cross over to vote for Wallace, either because they supported his platform or possibly to embarrass Reynolds. Since the Republican slate was uncontested, Republican voters could make this crossover without endangering their candidate.

4. *Birmingham News*, March 31, 1964.

5. Carter, *Politics of Rage*, 204–5. Wallace was even convinced to describe McCarthy as a "man before his time." Richard C. Haney, "Wallace in Wisconsin: The Presidential Primary of 1964," *Wisconsin Magazine of History* 61 (Summer 1978): 264.

6. On opposition for the Wisconsin Republican party, see Lesher, *George Wallace*, 211. On the other groups in Wisconsin that opposed Wallace, see 277 in the same volume.

7. Statements of this sort were reported glowingly in the Alabama press. *Alabama Journal*, March 7, 1964.

8. *Alabama Journal*, March 8, 1964. Reynolds made a number of similar statements throughout the campaign. See, particularly, *Newsweek*, March 30, 1964. Here he calls Wallace "a bigot . . . racist . . . demagogue, and a carpetbagger."

9. See both quotes in *Birmingham News*, April 5, 1964.

10. Martin, "George Wallace Shakes Up," 88.

11. *Birmingham News*, May 9, 1964.

12. Ibid., April 2, 1964; Carter, *Politics of Rage*, 206–7.

13. *Birmingham News*, March 22, 1964; *Montgomery Advertiser*, March 20, 1964; *Newsweek*, April 20, 1964; Martin, "George Wallace Shakes Up," 85.

14. For various election analyses, see *New York Times*, April 9, 1964; *Time*, April 12, 1964; *Newsweek*, April 20, 1964.

15. Michael R. Beschloss, *Taking Charge: The Johnson White House Tapes, 1963–1964* (New York, 1997), 309; Lesher, *George Wallace*, 285. The Reynold's quote is in *Newsweek*, April 20, 1964.

16. *Newsweek*, April 20, 1964.

17. Michael Rogin, "Wallace and the Middle Class: The White Backlash in Wisconsin," *Public Opinion Quarterly* (Spring 1966): 98. For a different opinion, see Seymour Martin Lipset, "Beyond the Backlands," *Encounter*, November 1964, 22. *Newsweek* saw quickly that it was the Republican crossover vote that gave Wallace his big numbers in Wisconsin. *Newsweek*, April 20, 1964.

18. Martin, "George Wallace Shakes Up," 86.

19. Nixon polled 17 percent, Goldwater 14 percent, and Rockefeller 13 percent. *Newsweek*, April 20, 1964.

20. Quoted in Stephen Ambrose, *Nixon*, vol. 1, *The Education of a Politician, 1913–1962* (New York, 1987), 580. See also Miller, *Henry Cabot Lodge*, 325.

21. *Newsweek*, April 13, 1964.

22. Roswell Perkins to George Hinman (May 29, 1964), Politics—NYC Office, Box 15/121, Rockefeller Papers, RFA, RAC; *Newsweek*, April 13, 1964. See also *Time*, June 12, 1964, for the Republican primary rundown.

23. Goldwater's son, Barry, Jr., spoke in Oregon on his father's behalf. Congressman Jack Westland and General Albert Wedemeyer also campaigned for Goldwater. Goldwater did make a few appearances in the first week of April. See various speaking schedules (April), 3H507, Barry Goldwater Collection, Center for American History, UT.

24. *Newsweek*, April 27, 1964. See also *Time*, June 12, 1964.

25. *Time*, May 11, 1964.

26. T. White, *Making of the President—1964*, 122; *Newsweek*, May 18, 1964.

27. *Saturday Evening Post*, May 29, 1964; *Newsweek*, May 4, 1964. The *New York Times*, however, gave Goldwater only 209 delegates in early May. *New York Times*, May 5, 1964.

28. See Evans, *Future of Conservatism*, 129–30; *Time*, July 24, 1964.

29. C. White, *Suite 3505*, 332, 349–50; Schadegg, *What Happened to Goldwater*, 117.

30. *Newsweek*, May 18, 1964.

31. Ibid., May 18, 1964.

32. Reinhard, *Republican Right*, 188.

33. *New York Herald-Tribune*, May 25, 1964.

34. Transcript of Rockefeller press conference (San Diego) (May 25, 1964), Politics—NYC Office, Box 21/159, Rockefeller Papers, RFA, RAC; *New York Times*, May 26, 1964.

35. These events are recounted in Wolf, *Scranton*, 105–9. See also, T. White, *Making of the President—1964*, 86–87.

36. *Newsweek*, April 20, 1964; Wolf, *Scranton*, 109.

37. Indiana voted Democratic in 1912, 1932, and 1936. The state would, however, fall to LBJ in the 1964 Democratic landslide.

38. *Birmingham News*, April 28, 1964; *Newsweek*, May 4, 1964; Carter, *The Politics of Rage*, 210.

39. See Welsh's explanation of all this, along with his contacts with the White House, in Mathew E. Welsh, "Civil Rights and the Primary Election of 1964 in Indiana: The Wallace Challenge," *Indiana Magazine of History* LXXV (March 1979): 4.

40. *Birmingham News*, April 25, 1964; *New York Times*, April 21, 1964. Welsh privately only hoped to keep Wallace's numbers below the Wisconsin results. Welsh quote in *Newsweek*, May 4, 1964.

41. *New York Times*, April 26 and May 4, 1964; *Birmingham News*, April 26 and 27, 1964; Beschloss, *Taking Charge*, 309.

42. *New York Times*, May 2, 1964.

43. See vote totals in *Newsweek*, May 5, 1964. Welsh received all of the state's fifty-one delegates and pledged them to LBJ. Wallace won big in Lake County, northwest Indiana, an area with a large black population and a recent history of riots. See Rogin, "Wallace and the Middle Class," 98.

44. Transcript of Brewster's *Today* show interview (May 6, 1964) in Alabama Governors' Speech Files, George Wallace, ADAH. A week later, in a confidential discussion with Hubert Humphrey, President Johnson remarked on Brewster's statements: "I was amazed. I didn't know that boy was as dumb as he is." Beschloss, *Taking Charge*, 355. *Alabama Journal*, March 2, 1964.

45. Branch, *Pillar of Fire*, 310. See also, *Birmingham News*, May 20, 1964; *Newsweek*, June 1, 1964; and *New York Times*, May 11 and 12, 1964. Gloria Richardson, a local leader of the SNCC, led the march. Stokley Carmichael was among the participants.

46. *Baltimore Sun*, May 20 and 21, 1964; *New York Times*, May 21, 1964. Wallace later insisted he had said "nigra" rather than "nigger." Lesher, *George Wallace*, 304. See also *Newsweek*, June 1, 1964.

47. Roland Evans and Robert Novak, "Big Crisis for Goldwater," *Saturday Evening Post*, May 30, 1964, 16.

48. This was in response to Rockefeller literature that asked, "Do you want a leader or a loner?" implying that all the other Republican candidates supported Rockefeller and that Goldwater was alone on the right. See Shedegg, *What Happened to Goldwater?*, 123.

49. Trotton Anderson and Eugene Lee, "The 1964 Election in California," *Western Political Science Quarterly* 18 (June 1965): 459–60; *Saturday Evening Post*, May 29, 1964; *Newsweek*, June 15, 1964; Shedegg, *What Happened to Goldwater?*, 126.

50. Harris poll quoted in Anderson and Lee, "1964 Election in California," 460.

51. *Time*, June 12, 1964; Schuparra, *Triumph of the Right*, 92; Evans, *Future of Conservatism*, 253–54.

52. Schuparra, *Triumph of the Right*, 94.

53. *Newsweek*, May 4, 1964; Hess, *In a Cause*, 85.

54. Goldwater, *Goldwater*, 158.

55. *Newsweek*, May 20, 1963.

56. Transcript of *Issues and Answers* (May 24, 1964) in Presidential Cam-

paign Material, 20/5, Goldwater Papers, AHF. Also quoted in *Newsweek*, June 8, 1964; and Shedegg, *What Happened to Goldwater?*, 125.

57. *Washington Post*, April 20, 1964. Shedegg, *What Happened to Goldwater?*, 124.

58. *Newsweek*, June 8, 1964; *Time*, June 12, 1964.

59. Schuparra, *Triumph of Conservatism*, 93.

60. Robert Welch, *The Politician* (Belmont, MA, 1963), 276–79. See also Himmelstein, *To the Right*, 66; Benjamin R. Epstein and Arnold Forster, *The Radical Right: Report on the John Birch Society and Its Allies* (New York, 1967), 11–46; and Daniel Bell, ed., *Radical Right: The New American Right* (New York, 1955), 422.

61. Goldwater, *Goldwater*, 160.

62. *Newsweek*, November 4, 1963.

63. Robert Welch, *The Blue Book of the John Birch Society*, 24th ed. (Appleton, WI, 1999, first published 1959), 109; Daniel, *Radical Right*, 422.

64. See, in particular, *National Review*, April 22, 1961, and February 13, 1962. See also Rusher, *Rise of the Right*, 119.

65. *National Review*, February 27, 1962; *Newsweek*, February 19, 1962.

66. Transcript of Press Conference, Concord, New Hampshire (January 7, 1964), "W" Series, 12/53, Goldwater Papers, AHF. Goldwater added here, "I disagree with about 90 percent of the things that Bob Welsh advocates and I have told him so. . . ." See also *Newsweek*, February 19, 1962. A similar statement in support of the JBS can be found in "The Public Record of Barry Goldwater," *Congressional Quarterly* (special report) September 20, 1963, 1615.

67. *New York Times*, September 29, 1961.

68. *Newsweek*, April 27, 1964. For additional and similar comments by Goldwater, see Bell, *Mr. Conservative*, 89. In 1961, Goldwater said that the members of the JBS "are the finest people in my community." *Time*, June 23, 1961. It was often argued that Goldwater wanted to steer the JBS toward moderation and toward a place in the Republican party. See *Time*, June 23, 1961.

69. Goldwater, *Goldwater*, 161.

70. *Life*, July 26, 1963.

71. Schuparra, *Triumph of the Right*, 86–87.

72. Goldberg, *Goldwater*, 159.

73. Rusher, *Rise of the Right*, 121. Kitchel resigned in 1960 following the publication of *The Politician*.

74. Schuparra, *Triumph of the Right*, 50, 60, 67, 76–78. In contrast, Rockefeller never received much support from Hollywood types. Jack Warner of Warner Brothers Studios was the only movie industry figure who campaigned for Rockefeller on a regular basis. See Press Release (May 25, 1964), George L. Hinman Files, Rockefeller Papers, RFA, RAC.

75. *Washington Post*, June 3, 1964; T. White, *Making of the President—1964*, 122–23; Edwards, *Goldwater*, 225–26; *Newsweek*, June 15, 1964. Cardinal James Francis McIntyre of the Diocese of Los Angeles also worked to influence Catholic voters to oppose Rockefeller on moral grounds. See Shedegg, *What Happened to Goldwater?*, 125; and Edwards, *Goldwater*, 226. Lou Harris had pre-

dicted that Goldwater would lose in California by a margin of 57 to 43 percent. *Time*, June 12, 1964. Rockefeller's own polling data showed, on May 30, that he was still in the lead, 44.8 to Goldwater's 36.9, and in control of all of California except the south. Opinion Research of California Politics (May 29–30, 1964), Politics: George L. Hinman Files, Rockefeller Papers, RFA, RAC. Rockefeller's people were told to "stay completely away" from the re-marriage issue. See "Analysis of Anticipated Goldwater Campaign in California," (n.d.), in same.

76. *Newsweek*, June 15, 1964; Robert D. Novak, *The Agony of the GOP: 1964* (New York, 1965) 414; Matusow, *Unraveling of America*, 136.

77. Hess, *In a Cause*, 147. *Washington Post*, April 20, 1964.

78. List of Dignitaries in California (n.d.), Goldwater Collection, 3H507, Center for American History, UT; *Saturday Evening Post*, May 29, 1964; Schuparra, *Triumph of the Right*, 94.

79. Lou Cannon, *President Reagan: The Role of a Lifetime* (New York, 1991), 11.

80. Rusher, *Rise of the Right*, 162. See vote tallies for the California primary in *Time*, June 12, 1964.

81. *Newsweek*, June 15, 1965.

82. Political scientists analyzing the California primary found the dividing line between the counties supporting Goldwater in the south and Rockefeller in the north at the Tehachapis River near Bakersfield. Anderson and Lee "1964 Election in California," 461. Goldwater won all the southern California counties except Santa Barbara. Schuparra, *Triumph of the Right*, 95.

83. Rockefeller's own accounting of the cost of the California primary is $2.4 million. He had budgeted $1.6 million. Rockefeller National Campaign Committee, Assets and Liabilities (January 31, 1965), Politics—NYC Office, Box 21/157, Rockefeller Papers, RFA, RAC. Anderson and Lee, in "1964 Election In California," have estimated that Rockefeller may have spent as much as $3.6 million. See page 459.

84. *Time*, July 24, 1964.

85. *Newsweek*, June 29, 1964.

86. Ibid., June 29, 1964.

87. Romney press release (June 7, 1964), Goldwater Collection, 3H508, Center for American History, UT.

88. C. White, *Suite 3505*, 364.

89. *Newsweek*, June 22, 1964.

90. C. White, *Suite 3505*, 367–68. Just one month earlier, Nixon had said that he would "have no part of a stop-Goldwater movement." *Newsweek*, May 18, 1964.

91. Quoted in Goldberg, *Goldwater*, 195.

92. *Time*, June 19, 1964.

93. Ibid., June 19, 1964.

94. Transcript of Rockefeller press conference (in Cleveland) (June 7, 1964) Politics—NYC Office, Box 21/159, Rockefeller Papers, RFA, RAC.

95. Schuparra, *Triumph of the Right*, 97; *Newsweek*, June 15 and 22, 1964.

96. Carter, *Politics of Rage*, 202; Lesher, *George Wallace*, 305–6.

97. Wallace to John Carnett (January 29, 1964), and Wallace to Calvin Poole (July 10, 1964), Administrative Files, SG22373, Wallace Papers, ADAH.

98. Lister Hill to John H. Thompson (February 3, 1964), in ibid. See letters from dozens of constituents complaining about the open slate plan in ibid.

99. Carter, *Politics of Rage*, 219–21. Wallace refused to endorse Goldwater, saying on *Meet the Press*, that such an endorsement would allow the press "to smear that candidate to death." Transcripts of *Meet the Press* George Wallace (October 25, 1964), Lawrence Spivak Papers, LC.

100. Transcript of *Face the Nation* (July 19, 1964), Alabama Governors' Speech Files, George Wallace, ADAH. Press reports claimed in this period that Goldwater had asked Wallace to drop out of the race, although neither Wallace nor Goldwater has ever acknowledged any type of contact on that issue. See, particularly, *New York Times*, July 13, 1964. Alan Matusow accepts that Goldwater asked Wallace to withdraw. Matusow, *Unraveling of America*, 139.

101. Wallace speech in Baton Rouge (June 17, 1964) and in Jackson, Mississippi (June 25, 1964), transcripts in Alabama Governors' Speech Files, George Wallace, ADAH.

102. *Washington Post*, July 19, 1964; *Time*, July 31, 1964; White House Press Release (July 29, 1964) WHCF: Aides—Moyers. LBJ Papers, LBJL.

103. Transcript of Brewster statement on the *Today* show (May 6, 1964), in WHCF: Aides—Moyers. LBJ Papers, LBJL.

104. Quoted in Birmingham News, *Wallace: A Portrait of Power*, 57.

105. See Wallace speeches on school prayer (April 30, June 27 and 28, 1964), Alabama Governors' Speech Files, George Wallace, ADAH. For a good contemporary analysis of Wallace's messages, see *U.S. News & World Report*, June 1, 1964.

106. *Newsweek*, April 20, 1964.

107. Poll conducted by *Newsweek*, see *Newsweek*, July 29, 1963.

108. *New York Times*, July 17, 1964. For similar statements, see transcript of *Issues and Answers*, Barry Goldwater (May 24, 1964), Presidential Campaign Files, 20/6, Goldwater Papers, AHF. Here Goldwater says, "I must agree with [Wallace] on states' rights. . . ." See also *Life*, July 12, 1963.

109. Loevy, *The Civil Rights Act of 1964*, 353–61; *Newsweek*, February 24, 1964; Gillion, *Politics and Vision*, 158. The quote is LBJ to Joseph Rauh of the ADA. Meeting Notes (January 21, 1964) Box 26/6, Joseph Rauh Papers, LC.

110. Rauh, "The Role of the Leadership Conference," 65; *Newsweek*, February 24, 1964. On Russell, see *Newsweek*, February 24, 1964.

111. *New York Times*, July 15, 1948.

112. Meeting Notes (January 21, 1964), Box 26/6, Joseph Rauh Papers, LC; Rauh, "Role of the Leadership Conference," 66.

113. *Newsweek*, April 13, 1964. *Newsweek* added that if Humphrey succeeds in ending the filibuster and passing the bill he will be Johnson's choice for vice president.

114. Dirksen's primary speech in opposition to the bill was read before the Senate on January 22, 1964. Copy in Alpha File, 19654, Dirksen Papers, DCC.

115. Dirksen Notebooks, f205, ibid.

116. *Washington Post*, June 1, 1964.

117. *Meet the Press* transcript (March 8, 1964), Lawrence Spivak papers, Box 218, LC.

118. Rauh, "Role of the Leadership Conference," 70.

119. Ibid., 70; Gillion, *Politics and Vision*, 160.

120. Rauh, "Role of the Leadership Conference," 71.

121. Remarks and Releases (June 10, 1964), Dirksen Papers, DCC.

122. *Time*, May 25, June 19 and 22, 1964; *Newsweek*, June 22 and 29, 1964. Bourke Hickenlooper of Iowa, John Tower of Texas, Edwin Meechum of New Mexico, Millward Simpson of Wyoming, and Norris Cotton of New Hampshire voted with Goldwater. *Newsweek*, June 29, 1964.

123. *Newsweek*, June 29, 1964. Goldwater had told Dirksen that he would vote against cloture. *Washington Post*, May 21 and 22, 1964. Just days before, on the television program *Issues and Answers,* Goldwater had told Howard K. Smith that his only reason for voting against cloture was that he did not "want to see the Senate destroy one of its very, very valuable rules." Transcript of *Issues and Answers* (May 24, 1964), Goldwater Papers, Presidential Campaign Files, 20/6, AHS. Following the vote, Goldwater was quoted in *Time*: "You cannot pass a law that will make me like you or you like me. This is something that can only happen in our hearts." *Time*, June 12, 1964.

124. *Newsweek*, June 29, 1964. In the same issue it is reported that Goldwater staffer told *Newsweek* in June that of the 279 southern delegates, "we've got 250, rock bottom."

125. Gallup poll cited in Nelson W. Polsby, "Strategic Considerations," in Milton C. Cummings, Jr., ed., *The National Election of 1964* (Washington, 1966), 91.

Chapter 7. Guillotine: The Jacobins Remove the Ancien Régime

1. T. White, *Making of the President—1964*, 191.

2. *New York Times*, July 13, 1964.

3. T. White, *Making of the President—1964*, 194.

4. Ibid., 192–94; *New York Times*, July 13, 1964.

5. Transcript of *Meet the Press* Scranton interview (July 12, 1964), Box 219, Spivak Papers, LC.

6. *Newsweek*, June 29 and July 17, 1964; *New York Times*, June 16, 1964; *Time*, June 21, 1964. The Rockefeller National Campaign Committee became the Rockefeller for Scranton Committee on June 19. Minutes of Rockefeller for Scranton Committee (July 2, 1964), Politics—NYC Office, Box 16/122, Rockefeller Papers, RFA, RAC. Rockefeller encouraged Romney to support Scranton. "The hour is late," he wrote, but if we unite, "the moderate cause can still be won." Rockefeller to Romney (June 15, 1964), Politics—Hinman Files, Box 94/647, Rockefeller Papers, RFA, RAC. Nixon withdrew from the campaign on July 3. A Nixon headquarters campaign release said he had "given up on his chances." Copy (dated June 21) WHCF: Aides—Moyers, LBJ Papers, LBJL.

7. *Newsweek*, June 29, 1964.

8. *New York Times*, July 11, 1964.

9. On Sunday, July 12, Eisenhower said in an interview on ABC-TV, "I may have made a mistake in saying I would remain neutral." Press Release (July 13, 1964),

WHCF: Aides—Moyers, LBJ Papers, LBJL. See also *New York Times*, July 17, 1964.

10. *Time*, June 26, 1964.

11. Transcript of NBC Scranton interview (July 30, 1964), Campaign files, 11/1, Goldwater Papers, AHF.

12. *Time*, July 3, 1964.

13. *Oakland Tribune*, July 13, 1964, press clipping in Goldwater Collection, 3H508, Center for American History, UT; *Time*, July 17, 1964.

14. Scranton Press Release (July 11, 1964), Goldwater Collection, 3H508, Center for American History, UT; *Time*, July 17, 1964.

15. Scranton Press Release (July 17, 1964); Goldwater Collection, see ibid.

16. Ibid.

17. C. White, *Suite 3505*, 389.

18. *New York Times*, July 11, 1964; *Der Spiegel*, July 8, 1964.

19. *Der Spiegel*, July 8, 1964.

20. *Time*, July 17, 1964.

21. *New York Times*, July 12, 1964; *Der Spiegel*, July 8, 1964.

22. Press Release (July 11, 1964), WHCF: Aides—Moyers, LBJ Papers, LBJL. See also Hess, *In a Cause*, 120; Barry M. Goldwater, *The Conscience of a Majority* (Englewood Cliffs, NJ, 1970), 180. Goldwater's friend was General William Quinn, commander of the U.S. Seventh Army stationed in Germany. See Goldberg, *Goldwater*, 223–25; *New York Times*, July 9, 1964; and Daniel Schorr, *Clearing the Air* (Boston, 1977), 7–8.

23. T. White, *Making of the President—1964*, 192; Rusher, *Rise of the Right*, 165. There was no thirteenth floor.

24. T. White, *Making of the President—1964*, 191.

25. Ibid., 192. See Rockefeller's statements before the platform committee in Politics—NYC Office (n.d.) Box 15/117, Rockefeller Papers, RFA, RAC.

26. *New York Times*, July 11, 1964; *Time*, July 17, 1964; C. White, *Suite 3505*, 387.

27. *Time*, July 17, 1964.

28. The platform is in *New York Times*, July 12 and July 13, 1964. There is an official copy in the Goldwater Collection, 3H508, Center for American History, UT.

29. *New York Times*, July 14, 1964. For Rockefeller's complaints about the RNC platform, see Rockefeller speech (July 12, 1964), Gubernatorial Press Office Files, Box 17/344, Rockefeller Papers, RFA, RAC.

30. *New York Times*, July 12 and 16, 1964. See Robinson's support for Rockefeller in Jackie Robinson press release (February 28, 1964), Politics—NYC Office, Box 21/159, Rockefeller Papers, RFA, RAC.

31. Scranton to Goldwater (July 12, 1964), 3H505, Goldwater Collection, Center for American History, UT. Another copy is in "W" Series, 8/1, Goldwater Papers, AHF. A more accessible copy is in C. White, *Suite 3505*, 434–36.

32. *New York Times*, July 15, 1964; *Time*, July 24, 1964.

33. *New York Times*, July 14, 1964. The letter was written by William Keisling, a twenty-eight-year-old speechwriter. It was signed by a receptionist authorized to sign Scranton's name. *Time*, July 24, 1964.

34. Transcript, *Campaign '64*, CBS News interview with William Scranton, n.p., n.d. Copy in Goldwater Collection, 3H505, Center for American History, UT.

35. *New York Times*, July 14, 1964.

36. Reinhard, *The Republican Right*, 192.

37. Evans, *Future of Conservatism*, 192.

38. T. White, *Making of the President—1964*, 198.

39. C. White, *Suite 3505*, 434–36.

40. Goldwater for President Committee, press release (July 14, 1964), "W" Series, 8/2, Goldwater Papers, AHF.

41. There is some argument as to whether Scranton was still being considered. Karl Hess, in his *In a Cause That Will Triumph*, argued that Scranton had been removed as a vice presidential contender long before the convention. See, Hess, *In a Cause*, 145. Clifton White, in his *Suite 3503*, wrote that the most disappointing aspect of the letter to Goldwater was that it eliminated Scranton from vice presidential contention. See C. White, *Suite 3505*, 391–92. See also Schuparra, *Triumph of the Right*, 98.

42. Hess, *In a Cause*, 147.

43. *New York Times*, July 15, 1964.

44. T. White, *Making of the President—1964*, 200.

45. Quoted in J. Tebbel and S.M. Watts, *The Press and the Presidency: From George Washington to Ronald Reagan* (New York, 1985), 476.

46. *New York Times*, July 15, 1964.

47. *Time*, July 24, 1964; *New York Times*, July 15, 1964; *New York Times Magazine*, August 8, 1964.

48. Republican National Committee, Official Report of the Proceedings of the Twenty-eighth Republican National Convention (n.p., n.d.), 216.

49. T. White, *Making of the President—1964*, 200.

50. Ibid., 200; Rusher, *Rise of the Right*, 166; C. White, *Suite 3505*, 398.

51. RNC, Official Report of the Proceedings of the Twenty-eighth Republican National Convention, 217–18; Transcript of Rockefeller's speech before Republican National Convention (July 14, 1964), Politics—NYC Office, Box 16/122, Rockefeller Papers, RFA, RAC. A second copy is in Gubernatorial Press Office Files, Box 17/344, Rockefeller Papers (as above). T. White, *Making of the President—1964*, 201; *New York Times*, July 15, 1964.

52. T. White, *Making of the President—1964*, 201.

53. C. White, *Suite 3505*, 399.

54. *New York Times*, July 15, 1964.

55. *Time*, July 24, 1964.

56. Jacob Javits, *The Autobiography of a Public Man* (Boston, 1981), 351.

57. *New York Times*, July 15, 1964; *Time*, July 24, 1964.

58. *Time*, July 24, 1964.

59. Ben Bradlee, *A Good Life: Newspapering and Other Adventures* (New York, 1995), 264.

60. *New York Times*, July 16, 1964.

61. C. White, *Suite 3505*, 403.

62. Matusow, *Unraveling of America*, 137. Matusow argues that Goldwater chose Miller to punish moderates further for opposing his candidacy. See also Reinhard, *Republican Right*, 195.

63. RNC Polls (August 1964) "W" Series, 4/5, Goldwater Papers, AHF.

64. RNC, Official Report of the Proceedings of the Twenty-eighth Republican National Convention, 413–19. A transcript of the speech is also in *New York Times*, July 17, 1964.

65. Ibid., July 17 and 24, 1964. Keating later said that he was simply trying to beat the traffic.

66. *Time*, July 24, 1964.

67. Reinhard, *Republican Right*, 198.

68. *New York Times*, July 17 and 18, 1964.

69. White House Press Release (July 20, 1964), WHCF: Aides—Moyers, LBJ Papers, LBJL.

70. *Time*, July 24, 1964.

71. Ibid., July 31, 1964.

72. Nixon, *RN*, 260.

73. Nixon to BMG (August 4, 1964), RNC Press Release, "W" Series, 5/1, Goldwater Papers, AHF. See the same exchange of letters in Goldwater Collection, 3H512, Center for American History, UT.

74. *Saturday Evening Post*, September 19, 1964.

75. *Time*, July 24, 1964.

76. Richard Rover, quoted in Richard Hofstader's *Paranoid Style in American Politics*, 112.

77. All quoted in *Time*, July 24, 1964.

78. Clifford interview, LBJLOHC.

79. Goldwater in *Arizona Republic*, February 16, 1992.

80. *Time*, July 31, 1964.

Chapter 8. LBJ's "Bobby Problem" and the Humphrey String-along

1. O'Donnell interview, LBJLOHC.

2. Clifford, *Counsel to the President*, 396.

3. *Newsweek*, August 10, 1964.

4. *Time*, August 7, 1964.

5. Evans and Novak, *Lyndon B. Johnson*, 465.

6. This topic is covered best in Shesol, *Mutual Contempt*, 183–84. Arthur Schlesinger has insisted that Kennedy was not behind the write-in campaign. See Schlesinger, *Robert Kennedy*, 680. See also O'Donnell interview, LBJLOHC. O'Donnell does not mention Corbin by name. And, Guthman, *We Band of Brothers*, 253–54; Beschloss, *Taking Charge*, 236–37. Beschloss insists that Corbin was acting on his own in New Hampshire.

7. *Newsweek*, March 16, 1964.

8. *Time*, March 20, 1964.

9. *Newsweek*, March 16, 1964.

10. *Time*, March 20, 1964; Evans and Novak, *Lyndon B. Johnson*, 441; Guthman, *We Band of Brothers*, 256.

11. Kearns, *Lyndon Johnson*, 199–200.

12. RFK interview (May 14, 1964) in Guthman and Shulman, *Robert Kennedy*, 418. Johnson was often being advised in this period that he needed a Catholic on the ticket. See, particularly, LBJ and John Connally, telephone conversation #4320 (July 23, 1964), LBJL.

13. Shesol, *Mutual Contempt*, 203; Dalleck, *Flawed Giant*, 137; Schlesinger, *Robert Kennedy*, 680.

14. LBJ and McNamara, telephone conversation #2961 (April 9, 1964), LBJL.

15. Robert S. McNamara, *In Retrospect: The Tragedy and Lesson of Vietnam* (New York, 1995), 123.

16. LBJ to McGeorge Bundy, telephone conversation #4419 (July 30, 1964), LBJL.

17. Clifford interview, LBJLOHC; Clifford, *Counsel to the President*, 398. McCarthy was deeply offended when Johnson finally dumped him for Humphrey just before the convention. It was the beginnings of a break between LBJ and McCarthy that would come back to haunt Johnson in the 1968 election. McCarthy rallied the anti-war forces and nearly beat Johnson in the New Hampshire primary, leading to the president's eventual withdrawal from the race.

18. *Newsweek*, August 31, 1964.

19. *Saturday Review*, August 22, 1964.

20. Evans and Novak, *Lyndon B. Johnson*, 461–63; O'Donnell interview, LBJLOHC; Clifford interview, LBJLOHC. For another analysis of the Humphrey decision, see Gerald Pomper, "The Nomination of Hubert Humphrey for Vice-President, *Journal of Politics* (August 1966): 639–59.

21. Clifford, *Counsel to the President*, 395.

22. Johnson and Valenti, telephone conversation #3674 LBJL (June 10, 1964); LBJ and RFK, telephone conversation #3699 (June 11, 1964), LBJL. See also, Jack Valenti, *A Very Human President* (New York, 1975), 141.

23. LBJ and RFK, telephone conversation #3784 (June 18, 1964), LBJL; Shesol, *Mutual Contempt*, 195; Ronald Steel, *In Love with the Night: The American Romance with Robert Kennedy* (New York, 2000), 112.

24. *U.S. News & World Report*, July 13, 1964; Steel, *In Love with the Night*, 112.

25. Schlesinger, *Robert Kennedy*, 688. There had been some talk in the press of a Kennedy run for Keating's New York Senate seat as early as May. See *Newsweek*, May 25, 1964.

26. LBJ and RFK, telephone conversation #4352 (July 27, 1964), LBJL.

27. Guthman, *We Band of Brothers*, 280.

28. O'Brien interview, LBJLOHC.

29. Clifford, *Counsel to the President*, 396.

30. Johnson, *Vantage Point*, 100.

31. Ibid., 100, 576–77; Shesol, *Mutual Contempt*, 205–7; Schlesinger, *Robert Kennedy*, 661.

32. *Time*, August 7, 1964.

33. Guthman, *We Band of Brothers*, 280; Evans and Novak, *Lyndon B. Johnson*, 445–46.

34. Clifford, *Counsel to the President*, 397–98.

35. Evans and Novak, *Lyndon B. Johnson*, 445–46.

36. T. White, *Making of the President—1964*, 315–17; Goldman, *Tragedy of Lyndon Johnson*, 236. Johnson stated also that he would exclude "those who meet regularly with the Cabinet. . . ." This eliminated Shriver and Stevenson from consideration as well. The speech is in *New York Times*, July 31, 1964; and *Time*, August 7, 1964.

37. Schlesinger, *Robert Kennedy*, 713.

38. O'Brien interview, LBJLOHC; Shesol, *Mutual Contempt*, 209; Goldman, *Tragedy of Lyndon Johnson*, 236.

39. This story is from several sources and varies somewhat with each. See Shesol, *Mutual Contempt*, 209–10; Schlesinger, *Robert Kennedy*, 691; Evans and Novak, *Lyndon B. Johnson*, 447; Miller, *Lyndon*, 500; Guthman, *We Band of Brothers*, 280; Clifford, *Counsel to the President*, 397. The journalists in attendance were Tom Wicker of the *New York Times*, Edward Folliard of the *Washington Post*, and Douglas Kiker of the *New York Herald-Tribune*.

40. LBJ and O'Brien, telephone conversation #4619 (August 1, 1964), LBJL.

41. White House Press Release, n.d. (early August, 1964?) WHCF: EX PL2, LBJ Papers, LBJL; *Time*, August 14, 1964.

42. Robert McNamara et al., *Argument Without End: In Search of Answers to the Vietnam Tragedy* (New York, 1999), 184.

43. *Public Papers of the Presidents, Lyndon B. Johnson, 1963–1964* (Washington, DC, 1964–1971), 927–28 (hereafter *PP, LBJ, 1963–64*).

44. Gallup, *Gallup Poll*, III, 1899; *New York Times*, August 12, 1964.

45. White House Press Release (August 5, 1964), WHCF: Aides—Moyers, LBJ Papers, LBJL. See also LBJ and McNamara, telephone conversation #4633 (August 3, 1964), LBJL.

46. Michael Carlton and Anthony Moncrieff, *Many Reasons Why: The American Involvement in Vietnam* (New York, 1978), 108.

47. Ibid., 117.

48. McNamara, *In Retrospect*, 141.

49. *Modern Maturity*, October–November 1993. See also Turner, *Lyndon Johnson's Dual War*, 83; and Dalleck, *Flawed Giant*, 148.

50. LBJ and BMG, telephone conversation #4715 (August 4, 1964), LBJL.

51. *PP, LBJ, 1963–64*, 927–28.

52. *New York Times*, August 5, 1964.

53. Ibid. Goldwater also quoted in White House Press Release (August 5, 1964), WHCF: Aides—Moyers, LBJ Papers, LBJL.

54. A good example is LBJ and Richard Russell, telephone conversation #3519 (May 27, 1964), LBJL.

55. By mid-August, Goldwater was saying in his campaign speeches that Johnson had made a mistake by warning the North Vietnamese of the attack in advance. However, he quickly dropped the point. See transcript of BMG speech (August 19, 1964) Goldwater Collection, Center for American History, UT.

56. White House Press Release (August 13, 1964), WHCF: Aides—Moyers, LBJ Papers, LBJL.

57. *New York Times*, October 6, 1964.

58. LBJ told Richard Russell as early as May that intervention would be necessary. See LBJ and Russell, telephone conversation #3519 (May 27, 1964), LBJL.

59. *PP, LBJ, 1963–64*, 1126.

60. Ibid., 1267.

61. Ibid., 1165.

62. Clifford interview, LBJLOHC. Johnson's heart attack was in 1955.

63. Martin, *Adlai Stevenson and the World*, 803. The story is a bit different in T. White, *Making of the President—1964*, 266.

64. O'Brien interview, LBJLOHC.

65. Valenti interview, LBJLOHC.

66. *Time*, August 7, 1964.

67. As it turned out, LBJ had great appeal in the Northeast, but in early August he believed he did not.

68. *Newsweek*, August 31, 1964.

69. Carl Solberg, *Hubert Humphrey* (New York, 1984), 240.

70. Evans and Novak, *Lyndon B. Johnson*, 443; Solberg, *Hubert Humphrey*, 242.

71. LBJ and Humphrey, telephone conversation #4441 (July 30, 1964), LBJL. Humphrey's account of this conversation is in Hubert Humphrey, *The Education of a Public Man: My Life in Politics* (Minneapolis, 1976, 1991), 222. As Michael Beschloss has pointed out, Humphrey's loyalty may have kept him from splitting with Johnson over Vietnam in 1968—and that may have cost Humphrey the election that year. See Bescholss, *Taking Charge*, 487.

72. Valenti interview, LBJLOHC.

73. Goldman, *Tragedy of Lyndon Johnson*, 239–40.

74. Evans and Novak, *Lyndon B. Johnson*, 457; Solberg, *Hubert Humphrey*, 246.

75. *Newsweek*, September 7, 1964. On the August 23 edition of *Meet the Press* McCarthy said he wanted the nomination. Humphrey, on the same program, insisted that he had never spoken to Johnson about the vice presidency. Transcripts of *Face the Nation* (August 23, 1964), Box 220, Spivak Papers, LC.

76. Humphrey did, however, tell his wife. The message from the White House came from James Rowe. Humphrey, *Education of a Public Man*, 223.

77. *Newsweek*, September 7, 1964; Evans and Novak, *Lyndon B. Johnson*, 459.

78. Johnson, *Vantage Point*, 101.

79. Valenti interview, LBJLOHC. Clifford had much the same opinion. See Clifford interview, LBJLOHC.

80. Humphrey, *Education of a Public Man*, 222.

81. Valenti interview, LBJLOHC; and ibid., 223.

82. O'Donnell interview, LBJLOHC. The interview is recounted best in Humphrey, *Education of a Public Man*, 224–25.

83. Ibid., 226; *Newsweek*, September 7, 1964.

84. Ibid., September 7, 1964.

Chapter 9. The King Is Dead. Long Live the King

1. Interview with O'Donnell, LBJLOHC. Hubert Humphrey made the same observation. See Humphrey, *Education of a Public Man*, 237.

2. A Gallup poll showed LBJ leading Goldwater by as much as 65 to 29 percent. *Time*, August 28, 1964.

3. T. White, *Making of the President—1964*, 275.

4. Ibid., 276–77. See similar complaints by Larry O'Brien. O'Brien interview, LBJLOHC.

5. T. White, *Making of the President—1964*, 276.

6. There were possibly as many as 90,000 votes cast here. See Branch, *Pillar of Fire*, 158; and David Burner, *Making Peace with the Sixties* (Princeton, NJ, 1996), 39. Robert Moses hoped that as many as 200,000 votes would be cast. See Branch, *Pillar of Fire*, 156.

7. For what is usually considered the semi-official account of these events, see Len Holt, *The Summer That Didn't End* (New York, 1965). Another important source is Howard Zinn, *SNCC: The New Abolitionists* (Boston, 1965), especially chapter 4. See also Joseph Sinsheimer, "The Freedom Vote of 1963: New Strategies of Racial Protest in Mississippi," *Journal of Southern History* LV (May 1989): 217–44.

8. Zinn, *SNCC*, 8–9.

9. Bill Higgs to Jack Minnis (January 15, 1964), Anne Romaine Papers, 2/ 12, King Library and Archives, Martin Luther King, Jr., Center for Nonviolent Social Protest, Atlanta, Georgia. Other early plans were reported in *New York Times*, March 13, 1964.

10. Documents pertaining to founding of the MFDP (April 26, 1964), SNCC Papers, Ser. XVI, 107/5, MLK Library and Archives. See also Robert Moses (and other MFDP coordinators) to "All Field Staff and Voter Registration Volunteers" (July 19, 1964), in same, XVI, 107/2. Other important leaders included James Farmer and Aaron Henry.

11. Allen J. Matusow, "From Civil Rights to Black Power: The Case of SNCC, 1960–1966," in *Twentieth-Century America: Recent Interpretations*, 2d ed., ed. Barton J. Bernstein and Allen J. Matusow (New York: 1972), 499.

12. Holt, *Summer That Didn't End*, 156, 162–63; Steven F. Lawson, *Black Ballots: Voting Rights in the South, 1944–1969* (New York, 1976), 301; *Jackson Clarion-Ledger*, August 26, 1964. Of the MFDP delegation, four were white.

13. David J. Garrow, *Bearing the Cross: Martin Luther King, Jr., and the Southern Christian Leadership Conference* (New York, 1986), 338.

14. *New York Times*, July 19–24, 1964; *Time*, July 31, 1964.

15. Hess, *In a Cause*, 206.

16. *Newsweek*, August 3, 1964.

17. Goldwater, *With No Apologies*, 192–93; *Time*, July 31, 1964; Goldberg, *Goldwater*, 215–16.

18. Hodges to LBJ (August 10, 1964), WHCF: EX PL6–77, LBJ Papers, LBJL.

19. White House Press Release (July 20, 1964), WHCF: Aides—Moyers, LBJ Papers, LBJL.

20. White House Press Releases (July 29 and August 14, 1964), in ibid.

21. Roy Wilkins, *Standing Fast: The Autobiography of Roy Wilkins* (New York, 1982), 304. For a discussion of LBJ's manipulation of these events, see Bruce Miroff, "Presidential Leverage over Social Movements: The Johnson White House and Civil Rights," *Journal of Politics* 43 (1981): 12–13.

22. James Farmer interview, LBJLOHC. On Wilkins and the SNCC, see Staff Meeting Minutes (June 9–11, 1964) SNCC Papers, Ser., VII, 11, MLK Library and Archives.

23. John Lewis, *Walking with the Wind*, 276.

24. Farmer interview, LBJLOHC.

25. Lewis, *Walking with the Wind*, 276. See also, *Time*, August 7, 1964; *New York Times*, July 30 and 31, 1964.

26. *New York Times*, July 30 and 31, 1964; *Time*, August 7, 1964.

27. Matusow, *Unraveling of America*, 140, 148. Matusow suggests that working-class Democrats worried more about Goldwater's economics than about race. See also Goldberg, *Goldwater*, 215–16.

28. White House Press Release (August 28, 1964), WHCF: EX PL6–1, LBJ Papers, LBJL.

29. Johnson and Reedy, telephone conversation #5176 (August 25, 1964), LBJL. See also George Reedy, *Lyndon B. Johnson: A Memoir* (New York, 1982), 59.

30. Johnson and Reuther (August 8, 1964) telephone conversation in Beschloss, *Taking Charge*, 510–11.

31. LBJ and Humphrey, telephone conversation #4918 (August 14, 1964), LBJL.

32. Casey Hayden to Robert Moses, Velma Hill, et al., (April 15, 1964) SNCC Papers, Ser. XVI, 107/4, MLK Library and Archives. On Rauh and the MFDP, see Mark Stern, *Calculating Visions: Kennedy, Johnson, and Civil Rights* (New Brunswick, NJ, 1992), 197–209.

33. Lewis, *Walking with the Wind*, 280.

34. Joseph Rauh interview, Anne Romaine Collection, MLK Library and Archives. Rauh explains here how badly he wanted Humphery to win the vice presidential nomination. See also Lee White to LBJ (August 13, 1964), WHCF: PL 1/ST 24, LBJ Papers, LBJL. This memo shows that the Johnson administration believed that Rauh was working in the interest of the White House.

35. John Lewis, *Walking with the Wind*, 275.

36. For Wallace's statements see "Testimony Prepared for Delivery by George C. Wallace Governor of Alabama Before the Platform Committee National Democratic Convention Atlantic City, New Jersey, August 21, 1964," Alabama Governor's Administration Files, George Wallace Papers, ADAH. Also, *New York Times*, August 22, 1964.

37. Cartha DeLoach, *Hoover's FBI: The Inside Story by Hoover's Trusted Lieutenant* (Washington, DC, 1995), 9; Matusow, *Unraveling of America*, 141. Eleven years later, after Watergate, this entire operation was investigated by a Senate subcommittee. See *Hearings Before the Senate Select Committee to Study Governmental Operations with Respect to Intelligence Activities* (November–

December 1975), 94th Cong., 2d sess., vol. 6, Federal Bureau of Investigation, passim.

38. Lewis, *Walking with the Wind*, 279.

39. *Jackson Clarion-Ledger*, August 22, 1964; Clayborne Carson, *In Struggle: SNCC and the Black Awakening of the 1960s* (Cambridge, MA, 1981), 123; *Washington Post*, August 23, 1964; *New York Times*, August 24, 1964; Rauh interview, Anne Romaine Collection, MLK Library and Archives. Transcript of Rauh's speech before the Credentials Committee (August 22, 1964), Box 29/6, Joseph Rauh Papers, LC.

40. Chana Kai Lee, *For Freedom's Sake: The Life of Fannie Lou Hamer* (Urbana, IL, 1999), 81; Fannie Lou Hamer interview, Mississippi Oral History Project, University of Southern Mississippi, Hattiesburg. Transcript of Hamer's speech before the Credentials Committee (August 22, 1964), Box 29/6, Joseph Rauh Papers, LC.

41. Kay Mills, *This Little Light of Mine: The Life of Fannie Lou Hamer* (New York, 1994), 119–21; Holt, *Summer that Didn't End*, 168–69.

42. *New York Times*, August 23, 1964. Transcript of Rauh's speech before the Credentials Committee (August 22, 1964), Box 29/6, Joseph Rauh Papers, LC.

43. Branch, *Pillar of Fire*, 459–60; Lee, *For Freedom's Sake*, 89–90.

44. LBJ and Russell, telephone conversation #5143 (August 24, 1984), LBJL.

45. White House Press Release (August 24, 1964), WHCF: Aides—Moyers, LBJ Papers, LBJL.

46. Reuther was in Detroit negotiating contracts with the big three auto makers. Clark Clifford made the call. Evans and Novak, *Lyndon B. Johnson*, 454.

47. White House Press Release (August 25, 1964), WHCF: Aides—Moyers, LBJ Papers, LBJL.

48. Transcript of Pastore speech in ibid. See also *New York Times*, August 26, 1964.

49. Rauh was constantly being made aware of this. See Rauh interview, LBJLOHC; Rauh interview, Anne Romaine Collection, MLK Library and Archives; Solberg, *Hubert Humphrey*, 239–56.

50. *New York Times*, August 26, 1964; *Newsweek*, September 7, 1964. *Newsweek* insisted that part of the deal was that the MFDP would reject the offer. *Newsweek*, August 31, 1964.

51. *New York Herald-Tribune*, September 3, 1964.

52. *New York Times*, August 27, 1964.

53. Walter Tillow interview, Anne Romaine Collection, MLK Library and Archives.

54. Rauh interview, ibid.

55. *Newsweek*, September 7, 1964.

56. Farmer interview, LBJLOHC.

57. *Jackson Clarion-Ledger*, August 26, 1964; *Washington Post*, August 27, 1964.

58. *Newsweek*, August 31, 1964; *New York Times*, July 26, 1964.

59. LBJ and John Connally (August 25, 1964) telephone conversation in Bescholss, *Taking Charge*, 535.

60. LBJ and Reedy, telephone conversation # 5176 (August 25, 1964), LBJL. Johnson said the same thing to Walter Jenkins. See also LBJ and Jenkins, telephone conversation #5177 (August 25, 1964), ibid.

61. Ibid. See also Reedy interview, LBJLOHC. Reedy finally concluded that threatening to resign was one of several ways LBJ controlled people. See also, Reedy, *Lyndon B. Johnson*, 59–60.

62. LBJ and Jenkins, telephone conversation #5177 (August 25, 1964), LBJL.

63. Entry August 25, 1964, "Diary of Lady Bird Johnson," LBJL. Lady Bird Johnson, White House Diary, 210.

64. LBJ, Humphrey, and Reuther, telephone conversation #5181 (August 25, 1964), LBJL.

65. *Newsweek*, September 7, 1964.

66. T. White, *Making of the President—1964*, 280; *Newsweek*, September 7, 1964. A first-hand account of floor activities is in a memo from Walter Adams (the Democratic party's sergeant-at-arms on the convention floor) to Walter Jenkins (September 1, 1964), WHCF: PL1/ST24, LBJ Papers, LBJL.

67. Hamer interview, Anne Romaine Collection, MLK Library and Archives.

68. T. White, *Making of the President—1964*, 281.

69. Donaldson, *Truman Defeats Dewey*, 162–64.

70. T. White, *Making of the President—1964*, 281.

71. Dan T. Carter, *George Wallace, Richard Nixon, and the Transformation of American Politics* (Waco, TX, 1991), 5.

72. Quoted in Harvard Sitkoff, *The Struggle for Black Equality, 1954–1980* (New York, 1981), 185.

73. Carson, *In Struggle*, 123–29. For a broader analysis of Carmichael and the radicalization of the movement as a result of the MFDP challenge, see Milton Viorst, *Fire in the Streets: America in the 1960's* (New York, 1979), 354–359; and Matusow, "From Civil Rights to Black Power," 506.

74. Lewis, *Walking with the Wind*, 283.

75. Rauh to Humphrey (September 7, 1964) 36/5, Joseph Rauh Papers, LC; Rauh interview, Anne Romaine Collection, MLK Library and Archives.

76. *Time*, September 4, 1964; Matusow, *Unraveling of America*, 140; Dalleck, *Flawed Giant*, 160. David Merrick, who produced the popular Broadway play *Hello Dolly*, threatened the Republicans with a $10 million lawsuit if they adapted the song "Hello Dolly" to "Hello Barry." Jerry Herman wrote the song. *New York Times*, July 18, 1964.

77. T. White, *Making of the President—1964*, 284–86.

78. Reedy interview, LBJLOHC.

79. *Time*, September 4, 1964.

80. *Richmond News Leader*, August 27, 1964.

81. *New York Times*, August 26, 1964; *Newsweek*, September 7, 1964; Guthman, *We Band of Brothers*, 287.

82. *Time*, August 28, 1964.

83. *Newsweek*, August 31, 1964.

84. Clifford interview, LBJLOHC; Clifford, *Counsel to the President*, 398.

85. *Newsweek*, September 7, 1964.

86. Evans and Novak, *Lyndon B. Johnson*, 462–63.

87. Schlesinger, *Robert Kennedy*, 718; *New York Times*, August 28, 1964; *Time*, September 4, 1964; *Newsweek*, September 7, 1964; T. White, *Making of the President—1964*, 248.

88. *Time* clocked it at a low of thirteen minutes; Schlesinger, *Robert Kennedy*, 665, and T. White, *Making of the President—1964*, 248, both estimated twenty-two minutes.

89. Edwin O. Guthman and C. Richard Allen, eds., *RFK: Collected Speeches* (New York, 1993), 114–17.

90. Russell, *Lady Bird*, 247.

91. Shesol, *Mutual Contempt*, 214.

92. Evans and Novak, *Lyndon B. Johnson*, 462–63.

93. Both quotes are in *Newsweek*, September 7, 1964.

94. Others agree. See Dalleck, *Flawed Giant*, 166; and Unger and Unger, *LBJ*, 327.

95. *PP, LBJ, 1963–64*, 1009–13.

96. T. White, *Making of the President—1964*, 281.

97. *New York Times*, August 28, 1964. Moyers wrote the speech. See Humphrey, *Education of a Public Man*, 226–27.

98. T. White, *Making of the President—1964*, 283.

99. Goldman, *Tragedy of Lyndon Johnson*, 218.

100. T. White, *Making of the President—1964*, 281, 293.

Chapter 10. Goldwater and Johnson in a Cause Predetermined

1. *Business Week*, September 5, 1964.

2. *Newsweek*, July 13, 1964.

3. O'Donnell to Jenkins (January 3, 1964), WHCF: EX PL2, LBJ Papers, LBJL. George Reedy, however, insisted that the election was never in doubt. See Reedy interview, LBJLOHC.

4. Harris Poll in *Washington Post*, July 21, 1964.

5. Copy in White House Press Release (July 13, 1964), WHCF: Aides—Moyers, LBJ Papers, LBJL.

6. *Newsweek*, August 31, 1964.

7. *Time*, August 14, 1964.

8. LBJ and John Connally, telephone conversation #430 (July 23, 1964), LBJL.

9. O'Donnell to LBJ (October 3, 1964), WHCF: EX PL2, LBJ Papers, LBJL.

10. Wilson to O'Brien (July 8, 1964), in ibid. There were similar fears expressed by Clark Clifford. See Clifford interview, LBJLOHC.

11. *Time*, April 22, 1957.

12. Ambrose, *Eisenhower*, 444, 464–65, 471–72; Reinhard, *The Republican Right*, 105, 144–45.

13. Piers Brendon, *Ike: The Life and Times of Dwight D. Eisenhower* (London, 1987), 411; Mary C. Brennan, *Turning Right in the Sixties: The Conservative Capture of the GOP* (Chapel Hill, NC, 1995), 79; Nixon, *RN*, 261–62.

14. Hess, *In a Cause*, 177; *Time*, August 21, 1964.

15. Hess, *In a Cause*, 177. A transcript of the Hershey meeting is also in Hess, 168–216. Another transcript of the Hershey meeting is in "The 1964 Presidential Campaign," *Cong. Rec.*, 89th Cong., 1st sess., pt. 3 ("Speeches, Remarks, Press Conferences and Other Papers of Senator Barry Goldwater"), 65–68.

16. Hess, *In a Cause*, 173.

17. Ibid., 174.

18. Ibid., 179–83.

19. Ibid., 203–4.

20. Ibid., 200.

21. Ibid., 206, 215.

22. *Time*, August 21, 1964.

23. White House Press Release (August 13, 1964), WHCF: Aides—Moyers, LBJ Papers, LBJL.

24. Hess, *In a Cause*, 216.

25. Nixon, *RN*, 262.

26. *Time*, August 21, 1964; *New York Times*, August 13, 1964.

27. Humphrey, *Education of a Public Man*, 227.

28. Ibid., 227.

29. Ibid., 229.

30. Ibid., 229.

31. See *Life*, Aug, 21, 1964.

32. Quoted in Solberg, *Hubert Humphrey*, 258.

33. Quoted in Evans and Novak, *Lyndon B. Johnson*, 471.

34. *PP, LBJ, 1963–64*, 1044.

35. Valenti to LBJ (September 7, 1964), WHCF: EX PL 2, LBJ Papers, LBJL.

36. *Time*, October 2, 1964.

37. Burch to Bailey (August 20, 1964), copy in RNC Press Release (August 20, 1964), "W" Series, 5/1, Goldwater Papers, AHF.

38. Transcript of Goldwater interview on the *Jack Paar Show* (January 31, 1964), "W" Series, 1/1, in ibid.

39. Paul Popple to Valenti (August 20, 1964), WHCF: EX PL 2, LBJ Papers, LBJL. Popple quotes Postmaster General John Gronouski here.

40. Bob Hunter to Douglass Cater (September 3, 1964), in ibid.

41. Valenti interview, LBJOHC.

42. Ibid.

43. Lee White to Bill Moyers (September 10, 1964), WHCF: EX PL 6–3, LBJ Papers, LBJL. This memo set up the committee. See also Evans and Novak, *Lyndon B. Johnson,* 767–829. Moyers to LBJ (July 17, 1964) and LBJ to Moyers (July 17, 1964), both in WHCF: Aides—Moyers, LBJ Papers, LBJL. See also, Meyer Feldman to Moyers (September 10, 1964), WHCF: EX PL 2, LBJ Papers, LBJL. This Five O'clock Club also compiled a list of Goldwater quotes and misquotes for use against the Republican candidate. See examples of this collection in Republican Files, WHCF: EX PL 2, LBJ Papers, LBJL. One of the White House spies was E. Howard Hunt. Goldberg, *Goldwater*, 212.

44. Valenti interview, LBJLOHC.

45. Humphrey, *Education of a Public Man*, 273.

46. O'Brien interview, LBJLOHC.

47. Valenti to Moyers (September 14, 1964), WHCF: EX PL 2, LBJ Papers, LBJL.

48. Valenti to LBJ (September 7, 1964), in ibid.

49. Valenti interview, LBJOHC.

50. O'Brien interview, LBJLOHC.

51. Larry Sabato, *The Rise of Political Consultants: New Ways of Winning Elections* (New York, 1983), 169–70; Richard Armstong, *The Next Hurrah: Communications Revolution in American Politics* (New York, 1988) 17; Polsby and Wildarsky, *Presidential Elections*, 191; Dalleck, *Flawed Giant*, 175; *Newsweek*, March 21, 1964.

52. Valenti interview, LBJLOHC. Humphrey claimed that he disapproved of the ad and insisted that it be pulled. See transcripts of *Meet the Press* (September 20, 1964), Spivak Papers, LC, Box 220.

53. Dirksen to Vincent T. Washilski (RNC Press Release) (September 12, 1964), "W" Series, 5/2, Goldwater Papers, AHF.

54. Edwin Diamond and Stephen Bates, *The Spot: The Rise of Political Advertising on Television* (Cambridge, MA, 1992), 127–29; *Newsweek*, March 21, 1964.

55. Quoted in Goldberg, *Goldwater*, 224.

56. *Time*, October 30, 1964.

57. Ibid.

58. Lee Edwards, a long-time Goldwater supporter and biographer, has said that the statement was made in the 1930s. See Edwards, *Goldwater*, 304. The Alsop article is "Can Goldwater Win in 1964?" in *Saturday Evening Post*, August 24, 1964. The Goldwater quote is on page 23.

59. Sabato, *Rise of Political Consultants*, 169–70; Manchester, *Glory and the Dream*, 1260; Diamond and Bates, *The Spot*, 132–36; Polsby and Waldarsky, *Presidential Elections*, 191; *Time*, October 23, 1964. Another commercial quoted Robert Cleal of the Alabama Ku Klux Klan: "The majority of people in Alabama hate niggerism, Catholicism, Judaism. I like Barry Goldwater. He needs our help." That spot, however, was finally cut from the collection and was never released. To view some of these ads, see www.pbs.org/30secondcandidate/timeline/years/1964b.html.

60. See RNC polling data (August 1964), "W" Series, 4/5, Goldwater Papers, AHF. Goldwater held a one-point lead in the South. Nationally, 12 percent responded as undecided. Only 9 percent saw the Bobby Baker scandal as significant.

61. Speech at Prescott, Arizona (September 3, 1964), 3H511,Goldwater Collection, Center for American History, UT.

62. *Time*, August 20 and 28, 1964; Speech at Prescott, Arizona (September 3, 1964) 3H511, Goldwater Collection, Center for American History, UT.

63. *Newsweek*, September 17, 1964.

64. Transcript of McNeil interview (September 10, 1964), Presidential Campaign Files, 11/2, Goldwater Papers, AHF. See particularly Goldwater's speech in St. Petersburg (September 15, 1964), Goldwater Collection, Center for American History, UT.

65. *Time*, October 30, 1964; Polsby and Wildavsky, *Presidential Elections*, 191; Diamond and Bates, *The Spot*, 144–45. On Goldwater's recollection of the ad, see Goldwater, *Goldwater*, 260.

66. T. White, *Making of the President—1964*, 332–33.

67. Edwards, *Goldwater*, 287; RNC Press Release (October 7, 1964), "W" Series, 5/2, Goldwater Papers, AHF. This press release gives the number of television ads planned for the last month of the campaign.

68. Quoted in Schuparra, *Triumph of the Right*, 99.

69. "Barry Goldwater Campaign Speeches" (September 8, 1964), vol. 3, manuscript collection, AHF.

70. *U.S. News & World Report*, September 21, 1964; Shedegg, *What Happened to Goldwater?*, 207.

71. *New York Times*, September 16–18, 20, 1964; *Time*, September 25, 1964.

72. Speech at Charlotte, North Carolina (September 21, 1964), 3H511, Goldwater Collection, Center for American History, UT.

73. Speech at Montgomery, Alabama, (September 16, 1964), in ibid.

74. Nadine Cohadis, *Strom Thurmond and the Politics of Southern Change* (New York, 1993), 356. It was Humphrey whose speech in favor of civil rights had forced a strong civil rights plank into the 1948 Democratic party platform. This, in turn, convinced southerners to form their own States' Rights party, the Dixiecrats. See Donaldson, *Truman Defeats Dewey*, 157–66.

75. *U.S. News & World Report*, September 24, 1964.

76. Speech at Fargo, North Dakota (September 19, 1964) 3H511, Goldwater Collection, Center for American History, UT; *New York Times*, September 16–20, 1964; Moyers to LBJ (September 2, 1964) WHCF: EX PL 6–3, LBJ Papers, LBJL. Stephen Shedegg, in his *What Happened to Goldwater?*, insists that most of these problems had to do with poorly motivated speechwriters, a point that contradicts my interpretation here. See Shedegg, *What Happened to Goldwater?*, 219. See also Shedegg's analysis of the various fiascos surrounding the writing of Goldwater's Fargo, North Dakota, speech in the same volume, 231–37. On his advisors' insistence that he not oppose price supports in Fargo, see, Hess, *In a Cause*, 159. For the other speeches in the South, see Presidential Campaign Files, 11/2, Goldwater Papers, AHF. For Charleston, West Virginia, speech (September 18), see "Barry Goldwater Campaign Speeches," vol. 2, manuscript collection, AHF. For Knoxville, Orlando, St. Petersburg, and Atlanta speeches see Presidential Campaign Files, 11/2, Goldwater Papers, AHF. Speaking in Atlanta (September 15), Goldwater complained about federal reapportionment. Atlanta had gained eleven state Senate seats and twenty-five House seats from reapportionment. On the entire September speaking fiasco, see Pam Rymer to Kitchel (September 23, 1964), Presidential Campaign Files, 11/2, Goldwater Papers, AHF.

77. Transcript of Gettysburg meeting (September 22, 1964), Presidential Campaign Files, 11/8, Goldwater Papers, AHF.

78. Polling data quoted in Dalleck, *Flawed Giant*, 177.

79. *New York Times*, September 30 and October 10, 1964; *Vital Speeches*, October 15, 1964, 5–7, and November 1, 1964, 36–38; Hess, *In a Cause*, 54; Goldwater, *Where I Stand* (New York, 1964), 57. In the mid-1960s there was a

growing conflict between the Soviet Union and the People's Republic of China over the manner in which communism should be exported to other parts of the world. This conflict ultimately resulted in a break between the two communist nations in 1966. Goldwater refused to accept that such conflicts existed.

80. A good example here is a speech Goldwater gave on August 25. Transcript is in Goldwater Collection, 3H511, Center for American History, UT; Goldwater televised speech (September 18, 1964), "Barry Goldwater Campaign Speeches," vol. 2, manuscript collection, AHF.

81. Moyers to LBJ (September 29, 1964) WHCF: EX PL2, LBJ Papers, LBJL. Also released in 1964 was *Seven Days in May*, a movie about a radical right-wing conspiracy that attempted to take over the U.S. government by force. The movie stared Burt Lancaster and Kirk Douglas and, like *Fail Safe*, was a box office hit.

82. *Time*, October 2, 1964.

83. See some of this in ibid., November 20, 1964.

84. *Time*, July 24, 1964.

85. For a taste of this, see Hess, *In a Cause*, 102–32.

86. Goldberg, *Goldwater*, 223. Goldwater was openly endorsed by about 50 percent of southern newspapers, the hightest endorsement of his campaign from any of the major national regions. His own campaign staff described endorsements from other regions of the nation as "overwhelmingly LBJ." Pam Rymer to Kitchel (September 22, 1964), "W" Series, 8/2, Goldwater Papers, AHF. It was Rymer's job within the Goldwater campaign structure to monitor and report on the press.

87. See James Keogh, *President Nixon and the Press* (New York, 1972), 172; Edith Efron, *News Twisters* (Los Angeles, 1971) 47; Nixon, *RN*, 330; and T. White, *Making of the President—1960*, 402–3.

88. Ronald Reagan, *An American Life* (New York, 1990), 209–10.

89. *Fact*, October 1964. See Goldwater's opinion on the *Fact* magazine article in Goldwater, *Goldwater*, 260–61.

90. For a discussion of this article and the importance it has had to Goldwater supporters since 1964, see Edwards, *Goldwater*, 319. Edwards was a Goldwater supporter. Following the election, Goldwater won a libel suit against the magazine's editor. The U.S. Supreme Court finally decided the case in 1970 in a five to two decision. See Edwards, *Goldwater*, 319. Goldwater's Papers at the Arizona Historical Foundation include a copy of the *Fact* issue, autographed by the magazine's editor. See Presidential Campaign Material, 20/7, Goldwater Papers, AHF.

91. *Time*, August 21, 1964.

92. T. White, *Making of the President—1964*, 106.

93. Ibid., 107.

94. *Time*, July 24, 1964. The *Saturday Evening Post* reported a similar situation in September. See September 19, 1964, edition.

95. Sam Donaldson, *Hold On, Mr. President!* (New York, 1987), 47. Donaldson was an admirer of Goldwater's.

96. *Time*, July 24, 1964.

97. Some examples include Harold Faber, and Staff of *New York Times*, eds.,

The Road to the White House: The Story of the 1964 Election (New York, 1965), 174; *Atlantic Monthly*, October 1964; and *New York Herald-Tribune*, October 4, 1964.

98. Schedegg, *What Happened to Goldwater?* 185–86; Rusher, *Rise of the Right*, 157–59; Brennan, *Turning Right*, 91. William Rusher has insisted that Goldwater did not like White because he believed that White had pushed him into an election he could not win. Rusher, *Rise of the Right*, 169. That White had been passed over, and that the campaign was damaged because of it, was apparent to many in the press. See, particularly, Roland Evans and Robert Novak, *New York Herald-Tribune*, July 21, 1964.

99. Goldwater, *No Apologies*, 169.

100. Brennan, *Turning Right*, 91; Goldberg, *Goldwater*, 173.

101. Shadegg, *What Happened to Goldwater?*, 168. Hess, Goldwater's main speechwriter, left the campaign shortly after the convention.

102. Rusher, *Rise of the Right*, 169.

103. Shedegg, *What Happened to Goldwater?*, 168.

104. Goldwater, *Goldwater*, 240.

Chapter 11. Home Stretch

1. Valenti interview, LBJLOHC. It was Henry Watson, one of LBJ's aides, who believed that the president was vulnerable in the campaign. See Watson to Lawrence O'Brien (July 8, 1964), WHCF: EX PL2, WHCF, LBJ Papers, LBJL. Others believed that the president's negative campaigning might cause a backlash. See O'Brien to LBJ (August 20, 1964) in same. The liberal magazine *Nation* also believed LBJ could lose. See *Nation*, October 26, 1964.

2. O'Donnell interview, LBJLOHC.

3. *Time*, October 16, 1964.

4. Valenti interview, LBJLOHC. See also Goldman, *Tragedy*, 272.

5. Ibid., 275.

6. Ibid., 274. Y.A. Tittle was a quarterback for the Greenbay Packers in the 1960s.

7. *PP, LBJ, 1963–64*, 1164.

8. *Time*, October 9, 1964.

9. Valenti interview, LBJLOHC.

10. *Time*, October 16, 1964.

11. Goldman, *Tragedy*, 275.

12. *PP, LBJ, 1963–64*, 1106.

13. Ibid., 1370.

14. *Time*, October 2, 1964.

15. Ibid., October 2, 1964.

16. Goldwater, *Goldwater*, 259.

17. RNC Press Release (October 6, 1964), "W" Series, 5/2, Goldwater Papers, AHF; *New York Times*, October 6, 1964.

18. "Barry Goldwater Campaign Speeches," (September 3, 1964, and September 10, 1964), vol. 3, unpublished manuscript collection, AHF.

19. Ibid. (October 1, 1964).

20. *New York Times*, October 11, 1964.

21. Ibid., October 17, 1964.

22. *Time*, October 9 and 16, 1964.

23. Gallup, *Gallup Poll, III*, 1894, 1896, 1898–99, 1901–03.

24. Valenti interview, LBJLOHC. On the lack of southern support, see also Cliff Carter to LBJ (August 15, 1964), WHCF: Ex PL2, LBJ Papers, LBJL. And LBJ and John Connally, telephone conversation #430 (July 23, 1964), LBJL.

25. See campaign schedules (n.d.), Presidential Campaign Files, 9/1; and "W" Series, 5/2. Both in Goldwater Papers, AHF.

26. *Time*, October 16, 1964.

27. Reedy interview, LBJLOHC.

28. Lady Bird, White House Diary, 195–96; Russell, *Lady Bird*, 251, 255.

29. *Time*, October 16, 1964.

30. Ibid.

31. Russell, *Lady Bird*, 258.

32. Ibid., 259. That night, following the confrontation in Charleston, Lynda told her father over the telephone that "We'll get a lot of sympathy reports because these people were bad. . . ." Lynda Bird Johnson and LBJ (October 7, 1964) telephone conversation in Michael Beschloss, *Reaching for Glory: Lyndon Johnson's Secret White House Tapes, 1964–1965* (New York, 2001), 48.

33. *PP, LBJ, 1963–64*, 1286. The *Public Papers* record "Negro, Negro, Negro."

34. Hale Boggs interview, LBJLOHC; Johnson, *Vantage Point*, 110; Miller, *Lyndon*, 485.

35. Ike only made about five speeches for Goldwater. See RNC Press Release (October 11, 1964), "W" Series, 5/3, Goldwater Papers, AHF. For Scranton's travel schedule, see RNC Press Release (October 5, 1964), in same. *Time*, October 16, 1964.

36. Nixon, *RN*, 263.

37. RNC Press Release (November 1, 1964), "W" Series, 5/4, Goldwater Papers, AHF; *Wall Street Journal*, October 6, 1964; *New York Times*, October 2, 1964; Nixon, *RN*, 263; Brennan, *Turning Right in the Sixties*, 97–99.

38. Valenti interview, LBJLOHC.

39. *Time*, October 23, 1964.

40. Ibid.; *U.S. News & World Report*, October 26, 1964. It was Jenkins's second arrest on the same charge. Clifford later said that Jenkins had "had quite a lot to drink." Clifford interview, LBJLOHC. See also LBJ's telephone conversation with FBI assistant director Cartha "Deke" DeLoach (October 14, 1964) in Beschloss, *Reaching for Glory*, 69–71.

41. *Time*, October 23, 1964; Clifford, *Counsel*, 399–400.

42. Clifford interview, LBJLOHC.

43. *Time*, October 23, 1964; *New York Times*, October 15 and 16, 1964.

44. LBJ and Abe Fortas, telephone conversation #5875 (October 14, 1964), LBJL. George Reedy is often identified as the one who delivered the news to LBJ. It was, however, more likely Fortas. See Reedy interview, LBJLOHC.

45. *Time*, October 23, 1964.

46. Valenti interview, LBJLOHC.
47. Evans and Novak, *Lyndon B. Johnson*, 480.
48. Goldwater, *Goldwater*, 258.
49. Goldwater said almost nothing on the topic and praised himself for his restraint in his autobiography. See Goldwater, *Goldwater*, 259. William Miller, however, mentioned the Jenkins incident often, and Dean Burch issued several press releases on the incident, focusing mostly on the question of compromised security in the White House, but Burch also used the incident to question the morals of the Johnson administration. See, particularly, Miller's speeches and several Burch statements and news conferences through mid-October, "W" Series, 6/4, 5/3, and 5/4, Goldwater Papers, AHF. Goldwater also sent an open letter to FBI chief J. Edgar Hoover asking why Jenkins had not been subjected to an investigation before he was allowed to work so close to Johnson. See BMG to J. Edgar Hoover (October 19, 1964), Goldwater Papers, AHF.
50. *Time*, August 21, 1964.
51. Ibid., August 28, 1964; *New York Times*, August 26, 1964.
52. *New York Times*, October 30, 1964.
53. Ibid.
54. Ibid., August 21, 1964.
55. *Time*, October 30, 1964.
56. *Time*, October 30, 1964.
57. Despite Keating's intransigence, Goldwater went to New York in early October and asked New Yorkers to vote for Keating. *Time*, October 2, 1964.
58. Ibid., October 30, 1964.
59. Polling data in Schlesinger, *Robert Kennedy*, 699; and Guthman, *We Band of Brothers*, 300.
60. *Time*, October 30, 1964.
61. LBJ and RFK, telephone conversation #5968 (October 26, 1964), LBJL; Schlesinger, *Robert Kennedy*, 699.
62. Guthman, *We Band of Brothers*, 300.
63. O'Donnell interview, LBJLOHC.
64. *New York Times*, October 15 and 16, 1964.
65. *PP, LBJ, 1963–64*, 1348.
66. Carter, *From Wallace to Gingrich*, xi.
67. *Time*, October 16, 1964.
68. Ibid.
69. Carter, *From Wallace to Gingrich*, xiii.
70. *Time*, October 16, 1964.
71. Ibid.
72. Anderson and Lee, "1964 Election in California," 462; *Saturday Evening Post*, May 29, 1964; *Time*, June 12 and October 16, 1964; Schuparra, *Triumph of the Right*, 103.
73. *Time*, June 12, 1964.
74. Ibid., October 16, 1964.
75. Schuparra, *Triumph of the Right*, 102–8; *Time*, September 25, October 16, and November 4, 1964.

76. Rusher, *Rise of the Right*, 173.

77. Cannon, *President Reagan*, 74, 282–84; William Pemberton, *Exit with Honor: The Life and Presidency of Ronald Reagan* (Armonk, NY, 1998), 29–36.

78. Schuparra, *Triumph of the Right*, 100; Cannon, *President Reagan*, 98–99; Shadegg, *What Happened to Goldwater?*, 252.

79. Goldwater, *Goldwater*, 266; Rusher, *Rise of the Right*, 173–74; Schuparra, *Triumph of the Right*, 100; Reagan, *An American Life*, 140–43.

80. Parts of the speech are quoted in Reagan, *An American Life*, 141–43; and Pemberton, *Exit With Honor*, 53–54. See also, Matthew Dallek, *The Right Moment: Ronald Reagan's First Victory and the Decisive Turning Point in American Politics* (New York, 2000), 64–69. And Perlstein, *Before the Storm*, 499–503.

81. Schuparra, *Triumph of the Right*, 101.

82. Edwards, *Ronald Reagan*, 77–80.

83. Rusher, *Rise of the Right*, 174; Hess, *In a Cause*, 139; Shadegg, *What Happened to Goldwater?*, 252.

84. Reagan, *An American Life*, 143.

85. *New York Times*, October 21 through October 28, 1964. Goldwater's schedules are in various RNC press releases, "W" Series, 5/4, Goldwater Papers, AHF. Full-page ads calling for strengthening and maintaining Social Security appeared in most national newspapers between October 31 and November 3.

86. Transcript of *CBS Nightly News* (November 3, 1964), Presidential Campaign Material 18/5, BMG Papers, AHS.

87. Goldwater, *Goldwater*, 279. Theodore White recalled that Goldwater said of Kennedy: "He would have debated me. It would have been good for the campaign. It would have been a good campaign." T. White, *Making of the President—1964*, 343.

88. *PP, LBJ, 1963–64*, 1546.

89. Ibid., 1496.

90. Valenti interview, LBJLOHC.

91. *PP, LBJ, 1963–64*, 1579.

92. Ibid., 1584–85.

93. Goldman, *Tragedy of Lyndon Johnson*, 301–4; *Time*, November 4, 1964.

Chapter 12. Analysis

1. *New York Times*, November 4, 1964.

2. *Time*, November 4, 1964, election edition.

3. T. White, *Making of the President—1964*, 389.

4. Ibid., 391–92.

5. *Newsweek*, November 16, 1964.

6. *PP, LBJ, 1963–64*, 1585–86.

7. FDR's 1936 popular vote victory is usually set at 60.8 percent. It is, however, occasionally rounded to 61 percent. The Electoral College margin was 523 to 8.

8. *Time*, November 4, 1964, election edition. *Time* insisted that Johnson received 100 percent of the California African-American vote.

9. O'Brien had hoped for this. See O'Brien to LBJ (August 22, 1964), WHCF: EX PL2, LBJ Papers, LBJL; O'Brien interview, LBJLOHC.

10. Ibid.

11. *Time*, November 13, 1964.

12. *Time*, November 4, 1964, election edition; *Newsweek*, November 16, 1964.

13. Ibid. Avery ran 5 percent ahead of the ticket; Boe 8, percent; Babcock, 10 percent; Knowles, 13 percent; Evans, 19 percent; Volpe, 26 percent; Chafee, 39 percent. Along with Romney, who ran 23 percent ahead of the ticket in Michigan, these can all be considered moderates in the party. See John H. Kessel, *The Goldwater Coalition: Republican Strategies in 1964* (Indianapolis, 1968), 308.

14. *Time*, November 4, 1964, election edition; *New York Times*, November 5, 1964; *Newsweek*, November 16, 1964; Polsby and Wildavsky, *Presidential Elections*, 190.

15. *New York Times*, November 5, 1964; *U.S. News & World Report*, November 16, 1964; Herbert Alexander, *Financing the 1964 Election* (New York, 1968), 7–17, 84–86, 98–99.

16. Reinhard, *Republican Right*, 216–17; *New York Times*, November 10, 1964; Gallup, *Gallup Poll, III*, 2091.

17. Evans, *Future of Conservatism*, 192.

18. In September, a Harris poll showed that 82 percent of the nation opposed the use of nuclear weapons in Asia, and 71 percent opposed going to war over the situation in Cuba. Polsby and Wildavsky, *Presidential Elections*, 306.

19. See particularly, C. White, *Suite 3305*, 410.

20. Hess, *In a Cause*, 1.

21. Transcript of news conference (November 4, 1964), Presidential Campaign Files, 11/6, Goldwater Papers, AHS; *Newsweek*, November 16, 1964.

22. *New York Times*, November 5, 1964.

23. *Time*, October 23, 1964.

24. *Newsweek*, November 16, 1964.

25. *Time*, November 20, 1964.

26. Ibid., November 13 and 20, 1964. For an analysis of the coup led by Romney, see Kessel, *Goldwater Coalition*, 309. The moderates accused the conservatives of hoarding $1.2 million left over from the campaign for the purpose of keeping control of the party.

27. *Time*, November 20, 1964.

28. Quoted in Kessel, *Goldwater Coalition*, 309.

29. *Newsweek*, November 16, 1964.

30. RNC Press Release (November 3, 1964), "W" Series, 5/4, Goldwater Papers, AHS.

31. These events are recounted in detail in Kessel, *Goldwater Coalition*, 314–20.

32. *New York Times*, November 4, 1964; Guthman, *We Band of Brothers*, 311.

33. *New York Times*, November 4, 1964.

34. Schlesinger, *Robert Kennedy*, 729.

35. Valenti, *Very Human President*, 150; Valenti interview, LBJLOHC. Kennedy did, however, thank Johnson personally on the night of the election. RFK and

LBJ telephone conversation #6142 (November 3, 1964), LBJL. The day after the election, LBJ complained to his advisors about Kennedy's speech. See LBJ and Bill Moyers and McGeorge Bundy (November 4, 1964) telephone conversation in Beschloss, *Reaching for Glory*, 114.

36. Schuparra, *Triumph of the Right*, 102–3; Dallek, *The Right Moment*, 48–61.

37. *Time*, November 20, 1964.

38. *Life*, September 8, 1964.

39. *Time*, November 13, 1964.

40. *New York Times*, November 6, 1964; *Newsweek*, November 16, 1964.

41. Reinhard, *Republican Right*, 219.

42. Himmelstein, *To the Right*, 69.

43. Evans, *Future of Conservatism*, 151.

44. Reinhard, *Republican Right*, 216.

45. *New York Times*, November 15, 1964.

46. Pemberton, *Exit with Honor*, 64.

47. *Time*, November 4, 1964.

48. RNC polling data (August 1964), "W" Series 4/5, Goldwater Papers, AHS.

Bibliography

Archival Collections

Alabama Governors' Speech Files, Alabama Department of Archives and History, Montgomery, Alabama

Diary of Lady Bird Johnson, Lyndon Baines Johnson Library, Austin, Texas

Everett M. Dirksen Papers, Dirksen Congressional Center, Pekin, Illinois

Barry M. Goldwater Campaign Speeches, Arizona Historical Foundation, Arizona State University, Tempe, Arizona

Barry M. Goldwater Collection, Center for American History, University of Texas, Austin, Texas

Barry M. Goldwater Papers, Arizona Historical Foundation, Arizona State University, Tempe, Arizona

Fannie L. Hamer Papers (1962–1976) Amistad Research Center, Tulane University, New Orleans, Louisiana

George L. Hinman Files, Rockefeller Archive Center, Pocantico Hills, North Tarrytown, New York

Lyndon Baines Johnson Papers, Lyndon Baines Johnson Library, Austin, Texas

Graham Molitor Papers, Rockefeller Archive Center, Pocantico Hills, North Tarrytown, New York

Ronnie Moore Collection, Amistad Research Center, Tulane University, New Orleans, Louisiana

Nelson Rockefeller Papers, Rockefeller Archive Center, Pocantico Hills, North Tarrytown, New York

Anne Romaine Papers, King Library and Archives, Martin Luther King, Jr., Center for Non-Violent Social Protest, Atlanta, Georgia

Joseph Rauh Papers, Library of Congress, Washington, DC

William Rusher Papers, Library of Congress, Washington, DC

Lawrence Spivak Papers, Library of Congress, Washington, DC

Student Non-Violent Coordinating Committee (SNCC) Papers, King Library and Archives, Martin Luther King, Jr., Center for Non-violent Social Protest, Atlanta, Georgia

George Wallace Papers, Alabama Department of Archives and History, Montgomery, Alabama

Interviews

Lyndon Baines Johnson Library Oral History Collection (LBJLOHC)
Hale Boggs
Clark Clifford
James Farmer
Abe Fortas
Orville Freeman
Hubert Humphrey
Lawrence O'Brien
Kenneth O'Donnell
Joseph Rauh
George Reedy
James Rowe
Arthur Schlesinger, Jr.
Jack Valenti
Anne Romaine Collection, King Library and Archives, Martin Luther King, Jr. Center for Non-violent Social Protest, Atlanta, Georgia
Fannie Lou Hamer
Joseph Rauh
Walter Tillow

Barry M. Goldwater interview with Robert Alan Goldberg
Fannie Lou Hamer interview, Mississippi Oral History Program, Hattiesburg, Mississippi

Magazines and Newspapers

Alabama Advertiser
Alabama Journal
Atlantic Monthly
Birmingham News
Businessweek
Der Spiegel
Esquire
Harpers
Jackson Clarion-Ledger
Life
Modern Maturity
National Review
Newsweek
New York Herald-Tribune
New York Post
New York Review of Books
New York Times
New York Times Magazine

Public Opinion Quarterly
Richmond News Leader
Saturday Evening Post
The Saturday Review
Time
U.S. News & World Report
Vital Speeches of the Day
Wall Street Journal
Washington Post

Books and Articles

Alsop, Joseph (with Adam Plant). *I've Seen the Best of It*. New York: W.W. Norton, 1992.

Alsop, Stewart. "Can Goldwater Win?" *Saturday Evening Post*, September 24, 1963, 19–24+.

Ambrose, Stephen. *Nixon.* Vol. 1. *The Education of a Politician, 1913⁻1962*. New York: Simon and Schuster, 1987.

———. *Eisenhower: Soldier and President*. New York: Simon and Schuster, 1990.

Anderson, Trotten. "The 1958 California Election." *Western Political Science Quarterly* (March 1959).

Anderson, Trotten, and Eugene Lee. "The 1964 Election in California." *Western Political Science Quarterly* (June 1965).

Andrew, John III. *The Other Side of the Sixties: Young Americans for Freedom and the Rise of Conservative Politics*. New Brunswick, NJ: Rutgers University Press, 1997.

———. *Lyndon Johnson and the Great Society*. Chicago: Ivan R. Dee, 1998.

Armstrong, Richard. *The Next Hurrah: Communications Revolution in American Politics*. New York: William Morrow, 1988.

Baker, Bobby (with Larry King). *Wheeling and Dealing: Confessions of a Capitol Hill Operator*. New York: W.W. Norton, 1978.

Bell, Daniel, ed. *The Radical Right: The New American Right*. New York: Anchor, 1964.

Bell, Jack. *Mr. Conservative: Barry Goldwater*. Garden City, NY: Doubleday 1962.

———. *The Johnson Treatment: How Lyndon Johnson Took over the Presidency and Made It His Own*. New York: Harper and Row, 1965.

Berman, William C. *The Politics of Civil Rights in the Truman Administration*. Columbus: Ohio State University Press, 1970.

Beschloss, Michael R. *Taking Charge: The Johnson White House Tapes, 1963–1964*. New York: Simon and Schuster, 1997.

———. *Reaching for Glory: Lyndon Johnson's Secret White House Tapes, 1964–1965*. New York: Simon and Schuster, 2001.

Birmingham News. *Wallace: A Portrait of Power*. Birmingham: Birmingham News, 1998.

Bradlee, Benjamin. *Conversations with Kennedy*. New York: W.W. Norton, 1975.

———. *A Good Life: Newspapering and Other Adventures*. New York: Simon and Schuster, 1995.

Branch, Taylor. *Pillar of Fire: America in the King Years, 1963–1965*. New York: Simon and Schuster, 1998.

Brauer, Carl M. *John F. Kennedy and the Second Reconstruction*. New York: Columbia University Press, 1977.

Brendon, Piers. *Ike, The Life and Times of Dwight D. Eisenhower*. London: Secker and Warburg, 1987.

Brennan, Mary C. *Turning Right in the Sixties: The Conservative Capture of the GOP*. Chapel Hill: University of North Carolina Press, 1995.

Burner, David. *John F. Kennedy and a New Generation*. New York: Harper Collins, 1988.

———. *Making Peace With the Sixties*. Princeton, NJ: Princeton University Press, 1996.

Cannon, Lou. *President Reagan: The Role of a Lifetime*. New York: Simon and Schuster, 1991.

Carlton, Michael, and Anthony Moncrieff. *Many Reasons Why: The American Involvement in Vietnam*. New York: Hill and Wang, 1978.

Carson, Clayborne. *In Struggle: SNCC and the Black Awakening of the 1960s*. Cambridge, MA: Harvard University Press, 1981.

Carter, Dan T. *George Wallace, Richard Nixon, and the Transformation of American Politics*. Waco, TX: Baylor University Press, 1991.

———. *Politics of Rage: George Wallace, the Origins of the New Conservatism, and the Transformation of American Politics*. Baton Rouge: Louisiana State University Press, 1995.

———. *From George Wallace to Newt Gingrich: Race in the Conservative Counterrevolution, 1963–1994*. Baton Rouge: Louisiana State University Press, 1996.

Clifford, Clark (with Richard Holbrook). *Counsel to the President: A Memoir*. New York: Random House, 1991.

Cohadis, Nadine. *Strom Thurmond and the Politics of Southern Change*. New York: Simon and Schuster, 1993.

Cook, James Graham. *The Segregationists*. New York: Appleton-Century-Crofts, 1962.

Crespi, Irving. "The Structural Basis for Right-wing Conservatism: The Goldwater Case." *Public Opinion Quarterly* (Winter 1965–66).

Cummings, Milton C., ed. *The National Election of 1964*. Washington, DC: Brookings Institution, 1964.

Dallek, Matthew. *The Right Moment: Ronald Reagan's First Victory and the Decisive Turning Point in American Politics*. New York: Free Press, 2000.

Dallek, Robert. *Flawed Giant. Lyndon Johnson and His Times, 1961–1973*. New York: Oxford University Press, 1998.

DeLoach, Cartha. *Hoover's FBI: The Inside Story by Hoover's Trusted Lieutenant*. Washington, DC: Regnery Press, 1995.

Diamond, Edwin, and Stephen Bates. *The Spot: The Rise of Political Advertising on Television*. Cambridge, MA: MIT Press, 1992.

Dickerson, Nancy. *Among Those Presents: A Reporter's View of Twenty-five Years in Washington*. New York: Random House, 1976.

Donaldson, Gary A. *Truman Defeats Dewey*. Lexington: University Press of Kentucky, 1999.

Donaldson, Sam. *Hold On, Mr. President!* New York: Faucett Crest, 1987.

Edwards, India. *Pulling No Punches: Memoirs of a Woman in Politics.* New York: Putnam, 1977.

Edwards, Lee. *The Conservative Revolution: The Movement That Remade America.* New York: Free Press, 1999.

———. *Goldwater: The Man Who Made a Revolution.* Washington, DC: Regnery Press, 1995.

———. *Ronald Reagan: A Political Biography.* Houston: Norland, 1981.

Efron, Edith. *The News Twisters.* Los Angeles: Nash, 1971.

Epstein, Benjamin R., and Arnold Forster. *The Radical Right: Report on the John Birch Society and Its Allies.* New York: Random House, 1967.

Evans, M. Stanton. *Revolt On Campus.* New York: McGraw-Hill, 1963.

———. *The Future of Conservatism: From Taft to Reagan and Beyond.* New York: Holt, Reinhart and Winston, 1968.

Evans, Roland, and Robert Novak. *Lyndon B. Johnson: The Exercise of Power.* New York: Signet, 1968.

Frady, Marshall. *Wallace.* 2d ed. New York: New American Library, 1976.

Gallup, George. *The Gallup Poll: Public Opinion, 1935–1971.* New York: Random House, 1972.

Garrow, David J. *Bearing the Cross: Martin Luther King, Jr., and the Southern Christian Leadership Conference.* New York: Vintage, 1986.

Gillon, Steven M. *Politics and Vision: The ADA and American Liberalism, 1947–1985.* New York: Oxford University Press, 1987.

Goldberg, Robert Alan. *Barry Goldwater.* New Haven, CT: Yale University Press, 1995.

Goldman, Eric F. *The Tragedy of Lyndon Johnson.* New York: Dell, 1968.

Goldwater, Barry. *Conscience of a Conservative.* Shepherdsville, KY: Victor, 1960.

———. "How to Win the Cold War." *New York Times Magazine,* September 17, 1961, 100+.

———. *Why Not Victory?: A Fresh Look at American Foreign Policy.* New York: McGraw-Hill, 1962.

———. *Where I Stand.* New York: McGraw-Hill, 1964.

———. *Conscience of a Majority.* Englewood Cliffs, NJ: Prentice-Hall, 1970.

———. *With No Apologies: The Personal and Political Memoirs of United States Senator Barry M. Goldwater.* New York: William Morrow, 1979.

——— (with Jack Casserly). *Goldwater.* New York: Doubleday, 1988.

Goodwin, Richard N. *Remembering America: A Voice From the Sixties.* New York: Harper and Row, 1988.

Griffin, Robert. *Politics of Fear: Joseph R. McCarthy and the Senate.* 2d ed. Amherst: University of Massachusetts Press, 1987.

Guthman, Edwin O. *We Band of Brothers.* New York: Harper and Row, 1971.

Guthman, Edwin O., and C. Richard Allen. *RFK: Collected Speeches.* New York: Viking, 1993.

Guthman, Edwin O., and Jeffrey Shulman, eds., *Robert Kennedy: In His Own Words.* New York: Bantam, 1988.

Halberstam, David. *The Fifties.* New York: Villard, 1993.

Haney, Richard C. "Wallace in Wisconsin: The Presidential Primary of 1964." *Wisconsin Magazine of History* LXI (Summer 1978): 258–78.

Harris, Lou. *Is There a Republican Majority?: Political Trends, 1952–1956.* New York: Harper and Row, 1954.

Henggeler, Paul R. *In His Steps: Lyndon Johnson and the Kennedy Mystique.* Chicago: Ivan Dee, 1991.

Hess, Karl. *In a Cause That Will Triumph: The Goldwater Campaign and the Future of Conservatism.* New York: Doubleday, 1967.

Himmelstein, Jerome L. *To the Right: The Transformation of American Conservatism.* Berkeley: University of California Press, 1990.

Hofstader, Richard. *The Paranoid Style in American Politics, and Other Essays.* New York: Vintage, 1967.

Holt, Len. *The Summer That Didn't End.* New York: William Morrow, 1965.

Hughes, Emmet John. *Ordeal of Power: A Political Memoir of the Eisenhower Years.* New York: Atheneum, 1963.

Hulsey, Byron C. *Everett Dirksen and His Presidents: How a Senate Giant Shaped American Politics.* Lawrence: University Press of Kansas, 2000.

Humphrey, Hubert. *The Education of a Public Man: My Life and Politics.* Minneapolis: University of Minnesota Press, 1991. First published 1976.

Javits, Jacob. *The Autobiography of a Public Man.* Boston: Houghton Mifflin, 1981.

Johnson, Lady Bird. *Lady Bird Johnson: A White House Diary.* New York: Holt, Reinhart and Winston, 1970.

Johnson, Lyndon Baines. *The Vantage Point.* New York: Holt, Reinhart and Winston, 1971.

Judis, John. *William F. Buckley, Jr.: Patron Saint of the Conservatives.* New York: Simon and Schuster, 1988.

Kearns, Doris. *Lyndon Johnson and the American Dream.* New York: Harper and Row, 1977.

Keogh, James. *President Nixon and the Press.* New York: Funk and Wagnalls, 1972.

Kessel, John H. *The Goldwater Coalition: Republican Strategies in 1964.* Indianapolis: Bobbs-Merrill, 1968.

Kleindienst, Richard G. *Justice: The Memoirs of Attorney General Richard Kleindienst.* Ottawa, IL: Jameson Books, 1985.

Kramer, Michael, and Sam Roberts, *"I Never Wanted to Be Vice-President of Anything!": An Investigative Biography of Nelson Rockefeller.* New York: Basic Books, 1976.

Larson, Arthur. *A Republican Looks at His Party.* New York: Harper and Row, 1956.

Lawson, Steven F. *Black Ballots: Voting Rights in the South, 1944–1969.* New York: Columbia University Press, 1976.

Lasky, Victor. *RFK: The Man and the Myth.* New York: Trident, 1968.

Lee, Chana Kai. *For Freedom's Sake: The Life of Fannie Lou Hamer.* Urbana: University of Illinois Press, 1999.

Lesher, Stephen. *George Wallace: American Populist.* Reading, MA: Addison-Wesley, 1994.

Lewis, John (with Michael D'Orso). *Walking with the Wind: A Memoir of the Movement.* New York: Simon and Schuster, 1998.

Lipset, Seymour, and William Schneider. *The Confidence Gap: Business, Labor, and Government in the Public Mind.* New York: Free Press, 1983.

Loevy, Robert E., ed. *The Civil Rights Act of 1964: The Passage of the Law That Ended Racial Segregation.* Albany: State University of New York Press, 1997.

McCarthy, Joseph. *America's Retreat from Victory: The Story of George Catlett Marshall.* New York: Devin Adair, 1951.

McDowell, Edwin. *Barry Goldwater: Portrait of an Arizonan.* Chicago: Regnery Press, 1964.

McNamara, Robert S., et al. *Argument Without End: In Search of Answers to the Vietnam Tragedy.* New York: Public Affairs Press, 1999.

————. (with Brian VanDeMark). *In Retrospect: The Tragedy and Lessons of Vietnam.* New York: Random House, 1995.

Mahoney, Daniel J. *Actions Speak Louder: The Story of the New York Conservative Party.* New York: Arlington House, 1968.

Manchester, William. *Death of a President.* New York: Harper and Row, 1967.

————. *The Glory and the Dream: A Narrative History of America, 1932–1972.* Boston: Little Brown, 1973.

Margolis, Jon. *The Last Innocent Year: America in 1964, The Beginning of the Sixties.* New York: William Morrow, 1999.

Martin, Harold H. "George Wallace Shakes Up the Political Scene." *Saturday Evening Post*, May 9, 1964, 89+.

Martin, John Bartlow. *Adlai Stevenson and the World: The Life of Adlai E. Stevenson.* Garden City, NY: Doubleday, 1977.

Martin, John Frederick. *Civil Rights and the Crisis of Liberalism: The Democratic Party, 1945–1976.* Boulder, CO: Westview Press, 1979.

Matusow, Allen J. "From Civil Rights to Black Power: The Case of the SNCC, 1960–1966." In *Twentieth Century America: Recent Interpretations*, ed. Barton J. Bernstein and Allen J. Matusow. 2d ed. New York: HBJ, 1972.

————. *The Unraveling of America: A History of Liberalism in the 1960s.* New York: Harper and Row, 1984.

Miller, Merle. *Lyndon: An Oral Biography.* New York: Ballantine, 1980.

Miller, William J. *Henry Cabot Lodge.* New York: James H. Heineman, 1967.

Mills, Kay. *This Little Light of Mine: The Life of Fannie Lou Hamer.* New York: Penguin, 1994.

Miroff, Bruce. "Presidential Leverage over Social Movements: The Johnson White House and Civil Rights." *Journal of Politics* 43 (1981): 2–23.

Nash, George. *The Conservative Intellectual Movement Since 1945.* New York: Basic Books, 1999.

Nixon, Richard M. *Six Crises.* Garden City, NY: Doubleday, 1962.

————. *RN: The Memoirs of Richard Nixon.* New York: Grosset and Dunlap, 1978.

Novak, Robert D. *The Agony of the GOP: 1964.* New York: Macmillan, 1965.

O'Donnell, Kenneth P., and David F. Powers (with Joe McCarthy). *"Johnny, We Hardly Knew Ye": Memoirs of John Fitzgerald Kennedy.* Boston: Little Brown, 1972.

O'Neill, Thomas P. (with William Novak). *Man of the House.* New York: Random House, 1987.

O'Reilly, Kenneth. *Nixon's Piano: Presidents and Racial Politics from Washington to Clinton.* New York: Free Press, 1995.

Oshinsky, David. *A Conspiracy So Immense.* New York: Free Press, 1983.

Parmet, Herbert. *JFK: The Presidency of John F. Kennedy.* New York: Dell, 1983.

Pemberton, William. *Exit with Honor: The Life and Presidency of Ronald Reagan.* Armonk, NY: M.E. Sharpe, 1998.

Perlstein, Rick. *Before the Storm: Barry Goldwater and the Unmaking of the American Consensus.* New York: Hill and Wang, 2001.

Permaloff, Ann, and Carl Grafton. *Political Power in Alabama: The More Things Change.* Athens: University of Georgia Press, 1995.

Polsby, Nelson W., and Aaron Wildavsky. *Presidential Elections: Strategies and Structures of American Politics.* 10th ed. New York: Chatham House, 2000.

Pomper, Gerald. "The Nomination of Hubert Humphrey for Vice-President." *Journal of Politics* 30 (August 1966): 639–59.

Rauh, Joseph L., Jr. "The Role of the Leadership Conference on Civil Rights in the Civil Rights Struggle of 1963–1964." In *The Civil Rights Act of 1964: The Passage of the Law That Ended Racial Segregation,* ed. Robert D. Loevy. Albany New York: State University of New York Press, 1997.

Reagan, Ronald. *An American Life.* New York: Simon and Schuster, 1990.

Reedy, George. *Lyndon B. Johnson: A Memoir.* New York: Andrews and McMeel, 1982.

Reichard, Gary W. *Politics as Usual: The Age of Truman and Eisenhower.* Arlington Heights, IL: Harlan Davidson, 1988.

Reinhard, Richard W. *The Republican Right Since 1945.* Lexington: University Press of Kentucky, 1983.

Republican National Committee. *Official Report of the Proceedings of the Twenty-eighth Republican National Convention.* n.p.: Graphis Arts Press, n.d. (1964?).

Rogin, Michael. "Wallace and the Middle Class: The White Backlash in Wisconsin." *Public Opinion Quarterly* (Spring 1966).

Rusher, William A. "Crossroads for the GOP." *National Review,* February 12, 1963.

———. *Rise of the Right.* New York: William Morrow, 1984.

Russell, Jan Jarboe. *Lady Bird: A Biography of Mrs. Johnson.* New York: Scribner, 1999.

Sabato, Larry J. *Rise of Political Consultants: New Ways of Winning Elections.* New York: Basic Books, 1983.

Schlafly, Phyllis. *A Choice, Not an Echo.* Alton, IL: Pere Marquette Press, 1964.

Schlesinger, Arthur M., Jr. *A Thousand Days.* Boston: Houghton Mifflin, 1965.

———. *Robert Kennedy and His Times.* New York: Ballantine, 1978.

Schorr, Daniel. *Clearing the Air.* Boston: Houghton-Mifflin, 1977.

Schuparra, Kurt. *Triumph of the Right: The Rise of the California Conservative Movement, 1945–1966.* Armonk, NY: M.E. Sharpe, 1998.

Shadegg, Stephen C. *Freedom Is His Flight Plan.* New York: Fleet Press, 1962.

———. *What Happened to Goldwater?: The Inside Story of the 1964 Republican Campaign.* New York: Holt, Reinhart and Winston, 1965.

Shesol, Jeff. *Mutual Contempt: Lyndon Johnson, Robert Kennedy, and the Feud That Defined a Decade.* New York: W.W. Norton, 1997.

Sinsheimer, Joseph. "The Freedom Vote of 1963: New Strategies of Racial Protest in Mississippi." *Journal of Southern History* LV (May 1989): 217–44.

Sitkoff, Harvard. *The Struggle for Black Equality, 1954–1980.* New York: Hill and Wang, 1981.

Solberg, Carl. *Hubert Humphrey.* New York: W.W. Norton, 1984.

Sorensen, Theodore C. *Kennedy.* New York: Harper and Row, 1965.

Steel, Ronald. *In Love with the Night: The American Romance with Robert Kennedy.* New York: Simon and Schuster, 2000.

Stern, Mark. *Calculating Visions: Kennedy, Johnson and Civil Rights.* New Brunswick, NJ: Rutgers University Press, 1992.

Taylor, Sandra Baxley. *Me 'n' George: A Story of George Corley Wallace and His Number One Crony, Oscar Harper.* Mobile, AL: Greenberry, 1988.

Thomas, Helen. *Dateline White House: A Warm and Revealing Account of America's Presidents from the Kennedys to the Fords.* New York: Macmillan, 1977.

Turner, Kathleen. *Lyndon Johnson's Dual War: Vietnam and the Press.* Chicago: University of Chicago Press, 1985.

Unger, Irwin, and Debi Unger. *LBJ: A Life.* New York: John Wiley and Sons, 1999.

Valenti, Jack. *A Very Human President.* New York: W.W. Norton, 1975.

Viorst, Milton. *Fire in the Streets: America in the 1960s.* New York: Simon and Schuster, 1979.

Welch, Robert. *The Blue Book of the John Birch Society.* 24th ed. Appleton, WI: Western Island Press, 1999. First published 1959.

———. *The Politician.* Belmont, MA: Western Islands, 1963.

Welsh, Mathew. "Civil Rights and the Primary Election of 1964 in Indiana: The Wallace Challenge." *Indiana Magazine of History* LXXV (March 1979): 1–27.

White, F. Clifton. *Suite 3505: The Story of the Draft Goldwater Movement.* New Rochelle, NY, Arlington House, 1967.

———. *Why Reagan Won: The Conservative Movement, 1964–1981.* Chicago: Regnery, 1981.

White, Theodore H. *The Making of the President—1960.* New York: Atheneum, 1961.

———. *The Making of the President—1964.* New York: Atheneum, 1965.

———. *The Making of the President—1972.* New York: Atheneum, 1973.

———. *America in Search of Itself: The Making of the President, 1956–1980.* New York: Harper and Row, 1982.

Wilkins, Roy (with Tom Matthews). *Standing Fast: Autobiography of Roy Wilkins.* New York: Viking, 1962.

Wiltcover, Jules. *The Resurrection of Richard Nixon.* New York: Putnam, 1970.

Wolf, George D. *William Warren Scranton: Pennsylvania Statesman.* University Park: Pennsylvania State University Press, 1981.

Zinn, Howard. *SNCC: The New Abolitionists.* Boston: Beacon, 1965.

Index

369

About the Author

Gary A. Donaldson is the Keller Family Foundation Chair in American History at Xavier University of Louisiana in New Orleans. He is the author of numerous books on American political and diplomatic history including *The Making of Modern America: The Nation from 1945 to the Present*; *Modern America: A Documentary History of the Nation Since 1945*; *The First Modern Campaign: Kennedy, Nixon, and the Election of 1960*; *American Foreign Policy: The Twentieth Century in Documents*; and *Truman Defeats Dewey*.